Constructivism
in Psychotherapy

Constructivism
in Psychotherapy

Edited by
Robert A.
Neimeyer

and

Michael J.
Mahoney

American Psychological Association ■ Washington, DC

Published by
American Psychological Association
750 First Street, NE
Washington, DC 20002

Copies may be ordered from
APA Order Department
P.O. Box 2710
Hyattsville, MD 20784

In the UK and Europe, copies may be ordered from
American Psychological Association
3 Henrietta Street
Covent Garden, London
WC2E 8LU England

Typeset in Goudy by Innodata Corporation, Publishing Services Division, Hanover, MD

Printer: Data Reproductions Corporation, Rochester Hills, MI
Jacket Designer: Grafik Communications, Ltd., Alexandria, VA
Technical/Production Editor: Molly R. Flickinger

Library of Congress Cataloging-in-Publication Data
Constructivism in psychotherapy / edited by Robert A. Neimeyer and Michael J. Mahoney.
     p. cm.
   Includes bibliographical references and index.
   ISBN 1-55798-279-1 (acid-free paper)
   1. Personal construct therapy. 2. Cognitive therapy. 3. Constructivism (Psychology)
I. Neimeyer, Robert A., 1954–   II. Mahoney, Michael J.
RC489.P46C66   1995
616.89′14—dc20   94-23952
                                                          CIP

British Cataloguing-in-Publication Data
A CIP record is available from the British Library.

Printed in the United States of America
First edition

To Eric and Michael,
who help keep alive my spirit of inquiry.

RAN

To Peg and Pat,
with much love and many thanks.

MJM

CONTENTS

CONTRIBUTORS

Mary Baird Carlsen, Seattle, Washington

Jay S. Efran, Department of Psychology, Temple University, Philadelphia, Pennsylvania

David Epston, Family Therapy Centre, Auckland, New Zealand

Robert L. Fauber, Department of Psychology, Temple University, Philadelphia, Pennsylvania

Guillem Feixas, Department of Psychology, University of Barcelona, Spain

Óscar F. Gonçalves, Department of Psychology, University of Minho, Portugal

Leslie Greenberg, Department of Psychology, York University, North York, Ontario, Canada

Vittorio F. Guidano, Centro di Psicoterapia Cognitive, Rome, Italy

Stephanie L. Harter, Department of Psychology, Texas Tech University, Lubbock, Texas

Hubert J. M. Hermans, Psychological Laboratory, Nijmegen, The Netherlands

Larry M. Leitner, Department of Psychology, Miami University, Oxford, Ohio

William J. Lyddon, Department of Counseling, University of Southern Mississippi, Hattiesburg

Michael J. Mahoney, Department of Psychology, University of North Texas, Denton

Greg J. Neimeyer, Department of Psychology, University of Florida, Gainesville

Robert A. Neimeyer, Department of Psychology, University of Memphis, Tennessee

Juan Pascual-Leone, Department of Psychology, York University, North York, Ontario, Canada

Michael White, Dulwich Centre, Adelaide, South Australia

PREFACE

Any project, whether personal or professional, can be viewed as having many origins. At the most obvious level, this volume on constructivism in psychotherapy grew out of our ongoing conversations with one another, with colleagues, with students, and with clients about a perspective that has come to inform our way of understanding human problems and the process of psychotherapy. Despite the different "voices" and contexts in which these conversations occurred—whether in the abstract discourse of the conference hall or classroom or the more concrete and urgent exchanges of the psychotherapy office—these dialogues turned on similar themes and addressed similar essential questions: How can we usefully understand the human penchant for meaning-making, especially in a world that provides no simple criteria for determining the validity of any one set of meanings or commitments relative to other possible contenders? How can we conceptualize both the idiosyncrasy of our personal stories and their embeddedness in larger familial, linguistic, and cultural narratives that enable as well as constrain our attempts to author our own biographies? More particularly, can we construe the infinite varieties of human distress as reflections of the same basic attempts at meaning-making on the part of both individuals and human communities? And, finally, can we envision forms of psychotherapeutic practice that offer new possibilities for reweaving the tangled narratives of people's lives? Although constructivism offers no final answers to any of these questions, it does provide a conceptual framework in which to articulate these deeply human concerns and to consider their implications for working with clients.

At a more personal level, this volume also reflects our own evolution as practitioners, theorists, and researchers of psychotherapy. After several years of working within the "secure bases" that provided a supportive scaffolding for our early careers—personal construct theory in the case of Neimeyer and cognitive–behavioral therapies in the case of Mahoney—we found ourselves exploring terrain at and eventually beyond the conventional boundaries of our respective training. The resulting odyssey eventually brought us into closer contact with one another and with a cadre of other travelers whose wanderings often started from quite different conceptual bases. Despite the diversity of backgrounds that distinguished us, we found that we all shared common concerns with the passion of knowing, the construction (and deconstruction) of identity, the role of narrative in the structuring of lives, the dialectical tensions between experiencing and explanation, the linguistic and social embeddedness of our most personal realities, and the daunting challenges of being reflective psychotherapists. Although our distinctive ways of approaching these constructivist themes are evidenced by the diversity of contributions to this book, our convergence on similar or complementary practices was often quite striking, suggesting that constructivist metatheory might serve as a kind of meeting ground for therapists of different traditions looking to add theoretical depth, diagnostic breadth, and experiential novelty to their practice of psychotherapy.

Finally, we acknowledge the importance to this project of the current postmodern zeitgeist—a contemporary spirit of inquiry that this book reflects and to which, we hope, it contributes. Postmodern emphases on the multiplicity of meaning, the rhetorical foundations of the human sciences, the social construction of knowledge, and interpretive and reflective methods of research are evident throughout this volume. That such emphases are transforming the field of psychotherapy is evident from the prominence of these topics at professional meetings of psychologists, marriage and family therapists, social workers, and mental health counselors. A particularly relevant example is the series of annual conferences titled *Constructivism in Psychotherapy*, which have been held in the United States, Portugal, Spain, and Argentina since 1990. Likewise, the 1994 inauguration of the *Journal of Constructivist Psychology* and the Society for Constructivism in Psychotherapy testify to the growing level of interest in constructivist conceptualizations of psychological issues, problems, and techniques, providing a forum for contributions to and critical appraisals of this perspective.

We believe that the authors contributing to this book reflect the scope and excitement of this postmodern clinical dialogue. Constructivism is not a monolithic ideology (if it is an ideology at all). On the contrary, a sense of iconoclasm, a distrust of absolute prescriptions for practice, and a recognition of the contingency of all knowledge claims are evident in the chapters that follow. But counterbalancing the critical thrust of these chapters is also an affirmative motivation to find points of contact with other schools of thought, to develop workable interventions to enrich the pragmatics of therapy, and to find personal and communal grounds for commitment. Taken together, the chapters that make up this volume suggest the distance that the discipline of psychotherapy has traveled, in its reluctant shift away from a conception of itself as an objective set of scientific techniques and toward a more (inter)personal engagement with the complex processes of human change and their facilitation.

In reflecting on the terrain that we have traversed since we first conceived of this project, we recognize the indeterminate directionality of both personal and professional change. Likewise, we realize that no set of articles (however carefully chosen or edited) could offer a definitive map of the creative possibilities afforded by constructive metatheory. Thus, our hope is only to illustrate some of those possibilities as they are expressed in the works and words of some of today's leading representatives and practitioners of constructivism in psychotherapy. We trust that some of the travelogues provided by the contributors to this volume will offer the allure of a good story and will hearten the reader in his or her own journey as a psychotherapist.

ROBERT A. NEIMEYER
MICHAEL J. MAHONEY

1

AN INVITATION TO CONSTRUCTIVIST PSYCHOTHERAPIES

ROBERT A. NEIMEYER

Who are we?

Who are we to reach
Toward that we cannot touch,
Illuminated only by the scintilla
Of a passing thought?

Who are we to claim knowledge
In the midst of our ignorance,
To impose an order, a human scale,
On the recalcitrant material of our worlds?

Who are we to stretch across the chasm
Of self-containment,
To indwell the otherness of a being so (un)like ourselves,
Supported only by the thin substantiality of flesh and words?

And yet,
How can we do otherwise,
Be otherwise,
Than to seek completion beyond the bounds of who we were?

What is constructivism, and what is its relevance for psychotherapy? Posed in this form, the question is on par with other similarly grand inquiries, such as "What is existentialism (or behaviorism, or cognitivism, or systems theory) and what are its psychological implications?" In a sense, this entire book represents an extended answer to the former question, with each subsequent chapter exploring one possible response or set of responses to this basic inquiry. Its goal is to make constructivist psychotherapy accessible to newcomers[1] to the approach and to deepen and broaden the understanding and application of constructivist psychotherapy for those who are already familiar with its terrain. My aim in this first, brief chapter is to provide a general working introduction to constructivism and an orienting framework for reading the more detailed chapters that follow.

To understand what constructivism is, it might be useful to ask what psychotherapy is, when viewed through constructivist spectacles. From the constructivist vantage point, *psychotherapy* can be defined as the variegated and subtle interchange and negotiation of (inter)personal meanings. This is done in the service of articulating, elaborating, and revising those constructions that the client uses to organize her or his experience and action. Such a definition emphasizes several features of the psychotherapy process, including the delicacy with which the therapist must grasp the contours of the experiential world of the client, the dialogical and discursive basis of their interaction, and the contributions of both to their mutual inquiry. These emphases in psychotherapy in turn reflect a more basic human quest to seek relatedness, connection, and mutuality of meaning in spite of our uniqueness, using the common grounding provided by our language and our embodiment to form an intersubjective bridge between our phenomenal worlds. Although psychotherapy conceived along these lines can have many different concrete objectives, at an abstract level all of these involve joining with clients to develop a refined map of the often inarticulate constructions in which they are emotionally invested and that define what they regard as viable courses of action and, then, extending or supplementing these constructions to enlarge the number of possible worlds clients might inhabit.

Importantly, no commitment is made in this definition to a particularly "cognitive" view of meaning (Kelly, 1955; Neimeyer, 1987); indeed, human affective experience is infused with significance and can itself be viewed as a refined form of knowing (Bannister, 1977; Guidano, 1991; Mahoney, 1991). Nor does this view of therapy endorse a solipsistic view of the isolated knower as encapsulated in a world of meanings solely of his or her construction. Although some constructivists do emphasize the role of the individual in "predicating" meanings and thereby framing experience (Rychlak, 1990), others stress that in doing so, the individual necessarily draws on—and, in a more radical sense, is constituted by—the linguistic conventions and cultural narratives in which he or she is embedded (Mair, 1988; Maturana & Varela, 1987). In this perspective,

---

[1]Newcomers to the field may find the glossary at the end of the book particularly helpful as they read through the chapters.

even such "personal" processes as remembering have their collective dimensions (Middleton & Edwards, 1990), and "mind" is in an important sense distributed through larger social and linguistic networks, with individuals operating as organizing foci for communal acts of meaning-making. Thus, constructivists can work meaningfully with both individuals and collectivities (such as families), as the various chapters in this book illustrate.

ORDER WITHOUT FOUNDATION

What joins constructivists is their commitment to a common epistemology, or theory of knowledge. Like Kant (1952), constructivists believe that "reality" is ultimately noumenal—that is, it lies beyond the reach of our most ambitious theories, whether personal or scientific, forever denying us as human beings the security of justifying our beliefs, faiths, and ideologies by simple recourse to "objective circumstances" outside ourselves. Instead, the hard-won organization that we impose on the world of our experience is a precariously human construction, supported by our private and shared quests for a modicum of order and predictability in our lives as well as by our need to find some grounding for our actions. At times, the meaning structures that we evolve to give pattern and direction to our lives seem all too frail, such as when a person must reconstruct a sense of self and future after suffering an invalidation of his or her assumptive world upon the traumatic death of a loved one. At other times, the constructions with which clients contend appear all too substantial, as in the case of an adolescent who struggles against her parents' (and perhaps therapist's) "diagnosis" of her as "acting out," "depressed," or "oppositional." Lacking any universal taxonomy of "disorders" that define the way in which our attempts at meaning-making may go awry, constructivist therapists seek to discover what is at issue or what is problematic for each client they serve. The interventions that result help the client explore possible avenues for movement while respecting the core organizing principles on which his or her views of life are built. Thus, psychotherapy can be viewed as a kind of collaboration in the construction and reconstruction of meaning, an intimate but temporary partnership in a developmental process that will continue long after formal therapy ends.

A BACKWARD GLANCE

A decade ago, constructivism was still in an inchoate stage of development in the area of psychotherapy, although it had already established itself as a postmodern intellectual force to be reckoned with elsewhere in the human sciences and humanities. Indeed, pioneering conceptions of psychotherapy as the reconstruction of personal and social realities had begun to appear independently in a variety of clinical traditions—ranging from the psychoanalytic and humanistic to the family systemic and cognitive-behavioral. But these developments were relatively isolated from one another, with theorists and practitioners in each tradition remaining largely unaware of the evolution of kindred perspectives in other specialties. As a result, a growing number of scholars and therapists were experimenting with novel narrative, conversational, developmental, and reconstructive models and methods, but without the benefit of dialogue with others who were grappling with similar problems and procedures.

In the space of 10 short years, this situation has begun to change perceptibly. In place of the intellectual isolation that characterized pockets of constructivism in the 1980s, there is now greater mutual awareness of converging trends in different therapeutic traditions, reflecting the more general enthusiasm for psychotherapy integration that has occurred in tandem with the upswell of interest in constructivism. As a result, constructivists working in historically autonomous fields have begun to explore such key issues as the transformative role of the therapeutic relationship, the subtle influence of therapeutic "languaging," and developmental constraints on therapeutic change from a common epistemological perspective. I hope that the present volume will both reflect and contribute to this ongoing dialogue.

SCOPE OF THIS BOOK

One hallmark of constructivism is its refreshing blend of high-level theory and experientially grounded practice, a balance that Michael Mahoney and I have tried to retain in inviting and editing the collection of manuscripts that make up this book. We hope that the publication of these diverse expressions of clinical constructivism will deepen and broaden the vigorous discourse and debate taking place across the psychotherapy landscape, and we invite the reader to "try on for size" the constructivist mantle and test how well it fits the contours of his or her own experience as a psychotherapist.

In undertaking this project, we have been fortunate to recruit many of the leading contributors to developmental, narrative, systemic, and personal construct psychotherapies, as well as some newer voices that are beginning to open up fresh elaborative possibilities in the ongoing constructivist conversation. In doing so, we have tried to fairly sample the diversity of approaches falling under the constructivist umbrella, giving greater prominence to the coverage of different perspectives than to the specific formats of therapy (e.g., individual, couple, family, or group) in which such perspectives might be applied. However, we have intentionally deemphasized some approaches—such as psychoanalysis, which has shifted strongly in the direction of a constructivist fascination with narrative—because it remains to be seen whether these developments are coherent with the larger corpus of psychoanalytic metatheory emphasizing unconscious drives, defenses, universal stages of development, and so on (Botella, in press). Likewise, we have devoted less attention to systemic family therapies claiming a social constructionist as opposed to constructivist base (Hoffman, 1992), because of our sense that more work needs to be done to tease out the intricate points of contact and conflict between these perspectives. In both cases, however, discussion of analytic and constructionist themes is incorporated into relevant chapters throughout the book, and kindred perspectives falling more clearly under the constructivist aegis are covered in detail.

Finally, in editing the volume, Dr. Mahoney and I chose to concentrate on conceptual developments of interest to psychotherapy practitioners and theorists and to treat more succinctly the intriguing methodological implications of constructivism for psychotherapy research. This decision was based both on the competent consideration of these research issues in other recent books (Martin, 1994; Polkinghorne, 1983; Toukmanian & Rennie, 1992) and on our opinion that relevant research strategies and challenges would better be presented in the context of chapters in which they were most pertinent (see especially chapters 2, 10, 12, and 14).

Even with these decisions to limit the scope of the volume, organizing the diversity of contributions that remained was itself a challenging task, one that we have tried to meet by dividing the contents of the volume into five thematically related sections.

In Part I, I first place constructivist psychotherapies in a postmodern context, outlining their core epistemological commitments, associated clinical strategies, and organizing metaphors for the therapeutic process. I then close with a consideration of three issues bearing on the future of clinical constructivism, including its implications for psychotherapy research, the synthesis of different psychotherapy models, and internal tensions within the constructivist camp that require more sustained critical appraisal. Michael Mahoney then situates the emergence of constructivist metatheory within the historical development of the cognitive sciences and psychotherapies, previewing some of the challenges posed by this perspective, which he develops further in the final section of the book. William Lyddon fine-tunes this discussion by providing a detailed consideration of the varieties of contemporary constructivism, using

Pepper's (1942) scheme of distinguishable root metaphors to understand their distinctive features at the levels of theory and practice. Vittorio Guidano completes this opening section on historical and conceptual foundations by underscoring the essential interplay between experiencing and explaining in our selfhood dynamics and outlining the role of inter-subjectivity in undergirding our life-span development. Taken together, these chapters provide a conceptual foundation for constructivist therapy as well as a way of organizing some of its diverse contemporary expressions.

Part II begins with the personal reflections of Greg Neimeyer on his role as a facilitator of constructive change for clients over several years of counseling practice. In particular, he sheds light on the critical importance of strategies and techniques that encourage experimentation with hypothetical change as a means of mitigating the phenomenological threat of precipitous transformation. Mary Baird Carlsen extends this basic perspective, emphasizing the continuous commitment to change reflected in the process of living and the problems and prospects of creative aging. Vittorio Guidano then details the self-observation method deriving from his model of the dynamic self, and he illustrates its use in reconstructing a client's affective style. Finally, Leslie Greenberg and Juan Pascual-Leone introduce their own dialectical constructivist model for conceptualizing and facilitating experiential change in psychotherapy. In combination, these four chapters lay the groundwork for a conception of psychotherapy as an arena for personal change and reconstruction.

Part III considers the narrative turn, a dimension of constructivist practice that has reverberated through many contemporary traditions of psychotherapy. Óscar Gonçalves opens the discussion with a panoramic portrayal of the evolution of human textuality in the progression from behaviorist, through cognitivist, to constructivist forms of therapy. I then consider the role of client-generated narratives (such as journals and poetic chronicles) in therapeutic change, arguing that they represent efforts to achieve a sense of continuity in the client's lived experience. Finally, Hubert Hermans develops a self-confrontation method grounded in valuation theory and illustrates its use in both identifying issues and tracking progress over the course of therapy. Given its diversity in level of abstraction and methodological specificity, this set of articles offers a broad sampling of the ways in which practice can be informed by constru-ing the self as text and therapy as a form of constructive hermeneutics.

In Part IV, Jay Efran and Robert Fauber provide an irreverent and engaging "manifesto" for radical constructivist therapists. By raising and responding to the most frequently posed questions about this novel orientation to practice, they dispel much of the ambiguity that surrounds discussions of language-based therapy, making a case for viewing interven-tion with individuals and families as a vigorous negotiation of client assumptions.[2] Guillem Feixas follows with an ambitious attempt to bridge the sometimes antagonistic traditions of individual and family therapy, finding conceptual linkages and the prospects for fruitful interchange between constructivists in both areas. David Epston and Michael White complete this part, taking issue with the "termination as loss" metaphor that undergirds many forms of therapy and offering a novel vision of graduation from therapy as a rite of passage into an alternative, less problem-saturated self-knowledge that the client can document in the context of significant relationships. As representatives of systemically informed constructivist thinking, these three chapters give the reader a glimpse of that area of therapy—namely, family therapy—that has been most thoroughly revolutionized by the adoption of a postmodern perspective.

Finally, Part V offers a personal view of the challenges posed by a constructivist model of practice. In the opening chapter of this part, Larry Leitner presents his reflections on working with severely traumatized clients who flee or defend themselves from the very forms of intimate relating that they most earnestly need. The intense therapeutic presence called for in such work leads him to consider the nature of "optimal therapeutic distance" and various forms of process validation for a therapist's interventions—two critical concepts for therapists of any persuasion attempting to transcend the tyranny of technique. In her subsequent chapter on "borderline" clients, Stephanie Harter extends this concern with the figural role of the therapeutic relationship into her work with a group of clients who press against our own borders and boundaries for what constitutes appropriate treatment. Perhaps because she construes such clients as individuals whose myths have been shattered and who have given up on the prospect of creating new ones, she uses an ancient but apropos myth of Western culture to understand their problematic position within the conventional mental health system. Finally, Michael Mahoney concludes this part, as well as the book, by considering the nexus of epistemological, existential, strategic, and ethical issues that personally challenge all therapists and counselors, but particularly those who adopt a constructivist credo. Ultimately, Mahoney conjures an image of the therapist as a fellow traveler, who, in accepting the invitation

---

[2]Efran and Fauber's chapter can also serve as a user-friendly introduction to the entire book for the reader who is quite unfamiliar with a constructivist perspective. This alternative introduction reveals the limitations on the universality of any given organizational scheme for a volume like the present one; ultimately, the best structure may be the one that the reader devises to meet his or her own needs and interests. Therefore, readers are encouraged to sample chapters in a sequence that corresponds to their own inclinations, perhaps using chapters 2 and 3 to provide a general backdrop for what follows, and drawing on the glossary as needed to "unpack" unfamiliar terminology as they encounter it.

to join in a client's personal quest, ventures into a genuine poetics of practice.

I hope that this volume provides an accessible point of entry into the rich but occasionally daunting field of constructivism for the newcomer to this perspective and that the seasoned traveler of these conceptual pathways will find fresh vantage points from which to view the varied terrain of psychotherapy.

REFERENCES

Bannister, D. (1977). The logic of passion. In D. Bannister (Ed.), *New perspectives in personal construct theory* (pp. 21–38). San Diego, CA: Academic Press.

Botella, L. (in press). Personal construct theory, constructivism, and postmodern thought. In R. A. Neimeyer & G. J. Neimeyer (Eds.), *Advances in personal construct psychology* (Vol. 3). Greenwich, CT: JAI Press.

Guidano, V. F. (1991). *The self in process.* New York: Guilford Press.

Hoffman, L. (1992). A reflexive stance for family therapy. In S. McNamee & K. J. Gergen (Eds.), *Therapy as social construction* (pp. 7–24). Newbury Park, CA: Sage.

Kant, I. (1952). *Critique of pure reason.* Chicago: Encyclopaedia Britannica.

Kelly, G. A. (1955). *The psychology of personal constructs.* New York: Norton.

Mahoney, M. J. (1991). *Human change processes.* New York: Basic Books.

Mair, M. (1988). Psychology as storytelling. *International Journal of Personal Construct Psychology, 1*, 125–137.

Martin, J. (1994). *The construction and understanding of psychotherapeutic change.* New York: Teachers College Press.

Maturana, H., & Varela, F. (1987). *The tree of knowledge.* Boston: New Science Library.

Middleton, D., & Edwards, D. (1990). *Collective remembering.* Newbury Park, CA: Sage.

Neimeyer, R. A. (1987). An orientation to personal construct therapy. In R. A. Neimeyer & G. J. Neimeyer (Eds.), *Personal construct therapy casebook* (pp. 3–19). New York: Springer.

Pepper, S. C. (1942). *World hypotheses.* Berkeley: University of California Press.

Polkinghorne, D. (1983). *Methodology for the human sciences.* Albany: State University of New York Press.

Rychlak, J. E. (1990). George Kelly and the concept of construction. *International Journal of Personal Construct Psychology, 3*, 7–19.

Toukmanian, S. G., & Rennie, D. L. (1992). *Psychotherapy process research: Paradigmatic and narrative approaches.* Newbury Park, CA: Sage.

I

HISTORICAL AND CONCEPTUAL FOUNDATIONS

2

CONSTRUCTIVIST PSYCHOTHERAPIES: FEATURES, FOUNDATIONS, AND FUTURE DIRECTIONS

ROBERT A. NEIMEYER

We can no longer rest assured that human progress may proceed step by step in an orderly fashion from the known to the unknown. Neither our senses nor our doctrines provide us with the immediate knowledge required for such a philosophy of science. What we think we know is anchored only in our assumptions, not in the bedrock of truth itself, and that world we seek to understand remains always on the horizons of our thoughts. (Kelly, 1977, p. 6)

Every significant stream of thought has many tributaries. In the case of constructivism, these include wellsprings of philosophic inspiration that can be traced at least as far back as Giambattista Vico, Immanuel Kant, and Hans Vaihinger (Mahoney, 1988)—each of whom emphasized the proactive, form-giving, or fictional character of human mentation and its role in configuring the very "realities" to which we respond. Other sources include the confluence of constructivist thinking within psychology in the first half of the twentieth century, as figures like Frederick Bartlett (1932), Alfred Korzybski (1933), and Jean Piaget (1971/1937) drew attention to the constructive and semantic processes of human memory, language, and cognition, breaking with the more associationist, objectivist, and determinist trends in their respective fields. Finally, by midcentury, a genuinely constructivist form of psychotherapy began to emerge, heralded by George Kelly's (1955) groundbreaking psychology of personal constructs.

11

Over the past few decades, the progression of constructivist thinking in psychotherapy has been more rapid and, in some respects, more turbulent as well. Like any stream of thought, the course that constructivism has taken has been responsive to the broader contours of the intellectual landscape that surrounds it. In this instance, the landscape has been shaped by the influence of postmodernism, with its iconoclastic penchant for celebrating the multiplicity of belief systems, resisting methodological prescriptions, and undermining faith in the "timeless truths" embedded in our social charters, cultural mores, masterworks of literature, and even science itself (W. T. Anderson, 1990; R. A. Neimeyer, 1993a). In this cultural context, contemporary constructivist psychotherapy has gained momentum— deepening, broadening, and occasionally being buffeted by contradictory crosscurrents originating in rather different disciplinary terrains.

In the current volume, various authors discuss these developments, at levels ranging from the epistemological to the applied. My goal in this chapter is to orient the reader to the family of therapies sharing basic constructivist commitments in a way that invites more detailed exploration of the chapters that follow. I begin by sketching some of the distinguishing features and foundations of these approaches, and I progress to outlining the basic therapeutic models or metaphors that are adopted by various schools of constructivist therapists. Finally, I close by concentrating on a cluster of issues—the role of constructivism in psychotherapy research and psychotherapy integration, and the sometimes divisive multiplicity of constructivist perspectives—that will help shape the form or forms that these therapies will take in the future.

CONSTRUCTIVISM AND OBJECTIVISM: DEFINITION BY CONTRAST

To understand the central constructivist themes of this volume, it is useful to view them in relief against the backdrop of an "objectivist" psychology conceived as a project of modernity. Embodying the Enlightenment faith in technological and human progress through the accumulation of legitimate knowledge, psychology in its first century largely concerned itself with the development of logical and empirical methods for discovering objective, verifiable facts about its specialized subject matter (Kvale, 1992). If successful, such a research program was presumed to be increasingly unified and progressive, leading to the discovery of generalizable laws of human behavior whose validity was established by their correspondence with observable, extratheoretical realities (Staats, 1991). At the core of this modern program was the belief in a knowable world and, with it, a knowable self (Gergen, 1992).

The postmodernist project turns nearly every aspect of this modern psychological program on its head. Gone is the faith in an objectively knowable universe and, with it, the hope that elimination of human bias, adherence to canons of methodology, and reliance on a pure language of observation would yield a "true" human science, mirroring psychological reality without distortion (Steier, 1991). Gone too is the modern notion of an essentialized self—an individual ego who is the locus of choice, action, and rational self-appraisal—at least in more radical social constructionist expressions of the postmodern trend (Lovlie, 1992). In their place is a panoply of perspectives cutting across the human sciences and humanities whose common threads include an acknowledgment of divergent realities, socially constituted and historically situated, that defy adequate comprehension in objectivist terms. Language, in this view, actually constitutes the structures of social reality (Maturana & Varela, 1987), requiring the cultivation of new approaches (hermeneutic, narrative, deconstructionist, rhetorical, and discursive) appropriate to analyzing the "text" of human experience in its social context (Edwards & Potter, 1992; Shotter & Gergen, 1989; Simons, 1989). The resulting image of psychological "science" is, in some respects, more humble than its modernist predecessor (Steier, 1991; aiming only for the production of "local knowledges" that are more bounded and closer to the domain of practice); yet, in other respects, it is more ambitious (involving more consistent self-criticism and reflexivity). It is also more disquieting—holding out the promise of only a shifting, fragmentary, and constructed knowledge, without the bedrock certainty of firm (logical or empirical) foundations. Even the self has been dethroned from a position of agency, freedom, and conscious self-determination in some constructionist and language-based approaches (Efran, Lukens, & Lukens, 1990; Sampson, 1989), vanishing into a proliferation of inconsistent social roles on the interpersonal and cultural stage.[1] If there is a positive thrust to this postmodern project, it is in the direction of developing viable (if not valid) knowledge and the pursuit of responsible social action. Table 1 summarizes some of the key epistemological commitments that inform the constructivist turn and distinguish it from a more familiar, objectivist

---

[1]Yet, several other constructivist (as distinct from constructionist) approaches continue to assign centrality to agentic "selfhood processes," however closely interwoven these may be with cultural and relational contexts (e.g., Kelly, 1955; Guidano, 1987, 1991; Mahoney, 1991; R. A. Neimeyer & Harter, 1988; Rychlak, 1990). Contributions have been solicited from representatives of both traditions in the present volume, in the hope of stimulating greater exploration and eventual integration of contemporary conceptions of the self and its ambient and interpenetrating social world. It may well be that a privileging of one aspect of this dialectic over the other has contributed to persistent difficulties in reconciling apparently contradictory accounts of human psychology, such as those polarized in their emphasis on (individual) free will versus (social) determinism, those endorsing (private) subjective versus (public) observable sources of data, and so on.

TABLE 1
Selected Epistemological Contrasts Between Objectivist and Constructivist Approaches to Psychology

Assumption	Approach	
	Objectivist	Constructivist
Nature of knowledge	Representation or copy of real world	Construction of subject's experience and action
Validation of knowledge	Correspondence theory of truth; veridical matching of knowledge claims and real world as revealed through senses	Coherence theory of truth; pursuit of viable knowledge through internal consistency and social consensus
Nature of truth	Singular, universal, ahistorical, incremental	Multiple, contextual, historical, paradigmatic
Goal of science	Unificationist; discovery of nomothetic laws	Pluralist; creation of local knowledges
Scientific method	Prescriptive; emphasis on quantitative measurement and controlled experimentation	Anarchistic; emphasis on qualitative methods and narrative–hermeneutic analysis
Human mentation	Reactive; "map" of actual events and relationships; mediational	Proactive; "plan" for organizing activity; predicational
Basic unit of meaning	Concept or schema assimilating events on the basis of similar inherent features	Construct or distinction establishing meaning through contrast
Relations between meanings	Associationist; cognitions as isolated self-statements or rules based on past contingencies	Systemic; constructions hierarchically arranged in self-organizing structure
Role of language	Mediates social reality; system of signs	Constitutes social reality; system of differentiations

approach to psychology. Expanded treatments of these philosophical contrasts can be found elsewhere (Mahoney, 1991; R. A. Neimeyer, 1993a, 1993b; R. A. Neimeyer & Feixas, 1990; Rychlak, 1990).

In a reflexive sense, the epistemological assumptions associated with constructivism can be read at two levels: on the one hand, referring to its stance toward the nature of abstract knowledge and scientific inquiry, and on the other hand, depicting the presumed knowing activities of individuals or human communities.[2] Thus, in a constructivist view, human beings are denied any direct access to an immediate reality beyond *language*, defined broadly as the entire repertory of symbolic utterances and actions afforded us by our culture (see Efran & Fauber's chapter in this volume). This existential condition relativizes knowledge, leading to the proliferation of diverse and often contradictory realities in various societal, family, and individual contexts. Nonetheless, most versions of constructivism also resist the urge toward an "anything goes" solipsism, insofar as human beings must nonetheless achieve an adequate coordination of their actions, or "fit," with their physical and social environments (Maturana & Varela, 1987). Thus, although we cannot aspire to a universally valid knowledge that corresponds in any direct sense with a "real world" external to us, we can and must draw on the symbolic resources of our place and time in formulating viable theories or useful fictions that enable us to negotiate our social world. The criteria for the adequacy of these personal or local knowledges vary from one constructivist theorist to another, but include the degree to which knowledges provide for meaningful anticipation of events (Kelly, 1955), promote a sense of agency and participation in one's life (White & Epston, 1990), or provide pragmatically useful organizing schemes for guiding human action (Polkinghorne, 1992).

Constructivism can also be distinguished by its operative assumptions about the structure of personal knowledge and its social embeddedness (R. A. Neimeyer, 1987). Human beings are viewed as being "set" to perceive patterns in the world around them (Popper, 1963). Confronted with the complexity of living in time and space, a person "attunes his ear to recurrent themes" to punctuate the unending flow of experience: "Like a musician, he must phrase his experience in order to make sense of it. The phrases are distinguished events. . . . Within these limited segments, which are based on recurrent themes, man begins to discover the bases for likenesses and differences" (Kelly, 1955, p. 52). Thus, the basic "act of meaning" is the framing of a difference (Bateson, 1972) that carves the experiential world into personally and communally

---

[2]This reflexive reading of the cells in the table is especially appropriate in comparing constructivist approaches to therapy with their more familiar cousins—"rationalist" versions of cognitive therapy. Some versions of both schools take the notion of "personal science" as a root metaphor for human functioning but interpret this metaphor quite differently, depending on their adherence to a "modern" view of science grounded in realism or to a somewhat more critical or relativized postmodern view of scientific inquiry. Contrast, for example, Kelly's (1977) constructivist rendering of personal science with Beck's (Beck et al., 1979) more rationalist interpretation. Some of these themes are elaborated below and are revisited in subsequent chapters of this book. For a more focused comparison of constructivism and the cognitive therapies, see R. A. Neimeyer (1993b, 1993c), as well as Mahoney (1991).

significant units. The bases of distinction that form these constructions are themselves predications (Rychlak, 1990, 1992) that organize subsequent experience and that comprise specific parts or functions of a larger self-organizing system or structure (Kelly, 1955; Mahoney, 1988; Maturana & Varela, 1987; Rychlak, 1990, 1992). Central to these meaning systems or personal theories are certain superordinate constructs (Kelly, 1955), deep structures (Guidano & Liotti, 1983), or core ordering processes (Mahoney, 1991) that define a person's sense of identity and mode of relating to others.

IMPLICATIONS FOR PSYCHOTHERAPY CONCEIVED AS A POSTMODERN PRACTICE

What implications do these philosophical and theoretical assumptions carry for the practice of psychotherapy? In a general sense, postmodernism is congenial to the "participatory epistemology" (Mahoney, 1989) that undergirds virtually all forms of clinical practice. Although the inherently fragmentary and perspectival, but pragmatically useful knowledge that guides clinical discourse and intervention may be derided by "modernists" within academic psychology, it can nonetheless be viewed as an affirmative, constructive approach to developing practical expertise (Polkinghorne, 1992). At this general level, nearly any model of psychotherapy can be a legitimate resource for the postmodern practitioner, as long as it is interpreted as a historically and culturally bounded set of provisional metaphors and guidelines rather than as an applied science that compels only a certain conceptualization of the problem and only a single approved form of intervention.

But in a more specific sense, a postmodern psychology tends to encourage certain strategies of intervention over others, insofar as these cohere with a broader constructivist view of human beings and their interaction. Several of these common clinical heuristics are outlined in Table 2, along with some selected techniques that are compatible with them. However, two aspects of intervention are worth emphasizing. First, these core strategic features are not universal among all constructivist therapies, in that these therapies compose a "fuzzy set" of approaches with indistinct boundaries (as illustrated by the diversity of subsequent chapters in this volume). Second, the relationship between abstract strategies or heuristics and concrete techniques or interventions is not a determinate one, particularly in view of the creativity and resistance to prescription that characterize constructivist therapists. Thus, these features and interventions are intended only to convey a general feel for therapies that are organized around constructivist themes, leaving to subsequent contributors to this volume the task of presenting specific

TABLE 2
Selected Strategic and Technical Preferences of Constructivist
Therapies

Area	Strategic Preferences	Representative Interventions
Assessment focus	Exploration of personal narratives, autobiography, personal and family construct systems and hierarchies	Identification of central metaphors, life review, repertory grids, laddering techniques
Goal of therapy	Creative rather than corrective; promotion of meaning-making and personal development	Fixed-role therapy, stream-of-consciousness technique, facilitation of meaningful accounts
Interpretation of emotion	Treatment of negative emotion as integral to constructive change; to be respected rather than controlled	Reprocessing of emotional schemata, systematic evocative unfolding, psychodramatic exploration
Level of intervention	Attention to selfhood processes, core role structures, family constructs or premises	Movieola technique, enactment of deep role relationship, circular questions, ritual prescription
Style of therapy	Personal rather than authoritative; empathic grasping of client's outlook as basis of negotiation	Credulous approach, adoption of "not-knowing" approach, elaboration of metaphor or story
Approach to resistance	To understand as a legitimate attempt to protect core-ordering processes; modulate pace of change	"Allowing" resistance, externalizing of the problem, identification of unique outcomes

frameworks for intervention. More detailed explication of the distinguishing strategic features of constructivist approaches to clinical assessment and psychotherapy can be found elsewhere (Mahoney & Gabriel, 1987; G. J. Neimeyer & Neimeyer, 1993; R. A. Neimeyer, 1993b).

The strategic preferences of constructivist therapists cohere with their epistemological commitments as outlined in Table 1. In keeping with their conceptualization of human beings as incipient theorists (Kelly, 1955) or narrators of their experience (Howard, 1991), constructivists envision the basic goal of therapy as the promotion of this meaning-making activity rather than the "correction" of presumed dysfunctions or deficits in the client's thinking, feeling, or behaving (Carlsen, 1989; R. A. Neimeyer, 1993a). Therefore, in assessment, constructivists concentrate on identifying and eventually reformulating the central metaphors that inform the client's self-narrative (Gonçalves, 1994; Woolum,

1994)[3] as well as personal and shared systems of meaning that prove impermeable in the face of novel experience (Kelly, 1955). This typically carries the constructivist therapist to relatively deep levels of intervention, or second-order change (Lyddon, 1990), with a focus on the basic selfhood processes (Guidano, 1991; Mahoney, 1991) that sustain an individual's sense of identity and essential relatedness to others. The therapist therefore remains alert to the threat that might be posed by moving too precipitously toward invalidating the assumptive bases of the client's self-theory and adopts an empathic, collaborative, respectful, and at times almost reverential, mode of relating to the client struggling with understandable "resistance" to change (Leitner, 1988; also see Leitner's chapter, this volume). As a process-oriented approach to therapy, constructivism encourages a delicate attunement to the often-inarticulate questions implicit in the client's behavior (R. A. Neimeyer, 1988b) and attempts to help the client weave through his or her experience threads of significance that lead either to provisional answers or toward better, more incisive questions (Kelly, 1969b). Ultimately, the aim of therapy is to create a personal and interpersonal atmosphere in which presenting problems can be reformulated and resolved in language (Loos & Epstein, 1989) and in which clients can recruit social validation for new, less "problem-saturated" identities (White & Epston, 1990).

METAPHORS FOR PSYCHOTHERAPY

Although these strategic tendencies characterize most forms of constructivist psychotherapy, different "lineages" or traditions of constructivism (R. A. Neimeyer, 1993a) tend to emphasize slightly different approaches to intervention, especially at a concrete technical level. Below, I outline four basic metaphors for therapy that are explicit or implicit in constructivist writing: (a) therapy as personal science, (b) therapy as selfhood development, (c) therapy as narrative reconstruction, and (d) therapy as conversational elaboration. I then conclude with a few observations about the possible futures of constructivist psychotherapy, foreshadowing themes developed further in some of the chapters to follow.

Therapy as Personal Science

The model of the person as scientist, actively formulating personal hypotheses and refining, revising, or elaborating these in the course of

---

[3]Sandy Woolum's (1994) videotape, *Exploring Personal Metaphors,* can be obtained from PsychoEducational Resources (P.O. Box 2196, Keystone Heights, FL 32656), as can information on a series of training videotapes in constructivist psychotherapy featuring many of the contributors to this volume.

ongoing experience, represents the cornerstone of personal construct theory, the first significant clinical constructivist theory. Since its proposal as the "fundamental postulate" of personal construct theory by Kelly (1955), the personal science paradigm has been adopted as an organizing metaphor for psychology and psychotherapy, not only by subsequent generations of personal construct theorists (cf. Epting, 1984; Fransella, 1972; Leitner & Dunnett, 1993; R. A. Neimeyer & Neimeyer, 1987), but also by a substantial number of constructivist therapists working largely outside the personal construct tradition (e.g., Guidano & Liotti, 1983; Mahoney, 1977). However, it has also proven attractive as a model to cognitive therapists of a more rationalist or objectivist persuasion. In many respects, this similarity in terminology has been unfortunate, in that the latter theorists have tended to interpret the notion of personal science in keeping with a "modernist," logical–empiricist conception of science that is concerned with eliminating distorted or invalid inferences (Beck, Rush, Shaw, & Emery, 1979), adhering to standards of rational disputation (Ellis, 1979), or promoting rule-governed behavior (Meichenbaum, 1977). In contrast, constructivist theorists who have adopted the metaphor adhere to a more contemporary, post-Kuhnian philosophy of science, emphasizing the inherently fictional nature of all theories and hypotheses (Vaihinger, 1924), the role of often-impassioned personal knowledge in scientific activity (Polanyi, 1958), and the parallels between periods of individual developmental crisis and the upheavals in basic assumptions that constitute a scientific paradigm shift (Mahoney, 1980). Moreover, the postmodern emphasis on neopragmatism or utility as a primary criterion for the adequacy of knowledge suggests that constructivists are more likely to envision the person as an "applied," rather than a "theoretical" scientist—one who is clearly invested in the implications of his or her experimentation for action in the real world. Thus, recent criticisms that the personal scientist metaphor (Wessler, 1987) is too cerebral and detached to offer a credible portrayal of human functioning appear to be principally directed at the more rationalist or logical–empiricist reading of the model, and such critics may actually support the view advanced by Kelly (1955) and subsequent constructivists.

In the present volume, this tradition of construing therapy as a sometimes terrifying relinquishment of the assumptive bases of one's life as well as a creative experimentation with new possibilities is especially represented in the chapters by G. J. Neimeyer, Leitner, and Harter. In addition to their mutual recognition that the pursuit of new significances poses formidable challenges for the client, these authors are also united in the inflection they place on the therapist's humble and personal participation in the process of change. Feixas's chapter on the integration of personal construct theory and the systemic therapies also reflects the influence of the personal science metaphor, although, in his case, individuals are cast more in the role of family theorists striving to develop and maintain an adequate construct system for interpreting and regulating family interactions. Nonetheless, in spite of the diversity of techniques, therapy formats, and client populations represented by these chapters, each of these contributors attempts to identify conditions conducive to a progressive revision of the client's personal paradigm and to deal empathically with the resistance to change that sometimes results.

Therapy as Selfhood Development

As indicated by Mahoney (1993; see also chapter 3 of this book), the cognitive revolution that reshaped the field of behavior therapy in the 1970s has further evolved as an increasing number of theorists and practitioners have begun to adopt constructivist tenets. Shifting away from the logocentrism and realism of previous formulations, onetime adherents to rational emotive or cognitive approaches—such as Wessler (1993), Young (1990), and Freeman (1993)—have begun to focus less on immediate cognitive or behavioral change and more on the emotionally charged "personal rules of living" or "early maladaptive schemas" that underlie serious psychological disturbance. This shift in focus has in turn fostered greater therapeutic attention to those early developmental stages (Freeman, 1993) or attachment relationships (Bricker, Young, & Flanagan, 1993; Liotti, 1987) in which various disordered self-schemas arose, a terrain once traversed mainly by psychodynamic therapists. This conceptual extension into a more developmental model of assessment (see also Lyddon & Alford, 1993) has necessitated a similar extension of therapeutic strategy and technique. Mahoney (1991), for example, has developed a variety of methods for helping both therapist and client observe the latter's selfhood processes. One such technique is the stream-of-consciousness method, "an exercise in which the client is invited to attend to, and as best one can, report ongoing thoughts, sensations, images, memories, and feelings" with minimal intrusion or interpretation on the part of the therapist (Mahoney, 1991, p. 295; see also R. A. Neimeyer, 1993d). Like the two-chair work and imagery techniques used by Bricker et al. (1993), such methods both facilitate the reaccessing of latent self-schemas in the session and permit their gradual modification. A hallmark of such approaches is their recognition that deep-going challenges to the self should be based on a careful, guided discovery rather than on a direct, confrontational and disputative stance (Freeman, 1993).

In the present volume, this model of therapy as an accelerated form of selfhood development is best represented in contributions by Guidano, Greenberg and Pascual-Leone, and Carlsen, although features of this approach permeate a number of the other chapters as well. Guidano (1987, 1991) in particular has elaborated on the "complexity of self," which he sees as coevolving with the capacity for intersubjectivity in human relationships. In contrast with a modernistic conception of an essentialized self as an entity comprising enduring traits, the self envisioned by Guidano (1991) is a dynamic process of "construction and reconstruction of a reality capable of making consistent the ongoing experience of the ordering individual" (p. 5). Central to this dynamic organization is the dialectical interplay between the experiencing *I* and the explaining *me*, resulting in a more or less continuous reordering of one's conscious sense of self and reality. From this vantage point, therapy becomes a necessarily emotional process of developmental analysis, with the client passing through the "movieola" of slow-motion replay a series of affectively charged scenes from his or her past that have been implicated in the construction of his or her current sense of self.

A parallel emphasis on the dynamics of self-development characterizes Greenberg and Pascual-Leone's contribution to this book. Wedding Pascual-Leone's attention to dialectical transformations in personal knowledge with Greenberg's traditional attention to specific emotional change events in therapy, the two theorists collaboratively "unpack" (systematically delineate) the way in which essential tensions within the individual's system of schemas set the stage for higher order experiential integrations. Among the distinctive characteristics of this hybrid perspective are its acknowledgment of real-world constraints on human adaptation and its attempt to detail the processes contributing to change within meaning systems. Like the reconstructive techniques of Clarke (1993) and Greenberg and Safran (1987), forms of treatment deriving from this model entail the reaccessing and reexperiencing of sometimes distressing emotions as a precondition to their therapeutic reconstruction. Although this reprocessing is calculated to facilitate more inclusive levels of knowledge about the self and world, it is nonetheless assumed that life-span development will be characterized by discontinuous and periodic challenges to the adequacy of one's personal organization—a theme elaborated by Carlsen in her contribution to this work and elsewhere (Carlsen, 1989). As such, one's sense of self is never fully consistent, because experience continues to perturb current patterns of self-explanation, pushing for their progressive refinement across the course of one's life.

Therapy as Narrative Reconstruction

A third constructivist metaphor for psychotherapy is of therapy as narrative reconstruction—the "rebiographing" (Howard, 1990) of life stories that have become constraining or incoherent, requiring significant editing or elaboration. Like constructivism itself, this model draws inspiration from intellectual trends far beyond the familiar domain of clinical practice, from such disparate fields as cognitive science (Abelson, 1989) and cultural psychology (Bruner, 1990). Across the human sciences and humanities, discipline after discipline has been "narrativized" in the past decade as scholars find that new facets are revealed when subject matter is viewed as a form of story construction or deconstruction.

Particularly in the domain of psychotherapy, the view of human beings as inveterate storytellers has powerful heuristic appeal. As narrators, the significance of our lives is dictated by the stories that we live and that we tell (Mair, 1989)—that is, by the ways that we link events in meaningful sequences (Vogel, 1994) and thereby constitute a sense of self as the protagonist of our own autobiography (Mancuso & Sarbin, 1983). But just as not all stories are comedies, not every storied life fulfills the criteria for a satisfying or profound "narrated or to-be-narrated quest" (MacIntyre, 1981, p. 203). Indeed, clients often seek or are referred to therapy when they are identified with their problems and subjected to a "dominant narrative" that disqualifies, delimits, or denies their personhood (White & Epston, 1990). Under such conditions, a constructivist therapist working within this metaphor "would not work word by word, proposition by proposition, testing each out against the current standards of evidence, but would instead proceed on a more holistic level whereby the adoption of a new language game would itself usher in new standards" (Russell, 1991, p. 250). Thus, in contrast with cognitive therapists who seek to dismantle distorted automatic thoughts, irrational beliefs, and illogical inferences in a piecemeal fashion, constructivist therapists attempt to articulate the thematic subtext that undergirds the plot of the client's life and to help him or her experiment with new plots that open possibilities for fresh chapters.

Among the growing cadre of therapists approaching their work from this metaphoric stance, White and Epston (1990) have been particularly creative in devising ingenious and practical "narrative means to therapeutic ends." The first crucial step in liberating clients from a story that subjugates and oppresses their lives is to "externalize the problem," anthropomorphizing the symptom or problem (e.g., depression) as something external to the identified client. The therapist then guides the client in detailing the "real effects" of the problem in his or her life (e.g., requiring a life of solitary confinement or forcing the client to disregard his or her own bodily needs). Having distanced from the problem in this way, the client is then better prepared to resist its demands on his or her life and to "perform an alternative story" charged with a greater sense of personal agency and fulfillment. Although the primary credit for reauthoring the client's life may go to the client, the therapist nonetheless plays a critical role in prompting and validating a new story through emphasizing those unique outcomes that fail to conform to the requirements of the externalized problem. To accomplish this, the therapist may draw on a broad repertory of narrative tools, such as conferring diplomas to formally certify the client's mastery of the problem, granting certificates attesting to the client's hard-won self-knowledge, or writing between-session letters that underscore the remarkable victories hinted at in the last interview or that express the therapist's curiosity about possible developments to be reviewed in the coming week (White & Epston, 1990). In their contribution to the current book, Epston and White expand on this theme, offering guidelines in the form of therapeutic rites of passage and inquiries that can help consolidate the gains the client has made over the course of therapy.

Among the other authors in this volume, Gonçalves, R. A. Neimeyer, and Hermans operate most explicitly within the narrative metaphor. Gonçalves is perhaps the most ambitious, using the narrative metaphor to understand the changing textuality of self associated with the progressive paradigm shifts from a behavioral, to a cognitive, to a constructivist ontology and epistemology. Therapy, in his view, then becomes a "rehearsing scenario" for life narratives, and hermeneutics can be used to understand in greater detail the role of the client in authoring his or her life. From a more applied perspective, R. A. Neimeyer then considers the unique role of client-generated narratives (e.g., personal journals, poetry, and written accounts) in both fostering and documenting therapeutic change, and Hermans illustrates an original form of clinical assessment with which to focus therapeutic discussion on emotionally problematic situations as well as help trace changes in client meanings over time.

Therapy as Conversational Elaboration

A final therapeutic metaphor that is closely aligned with a narrative model is of therapy as the elaboration of conversation. Proponents of this approach, particularly among the systemic family therapies, regard human systems as quintessentially language generating, defining their organization through discourse and negotiation. From this perspective, meaning arises through communicative action rather than residing within individual selves or knowers, and therapy itself becomes an exercise in cocreative "languaging" among all of the members of the "problem-organizing system" (H. Anderson & Goolishian, 1992).

If family construct systems (Feixas, 1990; Procter, 1987), family paradigms (Reiss, 1981), or family premises (Penn, 1985) are language determined, then the role of the therapist is to elucidate and subtly challenge those "contractual agreements, maintained in language," that solidify family members' (sometimes dysfunctional) realtionships to one another (Efran et al., 1990). Through the use of circular questions (Selvini-Palazzoli, Boscolo, Cecchin, & Prata, 1980) asked from an attitude of genuine curiosity and "not knowing" (H. Anderson & Goolishian, 1992), the therapist functions as a conversation manager in coconstructing a new story with the family that has a sense of coherence, that is relevant to the concerns of those struggling around the problem, and that provides a sense of elaborative possibility (Loos, 1993).

In the present volume, Efran and Fauber unpack the sometimes abstract presentation of this radical constructivist perspective and clearly spell out its implications for psychotherapy. Because they view problems as "unresolved quandaries" that are created and sustained in the domain of language, they regard problem-solving conversation as the necessary medium of all psychotherapy, regardless of the school of thought to which the therapist belongs. However, they broadly construe therapeutic conversation as an emotionally resonant form of symbolic exchange or performance, rather than as a thin line of verbal assertion distinguished sharply from affect and behavior. Epston and White's contribution extends this perspective, offering a taxonomy of provocative therapeutic questions that can be used by the therapist as conversational artist in elaborating a more constructive identity with the client and in recruiting social support for it. Finally, Feixas bridges the gap that sometimes separates more systemic and language-based expressions of constructivism from those that historically have focused more on the individual person. Efforts at integrating the various traditions of constructivism might lead toward a more comprehensive model of human change (see also Lyddon's chapter, this volume) and its facilitation in psychotherapy.

POSSIBLE FUTURES OF CONSTRUCTIVIST PSYCHOTHERAPY

Now that I have sketched the contours of constructivist psychotherapy conceived as a form of postmodern practice, it may be appropriate to close with a few reflections about the possible futures of this emerging clinical perspective. My treatment of these topics here is brief because some of these themes are developed further by Mahoney in the closing chapter of this volume. In particular, I hope to highlight (a) the relevance of constructivism for psychotherapy research, (b) its potential role in the exploration of psychotherapy integration, and (c) some of the unresolved internal tensions within the family of constructivist therapies that merit the attention of future scholars.

Constructivist Contributions to Psychotherapy Research

A brief review of the epistemological commitments of constructivists outlined in Table 1 is sufficient to raise significant questions about the place of constructivist thinking in psychology conceived as a scientific field of study. With their inherent distrust of objectivistic discourse about "knowable realities," their iconoclastic resistance to methodological prescription, and their pluralistic celebration of interpretive multiplism, constructivists would seem to be unlikely contributors to a research tradition characterized by a preoccupation with objectivity, experimental control, and the development of a secure knowledge base to guide applications to practice. Indeed, constructivists have come under fire for their ambivalence toward the premises, methods, and models underpinning traditional research—a charge I have considered in greater detail elsewhere (R. A. Neimeyer, in press). However, I believe that constructivists' "outsider status" to an objectivist approach may in some important respects be an advantage, allowing them to make at least two distinctive contributions to research in psychotherapy.

First, given conceptual and methodological developments in the larger discipline of psychology (Steenbarger, 1991), at least some forms of constructivist theory and method may be sufficiently familiar that they can be assimilated into current research practice within a "normal science" paradigm. For example, personal construct theory has generated thousands of publications, the majority of which make use of such methods as repertory grid technique to study individual conceptual structures and their modification (R. A. Neimeyer, Baker, & Neimeyer, 1990). In the context of psychotherapy research, such methods may help investigators address a range of questions about the role of personal meaning systems in therapeutic change, the nature of client–therapist or client–therapy matching, therapists' conceptualizations of therapy, and the relation of the therapy process to outcome (R. A. Neimeyer, Harter, & Alexander, 1991; Winter, 1990, 1992; see also Herman's chapter, this volume). Although empirical "horse race" studies of psychotherapy outcome or treatment preference studies pitting constructivist and nonconstructivist therapies against one another (Karst, 1970; Vincent & LeBow, in press) are conspicuously rare, researchers have been far more active in using constructivist methods to study the idiographic change processes that occur in therapy, irrespective of which theoretical orientation they follow (Caine, Wijesinghe, & Winter, 1981; Koch, 1983; Ryle, 1980). The diversity of interview-based assessment strategies arising within personal construct theory (Landfield & Epting, 1987), developmental therapy (Ivey, 1991), and kindred perspectives (Hoshmand, 1994; R. A. Neimeyer, 1993e) provides a rich trove of resources for psychotherapy researchers who share a concern with meaning reconstruction, whether in an individual or family systemic context (Rigazio-DiGilio, 1994; see also Feixas's chapter, this volume).

A second contribution that constructivists could make is toward the sophistication of psychotherapy process research, particularly in terms of work that adopts a "change events" perspective (Rice & Greenberg, 1984) or a narrative approach (Toukmanian & Rennie, 1992). Writing from the former perspective, Greenberg (1986) has argued that "increased understanding of therapy will emerge by discovering *what interventions make what type of impact at what particular client moments in therapy*" (pp. 717–718). This conceptual shift in research focus necessitates a parallel shift in units of analysis, concentrating on those observable "markers" of important in-session client processes (e.g., expression of internal conflict), followed by the therapist's intervention and the client's subsequent reaction or "performance." These events can then be studied in sequential detail, to elaborate a conceptual model of change and verify it against further observations of the same marker event in the same or among different clients. Among the aims of this research strategy would be to identify client markers that invite intervention, to specify therapist interventions that would facilitate change at these junctures, and to delineate client performances in response to these interventions that would promote both immediate and enduring change (Greenberg, 1986). Both Toukmanian's (1992) constructivist research on client perceptual systems and Greenberg's (1992) task analysis of intrapersonal conflict resolution provide examples of the heuristic and applied payoffs of this type of research. An advantage of this approach to studying therapy processes is that it is much closer to the grainy detail of clinical practice than to the more global correlational and experimental designs that tend to predominate in the study of psychotherapy.

Although a focus on change events departs in several important respects from conventional psychotherapy process research, it nonetheless can be considered to fit within a "paradigmatic" orientation concerned with discovering general laws or patterns by adapting externally applied coding systems to observable client performances or cognitive structures. In contrast, a "narrative" research strategy would be more hermeneutic and qualitative, concentrating on the client or therapist's own account of his or her intentions in a given therapeutic exchange (Rennie & Toukmanian, 1992). Rennie (1992) has provided an excellent example of this narrative thrust in investigating therapy process, using taped replays of therapy sessions to prompt clients' recollections of the experience of entire hours of psychotherapy. These spontaneous recollections are transcribed, yielding 40–80 pages of text per client, and are segmented into meaning units for grounded theory analysis. One result of Rennie's research has been his development of a detailed taxonomy of response categories that are hierarchically organized in terms of their levels of abstractness. For example, he has subsumed instances of client insight and contact with feelings into a superordinate category concerned with "the pursuit of meaning," whereas responses suggesting defensiveness or resistance are integrated under the heading "avoidance of meaning." These superordinate categories are themselves subsumed under the main category of "relationship with personal meaning," which is one of four such categories in the current system. Finally, at the highest level of abstraction is the "core category" of "clients' reflexivity," a heading that encompasses the clients' sense of self-awareness and agency.

Some of the more vigorous and intriguing programs of research into psychotherapeutic change combine aspects of the paradigmatic and narrative traditions. Martin's (1992) systematic series of studies is exemplary in this regard, mapping the gradual increments in the complexity and orderliness of clients' self-theories across the course of successful therapy. What makes this research an even more important contribution to theory and practice is its fit with an evolving model of how therapy works, predicated on the reciprocal interaction of memories and self-theories and their transformation in the crucible of therapeutic conversation (Martin, 1994).

Taken together, constructivist forays into the terrain of both paradigmatic (more objective or quantitative) research and narrative (more subjective or qualitative) research have begun to contribute to the understanding of processes of change in the therapy encounter. However, this dual allegiance to two somewhat irreconcilable epistemologies may be problematic at both a conceptual and a procedural level, despite the existence of some hybrid programs, such as those of Angus (1992) on metaphor and Martin (1992) on cognitive mediation. For example, Rennie and Toukmanian (1992) have argued that "each of the two approaches to explanation [the paradigmatic and narrative] entails a different logic of justification and attempts to bring both approaches under one roof could result in a weakening of each of them" (p. 246). Although it is clear that the methodological implications of a constructivist stance toward research are still evolving (Viney, 1988), it is equally clear that constructivist researchers are already contributing to the knowledge base regarding psychotherapy, in a way that is informative for academicians and practitioners alike (Hoshmand, 1994).

Constructivism and Psychotherapy Integration

Over the past few decades, growth in the area of psychotherapy has been prodigious, leading to the proliferation of literally hundreds of identifiable approaches to psychotherapy, with more "innovative" approaches being announced each year (Norcross, 1986). Perhaps somewhat ironically, this state of affairs has prompted an almost equally bewildering variety of calls for the integration or rapprochement of different perspectives (Mahrer, 1989), most of which share the goal of producing a unified body of knowledge that can guide both research and practice (Staats, 1991). Although such a goal is laudable in many respects, constructivists have embraced this trend with some ambivalence, raising both problems and prospects relevant to the further evolution of psychotherapy integration.

At one level, constructivists have expressed serious reservations about the epistemological näiveté of the most common approaches toward transcending or synthesizing different schools of therapy. For example, an intuitive form of eclecticism that selects techniques solely on the basis of their appeal can lead to a haphazard, atheoretical form of therapy, whereas the contrasting approach of theoretical integration of conceptually antagonistic models (e.g., behavior therapy and psychoanalysis) runs the risk of theoretical incoherence. Even appeals to "common factors" presumed to operate in all therapies or to a "common language" to transcend the jargon of different schools are not without problems, because they threaten to reduce multifaceted approaches to their "least common denominator" and to simplify theoretically rich discourse that is grounded in different traditions of thought (see R. A. Neimeyer, 1993c, for an extended discussion). In keeping with the epistemological commitments outlined in Table 1, constructivists tend to be pluralistic and perspectival in their approach to theory, and distrust moves toward the hegemony of any one approach or terminology. As Messer (1987) noted, "human nature being what it is, a diversity of theory and language is bound to continue, at least in those areas of the world where people are encouraged to think freely, creatively, and divergently" (p. 196).

In spite of their skepticism regarding a fully unified, universal system for psychotherapy, constructivists acknowledge the value in promoting greater dialogue across the sometimes arbitrary boundaries that have separated therapy traditions, as well as the importance of keeping any approach to therapy permeable enough to accommodate new developments. For this reason, I have tried elsewhere (R. A. Neimeyer, 1988a, 1993c; R. A. Neimeyer & Feixas, 1990) to develop a model of psychotherapy integration that avoids the pitfalls associated with atheoretical or purely data-driven forms of eclecticism, both of which disregard the thorny conceptual issues that must be confronted in the melding of different theories. This alternative approach, termed *theoretically progressive integrationism* (TPI), has as its goal the elaboration of a coherent theory that both explains and constrains psychotherapeutic interventions. Thus, like other systematic forms of eclecticism, it is an attempt to provide both a conceptualization of and a direction for clinical practice. Procedurally, it consists of three integrative dialectics: (a) between theory and practice, fostering an exchange in which each can enrich the other; (b) between a given school of psychotherapy and developments in another discipline (e.g., cognitive science and hermeneutics); and (c) between selected schools of psychotherapy. Because most enthusiasts for integration are principally concerned with this third area, I have devoted most attention to articulating those structural constraints on the blending of psychotherapeutic theories grounded in different intellectual traditions, arguing that "high level synthesis of any two theories of psychotherapy is only feasible to the extent that they share theoretical and metatheoretical assumptions" (R. A. Neimeyer, 1993c, pp. 144–145). In this view, some theories would be especially good candidates for bridge-building efforts (e.g., narrative and personal construct approaches, see above), whereas the attempted "integration" of abstractly incompatible models (e.g., psychoanalysis and structural family therapies) could be predicted to produce only a confusing assemblage of concepts that would resist any serious coordination or articulation.

Although a TPI model of integration could be advanced for any set of approaches that are congruent at metatheoretical or epistemological levels (witness the fruitful melding of mechanistic behavioral and information-processing trends, which have found expression in many forms of cognitive–behavioral therapy), constructivism itself seems to represent a particularly propitious meeting ground for potential integrationists. In the ideal case, a TPI model would suggest that the most progressive mergers would be between approaches that were congruent in their central assumptions about the nature of human beings, the processes of knowing, and so forth, but that were distinctive at more concrete technical levels—thereby contributing to the extension of therapeutic technique within a consistent, but enriched, theoretical framework (R. A. Neimeyer, 1993c). These ideal conditions are approximated in the case of constructivist therapies, which have converged at metatheoretical levels while bringing along their unique strategic and practical heritages. For example, Sass (1992) has detailed the postmodern turn in psychoanalysis, as such theorists as Schafer (1983) and Spence (1982) have abandoned the traditional view of "insight" as the discovery of repressed memories and, instead, have begun to view such memories as more invented than retrieved and as subject to the demand for narrative "smoothing." Parallel endorsements of this narrative view of historical interpretation can be found in personal construct theory (Kelly, 1969a), systemic family therapies (Efran et al., 1990), and other approaches founded on the analogy between text and treatment (White & Epston, 1990). Similarly, representatives of a broad range of therapies have been adopting constructivist tenets like those outlined in Table 1 (R. A. Neimeyer & Feixas, 1990), making the prospects for their cross-fertilization excellent, as is illustrated by Feixas's integration of personal construct and systemic therapies in this volume. Thus, constructivism seems well positioned to play more than a cautionary role in the evolution of psychotherapy integration, fostering the kind of conceptual interchange that should produce more comprehensive, but nonetheless bounded, theories of psychotherapy.

Internal Tensions Within the Constructivist Movement

In a sense, speaking of "constructivism" as a singular noun is more rhetorical than realistic, in that any close listening to the postmodern chorus reveals a polyphony of voices—not all of which are singing in the same key (R. A. Neimeyer, Neimeyer, Lyddon, & Hoshmand, 1994). Even within the more narrow scope of psychotherapy, constructivists have been energetically pluralistic in their postulates and procedures, as a reading of the subsequent chapters in this volume indicates. Although they may be united in their opposition to an objectivist epistemology, with its technological and power-based implications for the helping professions, postmodern practitioners display considerable divergence on important issues, occasionally to the point of contradiction.

One such area of conflict concerns the centrality of the self in constructivist discourse. For some authors (e.g., Guidano, 1991; Mahoney, 1991), the construction of an "evolving self" (Kegan, 1982) that consolidates the meaning of experience can be seen as the pivotal organizing principle of life, with challenges to one's core sense of selfhood triggering the sort of dynamic disequilibrium that brings clients into therapy. In contrast, other postmodern thinkers (Lather, 1992; Sampson, 1989) refer to the "death of the self," that is, the dissolution of any conception of individuality as a unitary and sovereign entity distinguishable from the "text" of the world. In their extreme moods, deconstructionist scholars celebrate the demise of personal subjectivity and idiosyncratic selfhood and their replacement by "the more anonymous sense of irreality carried by the flood of media images which surround us like an atmosphere" (Sass, 1992, p. 176). This in turn conjures a different set of existential issues confronted by the postmodern subject, whether in or out of therapy. As Sass (1992) observed:

> instead of the old pathos of distance . . . the condition of an inner self cut off from some unattainable reality—we enter into a universe devoid of both objects and selves: where there is only a swarming of "selfobjects," images and simulacra filling us without resistance. (Sass, 1992, p. 176)

In the domain of psychotherapy, this loss of individual agency carries the paradoxical implication that "life is a purposeless drift into which each speaker scatters a seemingly inexhaustible supply of causal inferences" (Efran et al., 1990, p. 97). Between these conceptual poles of self-centered and self-less psychologies is a range of more "agnostic" constructivist positions that ascribe no essential nature to human beings but that, nonetheless, accord them a measure of bounded autonomy in defining their own personhood in different cultural and historical contexts (Mair, 1977).

Closely allied with this essential tension regarding the role of the self is a debate regarding the locus of meaning—that is, whether it lies in an individual's "predication" or assertion of some organizing scheme in a given context (Rychlak, 1990) or in a communally defined language or symbol system from which "individual" acts of meaning are essentially derived (Gergen, 1985). Although such disputes may seem remote from the domain of clinical practice, they nonetheless carry implications for psychotherapeutic strategies: Proponents of the former, more individualistic perspective use procedures that invite more self-reflection by the client (Guidano, 1991; Mahoney, 1991; R. A. Neimeyer, 1993d), and proponents of the latter, more language-based perspective, emphasize more conversational procedures for coconstructing meaning in the therapeutic interaction (H. Anderson & Goolishian, 1992; Loos, 1993).

Myriad other differences (many of which are commented on throughout this book) distinguish the various versions of constructivism, including their advocacy or avoidance of cognitive terminology (cf. Bricker et al., 1993; Middleton & Edwards, 1990), their preference for respectful facilitation or vigorous negotiation of therapeutic change (cf. chapters by Leitner and by Efran & Fauber, this volume), their critical acceptance or rejection of ontological realism (Mahoney, 1991; Maturana & Varela, 1987), and their endorsement of a paradigmatic or narrative model of psychotherapeutic research (Rennie & Toukmanian, 1992). Indeed, these differences in inflection or ideology might be expected of proponents of postmodern pluralism, who sometimes seem to value intellectual iconoclasm over conceptual coherence. But such diversity nonetheless poses challenges for constructivist theorists and practitioners, as they struggle to maintain a meaningful dialogue across the divisions that separate some subgroups from others (R. A. Neimeyer, in press). Indeed, it is probable that this dialogue may grow more rather than less confusing in the immediate future, as one-time adherents to more rationalist or objectivist psychotherapies attempt to redefine themselves in constructivist and narrative terms (Ellis, 1993; Meichenbaum, 1993).

If there is a provisional "solution" to the challenge of this diversity, it lies in the direction of critical scholarship that seeks to articulate the nuances distinguishing different "varieties of constructivist experience," at both metatheoretical and applied levels (see Botella, in press, and Lyddon's chapter in this volume for an excellent beginning). Ultimately, the resulting internal as well as external dialogue could lay the groundwork for a more comprehensive constructivism that may help shape the future, as well as the present, of psychotherapy.

REFERENCES

Abelson, R. P. (1989). Psychological status of the script concept. *American Psychologist, 36*, 715–729.

Anderson, H., & Goolishian, H. (1992). The client is the expert: A not-knowing approach to therapy. In S. McNamee & K. J. Gergen (Eds.), *Therapy as social construction* (pp. 25–39). Newbury Park, CA: Sage.

Anderson, W. T. (1990). *Reality isn't what it used to be*. New York: Harper & Row.

Angus, L. E. (1992). Metaphor and the communication interaction in psycho-therapy. In S. G. Toukmanian & D. L. Rennie (Eds.), *Psychotherapy process research* (pp. 187–210). Newbury Park, CA: Sage.

Bartlett, F. C. (1932). *Remembering*. Cambridge, England: Cambridge University Press.

Bateson, G. (1972). *Steps to an ecology of mind*. New York: Dutton.

Beck, A. T., Rush, J., Shaw, B., & Emery, G. (1979). *Cognitive therapy of depression*. New York: Guilford Press.

Botella, L. (in press). Personal construct theory, constructivism, and postmodern thought. In R. A. Neimeyer & G. J. Neimeyer (Eds.), *Advances in personal construct psychology*. Greenwich, CT: JAI Press.

Bricker, D., Young, J. E., & Flanagan, C. M. (1993). Schema-focused cognitive therapy. In K. T. Kuehlwein & H. Rosen (Eds.), *Cognitive therapies in action* (pp. 88–124). San Francisco: Jossey-Bass.

Bruner, J. (1990). *Acts of meaning*. Cambridge, MA: Harvard University Press.

Caine, T. M., Wijesinghe, O., & Winter, D. A. (1981). *Personal styles in neurosis*. London: Routledge & Kegan Paul.

Carlsen, M. B. (1989). *Meaning-making: Therapeutic processes in adult development*. New York: Norton.

Clarke, K. M. (1993). Creation of meaning in incest survivors. *Journal of Cognitive Psychotherapy, 7*, 195–204.

Edwards, D., & Potter, J. (1992). *Discursive psychology*. Newbury Park, CA: Sage.

Efran, J. S., Lukens, M. D., & Lukens, R. J. (1990). *Language, structure, and change*. New York: Norton.

Ellis, A. (1979). Toward a new theory of personality. In A. Ellis & J. M. Whitely (Eds.), *Theoretical and empirical foundations of rational-emotive therapy* (pp. 7–32). Monterey, CA: Brooks/Cole.

Ellis, A. (1993). Reflections on rational-emotive therapy. *Journal of Consulting and Clinical Psychology, 61*, 199–201.

Epting, F. R. (1984). *Personal construct counseling and psychotherapy.* New York: Wiley.

Feixas, G. (1990). Personal construct theory and the systemic therapies: Parallel or convergent trends? *Journal of Marital and Family Therapy, 16,* 1–20.

Fransella, F. (1972). *Personal change and reconstruction.* San Diego, CA: Academic Press.

Freeman, A. (1993). A psychosocial approach for conceptualizing schematic development for cognitive therapy. In K. T. Kuehlwein & H. Rosen (Eds.), *Cognitive therapies in action* (pp. 54–87). San Francisco: Jossey-Bass.

Gergen, K. (1985). The social constructionist movement in modern psychology. *American Psychologist, 40,* 266–275.

Gergen, K. J. (1992). Toward a postmodern psychology. In S. Kvale (Ed.), *Psychology and postmodernism* (pp. 17–30). Newbury Park, CA: Sage.

Gonçalves, Ó. F. (1994). From epistemological truth to existential meaning in cognitive narrative psychotherapy. *Journal of Constructivist Psychology, 7,* 107–118.

Greenberg, L. S. (1986). Research strategies. In L. S. Greenberg & W. M. Pinsof (Eds.), *The psychotherapeutic process: A research handbook.* (pp. 707–734). New York: Guilford Press.

Greenberg, L. S. (1992). Task analysis. In S. G. Toukmanian & D. L. Rennie (Eds.), *Psychotherapy process research* (pp. 22–50). Newbury Park, CA: Sage.

Greenberg, L. S., & Safran, J. D. (1987). *Emotion in psychotherapy.* New York: Guilford Press.

Guidano, V. F. (1987). *Complexity of the self.* New York: Guilford Press.

Guidano, V. F. (1991). *The self in process.* New York: Guilford Press.

Guidano, V. F., & Liotti, G. (1983). *Cognitive processes and emotional disorders.* New York: Guilford Press.

Hoshmand, L. T. (1994). *Orientation to inquiry in a reflective professional psychology.* Albany: State University of New York Press.

Howard, G. S. (1990). Narrative psychotherapy. In J. K. Zeig & W. M. Munion (Eds.), *What is psychotherapy?* (pp. 199–201). San Francisco: Jossey-Bass.

Howard, G. S. (1991). Culture tales: A narrative approach to thinking, cross-cultural psychology, and psychotherapy. *American Psychologist, 46,* 187–197.

Ivey, A. E. (1991). *Developmental strategies.* Pacific Grove, CA: Brooks/Cole.

Karst, T. O. (1970). Initial study using fixed-role therapy and rational-emotive therapy in treating public speaking anxiety. *Journal of Consulting and Clinical Psychology, 34,* 360–366.

Kegan, R. (1982). *The evolving self.* Cambridge, MA: Harvard University Press.

Kelly, G. A. (1955). *The psychology of personal constructs.* New York: Norton.

Kelly, G. A. (1969a). The autobiography of a theory. In B. Maher (Ed.), *Clinical psychology and personality: The selected papers of George Kelly* (pp. 46–65). New York: Wiley.

Kelly, G. A. (1969b). Ontological acceleration. In B. Maher (Ed.), *Clinical psychology and personality* (pp. 7–45). San Diego, CA: Academic Press.

Kelly, G. A. (1977). The psychology of the unknown. In D. Bannister (Ed.), *New perspectives in personal construct theory* (pp. 1–19). San Diego, CA: Academic Press.

Koch, H. (1983). Changes in personal construing in three psychotherapy groups and a control group. *British Journal of Medical Psychology, 56,* 245–254.

Korzybski, A. (1933). *Science and sanity.* New York: International Non-Aristotelian Library.

Kvale, S. (1992). *Psychology and postmodernism.* Newbury Park, CA: Sage.

Landfield, A. W., & Epting, F. R. (1987). *Personal construct psychology: Clinical and personality assessment.* New York: Human Sciences Press.

Lather, P. (1992). Postmodernism and the human sciences. In S. Kvale (Ed.), *Psychology and postmodernism* (pp. 88–109). Newbury Park, CA: Sage.

Leitner, L. M. (1988). Terror, risk, and reverence: Experiential personal construct therapy. *International Journal of Personal Construct Psychology, 1,* 251–261.

Leitner, L. M., & Dunnett, N. G. (1993). *Critical issues in personal construct psychotherapy.* Malabar, FL: Krieger.

Liotti, G. (1987). Structural cognitive therapy. In W. Dryden & W. L. Golden (Eds.), *Cognitive–behavioural approaches to psychotherapy* (pp. 92–128). New York: Hemisphere.

Loos, V. (1993). Now that I know the techniques, what do I do with the family? In L. Leitner & G. Dunnett (Eds.), *Critical issues in personal construct psychotherapy* (pp. 239–263). Malabar, FL: Krieger.

Loos, V., & Epstein, E. S. (1989). Conversational construction of meaning in family therapy. *International Journal of Personal Construct Psychology, 2,* 149–167.

Lovlie, L. (1992). Postmodernism and subjectivity. In S. Kvale (Ed.), *Psychology and postmodernism* (pp. 119–134). Newbury Park, CA: Sage.

Lyddon, W. J. (1990). First- and second-order change: Implications for rationalist and constructivist cognitive therapies. *Journal of Counseling and Development, 69,* 122–127.

Lyddon, W. J., & Alford, D. J. (1993). Constructivist assessment: A developmental–epistemic perspective. In G. J. Neimeyer (Ed.), *Constructivist assessment: A handbook* (pp. 31–57). Newbury Park, CA: Sage.

MacIntyre, A. (1981). *After virtue: A study in moral theology.* Notre Dame, IN: University of Notre Dame Press.

Mahoney, M. J. (1977). Personal science. In A. Ellis & R. Grieger (Eds.), *Handbook of rational psychotherapy* (pp. 352–366). New York: Springer.

Mahoney, M. J. (1980). Psychotherapy and the structure of personal revolutions. In M. J. Mahoney (Ed.), *Psychotherapy process* (pp. 157–180). New York: Plenum.

Mahoney, M. J. (1988). Constructive metatheory, I: Basic features and historical foundations. *International Journal of Personal Construct Psychology, 1*, 299–315.

Mahoney, M. J. (1989). Participatory epistemology and the psychology of science. In B. Gholson, W. R. Shadish, R. A. Neimeyer, & A. C. Houts (Eds.), *Psychology of science* (pp. 138–164). Cambridge, England: Cambridge University Press.

Mahoney, M. J. (1991). *Human change processes*. New York: Basic Books.

Mahoney, M. J. (1993). Theoretical developments in the cognitive psychotherapies. *Journal of Consulting and Clinical Psychology, 61*, 187–193.

Mahoney, M. J., & Gabriel, T. J. (1987). Psychotherapy and the cognitive sciences: An evolving alliance. *Journal of Cognitive Psychotherapy, 1*, 39–59.

Mahrer, A. R. (1989). *The integration of psychotherapies*. New York: Human Sciences Press.

Mair, M. (1977). Metaphors for living. In A. W. Landfield (Ed.), *Nebraska symposium on motivation: 1976* (pp. 241–290). Lincoln: University of Nebraska Press.

Mair, M. (1989). *Between psychology and psychotherapy*. London: Routledge & Kegan Paul.

Mancuso, J. C., & Sarbin, T. R. (1983). The self-narrative in the enactment of roles. In T. R. Sarbin & K. Scheibe (Eds.), *Studies in social identity* (pp. 233–253). New York: Praeger.

Martin, J. (1992). Cognitive–mediational research on counseling and psychotherapy. In S. G. Toukmanian & D. L. Rennie (Eds.), *Psychotherapy process research* (pp. 108–133). Newbury Park, CA: Sage.

Martin, J. (1994). *The construction and understanding of psychotherapeutic change*. New York: Teachers College Press.

Maturana, H., & Varela, F. (1987). *The tree of knowledge*. Boston: New Science Library.

Meichenbaum, D. (1977). *Cognitive–behavior modification*. New York: Plenum.

Meichenbaum, D. (1993). Changing conceptions of cognitive–behavior modification: Retrospect and prospect. *Journal of Consulting and Clinical Psychology, 61*, 202–204.

Messer, S. B. (1987). Can the Tower of Babel be completed? A critique of the common language proposal. *Journal of Integrative and Eclectic Psychotherapy, 6*, 195–199.

Middleton, D., & Edwards, D. (1990). *Collective remembering*. Newbury Park, CA: Sage.

Neimeyer, G. J., & Neimeyer, R. A. (1993). Defining the boundaries of constructivist assessment. In G. J. Neimeyer (Ed.), *Constructivist assessment: A casebook* (pp. 1–30). Newbury Park, CA: Sage.

Neimeyer, R. A. (1987). An orientation to personal construct therapy. In R. A. Neimeyer & G. J. Neimeyer (Eds.), *Personal construct therapy casebook* (pp. 3–19). New York: Springer.

Neimeyer, R. A. (1988a). Integrative directions in personal construct therapy. *International Journal of Personal Construct Psychology, 1*, 283–298.

Neimeyer, R. A. (1988b). The origin of questions in the clinical context. *Questioning Exchange, 2*, 75–80.

Neimeyer, R. A. (1993a). An appraisal of constructivist therapy. *Journal of Consulting and Clinical Psychology, 61*, 221–234.

Neimeyer, R. A. (1993b). Constructivism and the cognitive therapies: Some conceptual and strategic contrasts. *Journal of Cognitive Psychotherapy, 7*, 159–171.

Neimeyer, R. A. (1993c). Constructivism and the problem of psychotherapy integration. *Journal of Psychotherapy Integration, 3*, 133–157.

Neimeyer, R. A. (1993d). Constructivist approaches to the measurement of meaning. In G. J. Neimeyer (Ed.), *Constructivist assessment: A casebook* (pp. 58–103). Newbury Park, CA: Sage.

Neimeyer, R. A. (1993e). Constructivist psychotherapy. In K. T. Kuehlwein & H. Rosen (Eds.), *Cognitive therapies in action: Evolving innovative practice* (pp. 268–300). San Francisco: Jossey-Bass.

Neimeyer, R. A. (in press). Problems and prospects in constructivist psychotherapy. *Journal of Constructivist Psychology.*

Neimeyer, R. A., Baker, K. D., & Neimeyer, G. J. (1990). The current status of personal construct theory: some scientometric data. In G. J. Neimeyer & R. A. Neimeyer (Eds.), *Advances in personal construct psychology* (pp. 3–22). Greenwich, CT: JAI Press.

Neimeyer, R. A., & Feixas, G. (1990). Constructivist contributions to psychotherapy integration. *Journal of Integrative and Eclectic Psychotherapy, 9*, 4–20.

Neimeyer, R. A., & Harter, S. (1988). Facilitating individual change in personal construct psychotherapy. In G. Dunnett (Ed.), *Working with people* (pp. 174–185). London: Routledge & Kegan Paul.

Neimeyer, R. A., Harter, S., & Alexander, P. C. (1991). Group perceptions as predictors of outcome in the treatment of incest survivors. *Psychotherapy Research, 1*, 149–158.

Neimeyer, R. A., & Neimeyer, G. J. (1987). *Personal construct therapy casebook.* New York: Springer.

Neimeyer, R. A., Neimeyer, G. J., Lyddon, W. J., & Hoshmand, L. T. (1994). The reality of social construction. *Contemporary Psychology, 39*, 458–463.

Norcross, J. C. (1986). Eclectic psychotherapy: An introduction and overview. In J. C. Norcross (Ed.), *Handbook of eclectic psychotherapy* (pp. 3–24). New York: Brunner/Mazel.

Penn, P. (1985). Feed-forward: Future questions, future maps. *Family Process, 24*, 299–310.

Piaget, J. (1971). *The construction of reality in the child.* New York: Basic Books. (Originally published in 1937)

Polanyi, M. (1958). *Personal knowledge.* New York: Harper.

Polkinghorne, D. E. (1992). Postmodern epistemology of practice. In S. Kvale (Ed.), *Psychology and postmodernism* (pp. 146–165). Newbury Park, CA: Sage.

Popper, K. R. (1963). *Conjectures and refutations*. London: Routledge & Kegan Paul.

Procter, H. G. (1987). Change in the family construct system. In R. A. Neimeyer & G. J. Neimeyer (Eds.), *Personal construct therapy casebook* (pp. 153–171). New York: Springer.

Reiss, D. (1981). *The family's construction of reality*. Cambridge, MA: Harvard University Press.

Rennie, D. L. (1992). Qualitative analysis of the client's experience of psychotherapy. In S. G. Toukmanian & D. L. Rennie (Eds.), *Psychotherapy process research* (pp. 211–233). Newbury Park, CA: Sage.

Rennie, D. L., & Toukmanian, S. G. (1992). Explanation in psychotherapy process research. In S. G. Toukmanian & D. L. Rennie (Eds.), *Psychotherapy process research* (pp. 234–251). Newbury Park, CA: Sage.

Rice, L. N., & Greenberg, L. S. (1984). *Patterns of change*. New York: Guilford Press.

Rigazio-DiGilio, S. A. (1994). A co-constructive developmental approach to ecosystemic treatment. *Journal of Mental Health Counseling, 16*, 43–74.

Russell, R. L. (1991). Narrative in views of humanity, science and action: Lessons for cognitive therapy. *Journal of Cognitive Psychotherapy, 5*, 241–256.

Rychlak, J. F. (1990). George Kelly and the concept of construction. *International Journal of Personal Construct Psychology, 3*, 7–19.

Rychlak, J. F. (1992). Oppositionality and the psychology of personal constructs. In R. A. Neimeyer & G. J. Neimeyer (Eds.), *Advances in personal construct psychology* (pp. 3–25). Greenwich, CT: JAI Press.

Ryle, A. (1980). Some measures of goal attainment in focused integrated active psychotherapy. *British Journal of Psychiatry, 137*, 475–486.

Sampson, E. E. (1989). The deconstruction of the self. In J. Shotter & K. Gergen (Eds.), *Texts of identity* (pp. 1–19). Newbury Park, CA: Sage.

Sass, L. A. (1992). The epic of disbelief: The postmodern turn in contemporary psychoanalysis. In S. Kvale (Ed.), *Psychology and postmodernism* (pp. 166–182). Newbury Park, CA: Sage.

Schafer, R. (1983). *The analytic attitude*. New York: Basic Books.

Selvini-Palazzoli, M., Boscolo, L., Cecchin, G., & Prata, G. (1980). Hypothesizing-circularity-neutrality. *Family Process, 19*, 3–12.

Shotter, J., & Gergen, K. (Eds.). (1989). *Texts of identity*. Newbury Park, CA: Sage.

Simons, H. W. (Ed.). (1989). *Rhetoric in the human sciences*. Newbury Park, CA: Sage.

Spence, D. (1982). *Narrative truth and historical truth*. New York: Norton.

Staats, A. W. (1991). Unified positivism and unification psychology. *American Psychologist, 46,* 899–912.

Steenbarger, B. (1991). All the world is not a stage: Emerging contextualist themes in counseling and development. *Journal of Counseling and Development, 70,* 288–296.

Steier, F. (1991). *Research and reflexivity.* Newbury Park, CA: Sage.

Toukmanian, S. G. (1992). Studying the client's perceptual processes and their outcomes in psychotherapy. In S. G. Toukmanian & D. L. Rennie (Eds.), *Psychotherapy process research* (pp. 77–107). Newbury Park, CA: Sage.

Toukmanian, S. G., & Rennie, D. L. (1992). *Psychotherapy process research: Paradigmatic and narrative approaches.* Newbury Park, CA: Sage.

Vaihinger, H. (1924). *The philosophy of "as if."* Berlin, Germany: Reuther & Reichard.

Vincent, N., & LeBow, L. M. (in press). Treatment preference and acceptability: Epistemology and locus of control. *Journal of Constructivist Psychotherapy.*

Viney, L. L. (1988). Which data-collection methods are appropriate for a contructivist psychology? *International Journal of Personal Construct Psychology, 1,* 191–203.

Vogel, D. (1994). Narrative perspectives in theory and therapy. *Journal of Constructivist Psychology, 7,* 243–261.

Wessler, R. L. (1987). Conceptualizing cognitions in the cognitive–behavioral therapies. In W. Dryden & W. L. Golden (Eds.), *Cognitive–behavioral approaches to psychotherapy* (pp. 1–29). New York: Hemisphere.

Wessler, R. L. (1993). Cognitive appraisal therapy and disorders of personality. In K. T. Kuehlwein & H. Rosen (Eds.), *Cognitive therapies in action* (pp. 240–267). San Francisco: Jossey-Bass.

White, M., & Epston, D. (1990). *Narrative means to therapeutic ends.* New York: Norton.

Winter, D. A. (1990). Therapeutic alternatives for psychological disorder. In G. J. Neimeyer & R. A. Neimeyer (Eds.), *Advances in personal construct psychology* (Vol. 1, pp. 89–116). Greenwich, CT: JAI Press.

Winter, D. A. (1992). *Personal construct psychology in clinical practice.* London: Routledge & Kegan Paul.

Woolum, S. (1994). *Exploring personal metaphors* [Videotape]. (Available from PsychoEducational Resources, P.O. Box 2196, Keystone Heghts, FL 32656.)

Young, J. E. (1990). *Cognitive therapy for personality disorders: A schema-focused approach.* Sarasota, FL: Professional Resource Exchange.

3

CONTINUING EVOLUTION OF THE COGNITIVE SCIENCES AND PSYCHOTHERAPIES

MICHAEL J. MAHONEY

In an era of heightened self-consciousness about the limits of historiography (the writing of history) and the fallible basis on which many historical interpretations are based, it is perhaps foolish to venture a narrative on the evolution of the cognitive sciences and their applied (service-focused) counterparts (the cognitive psychotherapies). It is clear, nevertheless, that these two related developments have captured the imagination and hopes of a whole generation of educators, psychologists, psychiatrists, social workers, and researchers who view the cognitive approaches as the latest and most promising contenders in a multicentury competition for the most adequate models of human experience and the most effective methods for servicing pathologies and problems in human adjustment (Dobson, 1988; Sperry, 1993). This chapter is intended to offer a necessarily personal synopsis of three related discussions: (a) developments in the cognitive sciences (and cognitive psychology) during the twentieth century, (b) the emergence and differentiation of the cognitive psychotherapies, and (c) a brief discussion of issues that are likely to challenge future developments in both areas in the twenty-first century.

In each of these three major topics of discussion, I propose that constructivism reflects some of the most exciting and viable developments in psychology and psychotherapy. As will be elaborated, I consider constructivism to be a multifaceted expression of a philosophical tradition that recognizes the individual as an active, anticipatory, and developing participant in his or her own life-span experience. This tradition, which has influenced a number of approaches to psychotherapy, seems uniquely suited to further evolution, and its clinical promise is gaining the interest of increasing numbers of health service providers in and beyond psychology. The premises and promise of constructivist theory in psychotherapy may be best understood in the context of the three discussions mentioned above.

TWENTIETH-CENTURY DEVELOPMENTS IN THE COGNITIVE SCIENCES

Future historians may find it interesting and challenging to identify a single individual, date, or event by which to mark the beginning of the so-called cognitive revolution (whether in psychology or in the sciences in general). That such a revolution took place in the second half of the twentieth century is undisputed. Where and when it started, how it was first expressed, and by whom it was inaugurated are matters that historiographers (writers of history) are already disputing. Consider, for example, the possible candidates for pioneers and pioneering contributions to the cognitive sciences from 1860 to 1970, which are summarized in the Appendix. The works listed also pre-date some of the important developments associated with postmodernism and postrationalism (Gergen, 1991; Guidano, 1991; Kvale, 1992; Madison, 1988; Mahoney, 1991a; Tarnas, 1991). Postmodernism and postrationalism are themselves reflections of developments that transcend philosophy and the academic disciplines; they are reflections of planetary life in the past decade of the twentieth century. Therefore, they are also reflections of the complexities and apparent paradoxes that challenge imminent developments in psychology and psychotherapy. The list in the Appendix is hardly exhaustive, of course, but it does render a sense of the wide range, diversity, and, in some cases, simultaneity of contributions that probably contributed to what modern observers consider the cognitive era in psychology, psychiatry, and many allied sciences.

Cybernetics and Information Processing

Although there were many precursors to the emergence of the cognitive revolution within and beyond psychology, historians of the cognitive sciences have suggested that these developments achieved critical mass and momentum sometime around midcentury. Bruner and Postman (1947a, 1947b) introduced the "new look" in perception in 1947, and Norbert Wiener's (1948) *Cybernetics* was published the next year (see Appendix). It was also in 1948 that the Hixon Symposium on Cerebral Mechanisms in Behavior provided a forum for such pioneers as John von Neumann, Warren McCulloch, and Herbert Simon to lay the foundations of information theory and to consider the promise of modeling theories of brain functioning by using computer analogies. Information processing soon became a respected field of research and development. Throughout much of the literature of the 1950s and 1960s, the terms *cognitive psychology* and *information processing* were often used synonymously. *Artificial intelligence*, in those decades, was a term and focus more radical and imaginative than was felt tolerable by mainstream gatekeepers in cognitive research.

There were, as always, personal and paradigmatic politics, the details and dynamics of which have barely been touched on in the most popular historiographies of the cognitive sciences (Baars, 1986; Gardner, 1985; Hirst, 1988). There were biases of method and traditions of metaphors that are now, historically, apparent. Gardner (1985), for example, asserted that the first three key features of cognitive science were its reliance on mental representation, its reliance on computation, and its "de-emphasis of such murky concepts as affect, context, culture, and history" (p. 42). All three of these so-called key features are topics of considerable controversy in the cognitive sciences of 1994, where metaphors of representation are under reappraisal; the limits of solely computational programs are increasingly recognized; and culture, affect, history, and context are among the most interesting topics in human knowing and experience (M. Johnson, 1987; Mahoney, 1991a; Merleau-Ponty, 1962, 1963; Miró, 1989; Salthe, 1985; Shanon, 1988; Tarnas, 1991; P. P. Wiener, 1974).

One must beware, however, of the tendency toward dichotomies in acceptance and rejection processes. These earliest efforts to develop more and more of a science of mind were themselves the engines of understanding and the generators of new ideas about human knowing. It will probably be centuries before their contributions to our inquiries are adequately appreciated. To be sure, the models and theories of these first decades of "black box" research tended to accentuate contrasts over continuities, states over processes, and physical metaphors over abstract orders. The black-box metaphor had been introduced to emphasize behaviorists' neglect of the inside story of experience. As long as functional relations could be demonstrated between stimulus and response, intervening processes were deemed irrelevant. In these early cognitive models, the mind was said to be a central way station—a relatively passive and usually consistent transducer of energy input (stimulation) and energy output (response). The Gallilean–Cartesian dream of certain and objective knowledge may have been fundamental to the development of psychology as a discipline separate from philosophy and experimental physiology in the eighteenth and nineteenth centuries. However, the more the pioneers in cybernetics and information processing began to look into and model the so-called black boxes of their experimental subjects (and, no doubt, themselves), the more complex were their impressions of human perception, learning, and memory, and the more pervasive became views of "opponent process" (essential tensions) and complex dynamics in motivation and learning (see below).

For all of their flaws and limitations, the cybernetic and information-processing traditions in the cognitive sciences served, and continue to serve, as an invaluable reference point and source of technological development. They are not yet history, and their presence is apparent in all other recognized perspectives in the cognitive sciences (Mazlish, 1993). Moreover, researchers associated with these traditions have continued to respond creatively to the challenges of increasing complexities in models and theories of the human mind. For this alone, the high regard of these traditions in the cognitive sciences is amply warranted.

Connectionism and Computational Neuroscience

Since the emergence and elaboration of modern cognitive sciences in the third quarter of the twentieth century, there have been significant and palpable evolutions within that successful revolution. One of these developments has been the emergence of a perspective called *connectionism*, which is a movement spanning the cognitive sciences, computer sciences, and neurosciences. Briefly put, connectionism is an approach to learning, memory, and development that relies on the computational capacities of supercomputers, which are essentially systems of systems with capacities for "massively distributed parallel processing" of information.

Like other such events, this evolution had at least some of its origins in events that occurred decades earlier. It is, for example, more than coincidental that modern connectionism shares its core metaphor with the turn-of-the-century learning theory of E. L. Thorndike (1898; also called *connectionism*). Then, in 1932, Tolman staggered the behaviorist majority with his book titled *Purposive Behavior in Animals and Men*. In 1943, Warren McCulloch and Walter Pitts published the seminal paper

"Logical Calculus of the Ideas Immanent in Nervous Activity." It was an incredible idea itself. And in 1948, Norbert Wiener published *Cybernetics*, a book on the cybernetic modeling of purposive behavior—the conceptual prototype later elaborated by Miller, Galanter, and Pribram (1960) as the TOTE (Test, Operate, Test, Exit). The TOTE was the essence of cybernetic logic: Test the current value of a variable, begin adjustment operations if necessary, test the variable again, and repeat this process until its values are acceptable.

In 1949, Donald O. Hebb published his classic theory of the organization of behavior, and the foundation for what is now known as connectionism was firmly in place. An unspoken rivalry began to develop between those drawn toward computer science metaphors and those drawn toward the organic processes of self-organization. The rivalry became a conscious skirmish after the 1962 publication of Frank Rosenblatt's *Principles of Neurodynamics*, a pathbreaking move toward the modeling of neuronlike learning systems. Rosenblatt's ideas were harshly criticized by "computophiles" Marvin Minsky and Seymour Papert (Minsky & Papert, 1969) and were functionally ignored by mainstream information scientists for more than a decade. But the ideas and technologies that would come to characterize connectionism continued to be elaborated. And they at least shared the following features: (a) a shift in emphasis from the computer to the living nervous system as the primary source of information about the structures and functions of human knowing; (b) a creative use of continuing developments in computer technology to refine models simulating human learning; and (c) a recognition that computational processes cannot adequately deal with a complexity of "subsymbolic processes" that operate pervasively in all human experience.

As its constituents have formed productive collaborations with leading neuroscientists—creating the sub-subspecialization of "computational neuroscience" (Sejnoski, Koch, & Churchland, 1988)—connectionists have become increasingly confident in the promise that the directions they are taking are leading toward truly revolutionary views of brain function and learning processes. Connectionism has become a movement of major proportions in late-twentieth-century cognitive science. It has both staunch defenders and harsh detractors (Feldman & Ballard, 1982; Fodor & Pylyshyn, 1988; Schneider, 1987; Seidenberg, 1993). And, perhaps most important, it has considerable interest as a theme of dialogue in contemporary cognitive science.

To reiterate, connectionism in its modern form is a mature and sophisticated type of stimulus–response associationism. It presumes that some form of computation is basic to learning and memory. With its concessions to "subsymbolic processes" and to the lessons of studying knowing systems in operation, connectionism may also represent a conceptual bridge from the centuries-old doctrine of associationism to the recent rise of constructivist and evolutionary theories of learning.

Constructivism and Evolutionary Epistemology

At about the same time that connectionism was coming together as a contemporary identity within cognitive science, another set of developments was taking place that would lead to an important differentiation within the cognitive sciences. These developments appeared to be relatively independent of a parallel set of developments in the cognitive psychotherapies in the period between 1950 and 1975.

At some point in all of this complexity, a coherent and viable perspective began to emerge. In 1952, the University of Chicago Press published a book that was initially ignored and yet remains in press more than 4 decades later. It was subtitled *Reflections on the Foundations of Theoretical Psychology*, and it was authored not by a psychologist, but by an economist. His name was Friedrich Hayek, and his book was *The Sensory Order* (1952). It was (and is) a masterpiece and classic expression of the modern transition from objectivist–naive and rationalist–passive-sensory metatheories of the human mind to more projectivist, postrationalist, and active motor-evolutionary perspectives. In his dense little volume, Hayek pushed the empiricist program to (and well beyond) its limits. In doing so, he demonstrated that the contents of experience—all frequencies, intensities, magnitudes, and diverse nuances—must be, neurologically and otherwise, the products of higher order categorization or classification processes that, with lessons from experience, participate in creating "the sensory order." The theoretical significance of Hayek's work has yet to be fully appreciated (Hamowy, 1987; Hayek, 1964; Mahoney & Weimer, 1994), but the power of its practical implications has already begun to be explored (Burrell, 1987; Ford, 1987; Mahoney, 1991a).

Constructivism is a tradition in the cognitive sciences that has been traced back at least as far as the writings of Vico, Kant, and Vaihinger in Western civilization, and its expressions in the literatures of Asiatic philosophies and religions are indisputable (Mahoney, 1988a, 1988b, 1991a). Essentially, constructivism is a family of theories and therapies that emphasize at least three interrelated principles of human experience: (a) that humans are proactive (and not passively reactive) participants in their own experience—that is, in all perception, memory, and knowing; (b) that the vast majority of the ordering processes organizing human lives operate at tacit (un- or super-conscious) levels of awareness; and (c) that human experience and personal psychological development reflect the ongoing operation of individualized, self-organizing processes that tend to favor the maintenance (over the modification) of experiential patterns. Although uniquely individual, these organizing processes always reflect and influence social systems. Pioneering expressions of constructivism can be found in the writings of Wilhelm Wundt (1896), Pierre Janet (1898), Charles Sherrington (1906), William James (1890), Jean Piaget (1926), and Frederic Bartlett (1932), to name some of the most familiar.

After midcentury, expressions of constructivist perspectives began to be elaborated. Berger and Luckman's (1966) classic, *The Social Construction of Reality*, ushered in a wave of writings on the social construction of everyday life and social processes in science (Gergen, 1985, 1991; Tarnas, 1991). Meanwhile, the beginnings of evolutionary epistemology—the study of developments in knowing systems—were established by Donald Campbell and others (Callebaut & Pinxten, 1987; Campbell, 1974; Dell & Goolishian, 1981; Radnitzky & Bartley, 1987). Because I have dwelt elsewhere on historical details and more recent expressions of constructivism and evolutionary epistemology within the cognitive sciences (Mahoney, 1988a, 1991a), I shall not reiterate them here. As the title and focus of this volume reflect, however, I remain appreciative of the past and future contributions of these metatheories to both the mind sciences and health services.

Hermeneutics and Narrative

In reflecting on the early days of the cognitive revolution, Jerome Bruner (1990) noted the following:

> It would make an absorbing essay in the intellectual history of the last quarter-century to trace what happened to the originating impulse of the cognitive revolution. . . . Very early on, for example, emphasis began shifting from "meaning" to "information," from the *construction* of meaning to the *processing* of information. These are profoundly different matters. The key factor in the shift was the introduction of computation as the ruling metaphor and of computability as a necessary criterion of a good theoretical model. (p. 4)

After introducing (with Postman) the "New Look in Perception" in 1947, Bruner went on to explore a "new look in knowing" as well. That look involved an acknowledgment that narrative processes are pervasive in human knowing. This view is now a popular and growing element in (and beyond) the cognitive therapies, as is its companion field of hermeneutics.

Hermeneutics is one of those terms that began to gain respect in the social and health sciences in the 1990s. It comes from the Greek *hermeneutikos*, meaning "interpretation," and it is associated with the

Greek god Hermes (synonymous with the Roman god Mercury), whose task was to serve as messenger of the gods. Not surprisingly, perhaps, the first formal appearance of hermeneutics as a specialization was in theology, where the interpretation of sacred scripture was of central importance. Through a tapestry of historical developments too intricate to trace here, however, hermeneutics became secularized in the twentieth century. It also began to cross-fertilize with linguistics, semiotics (theory of signs), analytic philosophy, literary criticism, psychoanalysis, and evolutionary epistemology (Carr, 1986; Dilthey, 1976; Freeman, 1993; Gadamer, 1975, 1976, 1988; Heidegger, 1927/1962, 1959/1971; Madison, 1988; Messer, Sass, & Woolfolk, 1988; Palmer, 1969; Stent, 1985; Wachterhauser, 1986).

Interestingly, one of the formative debates in hermeneutics was about validity and the objectivity of interpretations. Those championing objectivism argued that the meaning of a text literally resided within it; that is, the meaning was lying there waiting to be discovered and understood from an adequate reading of the text. Those championing other positions have ranged from relativists to radicals, and they have participated in a conceptual transformation of unprecedented proportions. They challenge, for example, traditional boundaries between subject and object, not to mention the presumed boundaries among author, text, and reader. Indeed, the postmodern reader is said to be "in the text" as an active and individualizing context for its "languaging" (which is a much more active and complex verb than "reading"; Fischer, 1987; Iser, 1978).

One can now see the striking parallels between narrative psychology and hermeneutics. Both have to do with stories and meanings that are personally interpreted. Both involve active generative processes and equally active reflective processes—"acts of meaning," as Bruner (1990) has called them. Both are reflections of the continuing human quest to understand—to experience and possibly express some of the order within the chaos. Narrative and hermeneutic approaches, in my opinion, have just begun to be appreciated for their possible contributions to psychotherapy. It will be interesting to observe their evolution in the coming decades.

Complex Systems Approaches

The last theme that I address as a development in twentieth-century cognitive science is the rise of the sciences of complexity and their contemporary cross-fertilization. Like other themes in the cognitive sciences, complexity can be traced to writers and works that long pre-dated the recent surge of popularity in the term (Bonner, 1988; Hamowy, 1987; Hayek, 1964; Lewin, 1992; Waldrop, 1992; Weimer, 1982). In recent decades, the appreciation for complexity and complex systems analyses has been stimulated by developments in the field of chaos. Although there have been varying interpretations about the boundaries of that field (Glass & Mackey, 1988; Gleick, 1987), chaos is a subspecialization within the broader context of studying complex systems. Chaos researchers and theorists have been primarily interested in the influence of initial conditions on subsequent system parameters—hence their affinity for the so-called butterfly effect, in which the minuscule air turbulence created by a butterfly in one hemisphere can—through the amplifications afforded by "strange attractors"—eventually influence the formation of a hurricane or tornado in another hemisphere. Complexity specialists are interested in the phenomena and processes of chaos, but their questions and emphases are much more diverse. They have been relatively more occupied, for example, with emergent properties, developing methods for modeling nonlinear dynamics (e.g., Morrison, 1991), and the essential tension between disequilibrium (disorganizing) and self-organizing processes in the development of open systems (e.g., Bienenstock, 1985; Bienenstock, Soulié, & Weisbuch, 1986; Hager, 1992).

Much of the early work in complex systems was authored by evolutionary biologists, organic chemists, thermodynamicists, and social systems experts (e.g., Campbell, Eccles, Eigen, Hayek, Jantsch, Pattee, Popper, Prigogine, Waddington, and Zeleny). The discovery of the self-replicating hypercycle and the demonstration of clear "dissipative" (self-organizing) structures in both living and nonliving systems led to conceptual leaps that are still in process (Depew & Weber, 1995; Jantsch, 1980, 1981; Mahoney, 1991b; Salthe, 1993; Varela, 1979; Weimer, 1987; Zeleny, 1980, 1981). In the last 2 decades, there have been exciting developments in this area, not the least of which are those formulated by Vittorio Guidano, Humberto Maturana, and Francisco Varela. As I elaborate toward the end of the next section, the evolution of constructivist psychotherapies from and toward the sciences of complexity is a trend worthy of note. (For contemporary expressions of the relationship between the sciences of complexity and the cognitive and computer sciences, see Glass and Mackey, 1988; M. H. Johnson, 1993; Kauffman, 1993; Lewin, 1992; Searle, 1992; and Waldrop, 1992.) It seems increasingly clear that future models of human experience (and hence, both education and psychotherapy) will be intimately linked with metaphors and models found useful in the study of adaptation and learning in other complex systems.

TWENTIETH-CENTURY DEVELOPMENTS IN COGNITIVE PSYCHOTHERAPIES

Like the foregoing narrative about developments in the cognitive sciences, this discussion on cognitive therapies is a limited and linear attempt to construct an order from which to view the history and current events of the cognitive psychotherapies. Having been a participant–observer of developments since the 1960s, I am sure that my reflections, recollections, and integration of developments in the cognitive psycho-therapies have been shaped by my experiences with them and their representatives over the last quarter century.

The Mind Cure Movement

Contemporary cognitive psychotherapy owes at least part of its practical legacy to the "psychology of healthy mindedness" and the so-called mind cure movement that swept through parts of western Europe and North America in the late-nineteenth and early-twentieth centuries (James, 1958; Mahoney, 1993; Meyer, 1965; Parker, 1973). It was out of that movement, for example, that Pierre Janet's (1898) "fixed ideas"—thought to be involved in neurotic disorders—were challenged by what would later come to be called "the power of positive thinking" (Peale, 1960). Active rituals of self-talk and healthy thinking were practiced, as were other health regimens. These practices were often packaged as part of a program for success and self-development that was aimed at Christian audiences.

Whatever their aim, the books on how to be healthy minded were a financial success. It takes only a casual stroll through an average bookstore almost anywhere on the planet to realize that the lay public have come to virtually equate psychology with self-help or self-improve-ment. Positive thinking and the psychology of optimism remain popular themes in the trade literature, and "feeling good" is now commonly associated with thinking right. This association is particularly apparent, I believe, in the literature devoted to rational emotive therapy.

Rational Emotive Therapy

Albert Ellis developed one of the most popular and influential forms of cognitive psychotherapy with his 1962 book *Reason and Emotion in Psychotherapy*, the "big book" founding rational emotive therapy. In it, he integrated the Stoic philosophy of Epictetus with a practical guide for identifying and eliminating a list of basic irrational ideas said to be responsible for a wide range of unnecessary human suffering. Ellis (with whom I have had the honor of working and the pleasure of friendship) soon became the nucleus of a worldwide network of centers and prac-titioners of rational emotive therapy. Thousands of his personal work-shops have drawn large audiences on five continents. Shocking to some, "Al" is quite direct and often provocative. He has not been a reticent participant in twentieth-century culture. He has inspired many to explore the relations between philosophy and psychotherapy and between thinking and feeling, as well as the meaning of living a theory. Because this chapter is meant to be a historiography of the cognitive therapies, I shall not venture into an evaluative review of rational emotive therapy (Mahoney, Lyddon, & Alford, 1989). More important for the present volume is the acknowledgment that Albert Ellis and rational emotive therapy have been and continue to be major and navigational elements in the continuing evolution of the cognitive psychotherapies.

Personal Construct Psychology

Another, even earlier classic in cognitive therapy was George Kelly's (1955) two-volume masterpiece *The Psychology of Personal Constructs*. Kelly did not call it "cognitive," however, and he was equally intentional in emphasizing that his system could not be adequately classified by any of the modern "isms" in psychology. Kelly was a master at metatheory—that is, conjectures at the level of superordinate processes (as contrasted, e.g., with the concrete particulars of "ordinary" experience). He was in the good company of his contemporary, Charles Osgood, in appreciating that the dimensions of human experience are carved from polar contrasts and that the measurement of meaning is fundamentally the measurement of personal dimensions of differences. This was but one of George Kelly's insights, however, and I shall resist elaborating themes here that may be quite familiar to readers of this volume. The contributions of Kelly and subsequent personal construct theorists have been elaborated by Neimeyer (1985) and are discussed in a number of other chapters in this volume.

Cognitive Behavior Modification

The approach called *cognitive behavior modification* is more difficult to describe than others, in part because it has continued to evolve over the decades since the 1970s. In my personal reconstruction of events, however, cognitive behavior modification seemed to appear on the heels of two earlier developments in behaviorism and behavior therapy. The first was the emergence of the conceptual and practical mutant known as *covert conditioning*, and the second was the surge of interest and activity in what was then called *behavioral self-management*. Covert conditioning was inaugurated by Lloyd Homme (1965). A student of Skinner, Homme proposed that human thoughts could be treated as "covert operants"—unobserved, internal responses "operating" on the environment—or "coverants," obeying the same principles of behavior and, therefore, susceptible to contingency management and thought-control strategies. My first interactions with Skinner were over Homme's proposal, about which he was skeptical. Skinner was, however, quite enthusiastic about behavioral self-control, to which he had devoted an entire chapter in his 1953 book.

Joseph Cautela (1966) published a more Pavlovian idea about thought control, proposing that images and words could be conditioned by other images and words, thereby permitting much of behavior therapy to be practiced in and with the client's imagination. Cautela believed that, rather than presenting painful stimuli in vivo, therapists could achieve comparable results by appropriately pairing imaginary stimuli and responses. Early research on the prospects and procedures of covert sensitization yielded ambiguous answers (Mahoney, 1974), and other perspectives and procedures began to receive increasing attention. Among these were the contributions of Donald H. Meichenbaum (1969, 1974, 1977), a University of Illinois graduate who, in his dissertation, had investigated thought patterns and their modification in hospitalized schizophrenics. Inspired by readings of Luria and Vygotsky, among others, Meichenbaum elaborated practical procedures for studying and possibly modifying the private, ongoing "self-statements" that lie beneath or behind people's behavioral and emotional difficulties. As his interests and activities have continued to diversify over the ensuing decades, Meichenbaum (1995) has contributed to health psychology, psychotherapy, and literatures in areas ranging from the unconscious to human narrative.

The book *Cognition and Behavior Modification* (Mahoney, 1974) was the result of several forces in my life. I had been working on the idea behind it since the late 1960s. The topic I proposed for my first term paper in graduate school was "an information processing analysis of behavior modification"; it was declined as lacking sufficient literature for a term paper. In 1973, as a young assistant professor at Pennsylvania State University, I spent a summer teaching in Brazil. That same year, at the annual convention of the American Psychological Association, in Montreal, I met B. F. Skinner for dinner. I was moved by the certainty with which Skinner pronounced cognitive psychology a regression to mysticism and an obstacle to scientific psychology. At the end of the evening, I paid my respects and expressed my appreciation to "Fred" for our conversation. I said that I disagreed about cognitive science, but that I would have to take a closer look at its models and the research on their practical value. He shook my hand warmly and said with a smile, "I think you'll be wasting your time, but I wish you well in the research."

Our interpretations of the results of that research were, of course, quite different. I concluded that the early cognitive sciences and therapies warranted some cautious optimism about their promise. Skinner and others called cognitive behavior modification an oxymoron (self-contradiction), and there began a long-standing tension between cognitive and behavioral emphases in postmodern (liberalized, or relativized) behavior therapy. The literatures of the 1970s and 1980s are scattered with skirmishes among various cognitivists and behaviorists. One of those skirmishes took place between Fred Skinner and myself. In 1987, he challenged psychology to come back to its identity as a science of behavior and to recognize the three major obstacles to the foundations and future of psychology as a science—namely, cognitive psychology, psychotherapy, and humanistic psychology. I responded with a candid criticism of what I experienced as an arrogance and elitism that seemed prevalent in "scientistic" and radical "objectivist" traditions in psychology (Mahoney, 1989). Some of Skinner's friends and admirers were incensed by my words, and—with encouragement and feedback from Skinner—Charles Catania (1991) wrote a response. Skinner, in the advanced stages of leukemia, worked to prepare the article that he presented with dignity just weeks before he died (1990). In it, he compared cognitive psychology to creationism and himself to Charles Darwin facing the conservative clergy of the previous century. It was a fitting and touching final narrative from the author of *Walden Two* (1948) and *Beyond Freedom and Dignity* (1971).

I was present at Skinner's last public appearance, and my admiration for him as a pioneering scientist was even further augmented. Even though I disagreed with his well-elaborated theory of learning and life, I admired his dignity and determination in the final hours of his exceptional life. It is no coincidence, I believe, that the last word uttered by Fred Skinner was "marvelous!" It was his response to a final drink of water. It might also express our collective gratitude to a human being who dared to challenge the mentalist tradition. After his death, I organized a tribute to Skinner by humanists, psychotherapists, and cognitive scientists (Mahoney, 1991b). I would like to think that the death of such an ideological giant might also signal an opportunity for the passing of animosities. Given the activity emphasis of contemporary cognitive science, I believe that the possibilities for a dialectical synthesis are substantial. In 1992, members of the European Association for Behavior Therapy voted to change the name of their organization to the European Association for Behavioral and Cognitive Therapies. Thus, there are promising signs that the behaviorist–cognitivist dichotomies are undergoing some kind of dialectical synthesis that preserves and elaborates the wisdom and praxis of both traditions.

Aaron T. Beck's Cognitive Therapy

One of the most visible representatives of the cognitive psychotherapies has been Aaron Timkin Beck, a Yale-trained psychiatrist whose theories, research, and practice wrought much of what came to be called "the cognitive revolution" in psychiatry, psychopathology, and psychotherapy. Originally trained as a psychoanalyst, Beck was interested in the dreams of depressed clients, and he soon began to study cognitive distortions in the thinking of his patients (Beck, 1963). After years of work and creative ideation, Beck published his classic (1967) treatise on depression and was soon thereafter outlining the basics of his cognitive therapy. More than a quarter of a century later, Beck's cognitive therapy—now applied to anxiety and personality disorders as well as to depressive disorders—is among the most popular and highly respected approaches in the world. Moreover, its potential applications continue to be explored in ways that promise to expand its domain of relevance.

I have known and respected Tim Beck for more than 2 decades now, and I continue to marvel at his enthusiasm for new research and theoretical developments. My favorite personal memory with him occurred in November of 1974. We had met less than a year before and had become fast friends. When my book *Cognition and Behavior Modification* (1974) came out in October, I made plans to visit Tim to personally deliver a copy. When I arrived at his office, he was surveying the partly finished chapters of his own forthcoming book, *Cognitive Therapy and the Emotional Disorders* (Beck, 1976). He was excited to see his project taking its final form after years of thinking and writing, and he showed me chapter headings devoted to belief systems, cognitive processes, and the like. I suddenly felt a sinking sensation in my stomach as I (erroneously, it turned out) imagined that I had unintentionally "scooped" the master. Tim noticed my face paling and asked what was wrong. I awkwardly explained that I felt like the young Alfred Russel Wallace in that moment in 1858 when he realized his impetuous synchrony with Charles Darwin. Tim looked at me warmly as I handed him my book, and he said, "How very generous of you to compare me with Charles Darwin!"

Constructivist and Complex Systems Therapies

Constructivism and motor-evolutionary developments in psychotherapy were almost totally independent of those taking place in the cognitive sciences until the last 2 decades. Prior to 1955, the main works on constructivist approaches were in the realm of theory, cognitive science, and psychobiology. Then, George Kelly (1955) published his brilliant principles of experiential construction, the basis for his book titled *The Psychology of Personal Constructs*. Kelly's ideas were not immediately noticed, let alone welcomed, by either theoretical or applied psychologists. Indeed, the current popularity of his ideas is more apparent internationally than in North America (Neimeyer, 1985; Neimeyer, Baker, & Neimeyer, 1990).

Besides the system outlined by G. A. Kelly (1955) and elaborated by his followers, constructivist psychotherapies have been proposed by logotherapist Viktor Frankl and by an international collection of scholars and practitioners (e.g., Luis Joyce-Moniz and Óscar Gonçalves, of Portugal; Guillem Feixas, Mayte Miró, and Manuel Villegas, of Spain; Giampiero Arciero, Vittorio Guidano, Gianni Liotti, and Mario Reda, of Italy; Juan Balbi and Héctor Férnandez-Alvarez, of Argentina; Humberto Maturana, Roberto Opazo, Alfredo Ruiz, and Tito Zagmutt, of Chile; Hubert Hermans, of the Netherlands; and, from North America, individuals like Jerome Bruner, Mary Baird Carlsen, Mark Burrell, Paul Dell, Don Ford, Harry Goolishian, Leslie Greenberg, Lynn Hoffman, Bradford Keeney, Hazel Markus, Juan Pascual-Leone, myself, Eleanor Rosch, Hugh Rosen, Jeremy Safran, Esther Thelen, and Paul Watzlawick). Needless to say, I have my biases about constructivism and complex systems psychotherapies. As a conceptual base camp, they provide what I personally find to be an accommodating and viable perspective from which to observe, understand, and, at times, facilitate human experience and the life-span dynamics of psychological development.

There are, however, problems with constructivism that deserve consideration. To begin with, there is the variety of meanings for the terms *constructive* and *construction*. Relatedly, there is the differentiation between the so-called radical and critical constructivists (Mahoney, 1991a; Maturana, 1970; Maturana & Varela, 1980, 1987; Mittenthal & Baskin, 1992; von Foerster, 1984; von Glasersfeld, 1984; Watzlawick, 1984). The radical constructivists contend that all experience is personal construction, and they reject not only objectivism but also all forms of realism. Critical constructivists admit to being hypothetical realists, but they deny that we can ever develop a metric of correspondence between ontological reality (the nature of things in themselves) and epistemological reification (the process of acting as if there were some orderly relation between the furniture of the universe and the architectural designs of our knowing processes).

There is also the disputed difference between constructivist and rationalist cognitive psychotherapies. For me, this apparent difference began to emerge in the context of dialogues with John Bowlby, Donald Campbell, Vittorio Guidano, Friedrich Hayek, Mario Reda, and Walter Weimer in the early and mid-1980s. It seemed increasingly clear that the model of human learning and psychopathology adopted by rationality-emphasizing cognitive psychotherapists was fundamentally different from that expressed in those cognitive therapies emphasizing epistemological, evolutionary, and self-organizing processes. When I wrote about my early impressions of this differentiation, however, I was surprised to learn that virtually every cognitive therapist I knew considered himself or herself to be constructivist rather than rationalist in preference (e.g., Ellis, 1988). Of course, if there are no rationalists to create such a contrast, then the proposed distinction between rationalist and constructivist cognitive therapies may have limited usefulness. This matter—the meaning and practical connotations of being a constructivist therapist—is likely to be one that will persist into the twenty-first century.

I close with a very brief glance toward the future. Will constructivism persist to shape and reflect future models of human experience? Yes, I think so. But I am not so sure that the label itself will survive. To the extent that everyone claims to be a constructivist, the label will serve little purpose. It is, perhaps, because of this terminological and conceptual ambiguity that I welcome the larger expanses of complex systems terminology in the continuing evolution of cognitive and constructivist psychotherapies (e.g., Pattee, 1973, 1977, 1978; Prigogine, 1980; Prigogine & Stengers, 1984; Salthe, 1993). Even though a parallel development is likely—that is, that increasing numbers of psychotherapists (cognitive and otherwise) will identify themselves as complex (vs. simple) systems specialists—I believe that the terrain and language of discourse in the sciences of complexity may be less cluttered with excess historical baggage than most (if not all) contemporary systems of theoretical psychology and psychotherapy.

FUTURE DIRECTIONS AND CHALLENGES

My personal hopes and fears about the future of constructivism as a force in psychotherapy cannot be separated from related reflections on the future of psychology and psychotherapy in general (Mahoney, 1993, 1995, in press-c, in press-e). To summarize those reflections, I welcome the diversity and dialogue that are being encouraged by the decline in the North American hegemony (domination and unchallenged leadership) and the emergence of both culturally contextualized and transcultural perspectives on psychotherapy (Feixas & Villegas, 1990; Férnandez-Alvarez, 1992; Fisher, 1989; Joyce-Moniz, 1985; Gonçalves, 1989; Guidano, 1987, 1991; Maturana, 1970; Moghaddam, 1987; Merleau-Ponty, 1963; Miró, 1989; Opazo, 1992; Reda, 1986; Rosenzweig, 1992). Beyond the differentiation of rationalist and constructivist cognitive therapies (a distinction that I continue to find useful in my attempts to understand the field), I (imperfectly, of course) anticipate the following developments.

1. I believe there will be an increasing appreciation of the role or roles of emotionality and emotional knowing pro-

cesses in the facilitation of enduring psychological change (e.g., Greenberg & Safran, 1987).

2. Beyond a simple acceptance, the tacit (unconscious) organizing processes of knowing and feeling will be increasingly appreciated, with the practical implication that, like our clients, we therapists know more than can be described in symbols (Ellenberger, 1970; Polanyi, 1958, 1966; Shevrin & Dickman, 1980).

3. Issues of embodiment—the bodily context that affords all forms of experiencing—will become increasingly central to therapeutic relevance; that is, embodied therapies will fare better than those therapies that are relatively disembodied (as in "talking heads" therapies; Berman, 1989; M. Johnson, 1987; Mahoney, in press-d; Montagu, 1978).

4. There will be an increasing appreciation of the centrality of personal identity (self) in real-life and everyday experience, with at least two corollary implications: (a) that all acts of counseling, education, parenting, and psychotherapy are necessarily acts of participation in individual "selving" processes (Guidano, 1987, 1991), and (b) that the psychological development of the self is most powerfully constrained and shaped—for better and for worse—by the intimate relationships that have had the most emotional power for the individual (Bowlby, 1988; Sroufe, 1979; Stolorow & Atwood, 1992).

5. There will be increasingly active involvement in explorations regarding eclecticism and the "psychotherapy integration" movement, in part because these explorations offer new opportunities for a diverse and rapidly changing world (Férnandez-Alvarez, 1992; Norcross & Goldfried, 1992; Opazo, 1992; Stricker & Gold, 1993).

6. The authoritarian (justificationist, objectivist, or positivist) domination of the social sciences will be superseded by alternatives that encourage active exploration and dynamic metrics of evaluation (Bernstein, 1983; Dell, 1982a, 1982b; Hermans, 1988, 1989; Mahoney, 1976).

7. Distinctions among the cognitive, behavioral, and affective approaches will recede, with an increasing acknowledgment of holism (wholeness) as an individuating factor in all cases of assessment, diagnosis, and therapy (Mahoney, in press-b).

8. The "cerebral primacy" and "rationalist supremacy" traditions of past decades will bow to somatopsychic and other-

wise embodied expressions of holism (M. Johnson, 1987; Lakoff & Johnson, 1980; Leder, 1990).

9. Issues of value—good–bad, right–wrong, and sacred–profane—will become increasingly central in psychotherapy, with the dimensions of religiosity and spirituality taking on new meanings in psychological assessment (T. A. Kelly & Strupp, 1992; Payne, Bergin, & Loftus, 1992; Sperry, 1988; Tarnas, 1991; Vaughan, 1991);

10. The fundamental promise and power of the child will be further documented in research and theory illustrating the continuity between early, intermediate, and later life experiences (Belsky & Nezworksi, 1987; Mahoney, in press-a, in press-b).

All of the above are speculations, of course, and I cannot honestly separate what I expect to happen from what I hope will happen. My sense is that this disability is not unusual.

CONCLUDING REMARKS

There is little doubt in my mind that the cognitive sciences and cognitive psychotherapies have evolved quite rapidly in the last half century. They are evolving as I write and you read these words. Models and theories of knowing, as well as therapies that are phenomenological in their epistemologies, are developing in leaps and bounds that are impossible to deny. The complexity, I believe, is much greater than that of contemporary meteorology, because changes in weather are substantially more accurate as the time interval increases (e.g., from seconds to seasons). This reflects the fact that contemporary cognitive sciences and the cognitive psychotherapies—which have historically been independent entities—are just now beginning to dialogue in ways that are stimulating changes in all parties involved. These changes require a considerable degree of resilience, flexibility, and openness on the part of the scientist and practitioner associated with these specializations. Being, as they are, in process, such changes also make it difficult to symbolically describe or survey those fields with any degree of finality. In this chapter I have ventured a brief historiography of the cognitive sciences and cognitive psychotherapies. In both of these domains, I have concluded that some of the most promising developments in both theory and practice have emerged from the tradition known as constructivism. The warrant for that conclusion and illustrations of constructivism in psychotherapy are elaborated in the other chapters of this volume.

REFERENCES

Baars, B. J. (Ed.). (1986). *The cognitive revolution in psychology*. New York: Guilford Press.

Bartlett, F. C. (1932). *Remembering*. Cambridge, England: Cambridge University Press.

Beck, A. T. (1963). Thinking and depression: I. Idiosyncratic content and cognitive distortion. *Archives of General Psychiatry, 9*, 324–333.

Beck, A. T. (1967). *Depression*. New York: Hoeber.

Beck, A. T. (1976). *Cognitive therapy and the emotional disorders*. New York: International Universities Press.

Belsky, J., & Nezworksi, M. T. (Eds.). (1987). *Clinical implications of attachment*. Hillsdale, NJ: Erlbaum.

Berger, P. L., & Luckman, T. (1966). *The social construction of reality*. Garden City, NY: Anchor Press.

Berman, M. (1989). *Coming to our senses*. New York: Simon & Schuster.

Bernstein, R. J. (1983). *Beyond objectivism and relativism*. Philadelphia: University of Pennsylvania Press.

Bienenstock, E. (1985). Dynamics of the central nervous system. In J. P. Aubin, D. Saari, & K. Sigmund (Eds.), *Dynamics of macrosystems* (pp. 3–20). New York: Springer-Verlag.

Bienenstock, E., Soulié, F. F., & Weisbuch, G. (Eds.). (1986). *Disordered systems and biological organization*. New York: Springer-Verlag.

Bonner, J. T. (1988). *The evolution of complexity by means of natural selection*. Princeton, NJ: Princeton University Press.

Bowlby, J. (1988). *A secure base*. New York: Basic Books.

Bruner, J. (1990). *Acts of meaning*. Cambridge, MA: Harvard University Press.

Bruner, J., & Postman, L. (1947a). Emotional selectivity in perception and reaction. *Journal of Personality, 16*, 69–77.

Bruner, J., & Postman, L. (1947b). Tension and tension-release as organizing factors in perception. *Journal of Personality, 15*, 300–308.

Burrell, M. J. (1987). Cognitive psychology, epistemology, and psychotherapy: A motor-evolutionary perspective. *Psychotherapy, 24*, 225–232.

Callebaut, W., & Pinxten, R. (1987). *Evolutionary epistemology: A multiparadigm program*. Boston: Reidel.

Campbell, D. T. (1974). Evolutionary epistemology. In P. A. Schilpp (Ed.), *The philosophy of Karl Popper* (Vol. 14, pp. 413–563). Peru, IL: Open Court.

Carr, D. (1986). *Time, narrative, and history*. Bloomington: University of Indiana Press.

Catania, A. C. (1991). The gifts of culture and of eloquence: An open letter to Michael J. Mahoney in reply to his article "Scientific psychology and radical behaviorism." *Behavior Analyst, 14*, 61–72.

Cautela, J. R. (1966). The treatment of compulsive behavior by covert sensitization. *Psychological Record, 16,* 33–41.

Dell, P. F. (1982a). Beyond homeostasis: Toward a concept of coherence. *Family Process, 21,* 21–41.

Dell, P. F. (1982b). In search of truth: On the way to clinical epistemology. *Family Process, 21,* 407–414.

Dell, P. F., & Goolishian, H. A. (1981). Order through fluctuation: An evolutionary epistemology for human systems. *Australian Journal of Family Therapy, 2,* 175–184.

Depew, D. J., & Weber, B. H. (1995). *Darwinism evolving: System dynamics and the genealogy of natural selection.* Cambridge, MA: MIT Press.

Dilthey, W. (1976). *Selected writings.* Cambridge, England: Cambridge University Press.

Dobson, K. S. (Ed.). (1988). *Handbook of cognitive behavioral therapies.* New York: Guilford Press.

Ellenberger, H. F. (1970). *The discovery of the unconscious.* New York: Basic Books.

Ellis, A. (1962). *Reason and emotion in psychotherapy.* New York: Lyle Stuart.

Ellis, A. (1988). Are there "rationalist" and "constructivist" camps of the cognitive therapies? A response to Michael Mahoney. *Cognitive Behaviorist, 10*(2), 13–17.

Feixas, G., & Villegas, M. (1990). *Constructivismo y psicoterápia* [Constructivism and psychotherapy]. Barcelona, Spain: Promociónes y Publicaciónes Universitarias.

Feldman, J. A., & Ballard, D. H. (1982). Connectionist models and their properties. *Cognitive Science, 6,* 205–254.

Férnandez-Alvarez, H. (1992). *Fundamentos de un modelo integrativo en psicoterápia* [Fundamentals of an integrative model of psychotherapy]. Buenos Aires, Argentina: Paidos.

Fischer, R. (1987). On fact and fiction—The structures of stories that the brain tells to itself about itself. *Journal of Social and Biological Structures, 10,* 343–351.

Fisher, D. (1989). Boundary work: A model of the relation between power and knowledge. *Knowledge: Creation, Diffusion, Utilization, 10,* 156–176.

Fodor, J. A., & Pylyshyn, Z. W. (1988). Connectionism and cognitive architecture: A critical analysis. *Cognition, 28,* 3–71.

Ford, D. H. (1987). *Humans as self-constructing living systems: A developmental perspective on behavior and personality.* Hillsdale, NJ: Erlbaum.

Freeman, M. (1993). *Rewriting the self: History, memory, narrative.* New York: Routledge, Chapman & Hall.

Gadamer, H. G. (1975). Hermeneutics and social sciences. *Cultural Hermeneutics, 2,* 307–352.

Gadamer, H. G. (1976). *Philosophical hermeneutics*. Berkeley: University of California Press.

Gadamer, H. G. (1988). *Truth and method*. New York: Crossroad.

Gardner, H. (1985). *The mind's new science: A history of the cognitive revolution*. New York: Basic Books.

Gergen, K. J. (1985). The social constructionist movement in modern psychology. *American Psychologist, 40,* 266–275.

Gergen, K. J. (1991). *The saturated self: Dilemmas of identity in contemporary life*. New York: Basic Books.

Glass, L., & Mackey, M. C. (1988). *From clocks to chaos: The rhythms of life*. Princeton, NJ: Princeton University Press.

Gleick, J. (1987). *Chaos: Making a new science*. New York: Viking Press.

Gonçalves, Ó. F. (Ed.). (1989). *Advances in the cognitive therapies: The constructivist–developmental approach*. Lisbon, Portugal: APPORT.

Greenberg, L. S., & Safran, J. D. (1987). *Emotion in psychotherapy*. New York: Guilford Press.

Guidano, V. F. (1987). *Complexity of the self: A developmental approach to psychopathology and therapy*. New York: Guilford Press.

Guidano, V. F. (1991). *The self in process: Toward a post-rationalist cognitive therapy*. New York: Guilford Press.

Hager, D. (1992). Chaos and growth. *Psychotherapy, 29,* 378–384.

Hamowy, R. (1987). *The Scottish Enlightenment and the theory of spontaneous order*. Carbondale: Southern Illinois University Press.

Hayek, F. A. (1952). *The sensory order*. Chicago: University of Chicago Press.

Hayek, F. A. (1964). The theory of complex phenomena. In M. Bunge (Ed.), *The critical approach to science and philosophy: Essays in honor of K. R. Popper* (pp. 332–349). New York: Free Press.

Hebb, D. O. (1949). *The organization of behavior*. New York: Wiley.

Heidegger, M. (1962). *Being and time*. New York: Harper & Row. (Original work published 1927)

Heidegger, M. (1971). *On the way to language*. New York: Harper & Row. (Original work published 1959)

Hermans, H. J. M. (1988). On the integration of nomothetic and idiographic research methods in the study of personal meaning. *Journal of Personality, 56,* 785–812.

Hermans, H. J. M. (1989). The meaning of life as an organized process. *Psychotherapy, 26,* 11–22.

Hirst, W. (Ed.). (1988). *The making of cognitive science*. Cambridge, England: Cambridge University Press.

Homme, L. E. (1965). Perspectives in psychology: XXIV. Control of coverants, the operants of the mind. *Psychological Record, 15,* 501–511.

Iser, W. (1978). *The act of reading: A theory of aesthetic response*. Baltimore: Johns Hopkins University Press.

James, W. (1890). *Principles of psychology*. New York: Henry Holt.

James, W. (1958). *The varieties of religious experience*. New York: New American Library. (Original work published 1902)

Janet, P. (1898). *Neurosis and fixed ideas*. Paris: Alcan.

Jantsch, E. (1980). *The self-organizing universe: Scientific and human implications of the emerging paradigm of evolution*. New York: Pergamon.

Jantsch, E. (Ed.). (1981). *The evolutionary vision: Toward a unifying paradigm of physical, biological, and sociocultural evolution*. Boulder, CO: Westview Press.

Johnson, M. (1987). *The body in the mind: The bodily basis of meaning, imagination, and reason*. Chicago: University of Chicago Press.

Johnson, M. H. (Ed.). (1993). *Brain development and cognition*. Oxford, England: Oxford University Press.

Joyce-Moniz, L. (1985). Epistemological therapy and constructivism. In M. J. Mahoney & A. Freeman (Eds.), *Cognition and psychotherapy* (pp. 143–179). New York: Plenum.

Kauffman, S. A. (1993). *The origins of order: Self-organization and selection in evolution*. Oxford, England: Oxford University Press.

Kelly, G. A. (1955). *The psychology of personal constructs* (2 vols.). New York: Norton.

Kelly, T. A., & Strupp, H. H. (1992). Patient and therapist values in psychotherapy: Perceived changes, assimilation, similarity, and outcome. *Journal of Consulting and Clinical Psychology, 60*, 34–40.

Kvale, S. (Ed.). (1992). *Psychology and postmodernism*. Newbury Park, CA: Sage.

Lakoff, G., & Johnson, M. (1980). *Metaphors we live by*. Chicago: University of Chicago Press.

Leder, D. (1990). *The absent body*. Chicago: University of Chicago Press.

Lewin, R. (1992). *Complexity: Life at the edge of chaos*. New York: Macmillan.

Madison, G. B. (1988). *The hermeneutics of postmodernity*. Bloomington: Indiana University Press.

Mahoney, M. J. (1974). *Cognition and behavior modification*. Cambridge, MA: Ballinger.

Mahoney, M. J. (1976). *Scientist as subject*. Cambridge, MA: Ballinger.

Mahoney, M. J. (1988a). Constructive metatheory: I. Basic features and historical foundations. *International Journal of Personal Construct Psychology, 1*, 1–35.

Mahoney, M. J. (1988b). Constructive metatheory: II. Implications for psychotherapy. *International Journal of Personal Construct Psychology, 1*, 299–315.

Mahoney, M. J. (1989). Scientific psychology and radical behaviorism: Important distinctions based in scientism and objectivism. *American Psychologist, 44*, 1372–1377.

Mahoney, M. J. (1991a). *Human change processes: The scientific foundations of psychotherapy*. New York: Basic Books.

Mahoney, M. J. (1991b). B. F. Skinner: A collective tribute. *Canadian Psychology, 32,* 628–635.

Mahoney, M. J. (1993). Theoretical developments in the cognitive psychotherapies. *Journal of Consulting and Clinical Psychology, 63,* 187–193.

Mahoney, M. J. (Ed.). (1995). *The cognitive and constructive psychotherapies.* New York: Springer.

Mahoney, M. J. (in press-a). *Constructive psychotherapy.* New York: Guilford Press.

Mahoney, M. J. (in press-b). *Constructive psychotherapy techniques.* New York: Guilford Press.

Mahoney, M. J. (in press-c). Developments and directions in psychology. *Boletín de Psicología.*

Mahoney, M. J. (in press-d). *Embodying the mind: Constructive health psychology.* New York: Guilford Press.

Mahoney, M. J. (in press-e). The modern psychotherapist and the future of psychotherapy. In B. Bongar & L. E. Beutler (Eds.), *Comprehensive textbook of psychotherapy: Theory and practice.* Oxford, England: Oxford University Press.

Mahoney, M. J., Lyddon, W. J., & Alford, D. J. (1989). The rational-emotive theory of psychotherapy. In M. E. Bernard & R. DiGuisepe (Eds.), *Inside rational-emotive therapy* (pp. 69–94). San Diego, CA: Academic Press.

Mahoney, M. J., & Weimer, W. B. (1994). Friedrich A. Hayek, 1899–1992. *American Psychologist, 49,* 63.

Maturana, H. R. (1970). *Biology of cognition* (Biological Computer Laboratory Report 9.0). Urbana: University of Illinois.

Maturana, H. R., & Varela, F. J. (1980). *Autopoeisis and cognition: The realization of the living.* Boston: Reidel.

Maturana, H. R., & Varela, F. J. (1987). *The tree of knowledge: The biological roots of human understanding.* Boston: Shambhala Publications.

Mazlish, B. (1993). *The fourth discontinuity: The co-evolution of humans and machines.* New Haven: CT: Yale University Press.

McCulloch, W. S., & Pitts, W. (1943). A logical calculus of the ideas immanent in nervous activity. *Bulletin of Mathematical Biophysics, 5,* 115–133.

Meichenbaum, D. (1969). The effects of instructions and reinforcement on thinking and language behaviors of schizophrenics. *Behaviour Research and Therapy, 7,* 101–114.

Meichenbaum, D. (1974). *Cognitive behavior modification.* Morristown, NJ: General Learning Press.

Meichenbaum, D. (1977). *Cognitive behavior modification.* New York: Plenum.

Meichenbaum, D. (1995). Changing conceptions of cognitive behavior modification: Retrospect and prospect. In M. J. Mahoney (Ed.), *Cognitive and constructive psychotherapies* (pp. 20–26). New York: Springer.

Merleau-Ponty, M. (1962). *Phenomenology of perception* (C. Smith, Trans.). London: Routledge & Kegan Paul.

Merleau-Ponty, M. (1963). *The structure of behavior* (A. L. Fisher, Trans.). Boston: Beacon Press.

Messer, S. B., Sass, L. A., & Woolfolk, R. L. (Eds.). (1988). *Hermeneutics and psychological theory: Interpretive perspectives on personality, psychotherapy, and psychopathology.* New Brunswick, NJ: Rutgers University Press.

Meyer, D. (1965). *The positive thinkers.* Garden City, NY: Doubleday.

Miller, G. A., Galanter, E., & Pribram, K. H. (1960). *Plans and the structure of behavior.* New York: Holt.

Minsky, M. L., & Papert, S. A. (1969). *Perceptrons.* Cambridge, MA: MIT Press.

Miró, M. (1989). Knowledge and society: An evolutionary outline. In Ó. F. Gonçalves (Ed.), *Advances in the cognitive therapies: The constructive-developmental approach* (pp. 111–128). Lisbon, Portugal: APPORT.

Mittenthal, J. E., & Baskin, A. B. (Eds.). (1992). *The principles of organization in organisms.* Reading, MA: Addison-Wesley.

Moghaddam, F. M. (1987). Psychology in three worlds. *American Psychologist, 42,* 912–920.

Montagu, A. (1978). *Touching: The human significance of the skin* (2nd ed.). New York: Harper & Row.

Morrison, F. (1991). *The art of modeling dynamic systems: Forecasting for chaos, randomness, and determinism.* New York: Wiley Interscience.

Neimeyer, R. A. (1985). *The development of personal construct psychology.* Lincoln: University of Nebraska Press.

Neimeyer, R. A., Baker, K. D., & Neimeyer, G. J. (1990). The current status of personal construct theory. In R. A. Neimeyer & G. J. Neimeyer (Eds.), *Advances in personal construct theory* (Vol. 1, pp. 3–22). Greenwich, CT: JAI Press.

Norcross, J. C., & Goldfried, M. R. (Eds.). (1992). *Handbook of psychotherapy integration.* New York: Basic Books.

Opazo, R. (Ed.). (1992). *Integración en psicoterápia* [Integration in psychotherapy]. Santiago, Chile: Centro Científico de Desarrollo Psicológico.

Palmer, R. E. (1969). *Hermeneutics: Interpretation theory in Schleiermacher, Dilthey, Heidegger, and Gadamer.* Evanston, IL: Northwestern University Press.

Parker, G. T. (1973). *Mind cure in New England.* Hanover, NH: University Press of New England.

Pattee, H. H. (1973). *Hierarchy theory: The challenge of complex systems.* New York: George Braziller.

Pattee, H. H. (1977). Dynamic and linguistic modes of complex systems. *International Journal of General Systems, 3,* 259–266.

Pattee, H. H. (1978). The complementarity principle in biological and social structures. *Journal of Biological and Social Structures, 1,* 191–200.

Payne, I. R., Bergin, A. E., & Loftus, P. E. (1992). A review of attempts to integrate spiritual and standard psychotherapy techniques. *Journal of Psychotherapy Integration, 2,* 171–192.

Peale, N. V. (1960). *The power of positive thinking.* Englewood Cliffs, NJ: Prentice Hall.

Piaget, J. (1926). *The language and thought of the child.* New York: Harcourt Brace.

Polanyi, M. (1958). *Personal knowledge: Towards a post-critical philosophy.* Chicago: University of Chicago Press.

Polanyi, M. (1966). *The tacit dimension.* Garden City, NY: Doubleday.

Prigogine, I. (1980). *From being to becoming: Time and complexity in the physical sciences.* New York: Freeman.

Prigogine, I., & Stengers, I. (1984). *Order out of chaos: Man's new dialogue with nature.* New York: Bantam Books.

Radnitzky, G., & Bartley, W. W. (Eds.). (1987). *Evolutionary epistemology, theory of rationality, and the sociology of knowledge.* Peru, IL: Open Court.

Reda, M. A. (1986). *Sistemi cognitivi complessi e psicoterápia* [Complex cognitive systems and psychotherapy]. Rome: Nuova Italia Scientifica.

Rosenblatt, F. (1962). *Principles of neurodynamics.* New York: Spartan Books.

Rosenzweig, M. R. (1992). Psychological science around the world. *American Psychologist, 47,* 718–722.

Salthe, S. N. (1985). *Evolving hierarchical systems.* New York: Columbia University Press.

Salthe, S. N. (1993). *Development and evolution: Complexity and change in biology.* Cambridge, MA: MIT Press.

Schneider, W. (1987). Connectionism: Is it a paradigm shift for psychology? *Behavior Research Methods, Instruments, and Computers, 19,* 73–83.

Searle, J. R. (1992). *The rediscovery of the mind.* Cambridge, MA: MIT Press.

Seidenberg, M. S. (1993). Connectionist models and cognitive theory. *Psychological Science, 4,* 228–235.

Sejnoski, T. J., Koch, C., & Churchland, P. S. (1988). Computational neuroscience. *Science, 241,* 1299–1306.

Shanon, B. (1988). Semantic representation of meaning: A critique. *Psychological Bulletin, 104,* 70–83.

Sherrington, C. S. (1906). *The integrative action of the nervous system.* New Haven, CT: Yale University Press.

Shevrin, H., & Dickman, S. (1980). The psychological unconscious: A necessary assumption for all psychological theory? *American Psychologist, 35,* 421–434.

Skinner, B. F. (1948). *Walden Two.* New York: Macmillan.

Skinner, B. F. (1953). *Science and human behavior.* New York: Macmillan.

Skinner, B. F. (1971). *Beyond freedom and dignity.* New York: Knopf.

Skinner, B. F. (1987). What ever became of psychology as the science of behavior? *American Psychologist, 42,* 786–789.

Skinner, B. F. (1990). Can psychology be a science of mind? *American Psychologist, 45,* 1206–1210.

Sperry, R. W. (1988). Psychology's mentalist paradigm and the religion/science tension. *American Psychologist, 43,* 607–613.

Sperry, R. W. (1993). The impact and promise of the cognitive revolution. *American Psychologist, 48,* 878–885.

Sroufe, L. A. (1979). The coherence of individual development: Early care, attachment, and subsequent developmental issues. *American Psychologist, 34,* 834–841.

Stent, E. S. (1985). Hermeneutics and the analysis of complex biological systems. In D. J. Depew & B. H. Weber (Eds.), *Evolution at a crossroads* (pp. 209–225). Cambridge, MA: MIT Press.

Stolorow, R. D., & Atwood, G. E. (1992). *Contexts of being: The intersubjective foundations of psychological life.* Hillsdale, NJ: Analytic Press.

Stricker, G., & Gold, J. (Eds.). (1993). *Comprehensive handbook of psychotherapy integration.* New York: Plenum.

Tarnas, R. (1991). *The passion of the Western mind.* New York: Ballantine Books.

Thorndike, E. L. (1898). Animal intelligence: An experimental study of the associative processes in animals [Monograph]. *Psychological Review, 2*(8).

Tolman, E. C. (1932). *Purposive behavior in animals and men.* New York: Appleton-Century-Crofts.

Varela, F. J. (1979). *Principles of biological autonomy.* New York: Elsevier North-Holland.

Vaughan, F. (1991). Spiritual issues in psychotherapy. *Journal of Transpersonal Psychology, 23,* 105–119.

von Foerster, H. (1984). On constructing a reality. In P. Watzlawick (Ed.), *The invented reality: Contributions to constructivism* (pp. 41–61). New York: Norton.

von Glasersfeld, E. (1984). An introduction to radical constructivism. In P. Watzlawick (Ed.), *The invented reality: Contributions to constructivism* (pp. 18–40). New York: Norton.

Wachterhauser, B. R. (Ed.). (1986). *Hermeneutics and modern philosophy.* Albany: State University of New York Press.

Waldrop, M. M. (1992). *Complexity: The emerging science at the edge of order and chaos.* New York: Simon & Schuster.

Watzlawick, P. (Ed.). (1984). *The invented reality: Contributions to constructivism.* New York: Norton.

Weimer, W. B. (1982). Hayek's approach to the problems of complex phenomena: An introduction to the theoretical psychology of *The Sensory Order.* In W. B. Weimer & D. S. Palermo (Eds.), *Cognition and the symbolic processes* (Vol. 2, pp. 267–311). Hillsdale, NJ: Erlbaum.

Weimer, W. B. (1987). Spontaneously ordered complex phenomena and the unity of the moral sciences. In G. Radnitzky (Ed.), *Centripetal forces in the sciences* (pp. 257–296). New York: Paragon House.

Wiener, N. (1948). *Cybernetics*. New York: Wiley.

Wiener, P. P. (Ed.). (1974). *Dictionary of the history of ideas: Studies of selected pivotal ideas*. New York: Scribner.

Wundt, W. (1896). *Outlines of psychology*. Leipzig: Engelmann.

Zeleny, M. (1980). *Autopoiesis, dissipative structures, and spontaneous social orders*. Washington, DC: Association for the Advancement of Science.

Zeleny, M. (1981). *Autopoiesis: A theory of living organization*. New York: Elsevier North-Holland.

(Appendix follows on next page)

APPENDIX

SELECTED INDIVIDUALS AND EVENTS IN COGNITIVE SCIENCE, 1860–1970

1860	Fechner published the first quantitative rule regarding the relationship between physical stimulation and psychological experience.
1874	Brentano inaugurated "act psychology," with an emphasis on psychological processes (in contrast with formerly popular structures).
1880	Galton published the first study of naturalistic memory ("what one had for breakfast").
1885	Ebbinghaus published his famous self-studies on memory.
1890	William James's *Principles of Psychology* anticipated many themes later central to cognitive science.
1896	Dewey published his famous critique of the reflex arc concept.
1907	Poincaré demonstrated the phenomenon of incubation in problem solving.
1912	Wertheimer published his early work on the phi phenomenon.
1916	de Saussure founded modern linguistics.
1926	Piaget's *The Language and Thought of the Child*.
1929	Cassirer's *Philosophy of Symbolic Forms*; Korzybski's Institute for General Semantics is founded.
1931	Lewin's field theory and topological psychology.
1932	Tolman's *Purposive Behavior in Animals and Men*; Bartlett's *Remembering*.
1934	Vygotsky's *Thought and Language*.
1940	von Bertalanffy's general systems theory.
1943	Hull's *Principles of Behavior*.
1946	Heider introduces balance (consistency) theory.
1947	Bruner & Postman announce the "new look" in perception (with emphasis on perceptual set).
1948	Hixon Symposium on Cerebral Mechanisms in Behavior.
1949	Hebb's *The Organization of Behavior*; Shannon & Weaver's *Mathematical Theory of Communication*.
1952	Hayek's *The Sensory Order*; Osgood's introduction of the semantic differential technique for measuring personal meaning.
1955	Cambridge Conference on Cognition; Kelly's *The Psychology of Personal Constructs*.
1956	Dartmouth Conference on Artificial Intelligence; Massachusetts Institute of Technology Conference on Cognition (including Austin, Chomsky, Miller, Newell, & Simon); Bruner,

Goodnow, & Austin's *A Study of Thinking*; Miller's "The Magical Number Seven"; Whorf's *Language, Thought, & Reality*; Newell & Simon's "The Logic Theory Machine."

1957   Chomsky's *Syntactic Structures*; Festinger's theory of cognitive dissonance.

1958   Broadbent's funnel (filter) theory of attention; Rosenblatt's perceptron theory.

1959   Frankl's logotherapy.

1960   Miller, Galanter, & Pribram's *Plans and the Structure of Behavior*.

1961   Luria's *The Role of Speech in the Regulation of Normal and Abnormal Behavior*.

1962   Harvard established its Center for Cognitive Studies; Rosenblatt's *Principles of Neurodynamics*; ellis's *Reason and Emotion in Psychotherapy*; Merleau-Ponty's *Phenomenology of Perception*.

1963   Bandura & Walters's *Social Learning and Personality Development*.

1966   J. J. Gibson's *The Senses Considered as Perceptual Systems*; Spielberger and colleagues demonstrated awareness in learning.

1967   Neisser's *Cognitive Psychology*; Beck's *Depression*.

1968   Atkinson & Shiffrin's model of information processing; Bever, Fodor, and Garrett's attack on associationism.

1969   Bandura's *Principles of Behavior Modification*; Minsky & Papert's critique of *Perceptrons*; Norman's *Memory and Attention*.

1970   Bower's work on imagery in memory; founding of the journal *Cognitive Psychology*.

4

FORMS AND FACETS OF
CONSTRUCTIVIST PSYCHOLOGY

WILLIAM J. LYDDON

Constructivism is an epistemological perspective based on the assertion that humans actively create the realities to which they respond (Mahoney, 1991; Neimeyer, 1993). Contemporary constructivist thought has its roots in a philosophical and psychological tradition that draws attention to the active role of the human mind in organizing and creating meaning—in literally inventing rather than discovering reality. The philosophical origins of constructivism include Vico's (1725/1948) *New Science* and concept of "imaginative universals," Kant's (1791/1969) analysis of the limits of derived knowledge, and Vaihinger's (1911/1924) neo-Kantian philosophy of "as if" (see Mahoney, 1988, for a detailed review), whereas formative contributions to constructivist thinking in psychology include Piaget's (1926) genetic epistemology, Bartlett's (1932) constructivist analysis of human memory, Hayek's (1952) treatise on the constructive nature of the human nervous system, Kelly's (1955) psychology of personal constructs, and Weimer's (1977) motor metatheory of mind.

Building on these early philosophical and psychological foundations, constructivist theories have come to play an increasingly significant

69

role in contemporary psychological science. In particular, constructivist thinking has emerged as a prominent perspective in such diverse psychological domains as cognitive psychology (Arbib & Hesse, 1986; Bruner, 1990; Bugaj & Rychlak, 1989; Coulter, 1983), developmental psychology (Berzonsky, 1990; Bronfenbrenner, Kessel, Kessen, & White, 1986; Feffer, 1988; Scarr, 1985), developmental psychopathology (Keating & Rosen, 1991), educational psychology (Black & Ammon, 1992; Cooper, 1993; J. W. Lerner, 1993), environmental psychology (Wicker, 1991), the psychology of emotion (Averill, 1985; Harré, 1986; Mandler, 1984, 1992), family therapy (Dell, 1985; Keeney, 1987; Mince, 1992; Reiss, 1981), feminist psychology and gender studies (Belenky, Clinchy, Goldberger, & Tarule, 1986; Hare-Mustin & Marecek, 1988; Unger, 1983, 1989; Wittig, 1985), narrative and discursive psychology (Bruner, 1990; Edwards & Potter, 1992; Howard, 1989, 1991; Mair, 1989; Polkinghorne, 1988; Sarbin, 1986), perception and memory (Collins & Hagen, 1979; Middleton & Edwards, 1990; Shaw & Bransford, 1977), personality (Hampson, 1988; Royce & Powell, 1983), psychotherapy and counseling (Guidano, 1991; Mahoney & Lyddon, 1988; Masterpasqua, 1989; McNamee & Gergen, 1992; Neimeyer, 1993); self-psychology (Cushman, 1990; Hermans, Kempen, & van Loon, 1992; Shotter & Gergen, 1989), and social psychology (Gergen, 1982, 1985).

Although constructivism's influence on the field of psychology has been pervasive, psychologists rarely distinguish among different forms of constructivist thought. When constructivist theories are examined in light of their assumptions about the nature of change and causation, for example, at least four forms of constructivist psychology may be distinguished. One viable framework for organizing constructivist theories along these dimensions of contrast is Pepper's (1942) root metaphor theory and his taxonomy of world hypotheses. With this framework in mind, I primarily have a threefold purpose in this chapter. First, I provide a brief overview of the root metaphors and causal assumptions that distinguish each of Pepper's four world hypotheses. Second, following from these contrasts, I differentiate four forms of constructivist psychology, giving contemporary theoretical exemplars of each form. Third, I discuss the implications of these differentiations for developing an integrative conception of constructivist psychology.

ROOT METAPHOR THEORY: PEPPER'S WORLD HYPOTHESES

At the center of Pepper's (1942) root metaphor theory is the notion of world hypothesis. A *world hypothesis* is a conjecture about the way the world works that operates according to a set of tacit assumptions derived from commonsense knowledge and understandings. Unlike hypotheses about specific aspects of the world, such as scientific hypotheses, world hypotheses are by definition unlimited in the range of observations they incorporate. Pepper identified four autonomous world hypotheses—formism, mechanism, contextualism, and organicism—each based on a particular organizing metaphor and related causal assumptions about world phenomena. Because the root metaphors and corollary causal assumptions are inherently connected to each world hypothesis, they are reviewed here in that context.

Formism is an analytical world hypothesis based on the root metaphor of similarity and is concerned primarily with classification and identification. The fundamental cognitive activity associated with the formistic world hypothesis is distinction making. Phenomena of the world are grouped into like and unlike categories, typologies, or ideal forms on the basis of their perceived similarities and differences. As a result, formism relies on the notion of material cause—the belief that intrinsic and stable properties of phenomena account for their functioning. Material causes are those influences that reflect the basic structure, or "essence," of a phenomenon and ultimately distinguish it from other phenomena (Altman & Rogoff, 1987; Rychlak, 1977).

Mechanism is based on the root metaphor of the machine and a view of the world as being composed of discrete entities—all with specific antecedent-consequent connections to each other. Although the mechanistic hypothesis is similar to formism in its analytic approach to distinguishing among objects and events, its attention to causal relations among objects and events seeks to organize the world into a working system rather than to focus only on structural identification and classification. As a result, mechanism depends on the concept of efficient cause—the assumption that phenomena may be understood in terms of their linear cause-and-effect relations. Efficient cause presumes that an antecedent variable is a "cause" if it is sytematically associated with changes in a consequent variable (Altman & Rogoff, 1987; Rychlak, 1977).

Differing sharply from both formism and mechanism, *contextualism* is based on the root metaphor of the historical event—the active event alive in its present context. Within the contextualist hypothesis, the world is seen as an infinite collection of events that are "all intrinsically complex, composed of interconnected activities and continuously changing patterns" (Pepper, 1942, p. 233). Because change and novelty are inherent features of contextualism, contextualist understandings emerge not from an analysis of discrete elements or causal relations but, rather, from a synthesis of the inseparable details of an act in its context. Accordingly, contextualism is associated with the notion of formal cause. Formal cause is a type of causal understanding that seeks to identify the temporal patterning, shape, or recognizable organization in the flow of events (Altman & Rogoff, 1987).

Organicism is based on the root metaphor of the organic process that is believed to characterize all developing, living systems. Pepper (1942) described *organismic development* as a dialectical process in which phenomena are periodically confronted by "oppositions" and "contradictions" that appear to impede progressive movement but that, in fact, give way to qualitative changes in the direction of increased complexity and integration. Each new integration forms the basis for a new thesis and subsequent antithesis (contradiction). The organismic notion that phenomena exist in anticipation of some new unfolding possibility is central to the concept of final cause. *Final cause* is a "telic" (or teleological) form of causal reasoning through which phenomena are understood to be in an ongoing process of developmental and structural change in the direction of some greater, albeit unspecifiable, whole (Altman & Rogoff, 1987).

FORMS OF PSYCHOLOGICAL CONSTRUCTIVISM

In recent years there has been growing interest in and greater application of Pepper's (1942) root metaphor framework in several areas of psychology, including applied behavioral analysis (Hayes, 1988; Morris, 1988), behavioral medicine and health psychology (Lyddon, 1987; Schwartz, 1984), clinical and counseling psychology (Kramer & Bopp, 1989; Lyddon, 1989; Lyddon & Adamson, 1992; Steenbarger, 1991), developmental psychology (R. M. Lerner, 1986; R. M. Lerner & Kauffman, 1985; Santrock & Bartlett, 1986), education (Geddis, 1982; Quina, 1982), environmental psychology (Altman & Rogoff, 1987), hypnosis and psychopathology (Sarbin & Coe, 1979), memory (Belli, 1986), organizational psychology (Payne, 1976), personality and social psychology (Johnson, Germer, Efran, & Overton, 1988), and theoretical psychology (Overton, 1984; Tyler, 1981). Causal assumptions associated with Pepper's (1942) philosophical framework can be used to differentiate among various forms of constructivist psychology. On the basis of these assumptions, I outline contrasts among material, efficient, formal, and final forms of constructivist psychology in the following section.

Material Constructivism

As previously noted, material causation is associated with the formistic world hypothesis and the assumption that intrinsic and structural properties of phenomena account for their functioning. Material constructivism is most evident in the "radical" perspectives espoused by von Glasersfeld (1979, 1984, 1987, 1991), von Foerster (1984), and Maturana and Varela (1987), suggesting that reality is exclusively a function of the structure of the human cognitive system.

According to von Glasersfeld (1984), the radical approach to constructivism

> is radical because it breaks with convention and develops a theory of knowledge in which knowledge does not reflect an "objective" ontological reality, but exclusively an ordering and organization of a world constituted by our experience. The radical constructivist has relinquished "metaphysical realism" once and for all. (p. 24)

Radical constructivists reject a representational theory of knowledge—that is, the view that people construct copies or representations of an external reality—and argue instead that reality results from the relatively durable perceptual and cognitive structures of the knower. This structure-determined view of reality is exemplified by von Foerster's (1984, p. 60) contention that "the nervous system is organized (or organizes itself) to produce a stable reality" and Maturana and Varela's (1987, p. 34) proposition that "all knowing depends upon the structure of the knower." It is important to note that radical constructivists, although bordering on phenomenology, do not deny the existence of some ontological reality but, rather, emphasize that "concepts . . . have no iconic or representational connection with anything that might 'exist' outside the cognizing system" (von Glasersfeld, 1991, p. 18).

Another important feature of radical constructivism is the fundamental role of distinction making in reality construction. From a radical constructivist perspective, reality is "brought forth" by the cognitive system's inherent capacity to draw distinctions (Maturana, 1988). If a distinction is not made, then the entity that this distinction would specify does not exist. Therefore, from a radical constructivist view, entities exist in the domain of cognitive distinctions only (Maturana & Varela, 1987).

The ontological and epistemological claims of radical constructivists ultimately lead to a view of living systems as (a) organizationally (not thermodynamically) closed and (b) not possessing inputs and outputs. Termed *autonomous* (or self-referencing), an organizationally closed system is one whose individual structure fully specifies how it will behave under any and all interactions (see in particular, Varela, 1979). Because it is the system (individual organism) that specifies how it will behave, information has no meaning apart from that given to it by the system. An important implication of the notion of organizational closure is that one system cannot instruct or determine the changes of another because all changes that a system undergoes are determined by its own organization (Maturana, 1988). Material constructivism has been embraced by systemic family therapists who conceptualize the family system as an informationally closed entity whose organizational structure (i.e., relations among family members) is maintained (sometimes dysfunctionally) within the interactional domain of language (cf. Efran, Lukens, & Lukens, 1990; Keeney, 1987; Mince, 1992).

To summarize, material constructivism—as a distinct form of constructivist thought—is exemplified by contemporary "radical" approaches to knowing and reality. Central features of this form of constructivist psychology entail (a) a view of reality as exclusively structure determined (materially caused); (b) the idea that reality is created through the basic formistic cognitive activity of distinction making; and (c) the notion that all living systems are fundamentally informationally closed, autonomous entities.

Efficient Constructivism

Although constructivist epistemology is generally antithetical to mechanism and the metaphor of knower as machine, some constructivist theories tend to exhibit bonds with the mechanistic world hypothesis through their endorsement of efficient causality. Efficient constructivism views knowing as an active process whereby environmental inputs are interpreted and stored as meaningful (and potentially useful) information. This form of constructivism is most evident in cognitive theories based on information-processing and social learning conceptualizations (Bandura, 1977; Bransford, 1979; Zimmerman, 1981).

Constructive Processing of Information

The constructivist flavor of the information-processing (IP) paradigm has been underscored by Merluzzi, Rudy, and Glass (1981), who contend that this approach to cognition

> views humans as active seekers and users of information. The cognitive system is seen as constantly active, adding to its environmental input and essentially constructing the mind's view of reality. (p. 81)

Using the theoretical metaphor of the "brain as computer," the IP perspective tends to emphasize (a) the "inward" flow of information from the environment to the sense organs and (b) the selective and sequential processing and storage of such information in organized forms, or schemata (J. R. Anderson, 1990). From this perspective, interactions with the world become a function of the cognitive system's capacity to identify potentially useful information, transform the information into meaningful cognitive patterns (schemata), and use these patterns in choosing appropriate responses. Schemata, in turn, influence (or bias) future information processing in a schema-consistent fashion (Fiske & Taylor, 1984; Lyddon, 1988).

Social Learning Theory

Paralleling IP portrayals of the relationship among environmental information, constructive cognitive processes, and behavioral responses, Bandura (1978) has stated that "in social learning theory, people play an active role in creating information-generating experiences as well as in processing and transforming informative stimuli" (p. 356). Social learning theory, as presented by Bandura, attempts to explain not only a person's interpretation of information but also how that person translates information into action and under what situations he or she will respond. Therefore, social learning theory is fundamentally cognitive (rule governed), constructivist (interpretive), and deterministic in the sense that cognition and behavior are thought to be causally linked in a reciprocal fashion to the environment (Zimmerman, 1981).

Although proponents of IP and social learning perspectives view human knowing as an active and constructive process, the present delineation of these perspectives as exemplars of efficient contructivism stems from their reliance on the ontological claim that what is known is to a large extent derived from the environment. In other words, central to both IP and social learning conceptualizations of human knowing is the notion that the environment functions as an antecedent variable that linearly directs the knowing process by providing the knowledge structures that humans must come to know. Accordingly, the primary role of the human cognitive system in IP and social learning theories is to reconstruct information that is preformed in external reality. Although it is important to note that recent descriptions of social cognitive theory assign a greater role to self-generated influences (Bandura, 1989), most contemporary IP and social learning models tend (a) to regard the environment as the primary source of information and (b) to evaluate the validity of people's schemata in terms of their accuracy, their degree of correspondence to external "reality" (i.e., social and environmental sources of information), or both. These features of efficient constructivism are particularly evident in models of psychotherapy that are based on the assumption that inaccurate and distorted information processing is at the root of many emotional and behavioral problems (cf. Beck, 1993; Ingram & Holle, 1992).

Formal Constructivism

As noted earlier, formal cause is associated with the contextualist world hypothesis and its root metaphor of the transitory historical event.

Similarly, formal constructivist theories assume that reality, rather than being static and categorically knowable, is instead active, ongoing, and both personally and socially constituted. Fundamental to this type of constructivism is the idea that meaning emerges from the organizational patterning (or form) of phenomena over time and within context. As Rosnow and Georgoudi (1986) stated:

> Human activity does not develop in a social vacuum, but rather it is rigorously situated within a sociohistorical and cultural context of meanings and relationships. Like a message that makes sense only in terms of the total context in which it occurs, human actions are embedded in a context of time, space, culture, and local tacit rules of conduct. (p. 4)

The contributions of William James (1890), Andras Angyal (1958), and others are historically significant because of their formal constructivist underpinnings. However, contemporary examples of formal constructivism include social constructionist theory (W. T. Anderson, 1990; Gergen, 1982, 1985, 1991; Lyddon, 1991) and emerging narrative approaches to psychology (Bruner, 1986; Howard, 1989, 1991; Mair, 1989, 1990; McAdams, 1993; Sarbin, 1986; Tappan, 1989; Vitz, 1990).

Social Constructionist Theory

Social constructionist thinkers seek to transcend endogenic and exogenic theories of knowledge by suggesting that knowledge does not reside exclusively in the minds of individuals (endogenic) or in the environment (exogenic) but, rather, in the social processes of symbolic interaction and exchange. According to Gergen (1982, 1985), *endogenic* refers to those theories of knowledge associated with the philosophies of Spinoza, Kant, Nietzche, and various phenomenologists that view the constructive and organizational processes of the mind as preeminent. In contrast, *exogenic* refers to the epistemic commitment reflected in the writings of such thinkers as Locke, Hume, the Mills, and various logical empiricists that impart priority to external reality. Pointing to significant conceptual limitations of the endogenic and exogenic perspectives when they are taken to their logical extremes (the problems of solipsism and justification, respectively), Gergen (Gergen & Gergen, 1991) has advocated a social constructionist epistemology that

> draws attention to the manner in which conventions of language and other social processes (negotiation, persuasion, power, etc.) influence the accounts rendered of the "objective" world. The emphasis is thus not on the individual mind but on the meanings of people as they collectively generate descriptions and explanations in language. (p. 78)

The notion that personal constructions of understanding are constrained by the social milieu—that is, the context of shared language and meaning systems that develop, persist, and evolve over time—is the essence of social constructionist thinking. This notion also forms the metatheoretical basis for critical revisions of a growing number of conceptual domains, including cognition (Arbib & Hesse, 1986; Coulter, 1983), emotion (Averill, 1985; Harré, 1986), gender (Bem, 1987; Hare-Mustin & Marecek, 1990), memory (Middleton & Edwards, 1990), personhood (Cushman, 1990; Gergen & Davis, 1985; Sampson, 1985), research and scholarly discourse (Edwards & Potter, 1992; Steier, 1991), and psychotherapy (Lyddon, in press; McNamee & Gergen, 1992; Owen, 1992).

Narrative Psychology

In recent years, several writers have suggested that the narrative, or story, is a potentially useful organizing principle for psychology and other human sciences (Bruner, 1990; Howard, 1989, 1991; Polkinghorne, 1988; Sarbin, 1986). According to Sarbin, narrative is founded on the contextualist root metaphor of the historical act and may be defined as a "symbolized account of human beings that has a temporal dimension" (1986, p. 3). Although the conceptual roots of narrative thinking in psychology include dramaturgical (Goffman, 1959, 1971), ethnogenic (Ginsberg, 1980; Harré & Secord, 1972), and social role (Sarbin & Allen, 1968) accounts of human behavior, perhaps the most familiar example of the application of the narrative and the historical act metaphor is the drama. As Sarbin has pointed out, in drama

> the actors' performances, the setting, the time and place, the nature of the audience, the script, the props, and so on, must all be taken into account to make sense of an episode or scene. The actors and the audiences play out their parts according to their individual and collective emplotments. Sense making in the drama is openly contextual. The meanings to be assigned to any actor's performance are a function of the context. (1986, p. 7)

Similar to drama, narrative psychology treats the narrative as an organizing context for human action. From a narrative psychology perspective, people impose socially constituted narratives (or roles) on the flow of their experience and, as a result, are both the authors of and actors in self-narratives—that is, their own personal dramas. In other words, narratives provide the contexts (and parameters) for people's constructions and descriptions of experience. Narrative knowing, conceptualized as a major mode of cognition that is qualitatively distinct from propositional thought (cf. Bruner, 1986; Spence, 1982; Tulving, 1983), forms the epistemic basis for emerging conceptualizations of attribution processes (Hilton, 1990), cultural differnces (Howard, 1991), moral development (Tappan, 1989; Tappan & Brown, 1989; Vitz, 1990), the self (Hermans & Kempen, 1993; Polkinghorne, 1991; Shotter & Gergen, 1989), and psychotherapy (Gilligan & Price, 1993; Oately, 1992; White & Epston, 1990).

Because they mutually emphasize the way in which shared language structures and roles "punctuate" the flow of human experience into organized and meaningful patterns, both social constructionist and narrative orientations to psychology reflect a commitment to formal constructivism. *Formal constructivism* represents a holistic approach to understanding human knowing—one that emphasizes the inseparable connection among psychological (personally constructed), contextual (socially constructed), and temporal dimensions of experience.

Final Constructivism

Final constructivism, associated with the organismic world hypothesis and organic process metaphor, is an epistemic position viewing knowledge as a constructed synthesis of the inevitable contradictions arising from person–environment interactions. Relying on the concept of final causation, this approach to constructivism views knowledge as dynamic and directional; that is, over time, knowledge structures are believed to undergo qualitative shifts or transformations in organization in the direction of increased complexity and abstraction. Cognitive–developmental (Kegan, 1982; Piaget, 1970, 1981), dialectical (Basseches, 1984a; Pascual-Leone, 1987; Riegel, 1979), and living systems approaches (D. H. Ford, 1987; Guidano, 1987; Jantsch, 1980; Olds, 1992; Prigogine & Stengers, 1984), as well as transpersonal approaches (Walsh & Vaughan, 1980; Weinhold & Hendricks, 1993; Wilber, Engler, & Brown, 1986) tend to exemplify forms of psychological constructivism based on the organic process metaphor.

Developmental and Dialectical Theories

According to Piaget (1970, 1981), equilibration is the fundamental organismic principle that guides cognitive development. *Equilibration* has been defined as

> a process of self-regulation which maintains a balance between "assimilation" and "accommodation," compensates for internal and external disturbances, and in doing so leads to the development of more and more complex, integrated and balanced structures. (Mischel, 1971, p. 323)

Piaget (1970) rejected the empiricist view that knowledge is imposed on the individual through experience and ultimately reflects the nature of the external world, like a mirror. Likewise, he rejected a priori claims that knowledge is a function of an innately given structure that people impose on the external world. Rather, Piaget contended that knowledge is actively constructed (and reconstructed) over time through the interplay of assimilative and accommodative processes. Although assimilation involves the ongoing integration of moment-to-moment experience into existing cognitive structures, accommodation entails a proactive and developmental change in the structures themselves in response to emergent discrepancies between ongoing reality and cognitive capacities. Although the form of knowledge is dictated by the structures of the mind, these structures are neither fixed nor innately given, but constructed. Furthermore, the role of experience within the Piagetian perspective is not to impose its form on knowledge but, rather, to create disequilibrium—disequilibrium that challenges the knower to actively construct new forms of understanding and to pursue equilibrium at a higher, more complex developmental level.

In recent years, the organismic notion that the self redefines (or reconstructs) its relationship to the world in a manner that is increasingly more coherent and integrated has become a foundational assumption associated with several life-span developmental thinkers (Basseches, 1984a; Guidano, 1987; Levinson, 1986). What has emerged from this line of thought are models of adult cognitive development that reach beyond Piaget's adolescent "formal operations" stage and describe various "postformal operations" and cognitive shifts (Alexander & Langer, 1990; Commons, Sinnott, Richards, & Armon, 1989). Cognitive development is viewed as an ongoing dialectical process whereby inevitable tensions and contradictions emerge from each resolution of previous thesis and antithesis tensions across the life span (Basseches, 1984a, 1984b; Kramer, 1989; Pascual-Leone, 1984). In short, cognitive development is conceived as a directional process whereby old forms of knowing give way to new, emergent forms as the knower continues to construct more epistemologically powerful (i.e., inclusive, viable, or integrated) ways of making sense out of the world.

Systems Perspectives

Paralleling developmental and dialectical approaches, contemporary descriptions of systems theory also differentiate between two types of dynamic changes that a system may undergo in adapting to both internal and external sources of stress: equilibrium and dissipative change. Whereas *equilibrium change* refers to a dynamically maintained (ordered) state that preserves the basic structure of a system, *dissipative change* represents a nonlinear transformation in system structures and a qualitative reformulation of the system and its capacities (cf. Capra, 1982;

Jantsch, 1980; Prigogine & Stengers, 1984). As applied to family systems, for example, equilibrium change is the essential structuring factor that maintains current organizational relations among family members (e.g., communication patterns and power relations). However, increases in family conflict and stress (i.e., system "perturbations") may lead to dissipative change and a new (and potentially more viable) family organization and state of equilibrium change (Dell & Goolishian, 1981).

The notion of systemic self-organization through dissipative change processes has become a significant feature associated with emerging psychological conceptualizations of humans as active, self-construing, open, and developing systems (Brent, 1978; D. H. Ford, 1987; Guidano, 1987; Mahoney, 1991; Sampson, 1985). For example, in his recent theoretical analysis of humans as self-constructing living systems, D. H. Ford (1987) stated:

> People display properties of self-construction, self-direction, self-control, and self-regulation, properties which give the appearance of purposive or goal-directed behavior. People's functioning appears to be directed towards maintaining and elaborating the effectiveness and complexity of their behavioral organization and the organization of their relationships with environments. To a considerable extent they are producers of their own development. (pp. 28–29)

D. H. Ford distinguished among three fundamental kinds of change processes: self-organizational, self-construction, and disorganizational–reorganizational. Self-organizational processes function to maintain existing patterns of organization in a dynamic equilibrium by assimilating new, but compatible information into existing schemata. Self-construction processes function to alter existing patterns of organization to accommodate new information that cannot be assimilated and, therefore, to elaborate behavioral options and capabilities. Disorganizational–reorganizational processes operate to transform patterns of functioning to a new dynamic equilibrium when disrupting influences are too great to be accommodated by existing capabilities (M. E. Ford & Ford, 1987).

Transpersonal Psychology

Emerging as the "fourth force" in psychology during the late 1960s (Sutich, 1968), transpersonal psychology has at its core a developmental conception of human potential and consciousness. As Washburn (1988) noted:

> Transpersonal psychology is the study of human nature and development that proceeds on the assumption that human beings possess potentialities that surpass the limits of the normally developed ego. It is an inquiry that presupposes that the ego, as ordinarily consti-

tuted, can be transcended and that a higher, transegoic plane or stage of life is possible. (p. v)

The developmental, or telic, emphasis of final constructivism is particularly evident in the transpersonal models of writers like Wilber (1981, 1986) who view humans (both individually and collectively) as in a process of evolution toward integral wholeness and spirit. In an attempt to bridge conventional (Western) and contemplative (Eastern) traditions, Wilber (1986) proposed a "full spectrum" developmental model composed of nine levels of self-development that are bracketed into three realms: prepersonal, or self-emergent; personal, or ego differentiation; and transpersonal, or self-transcendent. Because the first two realms of the full spectrum model only encompass traditional Western conceptualizations of development, it is important to note that even complete ego development or differentiation is considered to be a form of developmental arrest rather than a level of normalcy. From a transpersonal perspective, the highest level of development involves ego transcendence, which is believed to be essential to the full realization of human potential.

Transpersonal psychology—together with developmental, dialectical, and living systems perspectives—represents a contemporary example of final constructivism. Bound together by the root metaphor of the organic process and the concept of final causality, all of these constructivist theories view the human organism as an active, developing system capable of organizing and reorganizing itself throughout its life span.

TOWARD AN INTEGRATIVE CONSTRUCTIVIST PSYCHOLOGY

Up to this point, I have suggested that in spite of their common embeddedness in constructivist epistemology, constructivist theories do not reflect a similarly consistent philosophical base when contrasted along the dimension of causal assumptions. In particular, when examined in the context of the causal assumptions associated with Pepper's (1942) taxonomy of world hypotheses, four forms of psychological constructivism may be differentiated (see Table 1). First, material constructivist theories rely on the idea of material causation and the notion that knowledge is exclusively a function of the structures or basic materials of the knower. Ontologically, reality is structure determined and is knowable only by way of the closed organizational character of the human cognitive system. Second, efficient constructivist theories alternatively presume that an ontological reality exists independent of the knower in the form of environmental information—information that is acted on by the knower.

TABLE 1
Characteristics of Different Forms of Constructivist Psychology

Characteristic	Form of Constructivist Psychology			
	Material	Efficient	Formal	Final
Worldview	Formism	Mechanism	Contextualism	Organism
Root metaphor	Similarity	Machine	Historical event	Organic process
Causal assumption	Material cause: emanating from the substance or material of which a thing is made	Efficient cause: the impetus or force in events	Formal cause: the pattern, shape, outline, or recognizable organization in the flow of events	Final cause: that for the sake of which something occurs—the reason, purpose, intention, or telos of the events or actions
Theoretical exemplar(s)	Radical perspectives	Information-processing models Social learning theory	Social constructionism Narrative psychology	Developmental & dialectic theories Systems perspectives Transpersonal psychology

According to these theories, information tends to flow from the environment to the knower in a linear and efficient causal fashion, is actively "processed" (reconstructed), and becomes useful and adaptive to the extent that accurate or valid cognitive representations are developed. Third, formal theories of constructed knowledge are based on formal causal assumptions and the identification of meaningful patterns in the ongoing flow of moment-to-moment experience in context. From a formal constructivist perspective, personal realities are constrained by the socially and historically constituted roles, values, and narratives that make up the changing contexts of people's lives. Fourth, in contrast, final constructivist theories are based on the concept of final cause and the view that knowledge is fundamentally teleological, existing in anticipation of some larger unfolding structure. Central to final constructivism is the idea that new and more inclusive forms of knowledge emerge from the synthesis of the inevitable discrepancies, contradictions, and tensions resulting from person–environment interactions.

Although the distinctions drawn among forms of constructivist psychology may be somewhat unsettling (especially to constructivists unified around a common epistemic commitment to constructivism), this differentiation is not meant to preclude the possibility that all forms of constructivist psychology may reflect viable accounts of different aspects of human knowing. The advantage of this conjecture is its allegiance to the possibility that a more integrative and encompassing model of constructivist psychology may be developed. It is significant to note, for example, that Pepper (1942), in his delineation of root metaphor theory, suggested that all four world hypotheses offer unique and viable conceptual lenses for understanding world phenomena. Moreover, Aristotle—credited with first drawing the distinctions among the four types of causation—formulated his causal theory in an attempt to provide a full rendering of the nature of phenomena and their inherent properties of stability and change. According to Aristotle, a complete causal account of a phenomenon cannot be given until its material, efficient, formal, and final causal properties are addressed (Robinson, 1985).

When applied to constructivist views of human cognition and knowing, the contentions of Pepper (1942) and Aristotle may be instructive. A full understanding of the constructive nature of human knowing, for example, should consider those aspects of cognition that are more or less hardwired and reflect inherent feed-forward (or anticipatory) processes of the human nervous system (see Mahoney, 1991, pp. 100–102). These "material" forms of knowing may include but may not be limited to infant attachment processes, facial recognition, color vision, and the nervous system's ability to construct meaning through contrast and distinction. In a similar vein, an integrative constructivist psychology should include those aspects of cognition that reflect a capability to almost mechanically and efficiently process environmental information. Short-term and semantic memory processes and various forms of analog cognition (i.e., mental representations that have an underlying physiological analogy to the external stimulus) may be most obviously implicated here.

A more complete view of constructivist psychology should also be able to integrate that dimension to human knowing contained in the formal causal assertion that what we know of ourselves and the world may be historically and contextually situated. The implication here is that knowledge structures shared by individuals of a community may cohere into a patterned reality (social schema) external to each individual. In addition to material, efficient, and formal dimensions of human cognition, a more integrative constructivist psychology should encompass the telic nature of human knowing. The idea that construct systems (personal and social) evolve (or coevolve) in their developmental journeys through space and time places human knowing within a systems process framework of continual becoming. Final causal accounts of cognition, in addition to accentuating temporal and developmental features, help to underscore the agentic, purposeful, and generative (creative) aspects of human knowing and being (Howard, 1986).

Constructivism has emerged as a viable epistemic perspective in twentieth-century psychological science. As this perspective continues to influence the development of psychological theory, it will become increasingly important to distinguish among its various forms of expression. As suggested herein, however, such distinctions need not be divisive but, rather, may serve as catalysts for developing more integrative conceptions of the constructive nature of human knowing.

REFERENCES

Alexander, C. N., & Langer, E. J. (Eds.). (1990). *Higher stages of development: Perspectives on adult growth.* New York: Oxford University Press.

Altman, I., & Rogoff, B. (1987). World views in psychology: Trait, interactional, organismic, and transactional perspectives. In D. Stokols & I. Altman (Eds.), *Handbook of environmental psychology* (pp. 7–40). New York: Wiley.

Anderson, J. R. (1990). *Cognitive psychology and its implications.* New York: Freeman.

Anderson, W. T. (1990). *Reality isn't what it used to be.* San Francisco: Harper & Row.

Angyal, A. (1958). *Foundations for a science of personality.* Cambridge, MA: Harvard University.

Arbib, M. A., & Hesse, M. B. (1986). *The construction of reality.* Cambridge, England: Cambridge University Press.

Averill, J. (1985). The social construction of emotion: With special reference to love. In K. J. Gergen & K. E. Davis (Eds.), *The social construction of the person* (pp. 89–109). New York: Springer-Verlag.

Bandura, A. (1977). *Social learning theory*. Englewood Cliffs, NJ: Prentice Hall.

Bandura, A. (1978). The self system in reciprocal determinism. *American Psychologist, 33*, 344–358.

Bandura, A. (1989). Human agency in social cognitive theory. *American Psychologist, 44*, 1175–1184.

Bartlett, F. C. (1932). *Remembering*. Cambridge, England: Cambridge University Press.

Basseches, M. (1984a). *Dialectical thinking and adult development*. Norwood, NJ: Ablex.

Basseches, M. A. (1984b). Dialectical thinking as a metasystematic form of cognitive organization. In M. L. Commons, F. A. Richards, & C. Armon (Eds.), *Beyond formal operations: Late adolescent and adult cognitive development* (pp. 216–238). New York: Praeger.

Beck, A. T. (1993). Cognitive therapy: Past, present, and future. *Journal of Consulting and Clinical Psychology, 62*, 194–198.

Belenky, M. F., Clinchy, B. M., Goldberger, N. R., & Tarule, J. M. (1986). *Women's ways of knowing: The development of self, voice, and mind*. New York: Basic Books.

Belli, R. F. (1986). Mechanistic and organicist parallels between theories of memory and science. *Journal of Mind and Behavior, 2*, 63–86.

Bem, S. L. (1987). Gender schema theory and the romantic tradition. *Review of Personality and Social Psychology, 7*, 25–71.

Berzonsky, M. D. (1990). Self-construction over the life-span: A process perspective on identity formation. In G. J. Neimeyer & R. A. Neimeyer (Eds.), *Advances in personal construct theory* (Vol. 1, pp. 155–186). Greenwich, CT: JAI Press.

Black, A., & Ammon, P. (1992). A developmental–constructivist approach to teacher education. *Journal of Teacher Education, 43*, 323–335.

Bransford, J. D. (1979). *Human cognition: Learning, understanding and remembering*. Belmont, CA: Wadsworth.

Brent, S. B. (1978). Prigogine's model for self-organization in nonequilibrium systems: Its relevance for developmental psychology. *Human Development, 21*, 374–387.

Bronfenbrenner, U., Kessel, F., Kessen, W., & White, S. (1986). Toward a critical social history of developmental psychology: A propaedeutic discussion. *American Psychologist, 41*, 1218–1230.

Bruner, J. (1986). *Actual minds, possible worlds*. Cambridge, MA: Harvard University Press.

Bruner, J. (1990). *Acts of meaning*. Cambridge, MA: Harvard University Press.

Bugaj, A. M., & Rychlak, J. F. (1989). Pedicational versus mediational modeling and the directedness of cognition in impression formation. *Journal of Mind and Behavior, 10*, 135–152.

Capra, F. (1982). *The turning point.* New York: Bantam.

Collins, J. T., & Hagen, J. W. (1979). A constructivist account of the development of perception, attention, and memory. In G. A. Hale & M. Lewis (Eds.), *Attention and cognitive development* (pp. 65–96). New York: Plenum.

Commons, M. L., Sinnott, J. D., Richards, F. A., & Armon, C. (Eds.). (1989). *Beyond formal operations: II. Comparison of adolescent and adult developmental models* (pp. 133–159). New York: Praeger.

Cooper, J. D. (1993). *Literacy: Helping children construct meaning.* Boston: Houghton Mifflin.

Coulter, J. (1983). *Rethinking cognitive theory.* London: Macmillan.

Cushman, P. (1990). Why the self is empty: Toward a historically situated psychology. *American Psychologist, 45*, 599–611.

Dell, P. F. (1985). Understanding Bateson and Maturana: Toward a biological foundation for the social sciences. *Journal of Marital and Family Therapy, 11*, 1–20.

Dell, P. F., & Goolishian, H. A. (1981). Order through fluctuations: An evolutionary epistemology for human systems. *Australian Journal of Family Therapy, 2*, 175–184.

Edwards, D., & Potter, J. (1992). *Discursive psychology.* Newbury Park, CA: Sage.

Efran, J., Lukens, M., & Lukens, R. (1990). *Language, structure, and change: Frameworks of meaning in psychotherapy.* New York: Norton.

Feffer, M. (1988). *Radical constructionism: Rethinking the dynamics of development.* New York: New York University Press.

Fiske, S. T., & Taylor, S. T. (1984). *Social cognition.* New York: Random House.

Ford, D. H. (1987). *Humans as self-constructing living systems: A developmental perspective on behavior and personality.* Hillsdale, NJ: Erlbaum.

Ford, M. E., & Ford, D. H. (1987). *Humans as self-constructing living systems: Putting the framework to work.* Hillsdale, NJ: Erlbaum.

Geddis, A. N. (1982). Teaching: A study in evidence. *Journal of Mind and Behavior, 3*, 363–373.

Gergen, K. J. (1982). *Toward transformation in social knowledge.* New York: Springer-Verlag.

Gergen, K. J. (1985). The social constructionist movement in modern psychology. *American Psychologist, 40*, 266–275.

Gergen, K. J. (1991). *The saturated self.* New York: Basic Books.

Gergen, K. J., & Davis, K. E. (Eds.). (1985). *The social construction of the person.* New York: Springer-Verlag.

Gergen, K. J., & Gergen, M. M. (1991). Toward reflexive methodologies. In F. Steier (Ed.), *Research and reflexivity* (pp. 76–95). Newbury Park, CA: Sage.

Gilligan, S., & Price, R. E. (Eds.). (1993). *Therapeutic conversations*. New York: Norton.

Ginsberg, G. P. (1980). Situated action: An emerging paradigm. In L. Wheeler (Ed.), *Review of personality and social psychology* (Vol. 1, pp. 295–325). Beverly Hills, CA: Sage.

Goffman, E. (1959). *The presentation of self in everyday life*. New York: Doubleday.

Goffman, E. (1971). *Relations in public*. New York: Basic Books.

Guidano, V. F. (1987). *Complexity of the self: A developmental approach to psychopathology and therapy*. New York: Guilford Press.

Guidano, V. F. (1991). *The self in process*. New York: Guilford Press.

Hampson, S. E. (1988). *The construction of personality*. London: Routledge.

Hare-Mustin, R. T., & Marecek, J. (1988). The meaning of difference: Gender theory, postmodernism, and psychology. *American Psychologist, 43*, 455–464.

Hare-Mustin, R. T., & Marecek, J. (Eds.). (1990). *Making a difference: Psychology and the construction of gender*. New Haven, CT: Yale University Press.

Harré, R. (Ed.). (1986). *The social construction of emotions*. New York: Basil Blackwell.

Harré, R., & Secord, P. F. (1972). *The explanation of social behavior*. Totowa, NJ: Rowman & Littlefield.

Hayek, F. A. (1952). *The sensory order*. Chicago: University of Chicago Press.

Hayes, S. C. (1988). Contextualism and the next wave of behavioral psychology. *Behavior Analysis, 23*, 7–22.

Hermans, H. J. M., & Kempen, H. J. G. (1993). *The dialogical self*. San Diego, CA: Academic Press.

Hermans, H. J. M., Kempen, H. J. G., & van Loon, R. J. P. (1992). The dialogical self: Beyond individualism and rationalism. *American Psychologist, 47*, 23–33.

Hilton, D. (1990). Conversational processes and causal explanation. *Psychological Bulletin, 107*, 65–81.

Howard, G. S. (1986). *Dare we develop a human science?* Notre Dame, IN: Academic Publications.

Howard, G. S. (1989). *A tale of two stories: Excursions into a narrative approach to psychology*. Notre Dame, IN: Academic Publications.

Howard, G. S. (1991). Culture tales: A narrative approach to thinking, cross-cultural psychology, and psychotherapy. *American Psychologist, 46*, 187–197.

Ingram, R. E., & Holle, C. (1992). Cognitive science of depression. In D. J. Stein & J. E. Young (Eds.), *Cognitive science and clinical disorders* (pp. 187–209). San Diego, CA: Academic Press.

James, W. (1890). *The principles of psychology*. New York: Holt.

Jantsch, E. (1980). *The self-organizing universe: Scientific and human implications of the emerging paradigm of evolution*. New York: Pergamon.

Johnson, J. A., Germer, C. K., Efran, J. S., & Overton, W. F. (1988). Personality as the basis for theoretical predilections. *Journal of Personality and Social Psychology, 55,* 824–835.

Kant, I. (1969). *Critique of pure reason.* New York: St. Martin's Press. (Original work published 1791)

Keating, D. P., & Rosen, H. (Eds.). (1991). *Constructivist perspectives on developmental psychopathology and atypical development.* Hillsdale, NJ: Erlbaum.

Keeney, B. P. (1987). The construction of therapeutic realities. *Psychotherapy, 24,* 469–476.

Kegan, R. (1982). *The evolving self.* Cambridge, MA: Harvard University Press.

Kelly, G. A. (1955). *The psychology of personal constructs.* New York: Norton.

Kramer, D. A. (1989). Development of an awareness of contradiction across the lifespan and the question of post formal operations. In M. L. Commons, J. D. Sinnott, F. A. Richards, & C. Armon (Eds.), *Beyond formal operations: II. Comparisions and applications of adolescent and adult developmental models* (pp. 133–159). New York: Praeger.

Kramer, D. A., & Bopp, M. J. (Eds.). (1989). *Transformation in clinical and developmental psychology.* New York: Springer-Verlag.

Lerner, J. W. (1993). *Learning disabilities: Theories, diagnosis, and teaching strategies.* Boston: Houghton Mifflin.

Lerner, R. M. (1986). *Concepts and theories of human development* (2nd ed.). New York: Random House.

Lerner, R. M., & Kauffman, M. B. (1985). The concept of development in contextualism. *Developmental Review, 5,* 309–333.

Levinson, D. J. (1986). A conception of adult development. *American Psychologist, 41,* 3–13.

Lyddon, W. J. (1987). Emerging views of health: A challenge to rationalist doctrines of medical thought. *Journal of Mind and Behavior, 8,* 365–394.

Lyddon, W. J. (1988). Information-processing and constructivist models of cognitive therapy: A philosophical divergence. *Journal of Mind and Behavior, 9,* 137–166.

Lyddon, W. J. (1989). Root metaphor theory: A philosophical framework for counseling and psychotherapy. *Journal of Counseling and Development, 67,* 442–448.

Lyddon, W. J. (1991). Socially constituted knowledge: Philosophical, psychological, and feminist contributions. *Journal of Mind and Behavior, 12,* 263–280.

Lyddon, W. J. (in press). Cognitive therapy and theories of knowing: A social constructionist perspective. *Journal of Counseling and Development.*

Lyddon, W. J., & Adamson, L. A. (1992). Worldview and counseling preference: An analogue study. *Journal of Counseling and Development, 71,* 41–47.

Mahoney, M. J. (1988). Constructive metatheory: I. Basic features and historical foundations. *International Journal of Personal Construct Psychology, 1,* 1–35.

Mahoney, M. J. (1991). *Human change processes.* New York: Basic Books.

Mahoney, M. J., & Lyddon, W. J. (1988). Recent developments in cognitive approaches to counseling and psychotherapy. *The Counseling Psychologist, 16*, 190–234.

Mair, M. (1989). *Between psychology and psychotherapy: A poetics of experience.* New York: Routledge.

Mair, M. (1990). Telling psychological tales. *International Journal of Personal Construct Psychology, 3*, 121–135.

Mandler, G. (1984). *Mind and body: Psychology of emotion and stress.* New York: Norton.

Mandler, G. (1992). Cognition and emotion: Extensions and clinical application. In D. J. Stein & J. E. Young (Eds.), *Cognitive science and clinical disorders* (pp. 61–78). San Diego, CA: Academic Press.

Masterpasqua, F. (1989). A competence paradigm for psychological practice. *American Psychologist, 44*, 1366–1371.

Maturana, H. R. (1988). Reality: The search for objectivity or the quest for a compelling argument. *Irish Journal of Psychology, 9*, 25–82.

Maturana, H. R., & Varela, F. J. (1987). *The tree of knowledge.* Boston: Shambhala.

McAdams, D. P. (1993). *The stories we live by: Personal myths and the making of the self.* New York: Morrow.

McNamee, S., & Gergen, K. J. (1992). *Therapy as social construction.* Newbury Park, CA: Sage.

Merluzzi, T. V., Rudy, T. E., & Glass, C. R. (1981). The information-processing paradigm: Implications for clinical science. In T. V. Merluzzi, C. R. Glass, & M. Genest (Eds.), *Cognitive assessment* (pp. 77–124). New York: Guilford Press.

Middleton, D., & Edwards, D. (Eds.). (1990). *Collective remembering.* Newbury Park, CA: Sage.

Mince, J. (1992). Discovering meaning within families. In J. D. Atwood (Ed.), *Family therapy* (pp. 321–343). Chicago: Nelson-Hall.

Mischel, T. (Ed.). (1971). *Cognitive development and epistemology.* San Diego, CA: Academic Press.

Morris, E. K. (1988). Contextualism: The world view of behavioral analysis. *Journal of Experimental Child Psychology, 46*, 289–323.

Neimeyer, G. J. (Ed.). (1993). *Constructivist assessment: A casebook.* Newbury Park, CA: Sage.

Oately, K. (1992). Integrative action of narrative. In D. J. Stein & J. E. Young (Eds.), *Cognitive science and clinical disorders* (pp. 151–170). San Diego, CA: Academic Press.

Olds, L. E. (1992). *Metaphors of interrelatedness: Toward a systems theory of psychology.* Albany: State University of New York Press.

Overton, W. F. (1984). World views and their influence on psychological theory and research: Kuhn-Lakatos-Laudan. In H. W. Reese (Ed.), *Advances in child development and behavior* (Vol. 18, pp. 191–226). San Diego, CA: Academic Press.

Owen, I. R. (1992). Applying social constructionism to psychotherapy. *Counseling Psychology Quarterly, 5,* 385–402.

Pascual-Leone, J. (1984). Attentional, dialectical, and mental effort: Toward an organismic theory of life stages. In M. L. Commons, F. A. Richards, & C. Armon (Eds.), *Beyond formal operations: Late adolescent and adult cognitive development* (pp. 182–215). New York: Praeger.

Pascual-Leone, J. (1987). Organismic processes for new Piagetian theories: A dialectical causal account of cognitive development. *International Journal of Psychology, 22,* 531–570.

Payne, R. (1976). Truisms in organizational behavior. *Interpersonal Development, 6,* 202–221.

Pepper, S. C. (1942). *World hypotheses.* Berkeley: University of California Press.

Piaget, J. (1926). *The language and thought of the child.* London: Kegan, Paul, French, & Trubner.

Piaget, J. (1970). *Psychology and epistemology: Toward a theory of knowledge.* New York: Viking.

Piaget, J. (1981). *Intelligence and affectivity: The relationship during child development* (T. A. Brown & C. E. Kaegi, Trans.). Palo Alto, CA: Annual Review.

Polkinghorne, D. (1988). *Narrative knowing and the human sciences.* Albany: State University of New York Press.

Polkinghorne, D. (1991). Narrative and self concept. *Journal of Narrative and Life History, 1,* 135–153.

Prigogine, I., & Stengers, I. (1984). *Order out of chaos: Man's new dialogue with nature.* New York: Bantam Books.

Quina, J. (1982). Root metaphor and interdisciplinary curriculum: Designs for teaching literature in secondary schools. *Journal of Mind and Behavior, 3,* 345–356.

Reiss, D. (1981). *The family's construction of reality.* Cambridge, MA: Harvard University Press.

Riegel, K. F. (1979). *Foundations of dialectical psychology.* San Diego, CA: Academic Press.

Robinson, D. N. (1985). *Philosophy of psychology.* New York: Columbia University Press.

Rosnow, R. L., & Georgoudi, M. (Eds.). (1986). *Contextualism and understanding in behavioral science.* New York: Praeger.

Royce, J. R., & Powell, A. (1983). *Theory of personality and individual differences: Factors, systems, and processes.* Englewood Cliffs, NJ: Prentice Hall.

Rychlak, J. F. (1977). *The psychology of rigorous humanism.* New York: Wiley.

Sampson, E. E. (1985). The decentralization of identity: Toward a revised concept of personal and social order. *American Psychologist, 40,* 1203–1211.

Santrock, J. W., & Bartlett, J. C. (1986). *Developmental psychology: A life-cycle perspective*. Dubuque, IA: William C. Brown.

Sarbin, T. R. (Ed.). (1986). *Narrative psychology: The storied nature of human conduct*. New York: Praeger.

Sarbin, T. R., & Allen, V. L. (1968). Role theory. In G. Lindzey & E. Aronson (Eds.), *Handbook of social psychology* (Vol. 1, pp. 488–567). Reading, MA: Addison-Wesley.

Sarbin, T., & Coe, W. (1979). Hypnosis and psychopathology: Replacing old myths with fresh metaphors. *Journal of Abnormal Psychology, 88*, 506–526.

Scarr, S. (1985). Constructing psychology: Making facts and fables for our times. *American Psychologist, 40*, 499–512.

Schwartz, G. E. (1984). Psychobiology of health: A new synthesis. In B. L. Hammonds & C. J. Scheirer (Eds.), *Psychology and health* (pp. 149–193). Washington, DC: American Psychological Association.

Shaw, R., & Bransford, J. (Eds.). (1977). *Perceiving, acting, and knowing: Toward an ecological psychology*. Hillsdale, NJ: Erlbaum.

Shotter, J., & Gergen, K. J. (1989). *Texts of identity*. Newbury Park, CA: Sage.

Spence, D. P. (1982). *Narrative truth and historical truth: Meaning and interpretation in psychoanalysis*. New York: Norton.

Steenbarger, B. (1991). All the world is not a stage: Emerging contextualist themes in counseling and development. *Journal of Counseling and Development, 70*, 288–296.

Steier, F. (1991). *Research and reflexivity*. Newbury Park, CA: Sage.

Sutich, A. J. (1968). Transpersonal psychology: An emerging force. *Journal of Humanistic Psychology, 8*, 77–78.

Tappan, M. B. (1989). Stories lived and stories told: The narrative structure of late adolescent moral development. *Human Development, 32*, 300–315.

Tappan, M. B., & Brown, L. M. (1989). Stories told and lessons learned: Toward a narrative approach to moral development and moral education. *Harvard Educational Review, 59*, 182–205.

Tulving, E. (1983). *Elements of episodic memory*. New York: Oxford University Press.

Tyler, L. E. (1981). More stately mansions—psychology extends its boundaries. *Annual Review of Psychology, 32*, 1–20.

Unger, R. K. (1983). Through the looking glass: No Wonderland yet! *Psychology of Women Quarterly, 8*, 9–32.

Unger, R. (Ed.). (1989). *Representations: Social constructions of gender*. Amityville, NY: Baywood.

Vaihinger, H. (1924). *The philosophy of 'as if.'* New York: Routledge & Kegan Paul. (Original work published 1911)

Varela, F. J. (1979). *Principles of biological autonomy*. New York: Elsevier Science.

Vico, G. (1948). *The new science* (T. G. Bergin & M. H. Fisch, Trans.). Ithaca, NY: Cornell University Press. (Original work published 1725)

Vitz, P. C. (1990). The use of stories in moral development: New psychological reasons for an old educational method. *American Psychologist, 45*, 709–720.

von Foerster, H. (1984). On constructing a reality. In P. Watzlawick (Ed.), *The invented reality* (pp. 41–62). New York: Norton.

von Glasersfeld, E. (1979). Radical constructivism and Piaget's concept of knowledge. In F. B. Murray (Ed.), *The impact of Piagetian theory on education, philosophy, psychiatry, and psychology* (pp. 109–122). Baltimore: University Park Press.

von Glasersfeld, E. (1984). An introduction to radical constructivism. In P. Watzlawick (Ed.), *The invented reality* (pp. 17–40). New York: Norton.

von Glasersfeld, E. (1987). *The construction of knowledge*. Salinas, CA: Intersystems.

von Glasersfeld, E. (1991). Knowing without metaphysics: Aspects of the radical constructivist position. In F. Steier (Ed.), *Research and reflexivity* (pp. 12–29). Newbury Park, CA: Sage.

Walsh, R. N., & Vaughan, E. (1980). *Beyond ego: Transpersonal dimensions in psychology*. Los Angeles, CA: J. P. Tarcher.

Washburn, M. (1988). *The ego and the dynamic ground: A transpersonal theory of human development*. Albany: State University of New York Press.

Weimer, W. B. (1977). A conceptual framework for cognitive psychology: Motor theories of the mind. In R. Shaw & J. Bransford (Eds.), *Perceiving, acting and knowing* (pp. 267–311). Hillsdale, NJ: Erlbaum.

Weinhold, B., & Hendricks, G. (Eds.). (1993). *Counseling and psychotherapy: A transpersonal approach*. Denver, CO: Love.

White, M., & Epston, D. (1990). *Narrative means to therapeutic ends*. New York: Norton.

Wicker, A. W. (1991). Making sense of environments. In W. B. Walsh, K. H. Craik, & R. H. Price (Eds.), *Person–environment psychology: Models and perspectives* (pp. 157–192). Hillsdale, NJ: Erlbaum.

Wilber, K. (1981). *Up from Eden: A transpersonal view of human evolution*. Garden City, NY: Doubleday.

Wilber, K. (1986). The spectrum of development. In K. Wilber, J. Engler, & D. P. Brown (Eds.), *Transformations of consciousness: Conventional and contemplative perspectives on development* (pp. 65–105). Boston: New Science Library.

Wilber, K., Engler, J., & Brown, D. P. (1986). *Transformations of consciousness: Conventional and contemplative perspectives on development*. Boston: New Science Library.

Wittig, A. W. (1985). Metatheoretical dilemmas in the psychology of gender. *American Psychologist, 40*, 800–811.

Zimmerman, B. J. (1981). Social learning theory and cognitive constructivism. In I. E. Sigel, D. M. Brodzinsky, & R. M. Golinkoff (Eds.), *New directions in Piagetian theory and practice* (pp. 39–49). Hillsdale, NJ: Erlbaum.

5

CONSTRUCTIVIST PSYCHOTHERAPY: A THEORETICAL FRAMEWORK

VITTORIO F. GUIDANO

Contemporary cognitive psychology is still dominated by rationalist and objectivist perspectives, which have traditionally avoided or devalued the phenomenological realm and the complex nature of lived human experience. When reality is assumed to be an objective external order that exists independently from people's observations of it—an assumption common to objectivism, realism, and traditional rationalism—it is inevitable that people will overlook their own characteristics and processes as observers. The only possible themes of investigation in an objectivist world are to refine or perfect one's perceptions of that world and to modify one's mental representations in ways that reflect improved "contact" or compliance with objective reality.

A constructivist approach entails significant changes in these initial assumptions and in the possible themes of investigation. From such a nonobjectivist perspective, an essential task becomes understanding how people's characteristics as observers are involved in the process of observing, as well as how people otherwise participate in cocreating the dynamic personal realities to which they individually respond. This shift leads necessarily to a radical change in traditional formulations of human experience, human knowing, and professional helping.

BASIC FEATURES OF HUMAN EXPERIENCE

A proper framework for investigating such a problem, it seems, should rest on two basic points. One is the assumption of an evolutionary epistemological perspective—that is, a perspective that is based in the continuing study of evolving knowledge and knowing systems. Given that, as human beings, we cannot escape our particular way of being— which is fleshbound and animal—such a stance requires a central acknowledgment of the embodiment of human experience. The second basic point in this framework is that the ordering of our world is inseparable from our experiencing of it. We do, in fact, "experience it," or, more accurately, we "experience." The it is an objectification, however, and hence, implies a distancing between the experiencer and the living moment.

What is important to emphasize here is that there is no outside, impartial viewpoint capable of analyzing individual knowledge independent of the individual exhibiting this knowledge; there is no "God's eye point of view" (Putnam, 1981). Hence, knowledge should be considered from an ontological and epistemological perspective in which knowing, consciousness, and all other aspects of human experience are seen from the point of view of the experiencing subject. How an individual experiences is affected by the self-knowledge that he or she has been able to conjure. On the basis of these premises, I outline here some of the basic features inherent to the nature and the structure of human experience, with the aim of deriving from them a consistent methodology and strategy of intervention for cognitive therapy (cf. Guidano, 1991b, 1995).

Experiencing and Explaining

Given that we can perceive the reality in which we live only from within our perceiving order, we always find ourselves, as human beings, in the immediacy of our ongoing *praxis* of living, which is the absolute primary ontological condition. The praxis of living is one of those dimensions that is difficult (perhaps impossible) to put into words. It is the "living of living," if you will, or the "practice of practicing," which is a life-span project for all of us. Maturana (1986) pointed out:

> In these circumstances, whatever we say about how anything happens takes place in the praxis of our living as a comment, as a reflection, as reformulation; in short, as an explanation of the praxis

of our living, and as such it does not replace or constitute the praxis of living that it purports to explain. (pp. 3–4)

Human experience, therefore, appears as the emerging product of a process of mutual regulation continuously alternating between experiencing and explaining—that is, a process in which ongoing patterns of activity (immediate experience) become subject to linguistic distinctions and are reordered in terms of symbolic propositions distributed across conceptual networks. The level of symbolic reordering (explanation) makes possible new categories of experience, such as true–false, real–unreal, right–wrong, and subjective–objective, to name a few. This interdependence between subjective and objective, emotioning and cognizing, experiencing and explaining, and so forth, is constitutive of any human knowing process, just as is feeling ourselves to be alive.

In humans, as in all mammals (and especially all primates), affective-emotional activity corresponds to and depends on immediate and irrefutable apprehensions of the world. Hence, from a purely ontological point of view, feelings can never be "mistaken." It is through feelings that we experience our way of being in the world. In other words, we always are as we feel (Olafson, 1988). At the level of immediate experiencing, it is not possible to distinguish between perception and illusion (Maturana, 1986). For example, the perturbing feeling of having seen a ghost is, for the subject who is feeling it, a momentarily real and inescapable experience. Only by shifting to the level of "languaging" can the individual explain the felt experience in a variety of alternative manners, such as its having been a trick of light or an illusion, thereby making the experience consistent with his or her current appraisal of the world. In other words, errors can be noticed only a posteriori (after the experience) and depend on the point of view that we, as observers, take in reordering our experiencing. All rational-cognitive reordering involves expanding the coherence of symbolic rules to make the flow of immediate experience more consistent with the continuity of one's current appraisal of the world.

Rather than representing an already given reality according to a logic of external correspondence, knowledge is the continuous construction and reconstruction of a world by the ordering individual in an attempt to make ongoing experiences consistent (Arciero, 1989; Arciero & Mahoney, 1989; Maturana, 1988; Varela, 1987; Winograd & Flores, 1986).

Self and the Emotional Realm of Intersubjectivity

The evolutionary development of humans and their environments has always been fundamentally intersubjective. This is a relatively recent realization in global thinking. In fact, the phenomenon of "globalization" has sometimes been likened to the shrinking of the planet, bringing all of its inhabitants into more extensive contact. Most pertinent for this discussion is the fact that we humans are undeniably social beings. We need others (who, in turn, need us), and we participate in communities of identity and otherness that are crucial to our mutual well-being and development. We live in a complex interpersonal reality primarily structured and made consistent by language. Among other things, this fact implies that any knowledge of oneself and the world is always dependent on and relative to knowledge of others. The increasing complexity of the interpersonal dimension has afforded humans a range of skills in intersubjective learning (e.g., imitation and modeling) paralleled by an increase in the capacity for self-individuation (Kummer, 1979; Passingham, 1982). In fact, the ability to discriminate among individual others appears to be hardwired in primate organization, as evidenced by the central role of the face in the primate emotional system (Ekman, 1993; Reynolds, 1981). Hence, facial recognition has emerged as a neocortical process whose evolutionary progression closely parallels the emergence of a more complex interpersonal realm (e.g., closer mother–infant relationship and competition and social bonds) that requires incremental capacities for attunement with others' behaviors and intentions in order to viably adapt.

Facial recognition should therefore be regarded as a self-referent ordering of intersubjective experience that facilitates the possibility of self-individuation. On the one hand, the ability to discriminate between individual others allows one to anticipate their perceptions of one's action, thus improving interactional synchrony and reciprocity. On the other hand, simulating how others will interpret one's actions entails the capacity to view oneself from the perceived perspective of others. This enhances the possibilities for self-bordering (i.e., setting one's own psychological boundaries) and self-individuation.

The human dimension of intersubjectivity is a prerequisite for individuation and self-recognition (Gallup & Suarez, 1986), bringing about the differentiation of a sense of self—both as subject and as object. Language, in fact, affords the ability to make distinctions and references regarding the flow of immediate experience, making it possible to at least symbolically distinguish the self that is experiencing from the self that is appraising those experiences.

The experience of "being a self" is something intertwined with and arising from the endless flowing of one's praxis of living so that, as Gadamer (1976) explained, "the self that we are does not possess itself: one could say that it *happens*" (p. 55). In other words, the experiencing–explaining interdependence that underlies self-understanding is matched by an endless process of circularity between the immediate experience of oneself (the acting and experiencing *I*) and the sense of self that continually emerges as a result of abstractly self-referencing the ongoing experience (the observing and appraising *me*; James, 1890/1989; Mead, 1934; Smith, 1978, 1985). The self as subject (*I*) and the self as object (*me*) therefore represent the irreducible dimensions of a selfhood dynamic whose directionality depends on the continuous flow of our praxis of living. Indeed, the acting and experiencing *I* is always one step ahead of the current evaluation of the situation, and the appraising *me* becomes a continuous process of reordering one's conscious self-image.

Consider an emotional realm inherent to an intersubjective reality in which adaptation always transforms itself into a social relationship (e.g., the mother–infant bond). In a space–time dimension apprehensible in terms of proximity and distance from a safe base of emotional attachment, psychobiological attunement of and to caregivers allows the newborn human to order its sensory inflow into feelings that become recognizable only within an approach–avoidance continuum. In such a space–time dimension, attachment comes to exert a primary role in differentiating a range of decodable emotional tonalities (a) by regulating the rhythmic oscillation between arousal-inducing (exploration and play) and arousal-reducing (security and clinging) psychophysiological patterns and (b) by exerting a secondary role of modulating fear and anger by alternating between these same patterns (Fox & Davidson, 1984; Reynolds, 1981; Schore, 1994; Suomi, 1984). Alternatively, within an intersubjective reality, attachment exerts an organizational role in the development of a sense of self both as subject and as object.

Whereas the newborn's attunement to a synchronous source of regularities organizes his or her sensory inflow into a stream of recurrent psychophysiological rhythms, the emotional aspects of attachment transform feeling tonalities into specific emotional modules. Through regularities drawn from caregivers' behaviors and affective messages, the infant can begin to construct basic feelings that are inseparable from early perceptions, actions, and memories. The emergence of subjective experience is matched by the perception that one is an entity differentiated from other objects and people in the surrounding world. In other words, the initially ambivalent experience of being a self emerges with varying constraints of definition as a result of intersubjective experiences, especially those associated with intense emotional activity. Psychophysiological rhythms and emotional schemata become basic ingredients of infantile consciousness, a consciousness that is truly and fundamentally affective in nature and quality (Buck, 1984; Emde, 1984; Izard, 1980; Schore, 1994). The self-feeling immediately and tacitly perceived as an inner kinesthetic sense of *I* is therefore primarily organized around prototypical emotional schemata differentiated out of emotional reciprocity with caregivers.

The *I* comes to see himself or herself as a *me* (i.e., like other surrounding people) only through the consciousness that caregivers have of his or her behavior. Anticipating others' perceptions of one's actions facilitates the recognition of ongoing patterns of emotional schemata out of the stream of recurrent inner states, structuring them into specific emotional experiences connected to related intentions and goal-oriented behaviors. Evidence suggests that infants' perceptions of themselves, although dependent on their caregivers' behavior, are not confined to those situations in which their parents attempt to meet their basic needs. Indeed, it appears that parental imitation of infant behavior is very common from the earliest periods (Bretherton & Waters, 1985; Harter, 1983), and it is therefore very likely that such imitations are essential cues that allow the infant to recognize or internalize as his or her own those characteristics and attitudes that caregivers perceive as belonging to the infant as a person. In other words, self-consciousness emerges from a self-recognizability made possible only by the empathic ability to take the attitude of others onto oneself, subsequently elaborating a conscious self-image that consists of emotionally etching the profile of the *me* out of the experienced *I*.

Selfhood Dynamics and Life-Span Development

Individual life-span development should be regarded as a *hortogenetic progression*, meaning that it is an open-ended, spiraling process in which the continuous reordering of selfhood dynamics results in the emergence of more structured and integrated patterns of internal complexity. Self-regulating abilities reflect a dynamic equilibrium known as "order through fluctuations" (Brent, 1978; Dell & Goolishian, 1981; Prigogine, 1976). That is, continuous—both progressive and regressive—shifts of the point of equilibrium in *I–me* dynamics provide a scaffolding that enables one to maintain a coherent continuity of experiencing while allowing the assimilation of the perturbations that emerge from that experiencing. I now take a look at two essential variables involved in this lifelong process: the role of awareness in regulating and modulating challenging perturbations and the role of emotional activity in triggering them.

In strictly ontological terms, being aware of oneself means reaching an explanation for the ongoing experience of being a unique, irreducible, and often unpredictable *I*. Hence, awareness is a reflexive process for self-referencing immediate experience (*I*) in order to amplify consistent aspects of the perceived *me* while inhibiting discrepant aspects. Because the acting and experiencing *I* is always one step ahead of the current appraisal of the *me*, each person is in a position where it is possible to experience much more than the minimum required at that moment to maintain his or her own self-image consistency in that particular situation. As a consequence, the ability to manipulate immediate experiencing while self-referencing and reordering becomes essential. This ability is necessary to direct conscious attention in ways that contrast with the selected appraisal of the current situation. In this sense, one can say that no self-awareness can be viable without a necessary level of self-deception. Thus, it follows that excessive self-deception lowers the accuracy of decoding immediate experiencing (possibly to critical levels of uncontrollability), whereas limited self-deception, by failing to reject extraneous information, complicates the self-referencing process exponentially such that levels of complexity in selfhood dynamics are difficult to manage. Hence, any individual, although having critical emotional tonalities in immediate experiencing, is also endowed with specific self-deceiving abilities designed to manipulate their decoding so that it is consistent with the quality of awareness they have reached thus far. Through such procedures, individuals can appraise critical feelings and make them intelligible without questioning the total validity of the currently existing self-image.

Alternatively, attachment to significant others, although it shifts toward a more abstract level with maturation, maintains its fundamental interdependence with selfhood dynamics throughout the life span. This shift, it seems, explains the crucial role of affectivity in triggering significant perturbations. Although attachment is central to the stable differentiation of a sense of self, new patterns of attachment emerge (e.g., intimate love relationships) throughout maturational stages during adulthood, attachments that function to confirm, support, and further expand the pattern of self-coherence that has thus far been structured. It follows naturally that the influence of early attachments is subsequently manifested in later styles of attachment, which continue to differentiate along the entire developmental pathway (Bretherton, 1985). Indeed, the continuity of attachment throughout the life span is understandable if one considers that the perception of certain affective relationships as being unique to the self begins early in life and that subsequent adult bonds of love seem to grow out of these very first attachments (Hazan & Shaver, 1987; Marris, 1982; Shaver, Hazan, & Bradshaw, 1988; Weiss, 1982). Just as unique primary bonds seem to be necessary prerequisites for "perceiving a world" and "recognizing one's being in it," so in adulthood—though at a different level of abstraction—is building a unique relationship with a significant other an important way for one to perceive a consistent sense of uniqueness in his or her "being in the world." Hence, if working models of attachment figures are interdependent with ongoing patterns of self-perception, it is clear that any perceived modification of these models is matched by intense perturbations in immediate experiencing; these disruptions can trigger the emergence of I–me discrepancies, which in turn can challenge the current appraisal of the self. In fact, the importance of a balanced interplay of the individual's network of unique relationships throughout the life span is currently supported by evidence from various sources. First, life-events research has shown that the most disrupting emotions a person can experience in life are those triggered in the course of establishing, maintaining, and dissolving such relationships (Bowlby, 1977; Brown, 1982; Hafner, 1986; Henderson, Byrne, & Duncan-Jones, 1981). Second, recent epidemiological evidence has shown how the "social network index" should be regarded as a significant predictor of health on the basis of findings suggesting that social and affective isolation is a major risk factor for morbidity and mortality (House, Landis, & Umberson, 1988).

Structure and Dynamics of Therapeutic Change

The ontological approach briefly outlined thus far entails remarkable transformations in traditional perspectives on the conceptualization of change and therapeutic methodology (Gonçalves, 1989; Guidano, 1987, 1988, 1991a, 1991b; Mahoney, 1985, 1988, 1991, 1994, in press; Mahoney & Lyddon, 1988; Safran & Greenberg, 1991).

According to rationalist-cognitive approaches, which still regard knowledge as the representation of an objective and unequivocal order, emotional disturbances derive from an insufficiently valid correspondence between individual beliefs and external reality; that is, unpleasant feelings merely indicate distorted thinking, in accordance with the well-known saying "as you think, so shall you feel." Thus, traditional assessment is aimed at identifying "wrong" beliefs and irrational automatic thoughts. The client's affect, behavior, and thinking are compared with a set of standard rational axioms taken to be universally valid, and the basic principle of change revolves around one theme: To modify perturbing emotions, it is sufficient to change the corresponding "irrational" beliefs as these beliefs gradually come to light.

A rational supremacy of this kind results in the establishment of a self-control strategy centered on persuasion. The operational setting for such a procedure is a more or less pressing dialectical confrontation in which the therapist tries by every available means to convince the client to endorse more rational beliefs and to enact more appropriate attitudes while instructing him or her to control or eliminate negative emotions and dysfunctional behaviors. Moreover, because such a perspective is usually centered on an objective, immutable outside order that unequivocally rules and judges human events, it follows that the therapeutic relationship established in rationalist and objectivist psychotherapy cannot become other than an instrument—a more or less authoritarian instrument—for the reestablishment of a rational, realistic, and otherwise socially dictated order.

Alternatively, if the ordering of reality into personal experience is a self-referent construction—as is maintained by constructivists—then a therapist cannot invoke some objective outside point of view from which to evaluate a client's correctness, realism, or rationality in adaptation. From a constructivist perspective, rationality is intrinsically relativistic, and, as such, it can only refer to contextually and historically situated efforts to attain meaning and coherence. In terms of the ontological perspective presented by constructivists, it can thus be said that, through the continuing processes of reordering immediate experiencing into a conscious sense of self (*I*) and the world (including the *me*), an individual is able to structure a stable and yet dynamic and ever-developing demarcation between what is real and what is not real in his or her own personal and ongoing praxis of living. However, although the experiencing *I* can slip in and out of the momentary focus of consciousness, the possibility of the experiencing *I* being recognized as one's self-conscious self (*me*) depends on personally developed abilities in the abstractions of self-reflection. In this sense, a significant therapeutic modification often involves a change in the *me*'s appraisal of the experiencing *I*. This allows for a reordering of immediate experience in which negative affects previously perceived as extraneous and unreal may come to be appraised and embraced as real, with personal emotions being a vehicle of self-referral to one's conscious sense of ongoing continuity and individual uniqueness.

The structure and quality of psychological change experienced by any given individual depend in large part on the level and quality of self-awareness with which that person is capable of negotiating the reordering process. Such awareness is not a beam of light that reveals an already well arranged configuration of elements, merely acknowledging their presence. Awareness is a constructive self-referent ordering process that constrains the form that personal experience can immediately assume. Therefore, to attain a change in the *me*'s appraisal of the experiencing *I* capable of producing a viable assimilation of perturbing feelings, it is necessary for therapists to trigger progressive shifts in current patterns of self-awareness by increasing clients' comprehensions of the ways in which they tacitly participate in ordering their own ongoing experiences.

How are the above considerations reflected by the general methodology of a postrationalist, postobjectivist, and process-oriented constructivist psychotherapy? The crucial operational setting lies at the interface between immediate experiencing and its explicit reordering. The basic procedure consists of training clients, through methods of self-observation, to differentiate between immediate self-perception and conscious beliefs and attitudes and then to reconstruct the patterns of coherence that they use to maintain consistency with their feelings. The process of self-referring that characterizes the *me*'s appraisal of the *I* is carried out through a set of specific dimensions of elaboration (Guidano, 1987, 1991b, 1995; Lang, 1984; Schwartz & Trabasso, 1984), which is outlined below and illustrated in Figure 1.

First, valence, or polarity, accounts for a majority of the variance in affective reports and involves the therapist locating the client's perceived feelings within the pleasure–displeasure continuum. As a basic and immediate distinguishable property of affective arousal, it mainly entails the therapist's appraisal of the intensity with which the client's *me* is affected by his or her experiencing *I* and is consequently reflected by oscillations in approach–avoidance dispositions.

Second, the pattern and the directedness of the arousal, as a further elaboration, affect the client's appraisal of the quality of the experienced feeling, allowing a discrimination of the emotional content (i.e., imagery–memory modulation) as well as a patterning of psychophysiological responses (i.e., bodily sensations and motor activity).

Third, as a final step, the self–other distinction specifies whether the experienced affect is perceived as "internally bound" and recognized as belonging to one's self or as "externally bound" and attributed to causes other than the self, such as the environment or the body. In general, internal referencing brings about a control of emotion through understanding that, while expanding the range of articulated feelings, facilitates further elaborations in abstract self-referencing. External attributions, however, give rise to a control of emotions on the basis of their exclusion and are matched by a sense of being at the mercy of unpredictable events and impulses that adversely affect self-analytical abilities.

It is relevant to point out how cues for decoding valence and directedness derive directly from the emotional modulation carried out by the experiencing *I* whereas cues for self–other referencing mainly derive from the patterns of coherence enacted by the *me*. Alternatively, any reordering of immediate experience corresponds to a construction from the point of view of the *me* that is carrying it out and, consequently, is aimed at confirming the current appraisal of the world rather than at exploring the experiencing *I*. Given that immediate experience and its conscious appraisal are matched by different levels of knowing processes, feelings can exist in consciousness independently of cognition (Izard, 1977; Zajonc, 1984; Zajonc & Markus, 1984). In the absence of cognitive decoding, however, their activation tends to be directly realized through

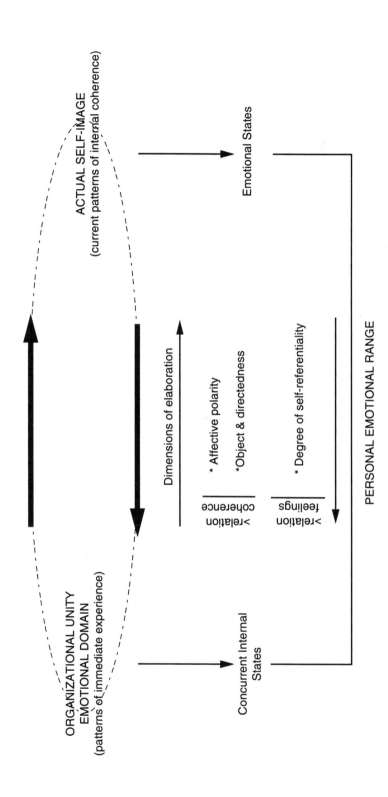

Figure 1. The set of specific dimensions of elaboration through which the process of self-referring that characterizes the *me's* appraisal of the *I* is carried out.

somatic and motor manifestations of emotion. As a consequence, a client will perceive an experienced affect as an externally bound perturbation to the extent that it does not fit with the range of decodability allowed by his or her current patterns of coherence.

It is important to emphasize here that there is no direct correlation between the type of strategic intervention carried out and the quality of change processes that occur, even though it is clear that therapeutic intervention has often triggered processes that have ultimately brought about reorganization. In other words, the therapist can only try to set forth "conditions" capable of triggering a reorganization, but she or he cannot determine or control either when or how clients organize the final outcome of the reorganization. The therapist tries to elicit and elaborate affect-laden events capable of modifying immediate experiencing in such a way that the client cannot avoid recognizing and self-referencing it (the change of the *me*'s appraisal of the *I*). The therapeutic relationship is the safe, secure, and specific context in which it becomes possible for the therapist both to accelerate affective change events and to guide the reorganization processes that they activate.

The increase in clients' comprehensions of the rules for ordering their realities is always paralleled by an appreciable degree of emotional modulation in which new tonalities of feelings are likely to emerge. However, modifications in clients' comprehensions are often at least partially related to explanations offered by the therapist, and, obviously, anything the therapist says or does can be considered an explanation, including training in methods of self-observation. Finally, the therapeutic relationship is a real, living interaction, and, as such, the structure and reciprocity of its emotional aspects produce a facilitating effect for the client's assimilation of new experiences or the reframing of existing ones.

CONCLUSION

In this chapter I have offered my best current attempt to communicate what I now understand about how people develop and how a constructivist (developmental process-oriented) psychotherapist might conceptualize and facilitate such development. I am the first to admit that this portrayal is preliminary and conjectural. At the same time, my 30 years of experience in the daily practice of psychotherapy and in the training and supervision of hundreds of psychotherapists bids me to assert that, at least in my own experience, the practice of "life-changing" psychotherapy is most successfully conducted by individuals who are themselves engaged in explorations of their capacities and willingness to work within the contexts of substantial ambiguity, complexity, and emotionality. This is not an easy task, and I do not claim to be an expert (only an aficionado) in these domains. I do, however, respectfully note the centrality of these challenges—ambiguity, complexity, and emotionality—to the enterprise of life counseling and psychotherapy.

REFERENCES

Arciero, G. (1989, October). *From epistemology to ontology: A new age of cognition.* Paper presented at the meeting of the American Association for the Advancement of Science, San Francisco, CA.

Arciero, G., & Mahoney, M. J. (1989). *Understanding and psychotherapy.* Unpublished manuscript, University of California, Santa Barbara.

Bowlby, J. (1977). The making and breaking of affectional bonds: I. Etiology and psychopathology in the light of attachment theory. *British Journal of Psychiatry, 130,* 201–210.

Brent, S. B. (1978). Prigogine's model for self-organization in nonequilibrium systems: Its relevance for developmental psychology. *Human Development, 21,* 374–387.

Bretherton, I. (1985). Attachment theory: Retrospect and prospect. In I. Bretherton & E. Waters (Eds.), *Growing points of attachment theory and research* (pp. 3–35). Chicago: University of Chicago Press.

Bretherton, I., & Waters, E. (Eds.). (1985). *Growing points of attachment theory and research.* Chicago: University of Chicago Press.

Brown, G. W. (1982). Early loss and depression. In C. M. Parkes & J. Stevenson-Hinde (Eds.), *The place of attachment in human behavior* (pp. 232–268). London: Tavistock.

Buck, R. (1984). *The communication of emotion.* New York: Guilford Press.

Dell, P. F., & Goolishian, H. A. (1981). "Order through fluctuation": An evolutionary epistemology for human systems. *Australian Journal of Family Therapy, 2,* 175–184.

Ekman, P. (1993). Facial expression and emotion. *American Psychologist, 48,* 384–392.

Emde, R. N. (1984). Levels of meaning for infants' emotions: A biosocial view. In K. R. Scherer & P. Ekman (Eds.), *Approaches to emotion* (pp. 77–107). Hillsdale, NJ: Erlbaum.

Fox, N. A., & Davidson, R. J. (Eds.). (1984). *The psychobiology of affective development.* Hillsdale, NJ: Erlbaum.

Gadamer, H. G. (1976). *Philosophical hermeneutics.* Berkeley: University of California Press.

Gallup, F. F., & Suarez, S. (1986). Self-awareness and the emergence of mind in humans and other primates. In J. Suls & A. G. Greenwald (Eds.), *Psychological perspectives on the self* (Vol. 3, pp. 23–36). Hillsdale, NJ: Erlbaum.

Gonçalves, Ó. F. (1989, November). *The hermeneutics of cognitive–behavioral narratives: From the object to the project.* Paper presented at 23rd annual convention of the American Association of Behavioral–Cognitive Therapy in the Clinical Roundtable "Hermeneutics and Behavior Therapy," Washington, DC.

Guidano, V. F. (1987). *Complexity of the self.* New York: Guilford Press.

Guidano, V. F. (1988). A system, process-oriented approach to cognitive therapy. In K. S. Dobson (Ed.), *Handbook of cognitive–behavioral therapies* (pp. 307–354). New York: Guilford Press.

Guidano, V. F. (1991a). Affective change events in a cognitive therapy system approach. In J. D. Safran & L. S. Greenberg (Eds.), *Emotion, psychotherapy, and change* (pp. 50–79). New York: Guilford Press.

Guidano, V. F. (1991b). *The self in process.* New York: Guilford Press.

Guidano, V. F. (1995). Self-observation in constructivist psychotherapy. In R. A. Neimeyer & M. J. Mahoney (Eds.), *Constructivism in psychotherapy* (pp. 155–168). Washington, DC: American Psychological Association.

Hafner, R. J. (1986). *Marriage and mental illness.* New York: Guilford Press.

Harter, S. (1983). Development perspectives on the self-system. In E. M. Hetherington (Ed.), *Handbook of child psychology* (Vol. 4, pp. 275–385). New York: Wiley.

Hazan, C., & Shaver, P. (1987). Romantic love conceptualized as an attachment process. *Journal of Personality and Social Psychology, 52,* 511–524.

Henderson, S., Byrne, D. G., & Duncan-Jones, P. (1981). *Neurosis and the social environment.* San Diego, CA: Academic Press.

House, J. S., Landis, K. R., & Umberson, D. (1988). Social relationships and health. *Science, 241,* 540–545.

Izard, C. E. (1977). *Human emotions.* New York: Plenum.

Izard, C. E. (1980). The emergence of emotions and the development of consciousness in infancy. In J. M. Davidson & R. J. Davidson (Eds.), *The psychobiology of consciousness* (pp. 193–216). New York: Plenum.

James, W. (1989). The consciousness of self. In *Principles of psychology* (Vol. 1). New York: Holt, Rinehart & Winston. (Original work published 1890)

Kummer, H. (1979). On the value of social relationships to nonhuman primates: A heuristic scheme. In M. Von Cranach, K. Foppa, W. Lepenies, & D. Ploog (Eds.), *Human ethology* (pp. 381–395). Cambridge, England: Cambridge University Press.

Lang, P. J. (1984). Cognition in emotion: Concept and action. In C. E. Izard, J. Kagan, & R. B. Zajonc (Eds.), *Emotions, cognitions and behavior* (pp. 192–226). Cambridge, England: Cambridge University Press.

Mahoney, M. J. (1985). Psychotherapy and human change processes. In M. J. Mahoney & A. Freeman (Eds.), *Cognition and psychotherapy* (pp. 3–48). New York: Plenum.

Mahoney, M. J. (1988). Constructive metatheory: I. Basic features and historical foundations. *International Journal of Personal Construct Psychology, 1*, 1–35.

Mahoney, M. J. (1991). *Human change processes: The scientific foundations of psychotherapy*. New York: Basic Books.

Mahoney, M. J. (Ed.). (1994). *Cognitive and constructive psychotherapies: Recent developments*. New York: Springer.

Mahoney, M. J. (in press). *Constructive psychotherapy*. New York: Guilford Press.

Mahoney, M. J., & Lyddon, W. J. (1988). Recent developments in cognitive approaches to counseling and psychotherapy. *Counseling Psychologist, 16*, 190–234.

Marris, P. (1982). Attachment and society. In C. M. Parkes & J. Stevenson-Hinde (Eds.), *The place of attachment in human behavior* (pp. 185–201). London: Tavistock.

Maturana, H. (1986). *Ontology of observing: The biological foundations of self-consciousness and the physical domain of existence*. Unpublished manuscript, University of Chile, Santiago.

Maturana, H. (1988). Reality: The search for objectivity, or the quest for a compelling argument. *Irish Journal of Psychology, 9*, 25–82.

Mead, G. H. (1934). *Mind, self and society*. Chicago: University of Chicago Press.

Olafson, A. F. (1988). *Heidegger and the philosophy of mind*. New Haven, CT: Yale University Press.

Passingham, R. (1982). *The human primate*. New York: Freeman.

Prigogine, I. (1976). Order through fluctuations. Self-organization and social systems. In E. Jantsch & C. H. Waddington (Eds.), *Evolution and consciousness: Human systems in transition* (pp. 93–133). Reading, MA: Addison-Wesley.

Putnam, H. (1981). *Reason, truth and history*. Cambridge, England: Cambridge University Press.

Reynolds, P. C. (1981). *On the evolution of human behavior*. Los Angeles: University of California Press.

Safran, J. D., & Greenberg, L. S. (Eds.). (1991). *Emotions, psychotherapy, and change*. New York: Guilford Press.

Schore, A. N. (1994). *Affect regulation and the origin of the self*. Hillsdale, NJ: Erlbaum.

Schwartz, R. M., & Trabasso, T. (1984). Children's understanding of emotions. In C. E. Izard, J. Kagan, & R. B. Zajonc (Eds.), *Emotions, cognition and behavior* (pp. 409–437). Cambridge, England: Cambridge University Press.

Shaver, P., Hazan, C., & Bradshaw, D. (1988). Love as attachment. In R. J. Stenberg & M. L. Barnes (Eds.), *The psychology of love* (pp. 68–99). New Haven, CT: Yale University Press.

Smith, M. B. (1978). What it means to be human. In R. Fitzgerald (Ed.), *What it means to be human* (pp. 49–64). Elmsford, NY: Pergamon Press.

Smith, M. B. (1985). The metaphorical basis of selfhood. In A. J. Marsella, G. DeVos, & F. L. K. Hsu (Eds.), *Culture and self* (pp. 56–88). London: Tavistock.

Suomi, S. G. (1984). The development of affect in rhesus monkeys. In N. A. Fox & R. J. Davidson (Eds.), *The psychobiology of affective development* (pp. 119–159). Hillsdale, NJ: Erlbaum.

Varela, F. (1987). Laying down a path in walking. In W. J. Thompson (Ed.), *Gaia, a way of knowing* (pp. 48–64). Great Barrington, MA: Lindisfarne Press.

Weiss, R. S. (1982). Attachment in adult life. In C. M. Parkes & J. Stevenson-Hinde (Eds.), *The place of attachment in human behavior* (pp. 171–183). London: Tavistock.

Winograd, T., & Flores, F. (1986). *Understanding computers and cognition.* Norwood, NJ: Ablex.

Zajonc, R. B. (1984). On primacy of affect. In K. R. Scherer & P. Ekman (Eds.), *Approaches to emotion* (pp. 259–270). Hillsdale, NJ: Erlbaum.

Zajonc, R. B., & Markus, H. (1984). Affect and cognition: The hard interface. In C. E. Izard, J. Kagan, & R. B. Zajonc (Eds.), *Emotions, cognition and behavior* (pp. 73–102). Cambridge, England: Cambridge University Press.

II

PERSONAL CHANGE AND RECONSTRUCTION

6

THE CHALLENGE OF CHANGE

GREG J. NEIMEYER

Potent life experiences are both magnetic and elastic—magnetic in the sense that they attract new meanings across time and elastic in that they expand to help structure and inform those new experiences. For me, a particular episode some years ago has gradually become a metaphor for understanding the experience of personal change, and I am periodically reminded of it whenever I am helping someone fashion significant life revisions.

In the Gulf Stream waters that course along the continental shelf on the eastern seaboard of North America, scuba divers are sometimes wont to do what is colloquially known as a "drift dive." They are transported by boat to the brink of the shelf, and an anchored line is set adrift in the swift waters, borne by a large fluorescent buoy. Drawn by the warm flow of the Gulf Stream currents, the line sweeps along the edge of the shelf at approximately a 100-foot depth, and the boat follows

This chapter is a slightly expanded version of the article "The Challenge of Change: Reflections on Constructivist Psychotherapy," by G. J. Neimeyer, 1993, *Journal of Cognitive Psychotherapy, 7*, pp. 183–194. Copyright 1993 by Springer Publishing. Adapted by permission.

vigilantly behind. Divers, eager to penetrate the unknown void, swiftly shuttle down the line to its terminus where instructors, "free-drifting" without a line, position banks of underwater lights to cast their luminescence out over the shelf in hopes of catching a glimpse of the unfathomable, aqueous canyon below.

My own memories of the experience are indelibly etched: the heart-pounding anticipation of the unknown as I drew myself deeper and deeper into darkness, the steely feel of the anchor as I reached the end of my lifeline, and the sudden flash of the underwater lights bolting through the watery midnight. My clearest, starkest memory, however, is of holding on to the drift line with one hand and stretching out toward the infinite void beneath me to see the fullest extent of the light's revelation. Unprepared for the outcome, I drew back in horror. There the lights ceased to penetrate; a thousand watts fell dead in space, failing to pierce the depths, failing to reveal what lay concealed in the vast depths before me.

The futility of those lights and my weightlessness in the fluid that surrounded me are vivid companions at critical points in my therapy practice now. Images of myself "on the brink" have acquired an almost surreal quality: clinging to a tendril being swept along the contours of nothingness, buoyed only by a cork tethering me to the familiar world above.

Clients, too, I remind myself, are similarly positioned in their own psychological space, struggling to relinquish the familiar in exchange for the unknown. It is those moments of perturbance, poised on the brink of significant change, when therapists and clients alike face their greatest challenges and responsibilities. Constructivist psychotherapies have, I think, some important contributions to make in this regard, and my thoughts in this chapter are aimed at exploring some of these. The thrust of my thoughts concerns the notion that both the preservation and alteration of meaning structures are central to being human. Constructivist psychotherapists respect this essential tension between retaining and relinquishing personal patterns of meaning and have devised methods of exploring alternative perspectives without first abandoning existing ones. I use the drift-diving metaphor to examine some of those methods as exemplars of three central features of constructivist therapy: the primacy of personal experience, the importance of novel enactments, and the role of "languaging" in developing new patterns of personal meaning.

EXPLORING THE UNKNOWN

Presenting problems represent windows onto the client's system of constructions. Clients' "effort after meaning"—as Bartlett (1932) so aptly phrased it—assures that they have struggled to understand the nature of their experience prior to therapy, and their presence in therapy speaks to the difficulty they have encountered along the way. When participating in a constructivist form of therapy, neither client nor therapist can enjoy the familiar moorings that anchor more realist or rationalist forms of therapy (see Mahoney & Lyddon, 1988; G. J. Neimeyer & Neimeyer, 1993; Parry & Doan, 1994). Gone is the certainty of a single "best," "right," or "functional" form of thinking, feeling, or behaving. Gone, too, is the directive, disputational comportment associated with that certainty, replaced by a more tentative, patient struggle aimed at developing a constructive process of exploration from within the individual (see Clark, 1989, 1993) that may lead to a more viable and developmentally progressive understanding of the world (Lyddon & Alford, 1993; R. A. Neimeyer, 1995).

There are many ways to encourage this kind of exploration and experimentation. For most constructivists, the nature of the therapeutic relationship itself is a figural feature in this process (Guidano, 1991; Lyddon & Alford, 1993; Mahoney, 1991). This relationship supports and contextualizes various forms of direct and indirect intervention. As Kelly (1969c) has noted,

> the relationships between therapist and client and the techniques they employ may be as varied as the whole human repertory of relationships and techniques. . . . It is the orchestration of techniques and the utilization of relationships in the on-going process of living and profiting from experience that makes psychotherapy a contribution to human life. (p. 223)

Constructivist approaches have contributed significantly in both of these regards, placing inflection on the nature of interpersonal and therapeutic bonds on the one hand, and sponsoring a wide variety of novel methods of intervention on the other. Mirror time, streaming, fixed-role therapy, controlled elaboration, tightening and loosening techniques, interpersonal transaction groups, bipolar sculptures, personal epilogues, repertory grid techniques, systemic bowties, time and place binding, laddering, and various forms of journaling have all emerged from constructivist traditions—and these are just a few techniques (see Mahoney, 1991; G. J. Neimeyer, 1993; R. A. Neimeyer & Neimeyer, 1987).

Still, constructivists are wary of an exclusive dedication to technique, preferring instead to emphasize the critical role of the therapeutic relationship in enabling and initiating human change. "I am not against technique," noted Mahoney (1991, p. 253), in a sentiment shared by many constructivists, "I am against technolatry."

This caveat contextualizes the discussion of methods that follows. All methods, all techniques, and all forms of intervention necessarily evolve from and reside within the context of a given relationship in a given time and place (Efran & Clarfield, 1993). In this sense, techniques can be regarded as coconstructed meaning rituals—vehicles for punctuating, initiating, or reorganizing experience—and, as such, they hold no power apart from the social and cultural contexts that inform them. Human change follows less from the application of a given technique per se than from the meaning that follows from its use in the therapeutic process. In a direct sense, therefore, a technique does not "do" anything for a person; rather, the person does something with the technique.

CONSTRUCTING A LIFELINE

For constructivists, psychotherapeutic technique occurs in relational contexts. For that reason, in most constructivist therapies a premium is placed on forging an intimate therapeutic bond between client and therapist. This bond enables them to participate jointly in conjuring a variety of alternative worlds to be explored and elaborated. These twin processes—exploration and elaboration—serve as the linchpins of the psychotherapeutic process, and both follow from the development of a strong working relationship.

Forging a Bond

Like Bowlby's (1988) "secure base," constructivists regard the therapeutic relationship as a kind of home base, or emotional tether, for the client to use in his or her personal exploration (Guidano, 1991). Although the ways in which this type of attachment may be formed can be quite varied, they converge in providing a kind of secure, permissive acceptance. Adopting what Kelly (1955) has referred to as a "credulous approach," the therapist takes the client's perspective seriously and respects it, even though she or he may not choose to be bound by it. Part of this credulous approach implies acceptance of the client, although acceptance takes on special meaning in this context: It is understood as a willingness to use the client's personal knowledge system, to see the problem and the world through his or her eyes, though not necessarily to be encapsulated by it. To this is added an attitude of inquiry—a curiosity or fascination with the client's perspective and its implications. From this the therapist develops a form of collaborative empiricism, establishing a working relationship that conveys a willingness to conjoin the client in an exploratory process that may seek to test or transcend the limitations of the client's personal worldview.

This kind of therapeutic relationship is qualitatively distinct from other forms of therapeutic alliances. As Kelly (1969b) observed,

> instead of assuming, on the one hand, that the therapist is obliged to bring the client's thinking into line, or, on the other, that the client will mysteriously bring his own thinking into line once he has been given the proper setting, we can take the stand that client and therapist are conjoining in an exploratory venture. The therapist assumes neither the position of judge nor that of the sympathetic bystander. He is sincere about this; he is willing to learn along with his client. He is the client's fellow researcher who seeks first to understand, and then to examine, and finally to assist the client in subjecting alternatives to experimental test and revision. (p. 82)

The constructivist therapist's attitude, therefore, is more inquisitive than disputational, more approving than disapproving, and more exploratory than demonstrative.

Beyond this, specific permission is sometimes given to remove the limits on what can be said and done in the therapy room. The therapist might emphasize, for example, that "this therapy room is a special kind of place for you. Here you can say things, express feelings and thoughts, and act out things that you might never even consider, much less do, in the outside world." This kind of explicit permissiveness again underscores the security of the therapeutic arena, and it begins to conjure the image of a hypothetical, "as if" world (Vaihinger, 1924) in which the client may fashion and test new meanings and behaviors.

Conjuring a World

Even as the nascent therapeutic world is conjured into existence, its function is already being partially fulfilled. Because it is a hypothetical place, a make-believe world, the client can feel free to experiment with changes without necessarily jeopardizing or assaulting existing meaning structures. New perspectives can be tried on without shedding present constructions, thereby circumventing much of the threat and anxiety associated with significant personal change.

A recent development in cosmetology provides a metaphorical marker for the power of this pretend world and illustrates its utility in facilitating personal change. Developed a few years ago, this technological advance enables cosmetologists to project the image of their clients' faces into a limitless assortment of different hairstyles. These projections transport people into whole new identities in swift succession, enabling them to peer out from within their make-believe worlds under the guise of a cast of different characters. From the copious curls of Dolly Parton to the shorn scalp of Sinead O'Connor, from the flowing tresses of Crystal

Gayle to the boyish coiffure of Lady Di—these computer-generated images permit a sort of smorgasbord sampling of identities, a playful means of engaging and disengaging a parade of alter egos without risking the more terminal, steely feel of actual scissors to scalp.

As a kind of metaphor for constructivist psychotherapy, this procedure pairs the exploratory, experiential features of significant change with important identity safeguards that protect extant personal meaning. After all, the comic value of Bill Clinton adopting the dreadlocks of Bob Marley or the electrified look of Don King would be matched only by the sheer terror that would, for Clinton, accompany that actual transformation. Radical reconstruction of current meanings, particularly those central to the self, is customarily and understandably resisted.

For most constructivists, the self constitutes an organized meaning unit, and events that signal profound changes in that system are threatening. Variously referred to as "personal construct systems" (Kelly, 1955), "personal meaning organizations" (Guidano, 1991), "cognitive structures" (Liotti, 1987), and "core ordering processes" (Mahoney, 1991), these interconnected networks of meaning are taken to constitute the individual. By jeopardizing the integrity of this worldview, change—particularly significant, core role change (Kelly, 1955)—produces massive threat and anxiety. In response, the individual understandably develops a self-protective approach that is commonly recast as "resistance" within the therapeutic context. "A cognitive structure that attributes meaning and causal relationships to an important class of emotional experiences," noted Liotti (1987, p. 95), "will be quite resistant to change if the individual does not develop alternative meaning structures." This self-protective theory of resistance is common to many diverse constructivist approaches (Guidano, 1991; Kelly, 1955; Liotti, 1987; Mahoney, 1991), and the development of a secure, "pretend world" in therapy is one means of cultivating these alternative meaning structures.

Central to this pretend world is the language of hypothesis. "There is something in stating a new outlook in the form of a hypothesis," noted Kelly (1969a, p. 156), "that leaves the person himself intact and whole." The use of this language, the development and exploration of alternative meanings, can occur alongside of rather than instead of existing meanings. It is the security associated with the preservation of existing meanings that often enables the exploration of new ones. Kelly (1969a) has characterized threat as

> the experience that occurs at the moment when we stand on the brink of profound change in ourselves and can see just enough of what lies ahead to know that so much of what we are now will be left behind forever, once we take that next step. (p. 156)

It is precisely at this point that the language of hypothesis can be most helpful, preserving the integrity of the client's current understandings, but momentarily suspending them as well, while alternative possibilities are explored. Having bracketed present perspectives, the person is free to envision alternative possibilities, to experience fresh perspectives from behind an assortment of masks. And these masks, Kelly (1969a) observed wryly, "have a way of sticking to our faces when worn too long" (p. 158).

For the constructivist psychotherapist, therefore, alternative perspectives are encouraged. Forged and tested within an as-if world, these various viewpoints are designed to dislodge the client from a strict allegiance to any single belief or conviction. "The psychologist is at his best," observed Kelly (1969a), "when he speaks the language of hypothesis rather than imposes psychological certainties on his clients" (p. 154).

That being said, techniques for encouraging this hypothetical exploration and personal revision must enable the client's active participation in the process of meaning making. In this regard, constructivist psychotherapy is an engaging, interactive vehicle for the negotiation of new meanings. Meaning is made through action, through participation, and through concrete and representational manipulations of the world. These manipulations yield novel experience, that is, perceived invalidations of present systems of knowing that require active efforts of meaning making to render them sensible within a coherent meaning structure (see Mahoney, 1991). This kind of "continuous self-reordering," noted Guidano (1991), "is inherently characterized, moment by moment, by a series of possible 'I'/'Me' discrepancies, that is, perceived gaps between immediate experience and self-consciousness that challenge ongoing patterns of self-control" (p. 69). One important means of fostering this kind of exploratory self-reordering is through various forms of interpersonal enactments.

Conducting the Exploration

Mahoney (1991) has noted "the importance of active exploratory behavior on the part of the changing individual . . . ," emphasizing that "there can be no real learning without novelty—that is, without a challenge to or elaboration of what has become familiar" (p. 19). Enactments, various forms of interpersonal role plays, constitute one important vehicle for introducing this novelty. Enactments can vary from very brief, unstructured, casual scenarios all the way to the formalized and enduring role plays that constitute fixed-role therapies. Regardless of their brevity or length, their spontaneity or formality, all enactment procedures share a common set of goals. Foremost among these is to provide for elaboration of the clients' personal worldview while protecting their core role structures from premature invalidation, to buffer them from assault until they are better able to consider abandoning them.

Casual enactments are brief, informal role plays designed to give the client an opportunity to experiment by trying on a part to see what it is like. Rarely more than a few minutes duration each, these enactments are aimed at discovery rather than demonstration, at exploration rather than rehearsal. An enactment is "designed, like a good experiment, to give the experimenter and his colleagues a chance to observe its outcomes" (Kelly, 1955, p. 1166).

Casual enactments have several salient features. Although brief, they can nonetheless present potent opportunities for discovery, even when they involve little or no actual conversation. Moreover, they foster a fleet-footed fluidity by enabling the client to move quickly among multiple perspectives.

Unverbalized casual enactments can be as potent as their more verbal counterparts. Clients often profit immensely from a brief enactment that casts them in a role that they are wholly unable or unwilling to enact or express in any overt way. "Just sitting there and feeling that he is cast in a certain part, or that he is perceived as being in a certain part," noted Kelly (1955), "is, in itself, a form of adventure which he is not likely to pass off lightly" (p. 1147).

One of my recent experiences with the potency of Kelly's (1955) insight came in an early session with "David," a client in his late 20s who was referred to me with alcoholism and alcohol-related difficulties. David had experienced several run-ins with the law at the time, having lost his driver's license and been placed on probation for a weapon's violation in the process. He had returned home to live with his parents because his life had been so "out of control," and he was contemplating a return to his private apartment. He spoke openly about how concerned his parents were about him and how they feared that returning to his apartment would again give him the license to drink that he could not exercise in their home. He was frustrated and angry that they did not trust him, and he felt a growing impasse that he could not resolve: either stay with them and sacrifice his adult freedoms, or return to his apartment and disappoint and provoke his parents, potentially jeopardizing their support of him.

I immediately cast David in his mother's role, pointed to a nearby empty chair, and said "Tell David what concerns you have. Tell him about your fears and worries for him." David, portraying his mother, talked fluidly for several minutes, detailing a set of concerns undoubtedly familiar to him. I then asked him to sit in the other chair and respond, as David, to his mom's concerns. He sat frozen. "I can't. I can't say anything!" he said. "I mean, she's right, I've always started drinking when

I got by myself and that started the cycle down. I mean, what can I tell her?" As he spoke, he flushed with emotion and turned to talk about how he was unwilling to provide her with the kind of false assurances that he had in the past. He spoke, too, of how justified her concerns were and how unjustified his own anger and frustration with her was, saying that "This has nothing to do with Mom in a sense, I mean, I've got to find some way of handling this thing myself." From here we turned to talking about possible safeguards, ways that he could reduce the ever-present temptation to start drinking and provide some tentative assurances to himself, as well as to his mother, en route.

In this and other uses of casual enactment, the client can be asked to shift perspectives. This provides one means of developing a contextual shift as discussed by Efran and Clarfield (1993). I have used a wide variety of such enactments productively in my practice, and Kelly (1955) has detailed a number of possibilities in this regard. In one form of enactment, for example, the client is asked to report to the therapist as if he or she were the client's best (real or imagined) friend. Simple prompts like "What concerns do you have about him or her?" or "What do you see going on from your perspective?" can initiate the enactment and help breathe life into the interaction. Another approach is to have the client portray the part of the therapist while the therapist enacts the part of another therapist who is being consulted about the client. This offers the additional advantage of indicating something about the client's constructions of the therapist and of the nature of the therapeutic enterprise. Yet another enactment that can have powerful effects is to ask the client to enact an admired or respected person, parent or otherwise, who has served as a source of inspiration or in the role of wise council for the client. In this variation, I typically ask clients to stand up, close their eyes, and imagine adopting the voice, movement, and mannerisms of that person. When they open their eyes they are to introduce the client and talk about specific aspects of the pride and concerns that they have regarding them. As with most casual enactments, roles can then be reversed to enable the client to shift perspectives within the same context or scenario.

In addition to brief, casual enactments, more elaborate enactment procedures can also be formulated within the therapeutic arena. Among the most elaborate of these is Kelly's (1955) fixed-role therapy. Like other enactments, the purpose of fixed-role therapy is primarily exploratory, to help dislodge the client from his or her adherence to an extant perspective by encouraging the adoption of an alternative one. Unlike the enactments described above, however, fixed-role therapy involves systematically developing a new, alternative identity, rather than simply co-opting an already available perspective.

The first step in fixed-role therapy is the development of the self-characterization sketch. The self-characterization sketch involves the client in a free-form description of himself or herself from the perspective of a close friend. Kelly (1955) would introduce the procedure by saying

> I want you to write a character sketch of Harry Brown, just as if he were the principal character in a play. Write it as it might be written by a friend who knew him very intimately and very sympathetically, perhaps better than anyone ever really could know him. Be sure to write it in the third person. For example, start out by saying, "Harry Brown is . . . ." (p. 323)

The phrasing of these instructions is designed to provide a supportive, exploratory perspective on the client and to enable the client to provide a window onto his or her system of personal constructions. Kelly (1955, pp. 330–359) discussed the self-characterization and its analysis in considerable detail. By attending to the particular constructs it includes, the organization of these constructs, and the recurrent themes that they suggest, the therapist develops an image of the client and aspects of the client's core role structure—those superordinate constructions that govern his or her identity and relationships with significant others.

The second step in fixed-role therapy is based on the self-characterization and involves the development of the fixed-role sketch. The purpose of the fixed-role sketch is to provide a viable alternative to the client's own perspective without invalidating that perspective, on the one hand, or simply recapitulating it, on the other. As with other enactments, the aim is less corrective than exploratory, so no attempt is made to fashion a sketch that corrects difficulties or "imperfections" in the client's current worldview. "The object was not to make a model human being" out of the client, Kelly (1955) reflected, "but to accomplish realistic therapeutic ends with as little disturbance to the client's personality as possible" (p. 369).

By and large this is accomplished by the therapist writing a sketch of a character that is decidedly different from, yet not completely foreign to, the client. Rather than simply writing a sketch that reflects the opposite of the client's salient self-perceptions, the therapist makes an effort to structure the sketch along different lines altogether. Rather than casting a timorous introvert into the role of a swashbuckling extrovert, for example, the therapist's fixed-role sketch might characterize an intensely curious individual for whom life is filled with intrigue. Whereas enacting the opposite would only familiarize the client with the (possibly feared or disdained) contrast to his or her existing system, the fixed-role sketch provides the basis for entering into qualitatively different kinds of relationships with people through entirely different conceptual paths. Throughout this and all subsequent stages of fixed-role therapy, the client is given the full protection afforded by the world of make-believe because, as Kelly (1955) was quick to point out, "this is probably man's oldest protective screen for reaching out into the unknown" (p. 373).

Once the fixed-role sketch is developed, it is presented to the client. Beginning with "Before we go into the problems which brought you here to the clinic," Kelly (1955) would invite the client "to spend at least two weeks doing some preparatory work. This will be something unusual. If it seems strange, so much the better" (p. 382). Then the sketch is presented and an "acceptance check" is conducted to determine whether the sketch presents a believable character from the client's perspective, a character that he or she might like to get to know.

Once the acceptance check is completed, the therapist initiates the rehearsal sequence. The therapist begins by inviting the client to pretend that he or she has gone on a 2-week vacation and that the character has stepped in in the meantime. The client is then instructed as follows:

> You are to *think* like him. You *talk* to your friends the way you think he would talk! You *do* the things you think he would do! You even *have his interests* and you *enjoy* the things he would enjoy! . . . Now let us do some rehearsing. (Kelly, 1955, p. 385)

Successful implementation of the fixed-role enactment requires adequate preparation, and that preparation involves rehearsing the character in each of five important life spheres: work situations, casual social relationships, situations involving the spouse or significant other, situations involving the parents, and situations involving life orientation and plan. Typically, one session is devoted to rehearsing interactions in each of these arenas. Originally, Kelly (1955) specified that rehearsals ordinarily required about six sessions within a 2-week period, including the presentations session, for the role to be adequately adopted.

During the enactment phase per se the client continues his or her sessions with the therapist, with these sessions being directed at troubleshooting the character and harvesting the insights of the client's enactment experience. Troubleshooting might mean rehearsing difficult interactions and elaborating or altering the character itself. Harvesting the insights of enactments means focusing attention on the differences that the client experiences in his or her behavior, thoughts, and feelings, as well as similar aspects of others in his or her social world.

"In evaluating progress," noted Kelly (1955), "the therapist should keep in mind that his purpose is to help the client set in motion a healthful psychological process rather than to create a fixed state of well-being at the termination of therapy" (p. 401). To this end, the client returns the fixed-role sketch to the therapist at the end of the designated enactment period, and therapist and client discuss the experience at length. The therapist does not attempt to encourage the client's continuation of the role, although aspects of the character do sometimes survive the enactment period. One of the most powerful indicators of the success of fixed-role therapy is when, following the enactment phase, the client says, "I feel as if that character was in some ways, the real me." This indicates not only that the client had successfully injected the role with spontaneity and life but also that the old self now seems somewhat cramped, foreign, or unnatural. "It means," noted Kelly (1955), "that he has accepted the point of view expressed in the fixed-role sketch or in his version of it" (p. 417), and "with this change in perspective there has never yet failed to occur a marked shift in the client's formulation of his problems, . . . [including] the tendency of the client to forget what he originally came for" (p. 413).

Adaptations of fixed-role therapy have been used in group therapy (Kelly, 1955) and marital therapy (Kremsdorf, 1985) and have been modified in a variety of ways in individual therapy as well (see Epting, 1984). Designed largely as a means of dislodging clients from adhering to a single, intransigent worldview, enactment procedures in general—and fixed-role procedures in particular—do have some hazards (see Kelly, 1955, Vol. 1). But they also illustrate several of the cardinal features of constructivist psychotherapy. These include emphases on embodied and active meaning-making, the importance placed on perspectival shifts, and the significance of language throughout the meaning-making process (see Parry & Doan, 1994).

RETURNING TO THE SURFACE

For many constructivists, psychotherapy constitutes a form of "accelerated living" (Kelly, 1955; Mahoney, 1991). Constructive change and development is endemic to life and to therapy, with the express goal of the latter being aimed at getting on with the former. "In fact, the task of psychotherapy," noted Kelly (1969c), "is to get the human process going again so that life may go on and on from where psychotherapy left off" (p. 223).

Determining when and how psychotherapy should let off presents particular challenges to the therapeutic enterprise. Because the therapeutic relationship is figural in many forms of constructivist psychotherapy, it is often explicitly invoked in the process of terminating therapy. Although "psychotherapy is a special form of human relationship, and the quality of that relationship appears to be a significant factor in influencing the lives of its participants," noted Mahoney (1991), "it is important to reiterate that the secure base provided by optimal psychotherapy is a base and not a permanent home" (p. 334). Facilitating transition from this base toward independence presents a powerful opportunity to underscore the nature of client change and its attendant process.

Just as no two therapeutic relationships are identical, no two therapeutic terminations are identical, and I am often guided by my clients in this regard. "There does not exist an unequivocal way in which things should unfold (including the therapy being carried out)," reminded Guidano (1991), "and the client remains, in the final analysis, the only one who can decide what is best for him or her to proceed along his or her life trajectory" (p. 164).

For this reason, I am less concerned about premature terminations than I once was, particularly if the quality of the therapeutic relationship has been good and the client remains open to, and invested in, continued personal development. For me, one marker of such development is the client's ability to spontaneously use a dialogue with me or with himself or herself to generate a shift in perspective. This perspectival shift itself relies on the capacity for self-reflection—intentional interrogation of immediate, or "sensed" reality.

Guidano (1991) has discussed the distinction between a priori first-order experiences and a posteriori second-order experiences in this regard. From his perspective, our moment-to-moment understandings of our worlds follow from a circular process in which immediate, and often tacit, experience becomes reordered into propositions and beliefs through processes of representation and languaging. As Guidano (1991) further explained, this "conscious-explicit restructuring makes new levels of abstraction available, transforming the continuous modulation of internal states into patterns of self-understanding that modify ongoing immediate experience and facilitate further articulation" (p. 7). This distinction between experiencing, on the one hand, and explaining, on the other, is critical to human growth and change. It is matched, for Guidano, by a similarly recursive process involving oscillations between the experiencing *me* and the explaining *I*, to use James's (1890) apt distinction:

> The self as subject ("I") and as object ("Me") therefore emerge as irreducible dimensions of a selfhood dynamic . . . the acting and experiencing "I" is always one step ahead of the current appraisal of the situation, and the evaluating "Me" becomes a continuous process of reordering and reconstructing one's conscious sense of self. (Guidano, 1991, p. 7)

One significant marker for me in gauging how prepared a client is to terminate therapy is his or her ability to harness this process. Becoming aware of, and capably intervening in, this otherwise seamlessly circular process is a sign of significant self-control, signaling the individual's capacity to continue generating self-change. This perspectival shift necessarily carries with it the emergence of new levels of abstract self-referring in construing past, present, and future experiences.

In negotiating the termination process, I will often explicitly empower clients by reminding them of their capacity to engage and disengage from experience at will, and I use this as an opportunity to encourage them to review and make sense of preceding therapeutic efforts. My open-door policy reminds them that even this termination is not necessarily terminal, echoing Mahoney's (1991) observation that "in having helped develop a secure base for the client's developmental explorations, the psychotherapist does not insist that base can never again be visited" (p. 318). I do, however, encourage my clients to symbolically ritualize the termination in some way of personal significance to them: a card or letter, a series of nonverbal sculptures reflecting perceived stages of our joint efforts, a token commemorating our relationship, or a simple hug and goodbye—any of which may serve to facilitate the leave-taking in a way that underscores and empowers the client's subsequent independence.

SUMMARY

In this brief chapter I have tried to emphasize the challenge of change. On the one hand, change is endemic to being human. But on the other hand, being human necessitates resisting change, at least to the extent that change threatens the consistency and continuity of core aspects of the self. Constructivist psychotherapy acknowledges the role of self-organization in meaning making and, for that reason, is fundamentally mindful of the limits and liabilities, as well as the profits and possibilities, associated with significant personal revision. "Significant psychological change is rarely easy or rapid," noted Mahoney (1991, p. 283), and for that reason, many constructivist psychotherapies present patient, respectful approaches to personal change that are deeply cognizant of the painful and sometimes measured progress that marks personal elaboration. Efforts to support and accept existing constructions, to provide nonthreatening vehicles for introducing experiential novelty, and to encourage active, interpersonal enactment all reflect the almost reverential regard that constructivists have for their clients' personal knowing systems. As psychotherapists, ours is a special position of privilege and responsibility—the privilege that attends our access to deeply personal human struggles and the responsibility to collaborate in efforts to transcend these struggles and, in so doing, to contribute to the ongoing process of human development.

REFERENCES

Bartlett, F. C. (1932). *Remembering*. Cambridge, England: Cambridge University Press.

Bowlby, J. (1988). *A secure base*. New York: Basic Books.

Clark, K. M. (1989). Creation of meaning: An emotional processing task in psychotherapy. *Psychotherapy, 26,* 139–148.

Clark, K. M. (1993). Meaning making in incest survivors. *Journal of Cognitive Psychotherapy: An International Quarterly, 7,* 195–204.

Efran, J. S., & Clarfield, L. E. (1993). Context: The fulcrum of constructivist psychotherapy. *Journal of Cognitive Psychotherapy: An International Quarterly, 7,* 173–182.

Epting, F. R. (1984). *Personal construct counseling and psychotherapy*. New York: Wiley.

Guidano, V. F. (1991). *The self in process: Toward a post-rationalist cognitive therapy*. New York: Guilford Press.

James, W. (1890). *Principles of psychology*. New York: Holt.

Kelly, G. A. (1955). *The psychology of personal constructs* (2 vols.). New York: Norton.

Kelly, G. A. (1969a). The language of hypothesis: Man's psychological instrument. In B. Maher (Ed.), *Clinical psychology and personality: The selected papers of George Kelly* (pp. 147–163). New York: Wiley.

Kelly, G. A. (1969b). Man's construction of his alternatives. In B. Maher (Ed.), *Clinical psychology and personality: The selected papers of George Kelly* (pp. 66–93). New York: Wiley.

Kelly, G. A. (1969c). Psychotherapy and the nature of man. In B. Maher (Ed.), *Clinical psychology and personality: The selected papers of George Kelly* (pp. 207–223). New York: Wiley.

Kremsdorf, R. (1985). An extension of fixed-role therapy with a couple. In F. R. Epting & A. W. Landfield (Eds.), *Anticipating personal construct psychology* (pp. 216–224). Lincoln: University of Nebraska Press.

Liotti, G. (1987). The resistance to change of cognitive structures: A counterproposal to psychoanalytic metapsychology. *Journal of Cognitive Psychotherapy: An International Quarterly, 1,* 87–104.

Lyddon, W. J., & Alford, D. J. (1993). Constructivist assessment: A developmental epistemic perspective. In G. J. Neimeyer (Ed.), *Casebook of constructivist assessment* (pp. 31–57). Newbury Park, CA: Sage.

Mahoney, M. J. (1991). *Human change processes: The scientific foundations of psychotherapy*. New York: Basic Books.

Mahoney, M. J., & Lyddon, W. J. (1988). Recent developments in cognitive approaches to counseling and psychotherapy. *The Counseling Psychologist, 16,* 190–234.

Neimeyer, G. J. (1993). The challenge of change: Reflections on constructivist psychotherapy. *Journal of Cognitive Psychotherapy, 7*, 183–194.

Neimeyer, G. J., & Neimeyer, R. A. (1993). Defining the boundaries of constructivist assessment. In G. J. Neimeyer (Ed.), *Casebook of constructivist assessment* (pp. 1–30). Newbury Park, CA: Sage.

Neimeyer, R. A. (1995). An invitation to constructivist psychotherapies. In R. A. Neimeyer & M. J. Mahoney (Eds.), *Constructivism in psychotherapy* (pp. 1–8). Washington, DC: American Psychological Association.

Neimeyer, R. A., & Neimeyer, G. J. (Eds.). (1987). *Personal construct therapy casebook.* New York: Springer.

Parry, A., & Doan, R. E. (1994). *Story re-visions: Narrative therapy in a postmodern world.* New York: Guilford Press.

Vaihinger, H. (1924). *The philosophy of 'as if.'* Berlin, Germany: Reuther & Reichard.

7

MEANING-MAKING AND CREATIVE AGING

MARY BAIRD CARLSEN

The ageless self maintains continuity through a symbolic, creative process . . . its definition is ongoing, continuous and creative. (Kaufman, 1987, p. 14)

Indeed, finally, I propose no solutions. It is a question of becoming familiar with the various roads and the regions into which they lead us. I deny that the North road is absolutely and for all purposes better than the South; but this is by no means to assert that each is always as good as the other. We need to devise maps showing how each road leads in a genuinely different and interesting direction. (Fingarette, 1962, p. 89)

"What do you mean by that?" is a frequent question in a therapy called *meaning-making*. Underlying that question is the assumption that there is no simple equation from a single word to a single interpretation or definitive meaning. Rather, meanings evolve and broaden from individual words and ideas into clusterings, elaborations, constructions, and reconstructions—systems that gain constructive power as they develop, intertwine, and transform in evolutions of personal meaning.

In similar fashion, I approach this discussion in a speculative, heuristic manner as I sort the frequently ambiguous meanings of aging, assemble clusterings of metaphor that radiate from such themes as "life as a journey" and "life as a story," introduce conceptions of human development and creative process, and propose a global therapeutic process called *meaning-making* that can alternately widen and narrow its focus according to

Portions of this chapter were drawn from *Meaning-Making*, by M. B. Carlsen, 1988, New York: Norton, and from *Creative Aging*, by M. B. Carlsen, 1991, New York: Norton. Copyright 1988 and 1991, respectively, by Norton. Adapted with permission.

client need. What I present is a tracking, a probing, a playing with ideas even as I am motivated by a variety of underlying questions: How do therapists undo simplicities of definition and interpretation in matters of aging? How do we serve the needs of people without segregating them or diminishing them because of age? How do we teach and stimulate the creativity that both constitutes and fosters wisdom? And how do we foster the engagement of life mystery (Smith, 1965) and the spirit of the never-ending question in the manner that Kelly (1979) has suggested (below)?

> If I had to end my life on some final note I think I would like it to be a question, preferably a basic one, well posed and challenging, and beckoning me on to where only others after me may go, rather than a terminal conclusion—no matter how well-documented. There is something exciting about a question, even one you have no reasonable expectation of answering. But a final conclusion, why that is like the stroke of doom; after it—nothing, just nothing at all! (pp. 51–52)

In this spirit of questioning, I start by exploring the ambiguous definitions of "aging."

WHAT DOES "AGING" MEAN?

"Definitions are tools, often weapons, not truths" (Achenbaum & Levin, 1989, p. 395), a conclusion warning that it is all too easy to create tidy classifications that can thrust any one person into stereotype. Indeed, rigid categories of chronological age can limit perspectives as well as suggest erroneous conclusions, especially at a time when "it is unclear just when later life or old age begins (after 50, 60, 70?), whether people feel a part of it, how social and cultural diversity may vary its development, and whether there is anything intrinsic and universal about it" (Manheimer, 1989, p. 232). What is more, the "rise of scientific gerontology and the decline of traditional, socially accepted beliefs about the meaning and purpose of later life has left a vacuous or fragmented sense of the place of old age in the life-course" (Manheimer, 1989, p. 231).

Categorical assignments continue, but the boundaries are shifting as increasing longevity expands the limits of life into the 80s, 90s, and 100s. As a result, the later years of life are being identified as much more complex, much more differentiated, than was originally thought. Because this is so, Schaie (1988) has categorized three successive age groups between 60 and 100 years of age: (a) those in their 60s and early 70s who are most similar to people in middle age—in terms of health and capability—although many are no longer in the workforce; (b) those in their late 70s and early 80s, a group composed largely of people who still live in their communities, but whose health and behavioral competence are beginning to fail; and (c) the "very-old," who are people in their late 80s and beyond. This third group "contains the largest proportions of frail and institutionalized elderly, even though a significant minority continue to function remarkably well" (Schaie, 1988, pp. 179–183).

Adding to the stage delineations are process descriptions of the sort suggested by Birren (Birren & Cunningham, 1985) when he wrote about senescing, eldering, and geronting. *Senescing* is the biological dimension of human aging involving those processes that increase physical vulnerability and the probabilities of dying. *Eldering* is the living out of social roles that have been most frequently age graded according to more traditional, normative definitions of aging—definitions that are in dramatic shift at the present time. *Geronting* is about self-regulation—for example, making choices, making meaning, and developing and maintaining interactions with others (Birren & Cunningham, 1985, p. 8).

Classification systems like those outlined above provide points of departure for ordering the sequences of aging, especially at a time in history when the outer limits of aging are being probed and tested. In many ways, such systems can be helpful. But I concur with developmental psychologist Marie Jahoda who, in her 80s at the time, threw up her hands at such finely delineated classifications. And I suggest that her protest against assigned "boxes" of age can serve as a reminder that it is all too easy to slip into *ageism*— that insidious "prejudice in thought and deed against the old" (*Oxford English Dictionary*, 1989, p. 247) that can lead to serious distortions in the perception of older people and in how they are treated (Butler, 1975; Carlsen, 1991, pp. 97–114). Even more, I suggest that these words from Dorothy Sayers (1938), written in her struggle against negative categorization, be remembered: "a category only exists for its special purposes and must be forgotten as soon as that purpose is served" (p. 33). Reinforcing these concerns, Bernice Neugarten (1982), over a decade ago, warned that

> policies and programs aimed at "the old," while they have been intended to compensate for inequity and disadvantage, may have the unintended effect of adding to age segregation, of reinforcing the misperception of "the old" as a problem group, and of stigmatizing rather than liberating older people from the negative effects of the label, "old." (p. 27)[1]

---

[1] In this chapter, I frequently use the descriptor *older*. It is true that this term is ambiguous; it is meant to be—to keep everyone pondering the question "What is meant by this?" The term *old* is too set, too determined, and too tangled with negatives; seniors seldom use this to describe themselves. Indeed, one of my older friends has heatedly insisted, "I will be old when I quit growing!"

What is increasingly evident is that chronological age as a defining variable does not tell much about human aging, a conclusion that echoes Neugarten's (Neugarten & Daltan, 1973) description of aging as a "seamless whole" and her later definition (Neugarten, 1977) of age as an "empty variable." What she saw as a vital influence was not chronological age per se but the biological and social events in a person's life that shape his or her identity. The constructivist psychologist would expand these influences to include those creative processes and learnings that shape meaning and activate the kinds of lifelong learning that can help a person live as creatively as possible. Baltes and Staudinger (1993) have emphasized personal growth into the "fundamental pragmatics of life," which they define as "wisdom": knowledge about possible pathways of life; knowledge about self, one's strengths and weaknesses; and the use of "management strategies aimed at optimizing the gain/loss ratio related to human development and at integrating the past, present, and future productively" (p. 77; cf. Alexander & Langer, 1990; Sternberg, 1990).

Interrupting the too-easy equation of chronology with definitive states of aging opens constructions of the reality of aging to wider, more flexible interpretation. In the process, categorical boundaries between "them" and "us" are softened. Also, this interrupts the automatic assumption that when one talks about aging one is talking about the final stages of life. By translating stage definitions into process descriptions, therapists are more able to conceptualize a long view of life; to become more sensitive to the importance of learning about aging early on; and to be more involved in stimulating those attitudes, outlooks, and learning patterns that creatively open our clients to life.

This duality of interpretation requires an ability to look two ways at once—a Janus-like position (Dorfman, 1994) from which therapists can view a client's past and future simultaneously and from which they can treat aging as both a lifelong process and a period of later life, as something that can be observed and experienced at all times. With delicious irony, Joan and Erik Erikson (1978) caught this duality when they described their roles at a conference on the humanities and aging: "We were the seniors in the senior group and thus, in a discussion on aging, were not only participant observers but also participants under observation"; both representatives of a "professional concern with the 'elderly,' but also this newly discovered human subspecies itself" (1978, pp. 1–2).

Kaufman (1993) found such a flexibility of self-definition when she worked with a group of older subjects. She discovered that when many older people talk about themselves,

> they express a sense of self that is ageless—an identity that maintains continuity despite the physical and social changes that come with

old age. They may, in passing, describe themselves as "feeling old" in one context and "feeling young" or "not old" in another. This is always variable. . . . *Old people do not perceive meaning in aging itself so much as they perceive meaning in being themselves in old age* [italics added]. (Kaufman, 1993, p. 14)

Metaphors are helpful in reframing people's viewpoints, transporting us into the less tangible domains of life as a journey and as a story to be told. Here are the expected and unexpected moments in the shaping of the scenario—the rise and fall of crisis and resolution and the interruptions of dreams and hopes by disenchantments and disappointments. Here is the working and reworking of the story that is "in some unspecifiable way what growth is about: turning around one's past and remaking it. It is the remaking that matters" (Bruner, 1984, p. 6).

METAPHORS AS TRANSPORTS INTO THE
MEANINGS OF LIFE

Metaphors facilitate the remaking of the story. Indeed, asserted Lakoff and Johnson (1980), people's conceptual systems play a "central role in defining our everyday realities" and are largely metaphorical: "the way we think, what we experience, and what we do every day is very much a matter of metaphor" (p. 3). "Metaphors are 'meaning transports' which extend our level of understanding by comparison, or some might argue by smuggling extra dimensions into our analysis" (Olds, 1992, p. 24). "When any aspect of our experience strikes us as worth understanding, either for the first time or in a new way, we begin to search for 'similar instances'" (Leary, 1990, p. 2). More than poetic figures of speech, metaphors shake and shape our systems of meaning. For these reasons, we do well to contemplate our conceptual systems in assembling their elements for thoughtful scrutiny; metaphors have a way of dropping below the surface of awareness to influence us in ways that we may not fully acknowledge or understand.

Life as a Journey and a Story to Be Told

When we use the language of "life as a journey," we incorporate clusterings of metaphor—what Gruber and Davis (1988) have called an "ensemble" of metaphors. These clusterings shape how we think about life and, in terms of what we are discussing, the unfolding conceptions of what we mean by aging. The metaphor of life as a journey suggests maps and turning points, barriers and breakthroughs, steps and stages, high points and low, and states of being lost and states of finding oneself.

Here is life as a path, as a "career," that engages our quests for purpose and meaning. Here, too, is life as a story that calls us to a tale that can be told.

> It is assumed that everyone's life is structured like a story, and the entire biographical and autobiographical tradition is based on this story. What do you do? You construct a coherent narrative that starts early in your life and continues up to the present. (Lakoff & Johnson, 1980, p. 172)

Indeed, much of a constructivist, meaning-making therapy is about uncovering, naming, and continually re-creating life as a story (Cochran & Laub, 1994; Neimeyer, 1995; White & Epston, 1990). Fairchild (1991) explained it this way:

> Everyone has, or lives, or is, a story. In the life review the plot line is not always clear. There are many subplots, detours, and wildernesses in each journey. But connections are made; we can remember pieces of our lives. Goethe noticed that "He is the happiest man who can see the connection between the end and beginning of life." (p. 40)

Life as the Way

The language of the "Way" was adopted by Confucius, who offered one of the earliest developmental models on record. He described his personal yet representational journey and indicated that "at 15 he had set his heart on learning; at 30 planted his feet firmly upon the ground; at 40 no longer suffered from perplexities; at 50 knew the biddings of heaven; and at 60 could 'follow the dictates of his own heart, for what [he] desired no longer overstepped the boundaries of right' " (summarized by Colarusso & Nemiroff, 1981, p. 4).

Confucian scholar Tu Wei-ming (1978) has added extra meaning to this shape for life: He wrote that Confucianism is "not so much a state of attainment as a process of becoming" (p. 125) with the analogy of the Way suggesting much more than a set of social norms or Confucius's life as the one and only norm. Rather, Wei-ming suggested, this master teacher inspired and instructed his followers to pursue the Way "by realizing humanity—or adulthood, if you will—in themselves" (1978, p. 125).

Wei-ming's (1978) restatement of the teachings of Confucius raises some interesting questions for those of us therapists who want to facilitate creative aging. If a goal for constructivist psychotherapies is to support clients' efforts "to realize humanity—or adulthood, if you will" (Wei-ming, 1978, p. 125), then we have to come to terms with what this means. We also have to face the reality that once we start sorting and articulating human possibilities we are addressing values questions as well as assumptions about our roles as therapists and the human potential inherent in our clients. Howard (1985) has reminded us that "the controversy is no longer about *whether* values influence scientific practice, but rather about *how* values are embedded in and shape scientific practice" (p. 255). At the same time, he challenged us to consider "what might occur if we viewed research in psychology as giving us knowledge regarding human *possibilities* rather than human realities or human necessities" (p. 262).

DEVELOPMENTAL PROCESS, DEVELOPMENTAL POSSIBILITIES

Adopting a framework of human possibilities orients primary therapeutic attention toward "ways of going right" over ways of going wrong; toward proactive, vital, and intentional kinds of living over passive, reactive, and predetermined living; and toward the shaping of coherence within the chaos of the unexpected. With that attention comes a search for models of health that go beyond those of the "OK"—the average, the well adjusted, or the reasonable—to those that reflect an ideal of what human living can be about (Korchin, 1976). The definition of such an ideal for life is closely intertwined with how one defines the developmental process.

Developmental Process

The metaphorical root meaning of *develop* is the "uncovering of the seed" (*Oxford English Dictionary*, 1989, p. 562). But this uncovering is more than the shedding of a skin or a shell—it is a process of moving through a series of intended forms. To use the words of the *Oxford English Dictionary* (1989; pp. 562–563), it is a growing "into a fuller, higher, or maturer, condition" (which must assume that there is such a state as a "more mature condition"). More than a result of the piling up of the cumulative years of life, developmental transformation occurs when there is a shaking apart of a system of processing personal reality—a shaking that challenges and interrupts old assumptions, beliefs, outlooks, and attitudes in a manner that changes a person's version of self and the world.

The cultivation of wisdom can be a part of such an evolution. But what is wisdom? And how can it be defined or even studied? Erikson (Erikson, Erikson, & Kivnick, 1986) has called wisdom a "truly involved disinvolvement" (p. 51) that results from a dialectical transcendence of the dichotomies within integrity and despair. Transcending the ego seems to be Erikson's point here—getting past limited perspectives on the self and its purposes to recognize a little piece of how one fits into the order of things, to see purposes and connections larger than the self. In a more contemporary interpretation, Baltes and Staudinger (1993) have characterized wisdom as an expert knowledge, a set of "cognitive pragmatics [that] can be conceived of as the 'software' of the mind; they reflect the kind of knowledge and information that cultures offer as bodies of factual and procedural knowledge about the world and human affairs" (p. 76). And, finally, if we are in dialogue with the insights of Huston Smith, wisdom might mean that we have arrived at a state of being when "less and less does our knowledge resemble floodlights progressively illumining reality's stage" (1965, p. 52)—that is, when we become increasingly aware and perhaps more accepting of "that which we not only *do* not know but *can* not know through normal modes of cognition" (1965, p. 52). Here we arrive at questions of the spiritual in human aging, a topic beyond the reach of this discussion, but one that every therapist who works with older people would do well to contemplate.

A Dialectic of the Unique and the Universal

Although each individual's life is a unique creation, this uniqueness is in dialectical interaction with the universal (Feldman, 1980). Indeed, one of the challenges for aging is to work with these paradoxical juxtapositions even as one heeds researchers who state that the real story in aging is "not in the average curves of maturation and decline, but in individual differences that cannot be attributed entirely to genetic functioning" (Hansson, 1989, pp. 29–30). Although I accept these qualifications, I nevertheless find windows into differing forms of human development by comparing and contrasting the varying developmental maps postulated by contemporary developmental theorists (Basseches, 1984; Erikson, 1961, 1968, 1974; Erikson et al., 1986; Gilligan, 1993; Kegan, 1982; Kohlberg, 1984; Levinson, 1978, 1986). Without locking into any one, I study them as suggested theories of life process, possible themes for the life story, and possible "universals" within which human uniqueness can develop (cf. Feldman, 1980). These developmental maps provide reference points for examining transitional passages of thought and emotion, of self and other, of work and love, of meaning and meaning-making, and of the evolutions of trust and hope into the states of wisdom that can transcend despair. In these developmental structurings are estimations of human potential, theoretical descriptions of an "apex of life," and the tracking of possible trajectories for life. Presumed in these models of the "uncovering of the seed" are portrayals of varying sorts of human ground plans. To illustrate just one definition of this, I quote Erikson (1974):

From the point of view of development, I would say: In youth you find out what you *care to do* and who you *care to be*—even in changing roles. In young adulthood you learn whom you *care to be with*—at work and in private life, not only exchanging intimacies, but sharing intimacy. In adulthood, however, you learn to know what and whom you can *take care of*. (p. 124)

When a therapist promotes such developmental goals as ideals for life, the specter of imposing a particular set of values on his or her client may be raised. On the other hand, if the therapist adopts the attitude that there are no standards by which to compare and contrast states of meaning-making—to "e-valuate," in other words—she or he enters the philosophical and psychological confusions explored so carefully in the final pages of Kegan's (1982) *The Evolving Self* (pp. 288–296). Indeed, if the specialist in creative aging throws away the idea that there are better ways to live in the later years of life, she or he would also have to throw away a conception of "creative aging" that has been affirmed by research into the lives of active, involved, creative older people (Carlsen, 1991; Hurwich, 1992; LeClerc, 1992). The therapist would have to throw away the viewpoint that "the study of wisdom involves the search for a better world. . . . wisdom is utopian in conception. And utopias are there to open minds to new possibilities" (Baltes & Staudinger, 1993, p. 75).

The Language of Transformation

The language of transformation is significant in this discussion. It is a language that suggests goals for a therapy for creative aging and that is linked to the evolutions of creative development and aging. Feldman (1988) called creativity "the construction and appreciation of crafted transformations"—a living out of the "transformational imperative" in human beings to create something new (pp. 285–295). This transformational creativity does not have to be evidenced by an artistic product. Rather, evidence for its presence can be found in the processes of self-creation, an applied creativity that tackles the never-ceasing negotiations of life: family, friends, associates, career, personal style, inner experience, general behavior, dress, character—whatever. More than an artistic product, creativity can be found in one's personal style and production of life.

It is in personal style, as an aspect of selfhood, that I find the ingredients of creativity. Openness to new ways of seeing, intuition, alertness to opportunity, a liking for complexity as a challenge to find simplicity, independence of judgment that questions assumptions, willingness to take risks, unconventionality of thought that allows odd connections to be made, keen attention, and a drive to find pattern and meaning—these, coupled with the motive and the courage to create, give us a picture of the creative self. (Barron, 1988, p. 95)

By entertaining questions about values, by studying the differing lifestyles that people adopt, and by playing with definitions of wisdom (Sternberg, 1990), the therapist is called on to compare and contrast the differing ways that a client can make the world cohere. Rather than running away from the demand, therapists need to evaluate their theories and frameworks—their "norms for growth"—to join their clients in comparing and contrasting alternative routes for life. Through such transformative dialogue—and Gardner (1989) calls Socratic questioning the "best-known classical instance of a 'transformative approach' " (p. 6)—the constructivist therapist seeks to stimulate the creative courage of clients to break open their patterns of thinking, feeling, and doing. The task is to help clients bring order out of personal chaos, that is, to help them transform personal confusions and pain into a more meaningful, fulfilling program for life.

CREATIVITY: A HUMAN RESOURCE FOR AGING

And what, again, is creativity? Many researchers have suggested answers (Amabile, 1989; Arieti, 1976; Barron, 1988; Feldman, 1988; Gruber & Davis, 1988; Russ, 1993; Sternberg, 1988). As a result we could go in various directions in examining this complex subject. I have done this in earlier writings, but for the purposes of this discussion I chose a summary that Barron developed for a brochure accompanying the Chevron exhibit "Creativity: The Human Resource" (1980). According to this, the creative person (a) challenges assumptions by "daring to question what most people take as truth"; (b) recognizes and creates new patterns by "perceiving significant similarities or differences in ideas, events, or physical phenomena" (which Silvano Arieti, 1976, called the "catching of similarity"); (c) sees new ways to take the commonplace to transform "the familiar to the strange, and the strange to the familiar"; (d) makes new and unusual connections in "bringing together seemingly unrelated ideas, objects, or events in a way that leads to a new conception"; (e) takes risks in "daring to try new ways or ideas with no control over the outcome"; (f) seizes the chance to take "advantage of the unexpected"; and (g) constructs networks to form "associations between people for an exchange of ideas, perceptions, questions, and encouragement."

Notice that these are process definitions that suggest the uniquely human capacity to transform the bits and pieces of experience into new patterns of significance and personal understanding—the capacity to go beyond old solutions, to transcend conventions, and to step into the uncharted territories of innovative thought and idea. What is more, these are demonstrations of the human capacity to exploit possibilities by being sensitive to materials, situations, self, and life, with an ability "to deal with the complexity and disorder such sensitivity brings, able to choose, reject, organize" (Tyler, 1978, pp. 191, 194). Such creativity requires a willingness to risk, an openness to the here and now, a searching for patterns, the making of connections, the challenging of assumptions, the taking advantage of change, and the seeing of a new way (Barron, 1988, p. 78). These are the outlooks, approaches, and processes that are helpful if creative aging is to be an operating program for life.

Much of what has been named above comes from the research studies of scientists and scholars who are specialists in the study of creativity. Their findings are guiding principles for this therapy of meaning-making that focuses on creative aging. But there are other demonstrations of creative living and creative outlook that are revealed in the daily processing of personal experience in the lives of people who come into my office, whom I meet on the street, who sit in my college class, or whom I meet secondhand through the stories in media reports or in the obituaries that appear weekly in my newspaper. Drawing on studies in adult development, I conclude that these people are modeling, or have modeled, a personal maturity and a set of accomplishments that manifest the following: a courage to create (cf. May, 1975) that enables them to risk; a kind of wisdom and integrity that triumphs over ignorance and despair; a caring for the generations, for their culture, and their world that helps them overcome narcissistic preoccupation; an openmindedness that reduces rigid, closed thinking and allows them to entertain new ideas in an exploratory, playful manner; and the kinds of fulfilled, mutually enriching relationships that take them beyond the extremes of either self-absorption or the loss of identity within that of another (cf. Carlsen, 1988, p. 228).

Support for these descriptive definitions comes from two independent studies by Hurwich (1992) and LeClerc (1992) that name characteristics of a group of subjects who are growing older in a creative, healthful manner. These creative older people (a) experience life as meaningful, (b) hold an optimistic perception of health, (c) maintain close relationships, (d) continue to grow, (e) live in the present, (f) practice spiritual development, (g) have developed an attitude of forgiveness toward themselves, (h) see themselves as still developing, and (i) are active mentally and physically. In this manner, many of these older subjects model the integrity that Erikson (1961) defined as the ability to "envisage human problems in their entirety" (p. 161). This reflects qualities that represent a coming into wisdom—a wisdom that contains a sense of coherence and wholeness that can sustain an individual's capacity to keep the human spirit alive and growing, even into death (Erikson, Erikson, & Kivnick, 1986, p. 37).

One human capacity that can activate the creative process is what contemporary researchers (Alexander & Langer, 1990; Chanowitz & Langer, 1981; Langer, 1989) have called *mindfulness*. It is a state of mind combining emotion and cognition within a "state of alertness and lively awareness" (Strickland, 1989, p. 6): a state characterized by and expressed through an active information process or a state that includes an awareness of context and a flexibility of thinking that can "lead a person to the creation of multiple perspectives and new ways of looking at things" (Strickland, 1989, p. 6). It is what Harold Rothbart (1972) described as the "dynamic experience of learning, as opposed to the passive reception of ideas or other people's work. Creating is doing" (pp. xi–xii).

Studies of older people (Alexander, Langer, Newman, Chandler, & Davies, 1989; Rodin & Langer, 1977) have found that some sense of control over the choices in one's life—whether a choice of a plant for one's nursing home room or a choice of treatments for pain control—can increase personal mindfulness, and, alternatively, mindfulness can contribute to a sense of control. These interactive dynamics contribute to the ability to attend to the experiences of the here and now, to be able to make a difference in those experiences, and to personally encourage a psychological state that increases health and well-being. This brings up a point that is significant for creative aging.

> Many, if not all, of the qualities that make up a mindful attitude are characteristic of creative people. Those who can free themselves of old mindsets, who can open themselves to new information and surprise, play with perspective and context, and focus on process rather than outcome are likely to be creative, whether they are scientists, artists, or cooks. (Langer, 1989, p. 115)

Mindfulness breaks open categorical assignments as it also affirms and encourages the proactive capabilities of the human being. Mindfulness enables each person to interrupt deeply worn habits of thinking and doing—to build in pauses between stimuli and their responses. Rollo May (1981) has called this ability to pause a vital goal for therapy when transformative pauses can be created not only by the identification of learned responses but by an imaginative, affirmative effort to reshape these responses:

> The pause is especially important for the freedom of being, what I have called essential freedom. For it is in the pause that we experience the context out of which freedom comes. In the pause we wonder, reflect, sense awe, and conceive of eternity. (May, 1981, p. 164)

In such a creative manner, both the therapist and the client can act on the premise that life is not completely determined, that the individual has the potential to transcend life difficulties, and that the behaviors of everyday life can be creatively enriched by proactive efforts to name, understand, and direct them (cf. Mahoney, 1991, pp. 100–104).

In negative contrast, "mindlessness" occurs when "people treat information as though it were context-free—true regardless of circumstance. For example, take the statement: Heroin is dangerous. How true is this for a dying individual in intolerable pain?" (Langer, 1989, p. 3). Mindlessness is seen in a "state of reduced attention, expressed in behavior that is rigid and rule governed. Mindlessness is inflexibility by default rather than by design" (Strickland, 1989, p. 6). Finally, mindlessness is a cognitive state in which the individual relies on categories already formed and distinctions that have already been drawn (Alexander et al., 1989).

On the other hand, mindlessness may be a cognitive turn that people take to help them survive when they cannot face rejection, discounting, neglect, or emotional or physical abuse. We shut down our minds because the full processing of experience could well drive us into madness. When I hear of the depressions and addictions of many older people, I wonder about such things as I imagine myself as an older person in worst-case scenarios where my requests go unheard, where my frailty results in my being tied in a chair, and where my attempts at communication bring me to breaking points of frustration and despair. Wouldn't it be my normal human response to withdraw into silence and depression to avoid more pain? Wouldn't that choice reflect some sense of my own identity and autonomy? With scenes like this haunting me (especially after observing my mother-in-law's last years in a nursing home), I add to my therapeutic role an attention to what is happening in our culture, an effort to work on behalf of better, more creative environments for older people that move them out of mindlessness and into mindfulness.

MEANING-MAKING AND THE PROCESSES OF PSYCHOTHERAPY

Under the overarching umbrella of transformational meaning-making and with sensitivity to developmental passages in lifelong aging, therapy is viewed as moving along a continuum from the continuous—that is, that which works for all ages—to the discontinuous, when therapeutic attentions are focused on particular problems, contexts, or interactive dynamics more attuned to the concerns of a particular period of life. These applied specifics take shape in response to the unique requirements of individuals, their environments, and their relationships—all as the therapist adopts a willingness to attend to the uniqueness of each person, not only in terms of problems, personality, temperament, and style, but in terms of how each client makes sense of his or her world. It is a matter of careful listening, of respect and openness. And, very importantly, it is a matter of heeding the suggestion that therapy's purpose is not to psychologize, pathologize, or simplistically categorize, but to teach, stimulate, and encourage the individual client regardless of age or stage.

Therapy as a Proactive, Creative Process

In breaking free from categorical assignments and interpretation, therapist and client engage a proactive process that can open thinking to the "gerunds of human experience": reconstruing over bounded constructions; "faith-ing" over fixed tenets of faith (Parks, 1980); and meaning-making over the adoptions of firmly established meanings, careers, and goals that are supposed to serve for life. With such dialectical construction, the therapist can guide the client beyond black–white, success–failure, and right–wrong models that suggest some sort of ultimate path. In matters of aging, such a process orientation carries the potential to redirect a person from a state of fear about the future to an engagement with what Whitehead has called the "Sacred Present" (cited in McLeish, 1983, p. 37): an engagement with the "Grand Perhaps" that enjoys "the doubt, the uncertainty, the magnificent issue of the game" (Robert E. Lee, quoted in Berman, 1989, p. 71). Here, certainly, is the poignant stimulus of the unanswered question.

The challenge for psychotherapy is to encourage such creative enjoyments of the question, of the growing, and of the avoidance of any fixed conclusions about what life is all about. By making encouragements of this kind a goal, the therapist can point the client toward the creative preparations, incubations, illuminations, and verifications that can lead to new insights that interrupt and transform old systems of meaning (Langley & Jones, 1988). In this manner, therapy becomes a series of movements through the formings and transformings of personal reality (cf. Loder, 1981).

A Natural Evolution in Therapy

In practicing psychotherapy, I have discovered a relatively natural evolution that occurs as therapist and client first come to know each other, to name the varieties of experiences and variables that influence the presenting conflict, and then to begin the explorations and patternings that open the client to new solutions and new conceptions. Out of my experience, I have identified the following overlapping, recycling stages: (a) the *establishment stage*, when the therapist creates a relationship with the client as they begin to name the problems; (b) the *data-gathering stage*, when therapist and client work together to assemble the historical data that feed into the current moment in time; (c) the *patterning stage*, involving active work to find and reshape the patterns of personal experience and knowing; and, finally, (d) *closure*, an arrival at those reconciliations and resolutions that free the client to leave the therapist and the therapy room.

In the establishment stage, the therapist first meets the client and does the important work of inviting the person into the therapy room and setting a tone for therapy. Very typically, some sort of unresolved conflict, identity confusion, or crisis experience brings the person to expose his or her private self to a stranger. What is needed, therefore, is an atmosphere of acceptance, respect, and personal safety. As this is established, the tentative, exploratory activities of sharing, questioning, and answering are begun as the therapist continues to cultivate a receptive environment. Within this receptivity, the roots of trust are planted and nurtured toward growth.

A client's initiating concerns and the establishment of a mutuality of pace, purpose, and rapport move therapy into a variety of forms of data gathering. This is what Loder (1981) has called the "scanning of the environment," when therapist and client "*scan* the client's psychic terrain, making new connections in a genuinely creative way" (p. 54). Through differing intensities of therapeutic dialogue, therapist and client work together to bring into awareness bits and pieces of problem definition, personal statement, and emotional expression. In addition to this dialogue, every type of exploratory technique is used to facilitate the therapeutic process: testing, autobiographical exercise, selected readings to stimulate thought, role playing, imaging, relaxation and meditation, behavioral assignments, new experiments in living and learning—all used to open both conscious and unconscious processes to the light of naming and understanding (cf. Carlsen, 1991).

At all times in therapy, careful attention is paid to emotions; they are considered "barometers of meaning"—affective feedback on hidden states of mind, body, and spirit (cf. Frijda, 1988). Certainly, for the older person experiencing progressive losses, and sometimes frightening and anxiety-producing changes, emotions are pain responses to the "hot burners" of such personal upheaval. For this reason, psychotherapy for creative aging requires sensitive attention to the emotional life of the client, an attention that joins rather than imposes and that engages in dialogue rather than in assignments of diagnosis and judgment.

The therapeutic dialogue (and all that the phrase implies in terms of the therapeutic relationship) remains central, adding its own momentum to data gathering with a mix of statement and response, of question and answer, of feeling and reaction. It is through such dialogue that the therapist can both confirm and constructively contradict in arousing the energy of exploration. These explorations encourage clients to become more aware of the differing ways that personal experience is defined—to do the work of "uncluttering their attics" (as one of my clients so poetically described his work with cognitive confusion), to walk into their emotional pain, to experiment with new scenarios, and to reconstrue their shaping stories. And as the recyclings of establishment and data gathering continue (there are no neat-and-tidy stages), patternings of the bits and pieces may emerge, develop, and accelerate. Ideally, this is an assembling of the pieces of the puzzle—not in the old way, but in a new, more complex emergence of personal knowledge and awareness. This can be the novice becoming an expert in the matters of self (Glaser, 1984) as insights collect and transform. What I mean by this is that the bits and pieces of knowledge assembled by the novice begin to knit themselves into a fabric of interconnected expertise through the synthesizing, systems-making processes of learning. To maintain the emergent expertise requires an ongoing process of renewal: through the creative life engagements I have described; through the emergence of the cognitive pragmatics of wisdom (Alexander & Langer, 1990; Baltes & Staudinger, 1993; Sternberg, 1990); and through the ongoing building and expansion of expertise that require reinvestments, progressive problem solving, and a "working at the edge of competence" (Bereiter & Scardamalia, 1993, pp. 244–245).

> In all lines of work that involve design, planning, leadership, teaching, or helping people with their problems, the potential complexity of problems to be addressed exceeds anyone's capacity. Thus . . . people must simplify. But people have a choice of how much they will simplify. They can simplify to the maximum that conditions permit, reducing the work as much as possible to undemanding routines. Or they can simplify to the minimum that their knowledge and talent will permit. (Bereiter & Scardamalia, 1993, p. 20)

For the person who is growing older, the dilemmas of "working at the edge of competence" require a careful sorting if creative vitality is to be maintained.

As therapeutic insights are created, named, and developed, they need to be integrated into the behaviors, cognitive constructions, and emotional expressions of the person. This integration constitutes a kind of "reconciliation" of the new with the old, of the present with the past (Loder, 1981). New understandings are thus integrated with the old in an important reforming of the personal system. Not a simple cumulative process but a transformational one, this period of reconciliation and integration is also a time for practicing new behaviors and outlooks, an integrative time that includes the "remembrance and inner replaying of past traumatic conflicts" in the service of personal creativity (Arieti, 1976, p. 377). As one remembers, acknowledges, and integrates former conflicts, they can be seen through new eyes—all this in the service of creative growth (Arieti, 1976, pp. 372–383). (Note that the work of narrative takes on extra meaning as a resource for these processes.)

Therapists must realize that insights do not always collect and transform. Resistances may be activated that fight new patternings. The client may be afraid of breaking loose from old systems of knowing in the creation of the new, to interrupt the foundations of personal identity that have already been laid. Thus, fear, denial, or rigidity of thinking may lead a client to fight back. And if cognitive patternings are fairly well fixed in black–white or either–or constructions, it may be much more difficult to bring about change. It is the therapist's important task to respect this resistance even as he or she works with it. In engaging this paradoxical challenge, therapists retain their goals to name, examine, and shake personal reality in the service of creative, transformational development.

This kind of psychotherapy frames closure as a kind of revolving door that respects the reality that the developmental process never ends and new experiences of living can further challenge personal integrity (cf. Freud, 1937). What the therapist seeks to do within this model is teach clients to handle these future transitional experiences with new understandings and new security so that they are independent of the therapist, more able to order and create their lives, and more capable of regulating their lives by stepping outside of their own problems to work with those same problems.

Levels of Change

The ability of a client to reflectively ponder the way he or she thinks is a remarkable outcome for a constructivist psychotherapy. Kegan (1982) has called this a "subject–object" transition, and Lyddon (1990) called it "third-level change" (see below). In an era when "brief therapy" seems to be the name of the therapeutic game, therapists need to understand these kinds of change as they aim to facilitate as well as to sort those therapies that are possible and appropriate for their goals. To further understanding, below I share Lyddon's portrayal of what he called *first-level, second-level,* and *third-level change*. From Lyddon's viewpoint, first-level change takes place by means of

> rationalist strategies to modify "maladaptive" cognitions, behaviors, or emotions. Based on the counselor's assessment, these individuals would seem to be comfortable with their core assumptions about

reality, self, and world and may only require peripheral adjustments in their system. (Lyddon, 1990, p. 125)

In contrast, second-level change represents a shift in outlook and reality construction—a new patterning, in other words, that is born of the emerging disintegration of one system of meaning that is transforming into a new one (cf. Watzlawick, Weakland, & Fisch, 1974). This birth is most frequently unpredictable, is often difficult, and is not particularly amenable to precise planning for its resolution. Presenting the potential for both opportunity and danger (in the same manner that the Chinese portray "crisis"), second-order change may bring either progressive or regressive identity reorganization (Guidano, 1987; Lyddon, 1990; Mahoney & Lyddon, 1988).

Lyddon's (1990) third level of change becomes evident when the client is able to describe personal passages of change—an ability that demonstrates a "self-conscious discussion of the procedures by which the pieces of the jigsaw are put together" (Bateson, 1958, p. 281) or one that further demonstrates the person's transformed capability to self-regulate personal growth with a type of "metacognitive awareness" (Lyddon, 1990). Where the person used to be the problem, he or she can now step back from the problem to name it and to have it (what Kegan, 1982, has called a *subject–object transition*). This last achievement can represent the reconciliation stage of therapy, in which a client is able to look in on his or her self, to see how he or she thinks, to make adjustments in those processes, or to transform into new forms of processing. This last achievement can also lead to the "truly involved disinvolvement" that Erikson (Erikson et al., 1986, p. 51) has named *wisdom*.

Third-level change is illustrated in these statements made by two clients in the reconciliation and closure phase of their therapies:

> You have helped me to that one step further in my thinking so that I can get out of whichever circle I'm caught in. Of course, after so many years of "circling," I still need a lot of practice on actually using the exits. (Quoted in Carlsen, 1988, p. 70)

> Things are coming together. I'm connecting up with the person I have always been. Images of my child are connecting with me now. And this child is exuberant, enthusiastic, with a place, a passion, a celebration. . . . Things are not as cut and dried; the hard edges are softening in lots of areas; I am transforming; trying not to see things just from my perspective; I have talked about it in a cognitive way, now I can laugh about it. I feel more myself—more integrated, a lot more self-accepting. I don't think I can go back but it is interesting to look back.

ADJUSTING THE THERAPEUTIC FOCUS TO NEEDS IN LATER AGING

This meaning-making emphasis does not neglect physical problems, defeating psychological patterns, or the griefs that can come with losses resulting from growing older. What this approach does do is shift emphasis from the reactive to the proactive, from the pathological to the healthful, and from aging as noun to aging as process, even as it pays attention to human intangibles like love, care, and wisdom (Erikson's [1961] listing of virtues for adult life); emotion and interior processing; and the possible lifelong cultivations of a wisdom that can eventually "balance the despair of a limited life coming to a conscious conclusion" (Erikson, 1961, p. 161).

In this psychotherapy I call "meaning-making" (cf. Carlsen, 1988, 1991), a sequence of establishment, data gathering, patterning, and reconciliation or closure is adapted according to need—its processes expanded and contracted in response to each client. Some clients may never want, engage, or complete a long-term sequence. Many will only want or need some sort of behavioral modification, and what they achieve on that level can be very helpful. Others will have insights and awakenings but may never fully integrate them into a scenario of life; nor will they learn the metacognitive skills to step outside of their problems to more effectively self-regulate themselves. Again, that may be all that is needed or desired at the time. And certainly, ideological outlooks, influences of discrimination and prejudice, boundaries of available time and money, dynamics of environmental contexts and states of health will affect opportunity, desire, and possible accomplishment.

Nevertheless, the sequences of meaning-making outlined above are readily adaptable to the therapeutic needs of older people in a variety of settings and circumstances. Establishment becomes particularly important with people of differing ages as the therapist adapts the style of therapy to the capabilities of the client. Data gathering can go in the various directions that any therapy can take—testing, storytelling, role playing, structuring of genograms (McGoldrick & Gerson, 1985), or the playing off of the past against the present and one's vision of the future. Patternings can expand not only into the realms of cognitive construction but also into artistic exploration, possible career choices, varieties of volunteering, or investments in lifelong learning. Reconciliations may take the form of "life review"; family therapy; or integrating emerging insight into the demands of caregiving, of illness, of preparations for death. *Closure* can mean returning control to the person after providing the necessary assistance and support in a time of need. In this manner, we therapists can "optimize or maximize the adaptive capacity of the individual" (Eisdorfer, 1974), even as we are available in an ongoing, dependable way.

A repertoire of therapies is thus available to assist the client—a "systemic eclecticism" (cf. Allport, 1968, pp. 3–27) organized within the paradigmatic principles and structures of constructivist meaning-making. Many of these therapies do take the client into the realms of constructivist meaning-making. Others move into more concrete kinds of activity in which active participations stimulate minds, bodies, and spirits: for example, into classes in wellness, autobiography, theater, and history at lifetime wellness centers, community colleges, and private schools; into Elderhostel programs that take the person to a variety of places, near to home or across the world; or into performances in intergenerational theater, in which octogenarians and eight-year-olds share performances. In previous research, I have discovered the usefulness of forms of pet therapy, in which animals are brought to nursing homes or into private homes. It is important for people to touch something soft, warm, and responsive when all too often there is no one to touch. There is also objective evidence that animals are calming, that they can dramatically lower heart rate and blood pressure, ease loneliness and depression, and serve as social catalysts, providing a common ground for conversation. In passing, I also mention the gardening programs for disabled partici-pants—another imaginative effort to stimulate the creativities of older people. Anything that adds to a repertoire of personal possibility and meaning is of value in dealing with the uncertain, evolving states of the later years of life.

To most effectively facilitate these explorations and stimulations, a therapist needs to be an educated, supportive advocate in matters of aging, open to the complexities of both the practical and the intangi-ble—a person willing to serve variously as listener, teacher, coach, and sensitive guide. In the midst of such complexity, the therapist would do well to remember the suggestion from Robert Butler (Butler & Lewis, 1982) that "realistic and appropriate treatment is greatly facilitated by a fairly sophisticated understanding of social, psychological and medical phenomena" (p. 4). For these reasons, the therapist also needs to continu-ously study the research literature, especially at a time when many new findings are interrupting old assumptions about the capabilities of age. Increasingly, qualitative research is balancing the quantitative (Man-heimer, 1989), ethnographic studies are complementing the empirical, and many studies are offering a broader, more human portrait of the older person. I for one am encouraged that gerontological paradigms are being leavened with fresh "resource perspectives" (Tornstam, 1992) in which the potential of the older person is being affirmed. This means that more recognition is being given to the proactive values and aspirations of older people (Dorfman, 1994), and we are seeing increasingly sophisti-cated study of the achievements of wisdom (Alexander & Langer, 1990;

Baltes & Staudinger, 1993; Sternberg, 1990). But paradigms take time to change, a fact that Tornstam (1992) addressed when he dared therapists to examine and shake their models of aging:

> It might quite possibly be that we—starting from the predominating ontological assumptions within gerontology—carry out research work and care that in certain cases are *incompatible* [italics added] with the metatheoretical paradigm that defines reality for individuals who have come far in their individuation process—who have approached a condition of gerotranscendence. *Perhaps we force upon elderly people a positivist paradigm that they themselves no longer live in* [italics added]. (p. 324)

Tornstam (1992) has asked those of us who work in the field of aging to question our attitudes and approaches: Do we transcend ageist expectation when we work with people with gray hair, sagging skin, and age spots? Are we able to separate the person from outward appearances and to defuse our own denials of growing older? Do we respect these people whose status in the world is shifting? Are we able to adapt to shifts in aging memory if they occur? Are we willing to accept and learn from those who are older than we are? Do we really believe that these people are capable of proactive, ongoing construction and reconstruction of their personal realities? To fully enter the meaning-makings of our senior clients requires an attitude of acceptance, respect, and appreciation that adapts to the rhythms of each client. To come in with a set of interventions—a stereotyped set of assumptions about what this "old person" requires—is to undermine the therapeutic relationship and do more harm than good. For these reasons, it is necessary for each constructive psychotherapist to ask "Are we preserving the humanness of our clients within our therapies?" (Frankl, 1969, p. 16).

With these questions in mind, I use a case description to illustrate the significant role that therapists assume in simply listening to, believing in, and encouraging older clients. In addition, I hope to emphasize the important service that therapists can provide in helping seniors pragmatically deal with the stressful impacts from a contemporary Western culture that does not always treat them very well or like them very well.

My client is a woman in her mid-70s, someone I have been working with for about 6 months. In many ways she is living quite effectively, reducing the depression that first brought her to see me. Although alone in her home, she maintains active interactions with friends and family. To fend off the depression that all too easily takes over, she attends classes, goes on Elderhostel tours when money is available, and works hard to maintain harmonious family relationships (not always easy!). Therapy provides a source of the acknowledgment and affirmation that is frequently missing in her life. She needs me to listen to her angers and frustrations before they translate into depression. She also needs me to provide a reality check in her problem solving as she struggles with recurring medical insensitivity, a noisy apartment, and her inclination to adopt the "packrat" tendencies of a mother who was an alcoholic. Moreover, there are developmental needs that feed an intense desire to keep growing and learning in some way. She makes delighted exclamations when a new idea opens her thinking; when her speculations are affirmed; when she realizes she is changing the packrat scenario modeled by her mother; or when she feels her bottled-up feelings softening into a new perspective on life. In such developments are her emerging wisdoms.

And so it is that constructivist therapy is carried out as it implements the following goals for creative aging: (a) the stimulation of creative process and, thus, creative aging; (b) the activation of the hopeful and the imaginative; (c) the reworking of the past in the creation of the new; (d) the encouragement of mindfulness (cf. Langer, 1989); (e) the encouragement of proactive capabilities to shape alternatives within the "givens" of life; (f) the building of a flexible repertoire of response that includes the differing creative, constructive capabilities named in this discussion; (g) the teaching, and stimulation, of those forms of thinking that help each person step outside of the self to look in on the self—in other words, to be more capable of self-regulating personal approaches to life; and (h) the growth of a wisdom and integrity that can transcend the losses that come with age.

Those clients who do achieve a more detached perspective on themselves—a kind of third-order level of change—seem to be able to incorporate many of these skills, developing a cognitive ability to work with their own psychic, emotional, and behavioral resources in maintaining an ongoing program for life. New awareness on this metacognitive level enables them to compare and contrast new ways of knowing and being with previous ways they have shaped and made meaning of their worlds. These people seem to be in process toward the wisdom that will enable them to "envisage human problems in their entirety (which is what integrity means)" and, ultimately, "to balance the despair of a limited life coming to a conscious conclusion" (Erikson, 1961, p. 161).

> Wisdom seems to emerge as a dialectic that, on one pole, is bounded by the transcendence of limitations and, on the other, by their acceptance. Wisdom is tested by circumstances in which we have to decide what is changeable and what is not. . . . [wisdom is] an emergent property of an individual's inward and external response to life experiences. A wise person has learned to balance the opposing valences of the three aspects of behavior: cognition, affect, and volition. A wise person weighs the knowns and unknowns, resists overwhelming emotion while maintaining interest, and carefully

chooses when and where to take action. (Birren & Fischer, 1990, pp. 324, 332)

REFERENCES

Achenbaum, W. A., & Levin, J. S. (1989). What does gerontology mean? *The Gerontologist, 29*, 393–400.

Alexander, C. N., & Langer, E. J. (Eds.). (1990). *Higher stages of human development: Perspectives on adult growth.* New York: Oxford University Press.

Alexander, C., Langer, E., Newman, R., Chandler, H., & Davies, J. (1989). Transcendental meditation, mindfulness, and longevity: An experimental study with the elderly. *Journal of Personality and Social Psychology, 57*, 950–964.

Allport, G. (1968). *The person in psychology.* Boston: Beacon Press.

Amabile, T. M. (1989). *Growing up creative: Nurturing a lifetime of creativity.* New York: Crown.

Arieti, S. (1976). *Creativity: The magic synthesis.* New York: Basic Books.

Baltes, P. B., & Staudinger, U. M. (1993). The search for a psychology of wisdom. *Current Directions in Psychological Science, 2*, 75–80.

Barron, F. (1988). Putting creativity to work. In R. Sternberg (Ed.), *The nature of creativity* (pp. 76–98). Cambridge, England: Cambridge University Press.

Basseches, M. (1984). *Dialectical thinking and adult development.* Norwood, NJ: Ablex.

Bateson, G. (1958). *Naven* (2nd ed.). Stanford, CA: Stanford University Press.

Bereiter, C., & Scardamalia, M. (1993). *An inquiry into the nature and implications of expertise.* Chicago: Open Court.

Berman, P. L. (Ed.). (1989). *The courage to grow old.* New York: Ballantine Books.

Birren, J. E., & Cunningham, W. (1985). Research on the psychology of aging: Principles, concepts, and theory. In J. Birren & K. W. Schaie (Eds.), *Handbook of the psychology of aging* (2nd ed., pp. 3–34). New York: Van Nostrand Reinhold.

Birren, J. E., & Fischer, L. M. (1990). The elements of wisdom: Overview and integration. In R. J. Sternberg (Ed.), *Wisdom* (pp. 317–332). Cambridge, England: Cambridge University Press.

Bruner, J. (1984). *In search of mind: Essays in autobiography.* Cambridge, MA: Harvard University Press.

Butler, R. (1975). *Why survive? Being old in America.* New York: Harper & Row.

Butler, R., & Lewis, M. (1982). *Aging and mental health: Positive psychosocial and biomedical approaches* (3rd ed.). St. Louis, MO: C. V. Mosby.

Carlsen, M. B. (1988). *Meaning-making: Therapeutic processes in adult development.* New York: Norton.

Carlsen, M. B. (1991). *Creative aging: A meaning-making perspective.* New York: Norton.

Chanowitz, B., & Langer, E. (1981). Premature cognitive commitment. *Journal of Personality and Social Psychology, 41,* 1051–1063.

Cochran, L., & Laub, J. (1994). *Becoming an agent: Patterns and dynamics for shaping your life.* Albany: State University of New York Press.

Colarusso, C. A., & Nemiroff, R. A. (1981). *Adult development: A new dimension in psychodynamic theory and practice.* New York: Plenum.

Dorfman, R. A. (1994). *Aging into the 21st century: The exploration of aspirations and values.* New York: Brunner/Mazel.

Eisdorfer, C. (1974). The role of the psychiatrist in successful aging. In Eric Pfeiffer (Ed.), *Successful aging* (pp. 60–67). Durham, NC: Duke University, Center for the Study of Aging and Human Development.

Erikson, E. (1961). The roots of virtue. In J. Huxley (Ed.), *The humanist frame* (pp. 150–165). New York: Harper & Brothers.

Erikson, E. (1968). *Identity, youth and crisis.* New York: Norton.

Erikson, E. (1974). *Dimensions of a new identity.* New York: Norton.

Erikson, E. H., & Erikson, J. M. (1978). Introduction: Reflections on aging. In S. Spiker, K. Woodward, & D. Van Tassel (Eds.), *Aging and the elderly: Humanistic perspectives in gerontology.* Atlantic Heights, NJ: Humanities Press.

Erikson, E. H., Erikson, J. M., & Kivnick, H. Q. (1986). *Vital involvement in old age: The experience of old age in our time.* New York: Norton.

Fairchild, R. W. (1991). Re-visioning our ministry with older adults. *Pacific Theological Review, 24,* 40–48.

Feldman, D. H. (1980). *Beyond universals to cognitive development.* Norwood, NJ: Ablex.

Feldman, D. H. (1988). Creativity: Dreams, insights, and transformations. In R. Sternberg (Ed.), *The nature of creativity* (pp. 271–297). Cambridge, England: Cambridge University Press.

Fingarette, H. (1962, Fall). On the relation between moral guilt and guilt in neurosis. *Journal of Humanistic Psychology, 2,* 75–89.

Frankl, V. (1969). *The will to meaning.* New York: World.

Freud, S. (1937). *Analysis terminable and interminable* (Standard ed. 23:216). New York: Norton.

Frijda, N. H. (1988). The laws of emotion. *American Psychologist, 43,* 349–358.

Gardner, H. (1989). *To open minds: Chinese clues to the dilemma of contemporary education.* New York: Basic Books.

Gilligan, C. (1993). *In a different voice: Psychological theory and women's development* (Rev. ed.). Cambridge, MA: Harvard University Press.

Glaser, R. (1984). Education and thinking: The role of knowledge. *American Psychologist, 39,* 93–104.

Gruber, H. E., & Davis, S. N. (1988). Inching our way up Mount Olympus: The evolving-systems approach to creative thinking. In R. Sternberg (Ed.), *The nature of creativity* (pp. 243–270). Cambridge, England: Cambridge University Press.

Guidano, V. F. (1987). *Complexity of the self: A developmental approach to psychopathology and therapy*. New York: Guilford Press.

Hansson, R. O. (1989). Old age: Testing the parameters of social psychological assumptions. In S. Spacapan & S. Oskamp (Eds.), *The social psychology of aging* (pp. 25–51). Newbury Park: Sage.

Howard, G. (1985). The role of values in the science of psychology. *American Psychologist, 40,* 255–265.

Hurwich, C. (1992, March). *Late-life potential*. Panel discussion presented at the annual meeting of the American Society on Aging, San Diego, CA.

Kaufman, S. R. (1987). *The ageless self: Sources of meaning in late life*. New York: New American Library.

Kaufman, S. R. (1993). Reflections on "The ageless self." *Generations, 17*(2), 13–16.

Kegan, R. (1982). *The evolving self*. Cambridge, MA: Harvard University Press.

Kelly, G. (1979). The autobiography of a theory. In B. Maher (Ed.), *Clinical psychology and personality* (Rev. ed., pp. 46–65). Huntington, NY: Robert E. Krieger.

Kohlberg, L. (1984). *Essays on moral development: Vol. 2. The psychology of moral development*. San Francisco: Harper & Row.

Korchin, S. J. (1976). *Modern clinical psychology*. New York: Basic Books.

Lakoff, G., & Johnson, M. (1980). *Metaphors we live by*. Chicago: University of Chicago Press.

Langer, E. (1989). *Mindfulness*. Reading, MA: Addison-Wesley.

Langley, P., & Jones, R. (1988). A computational model of scientific insight. In R. Sternberg (Ed.), *The nature of creativity* (pp. 177–201). Cambridge, England: Cambridge University Press.

Leary, D. E. (1990). *Metaphors in the history of psychology*. Cambridge, England: Cambridge University Press.

LeClerc, G. (1992, March). *Late-life potential*. Panel discussion presented at the annual meeting of the American Society on Aging, San Diego, CA.

Levinson, D. J. (with Darrow, C. N., Klein, E. B., Levinson, M. H., & McKee, B.). (1978). *The seasons of a man's life*. New York: Knopf.

Levinson, D. J. (1986). A conception of adult development. *American Psychologist, 4,* 3–13.

Loder, J. (1981). *The transforming moment*. San Francisco: Jossey-Bass.

Lyddon, W. J. (1990). First- and second-order change: Implications for rationalist and constructivist cognitive therapies. *Journal of Counseling and Development, 69,* 122–127.

Mahoney, M. J. (1991). *Human change processes: The scientific foundations of psychotherapy*. New York: Basic Books.

Mahoney, M. J., & Lyddon, W. J. (1988). Recent developments in cognitive approaches to counseling and psychotherapy. *Counseling Psychologist, 16,* 190–234.

Manheimer, R. J. (1989). The narrative quest in qualitative gerontology. *Journal of Aging Studies, 3,* 231–252.

May, R. (1975). *The courage to create*. New York: Norton.

May, R. (1981). *Freedom and destiny*. New York: Norton.

McGoldrick, M., & Gerson, R. (1985). *Genograms in family assessment*. New York: Norton.

McLeish, J. A. B. (1983). *The challenge of aging: Ulyssean paths to creative living*. Vancouver, British Columbia: Douglas & McIntyre.

Neimeyer, R. A. (1995). Client-generated narratives in psychotherapy. In R. A. Neimeyer & M. J. Mahoney (Eds.), *Constructivism in psychotherapy* (pp. 231–246). Washington, DC: American Psychological Association.

Neugarten, B. L. (1977). Adult personality: Toward a psychology of the life-cycle. In L. Allman & D. Jaffe (Eds.), *Readings in adult psychology: Contemporary perspectives* (pp. 41–48). New York: Harper & Row.

Neugarten, B. L. (1982). *Age or need? Public policies for older people*. Beverly Hills, CA: Sage.

Neugarten, B. L., & Daltan, N. (1973). Sociological perspectives on the life cycle. In P. B. Baltes & K. W. Schaie (Eds.), *Life-span developmental psychology: Personality and socialization* (pp. 53–69). San Diego, CA: Academic Press.

Olds, L. (1992). *Metaphors of interrelatedness: Toward a systems theory of psychology*. Albany: State University of New York Press.

Oxford English Dictionary (2nd ed.). (1989). Oxford, England: Clarendon Press.

Parks, S. (1980). *Faith development and imagination in the context of higher education*. Unpublished doctoral dissertation, Harvard University, Cambridge, MA.

Rodin, J., & Langer, E. (1977). Long-term effects of a control-relevant intervention among the institutionalized aged. *Journal of Personality and Social Psychology, 35,* 897–902.

Rothbart, H. A. (1972). *Cybernetic creativity*. New York: Robert Speller & Sons.

Russ, S. W. (1993). *Affect and creativity: The role of affect and play in the creative process*. Hillsdale, NJ: Erlbaum.

Sayers, D. (1938). Are women human? Address given to the Women's Society. In R. K. Sprague (Ed.), *A matter of eternity: Selections from the writings of Dorothy L. Sayers*. Grand Rapids, MI: Eerdmans.

Schaie, K. W. (1988). Ageism in psychological research. *American Psychologist, 43,* 179–183.

Smith, H. (1965). *Condemned to meaning*. New York: Harper & Row.

Sternberg, R. J. (Ed.). (1988). *The nature of creativity: Contemporary psychological perspectives*. Cambridge, England: Cambridge University Press.

Sternberg, R. J. (Ed.). (1990). *Wisdom: Its nature, origins, and development*. Cambridge, England: Cambridge University Press.

Strickland, B. R. (1989). Internal–external control expectancies: From contingency to creativity. *American Psychologist, 44*, 1–12.

Tornstam, L. (1992). The quo vadis of gerontology: On the scientific paradigm of gerontology. *The Gerontologist, 32*, 318–326.

Tyler, L. (1978). *Individuality: Human possibilities and personal choice in the psychological development of men and women*. San Francisco: Jossey-Bass.

Watzlawick, P., Weakland, J., & Fisch, R. (1974). *Change: Principles of problem formation and problem resolution*. New York: Norton.

Wei-ming, T. (1978). The Confucian perception of adulthood. In E. H. Erikson (Ed.), *Adulthood* (pp. 113–127). New York: Norton.

White, M., & Epston, D. (1990). *Narrative means to therapeutic ends*. New York: Norton.

8

SELF-OBSERVATION IN CONSTRUCTIVIST PSYCHOTHERAPY

VITTORIO F. GUIDANO

Self-observation is the essential method for carrying out the primary tasks of both assessment and intervention in constructivist psychotherapy (Guidano, 1991). This chapter represents an attempt to move beyond the basic theoretical framework of contructivism (chap. 5) and into the realm of clinical practice. Here I discuss the dynamics of development in the lifelong relationship between the *I* and the *me*—that is, between immediate and reflective experience, between what is momentary, bodily reality and what are more symbolically organized reflections on the meanings of bodily experiences.

Self-observation provides the raw materials that are necessary in the attempted reconstruction of events of therapeutic interest, working at the interface between immediate experiencing and symbolic explaining. It permits the exploration and analysis of three levels of processing: immediate awareness, mediated explanations, and the dynamic and ever-developing relationship between these basic contrasts.

In this sense, therefore, self-observation is clearly differentiated both from introspection (e.g., the free-association technique), in which the level of immediacy is privileged, and from self-monitoring techniques (e.g., detection of automatic thoughts), in which the explicit level is privileged.

The crucial feature characterizing the therapist's attitude in self-observation is his or her ability to differentiate between immediate experiencing and its more reflective explanation. This is certainly one of those tasks that is more easily assigned than accomplished. Here the therapist is dealing with the well-known problem of distinguishing fact from theory, a problem contemplated by Ritter (1979):

> I often have the impression that scientists forget what is fact and what is theory. The frequency of light waves, for example, has been associated with the experience of color. Some scientists seem to think that light waves constitute the real world and the conscious experience of color associated with them some kind of unreliable, shadow events. But it is the light waves which are hypothetical (no one has ever seen them). Color is a fact. Scientific theories are held with varying degrees of confidence, and an essential tenet of science is that theories can in principle never be entirely proven. Such is not the case with conscious experience. That we experience color is not an idea to be held with varying degrees of confidence: it is a fact of human existence. Indeed, all conscious experiences are facts and represent the only things we can be certain of. (p. 208)

In other words, the point to bear in mind is that the "facts" correspond to the client's immediate experiencing, whereas his or her explaining and reasoning provide ways for self-referencing those facts to make them understandable (as in the case of light waves). As a consequence, while assessing a given situation (e.g., a marital quarrel), the therapist should not focus only on the way in which the client talks about what happened. Quite the contrary. While reconstructing the event with the same meticulousness with which one would reconstruct a scene from a film, the therapist should be able to continually shift his or her focus from one level to another.

On the first level, the therapist would consider how the client's experience happened in the situation. In the case of a marital quarrel, this would mean considering such issues as perception of discrepancy in the spouse's attitude, how the discrepancy was felt when it triggered anger, the experience of anger and related feelings, the emotional effects of becoming aware of being angry, and so on.

At the second level, the therapist asks how the client self-references and explains what is happening in the situation. One might consider, for example, contingent reasons adopted for the quarrel that exclude, or at least reduce, responsibility for it; explanations of the client's aggressive behavior in terms of personality traits or disposition; or inferences about intentions and moods of the spouse.

A basic distinction between these two levels is not that the latter has truth value whereas the former does not. Immediate experiencing simply expresses one's current and inescapable way of being in the world and, as such, can never be mistaken. Explanations, because they belong to a semantic metalevel, can be erroneous when compared with the experiences that they are intended to explain. Thus, in the quarrel example, even if the explanations and reasons adopted turn out to be irrelevant and inconsistent with respect to the experiential situation, the therapist should not limit herself or himself to the presumption that her or his primary professional responsibility is to suggest more suitable or satisfactory interpretations of a client's developmental crises. Rather, the responsibility of the constructivist therapist is to create a safe interpersonal context for the exploration of possibilities. This is important because different clients explore at different paces and through different and evolving patterns.

THE MOVIEOLA TECHNIQUE

I now momentarily focus on the essential aspects of self-observation methods and the basic instructions given to the client. First of all, one must always start with an event or a series of events that may then be analyzed in detail. Any problem presented by a client may be reformulated in terms of the events that produced or maintain it. Adopting a kind of "cinematographic language," because of its familiarity, the therapist reconstructs with the client the succession of scenes in the event under investigation. Then, as if one were in an editing room, the client is trained to "pan" the succession of scenes, going back and forth in slow motion, thereby allowing him or her to "zoom in" on a single scene, to focus on particular aspects, to "zoom out" and reinsert the same (now enriched) scene into the narrative sequence, and so on—a process that I call the *movieola technique*. Whenever a scene enriched with details is reinserted into the sequence, the sequence itself begins to mutate, taking on new connotations and permitting the emergence of other details in other scenes. Sequentially, this might unfold as follows: viewing Scene 1, Scene 2, Scene 3, Scene 4, and Scene 5; zooming in and out, to gain local, private versus distant, and social perspectives; and panning. As can be seen, the basic procedure is relatively simple. It should be clear, however, that self-observation is essentially a method, and, as will be shown, it can be carried out at even more structured levels as one proceeds through the phases of constructivist psychotherapy, especially when the client develops more efficient and articulated self-observational skills.

In the initial phases of constructivist therapy, when it is necessary to guide the client toward an understanding and appreciation of the difference between immediate experiencing and his or her self-referencing and explanations of that experience, the basic scene analysis consists of (a) reconstructing the patterns of immediate experience that occurred in the situation, with an emphasis on concrete and detailed phenomenology, and (b) reexamining the emotions consciously experienced as the client relives the situation and speculates about the interpretation rules by which that situation called forth those emotions. These aspects can be reconstructed directly from clients' reports.

In addition to considering how they talk to themselves or others about their emotions and how they conceptualize their feelings after an event, clients should be trained to focus on the structure of their immediate experience as it unfolds in the course of their perturbing situation. A simple way to do this is to point out that, in investigating an emotional experience, there are two types of questions one can explore: (a) the *why* of that experience, which yields data on how a person self-references and self-explains what has been felt; and (b) the *how* of the composition of what was felt, that is, its structure (e.g., imagery modulation, basic affective tonalities and related feelings, and the sense of self throughout). Assuming that the therapist is able to make this differentiation in his or her own emotional experiences, he or she should be able to guide clients in shifting their points of view from the *why* to the *how*, while reconstructing the type of difficulty experienced by them in such shifting.

The moment this differentiation gets under way, clients can begin to see themselves from two alternative points of view: one in which they are carrying out a given scene in the first person (subjective viewpoint), and one in which they are looking at self in that scene from without (objective viewpoint). The client's flexibility in subjective–objective differentiation further improves the possibilities of reconstructing the immediate experience, given that from an objective viewpoint, the client is now able to make inferences about the possible structure of the subjective viewpoint experienced in the situation. This is more or less what takes place when one thinks about a scene from a film: Starting with the words and actions of a character, one tries to reconstruct his or her moods, affective motivations, secret intentions, and so on.

This same procedure can also be used in more advanced phases of constructivist therapy when reconstruction of developmental history is being undertaken. Because of the client's more advanced skills at this stage, the reconstruction of the subjective viewpoint with which the event was experienced at a certain age can be carried out from two different objective viewpoints: (a) as one would have seen oneself as an "observer from without" at the same age and (b) as one sees oneself now as an observer from without while focusing on that age.

As can be seen, rather than the simple modification of ways of thinking judged to be erroneous, the essential aspect of constructive self-observation methods consists of the client's gradual acquisition of an appreciable degree of flexibility in assessing his or her selfhood dynamics. Both the increase in emotional openness and self-revelation (focusing on immediate experiencing) and the possibility of being able to see oneself from the symbolic distance of a hypothetical other inevitably modify the individual's current sense of self (Clark & Reis, 1988; Csikszentmihalyi & Figurski, 1982; Miall, 1986). Moreover, repeatedly viewing the same affect-laden scene in slow motion—going back and forth from many points of view—brings about a modification of the way the scene is appraised and self-referenced, with a consequent change in the current relationship between "episodic" and "semantic" memory (Tulving, 1985). Inevitably, all of this becomes translated into a reframing of the same scene, which triggers the emergence of other feeling tonalities. Hence, as such flexibility increases, the usual viewpoint of oneself (*me*) is gradually challenged so that new aspects of the experiencing *I* can come into the picture.

Therefore, the basic therapeutic effect resulting from an increased flexibility in selfhood dynamics consists of a gradual changing in the appraisal of *me* by the *I*, matched by a consistent degree of emotional restructuring. That is, new feeling tonalities in one's ongoing immediate experiencing are recognized and self-referenced, thus becoming essential ingredients in one's perceived range of conscious emotions.

THE THERAPEUTIC PROCESS

The therapeutic approach outlined in this final section usually involves weekly sessions. The entire strategy consists of three main phases following in sequence:

- Phase 1: Preparing the clinical and interpersonal context.
- Phase 2: Construing the therapeutic setting.
- Phase 3: Undertaking the developmental analysis.

Needless to say, psychotherapy is an inherently complex and multi-directional process that unfolds simultaneously across many levels. For that reason, the attempt to identify a sequence of phases where, in fact, there is a network of processes is an explicatory artifice aimed at exemplifying an operative praxis.

Preparing the Clinical and Interpersonal Context

This first phase includes the initial sessions, usually lasting from a minimum of 1–2 sessions to a maximum of 7–8. The outset is generally marked by the classic question "What problem has brought you here?" and the client, as is usually the case, replies by laying out his or her clinical picture. At this point, faced with the set of disturbances that the client has described, the therapist must reach a reformulation of the problem, which he or she presents in terms that will allow operation at the experiencing–explaining interface (self-observation method) while at the same time excluding interpretations that are disease based and that imply an external causal attribution. The basic operation is therefore to redefine the presented problem as internal (i.e., feelings inherent to one's way of being that acquire perturbing qualities because they are not sufficiently recognized and explained), as opposed to the external definition that clients often experience and exhibit (as when they view their symptoms as foreign or forced on them rather than being connected to their personal way of being).

The therapist should not be concerned with the correctness or truthfulness of the client's affirmations and should thereby avoid arguments in this domain. On the contrary, when working toward a formulation, the therapist begins by defining the interpersonal context as a reciprocal collaboration and the therapeutic relationship as a tool of exploration for construing a comprehension that is not available at the moment, thereby starting to dispel the client's usual expectations of finding in the therapy a place for being reassured and provided with technical solutions (the common search for an external solution). In this way, rather than focusing on the validity of the contents put forward by the client, the therapist—together with the client—instead begins to investigate the overall meaning of the contents, thus trying to construct a point of view that is both novel and plausible enough to shift the client's focus onto other aspects of himself or herself.

As an example, the problem exhibited by the usual phobic client is experienced as "extraneous" (e.g., panic attacks striking him or her like unpredictable somatic breakdowns) and attributed to an external cause (e.g., cardiac disease). By reconstructing the characteristics of the panic attacks, using the movieola technique, the client starts to realize that attacks may not crop up "at random" in a bizarre and unpredictable manner but, instead, seem to occur within two essential experiential domains: either situations perceived to be constricting—that is, felt as limiting one's freedom of movement (e.g., traffic jams, elevators, crowded places, or buses or subways from which one cannot escape at will)—or situations marked by the absence of a trustworthy companion in the immediate surroundings and perceived as leaving one insufficiently protected (e.g., being alone at home or in a public place where nobody is known).

All this gradually permits an internal reformulation of the problem. In comparison with its presentation as an illness, now the experience of panic can be discussed in terms of the client's feelings and attitudes toward life (i.e., his or her inclination to perceive situations as constrictive or lacking protection). Through such reformulation it now becomes possible to define a corresponding self-observational setting for the subsequent phase of the therapy: to put into focus in a movieola setting the how and when of all the client's perceptions of danger and related fears, reconstructing as well the makeup of all senses of constriction and non-protection. The trend of the reformulation is not as linear as it might seem in this brief description, and, furthermore, it is often interrupted many times by requests for reassurance and by more or less explicit attempts by the client to divert attention to such themes as illness, medicines, and so on. The constructive therapist should not refuse the assurance requested or criticize the requests but, rather, should use them to advance the process. Hence, while supplying the reassurance requested, the therapist points out to the client how these sudden shifts from talking about his or her own moods and oversensitivities to talking in terms of illness and curability show a curious extraneous attitude toward his or her own emotions that should be gradually focused on in the next phases and reformulated just as is being done with other aspects of the problem.

Finally, it is interesting to note that, in contrast to succeeding phases, these first sessions are critical because they do not allow for any kind of error. Later stages of therapy, although longer and more demanding, nonetheless permit the therapist to err without such serious consequences because there is already an established relationship. Indeed, any error in the initial phase of therapy reflects on the very structure of the emotional–relational setting (i.e., in the process of formation) and may thus have pervasive effects over time. Analogous to what occurs in the formation of any significant bond, during Phase 1 there are gradually defined—mostly implicitly (as in any affective relationship)—roles and relational rules that will constrain the structure of the relationship from that moment on.

Construing the Therapeutic Setting

This is the central phase of the overall therapeutic strategy in which fairly stable and often complete remission of initial disturbances usually occurs. Schematically, this phase consists of two consecutive stages, each lasting from a minimum of 3–4 months to a maximum of 7–8 months. In the first of these two stages, the primary focus is on reordering immediate experiencing patterns. In the second, the emphasis shifts toward reconstructing the client's affective style. I deal with these stages in sequence.

Focusing and Reordering Immediate Experiencing

This first stage of Phase 2 immediately follows the Phase 1 therapeutic sessions and may last as long as 4 to 8 months. It begins with the therapist asking the client to focus on the events of a week that both have chosen as meaningful in the preceding sessions on the basis of their working and collaborative reformulation of the problem. Continuing with the example of the phobic client, the events to be focused on would be all of the weekly situations that were capable of triggering even minimal feelings of constriction or nonprotection in the client. The goal would be to reconstruct how the client's oversensitivity to and inclinations toward these specific experiential domains unfold.

During the introductory sessions of Phase 2, it is absolutely essential that the therapist repeatedly instruct the client to use the movieola technique for each scene and to focus on the difference between immediate experiencing and his or her explanation of the experience both during and after the scene. Clients are not able to make this differentiation easily, if for no other reason than because this process is so different from their usual manner of living and thinking about themselves. While supplying many explanations, which is necessary to carry on a work of gradual reconstruction, the therapist should constantly train the client to be flexible in shifting his or her viewpoint from the why to the how, while discussing the client's difficulties in making this shift. In the usual phobic client, difficulties derive from his or her sensory reading of subjective experience, so much so that any emotional state is usually perceived only in terms of physiological reactions (tachycardia, respiratory difficulties, etc.), making it difficult (if not phenomenologically impossible) to differentiate the feelings from actual medical causes or symptoms.

One usually notices that clients are able to put into practice an experiencing–explaining differentiation when, after applying it correctly (more or less) during the week, they begin to increase the focus on their subjective experience and gradually extend these differentiations to other domains. In the example of the phobic client, this increased focus is paralleled by a greater ability to differentiate which external situations elicit feelings of constriction or nonprotection. Going beyond the sensorial domain, the client begins to recognize other aspects of his or her perturbing feelings. For example, the client may begin to notice that, rather than his or her responses being simple and almost automatically brought about by "objectively" dangerous external situations, these responses—which he or she experiences as disturbing—have a sort of daily rhythmic oscillation: Perhaps they emerge when he or she is leaving home (nonprotection) or returning home (constriction). Therefore, his or her feelings are in some way connected to the activity and his or her manner of experiencing affective contexts of reference.

By this time, the client has passed from an externally bound to a more internally bound attitude: He or she has gone from putting up with an objective problem to seeing that problem as consisting of how he or she manages or participates in the unfolding of his or her subjective experience. This process is enhanced by a growing capacity to bring critical feelings into focus, and, as a rule, it is matched by an increased distancing from the immediacy of the experience, which in turn even further increases the focusing ability. By using the movieola technique, the client shifts his or her focus more and more toward the emerging discrepancy between immediate experience and its explicit reordering, with the agreed objective being to reconstruct the actual pattern of coherence on which the discrepancy depends. Once again, in the case of the phobic client, the remaining work at this stage would consist essentially of reconstructing the process whereby self-deceiving patterns for maintaining current self-image prevented the client from recognizing a change in his or her way of experiencing marital and family context.

At this point, usually about 4 to 8 months after beginning therapy, clients have gone through an appreciable change in their views of themselves, accompanied, it is hoped, by a remarkable remission of the disturbances that led them to therapy in the first place. This change—in the *me's* appraisal of the *I*—brings about a reordering of immediate experiencing matched by a first-level restructuring of the range of perceivable emotions. Besides recognizing and self-referencing feelings previously neglected or excluded from consciousness, the client is now able to focus on more complex emotional states and to perceive the connection between different feelings and affects, such as concurrent relationships among attachment, fear, and anger. In fact, in the course of the work done in this stage, there is an implicit reformulation of the original problem in the sense that clients become progressively more capable of realizing how current critical emotional states are interwoven with a perceived imbalance in an affective relationship experienced as an essential part of their current life structure.

Reconstructing the Client's Affective Style

The second stage of Phase 2 in constructive psychotherapy may last from 3 to 7 months, and it is most characteristically associated with therapeutic work from the 6th month (plus or minus 2 months) to the 11th month (plus or minus 4 months). The therapist begins the second stage of Phase 2 by trying to explicate the reformulation thus far achieved and by highlighting the relations between the client's perceived affective imbalance and concurrent changes in his or her images of self and significant others. Thus, it becomes increasingly apparent that the original problem was associated with the self-deceptive reordering of challenging feelings triggered by a major affective oscillation. It is also necessary at this point to shift the focus of therapeutic work to how the client constructs his or her image of an attachment figure so as to make that figure consistent with his or her sense of self. In addition, it is important to address the strategies that the client uses to cope with any discrepancies that may occur. The therapist can then begin to analyze the client's affective style, reconstructing with him or her the recurrent patterns of coherence underlying its unity and continuity and thereby widening the focus of exploration and the reach of comprehension in self-observational practices.

The reconstruction of affective style takes up the entire second stage and begins with a detailed analysis of the client's affective history. Several aspects of this history should be investigated. Of particular importance are the variables that underlie the "sentimental debut" in relation to the original attachment figure and the ways in which the relationship was experienced, appraised, and self-referenced by the client as a child. Among these variables would be developmental context, personal attitudes, and social network. The sentimental debut is important because it corresponds to a kind of "dress rehearsal" for a potential career of building loving relationships. A look at this rehearsal permits a glimpse at the basic ingredients that are likely to be part of the client's affective style. In addition, the client's perceived outcome of the rehearsal will influence the way in which those ingredients will recombine at a later date to give rise to a more specific and defined affective style.

Also of paramount importance is the sequence of meaningful relationships that have taken place since the debut relationship. A review such as this can enable the client to reconstruct the significant criteria that he or she uses to differentiate between meaningful and nonmeaningful relationships. Such criteria permit clients to highlight which patterns of assortative mating were consistent with the bonding style that was gradually structured. It is also important for the client to examine the way in which each meaningful relationship was formed, maintained, and broken, as well as the ways in which each was experienced, appraised, and self-referenced. In doing this, it is possible to reveal the coherence exhibited by the client's affective style, that is, how this style produces recurrent emotional experiences that confirm and stabilize his or her current sense of self.

Passing through the sequences of significant scenes that characterize each relationship by using the movieola technique, the client is gradually able to reconstruct the invariant thread that unifies and gives continuity to his or her affective "career." For the phobic client, this thread might connect appraisals that attachment primarily fulfills a need for protection yet is experienced with an equally strong need for independence. In other words, the sense of feeling protected by a reference (i.e., attachment) figure appears to be the necessary condition for beginning a relationship. As soon as this sense of or need for protection goes beyond a certain limit, feelings of being constrained and needing independence may trigger processes that bring about the deterioration of the situation or attachment.

Going back and forth through critical events with the movieola technique to study the formation of the client's affective style brings about a gradual reordering of immediate experiences paralleled by a reframing of these same events. This in turn initiates further appreciable change in the client's viewpoint of himself or herself—a change in the me's appraisal of the I—this time, however, at the more complex, second level of restructuring of perceivable emotions. Basically, the client can now recognize and appreciate how different emotional states combine and recombine as a person establishes an affectional bond. The client also begins to appreciate how the perception of a significant other comes to regulate and influence his or her self-perception. On the other hand, the client is now ready to experience how these recombinations of emotions and perceptions of significant others unfold to create a pattern of coherence, the traces of which are now discernible from early developmental periods.

Accompanied by a near complete disappearance of the original presenting problems, this kind of change in the viewpoint of oneself also initiates the emergence of new abstract levels of self-referencing in ordering past and present experiences. Perhaps more important, this new self-perspective encourages a different attitude toward reality with the discovery of new experiential domains. It is therefore understandable that more than half of all clients prefer to stop constructivist treatment at this point and maintain a relationship with the therapist through check-up sessions that gradually decrease in frequency until they cease altogether, generally within 1–2 years.

Clearly, the therapist should have no qualms about the client terminating therapy at this point. Indeed, a correct way for things to unfold—including the therapy being carried out—does not exist and, in the final analysis, the client remains the only one who should decide what is the best way to proceed along his or her life trajectory.

Undertaking the Developmental Analysis

The third phase of the kind of constructivist psychotherapy that I am outlining lasts between 3 and 6 months and thus takes place during the second year of therapy. Generally, this phase is only necessary to clarify the work of self-observation that has been and is going to be undertaken. By this time, it should be clear to clients that their goal is to reconstruct the way in which their developmental pathway has influenced the processes that eventually came to make up the structure and pattern of coherence that, ideally, became evident to them during the second phase of constructivist therapy.

In contrast with the preceding phases, in which one is working with recent experiences that are more vivid and richer in detail, and thus more easily reconstructed, in this third phase—the developmental analysis—one is working with material that is much more vague and less detailed. Moreover, the fact that the client usually endorses a particular version of his or her past history—a version that has been "tidying itself up" over the years with ad hoc explanations in keeping with a specific image of oneself—is germane to this developmental analysis.

The client's ability to focus on the past from a new level of self-appraisal and self-referencing will probably have added to his or her growing awareness of his or her functioning as the crucial variable that allows the reconstruction of the past to be carried out with an appreciable level of reordering. On the contrary, if the client were not able to use another point of view of himself or herself as a fulcrum from which to "re-view" his or her life, he or she would arrive at a mere "biographical account." Such an account would be not only useless but also potentially harmful because of its tendency to confirm and legitimize the versions of self and reality heretofore unquestioningly endorsed by the client.

On a more practical level, the first stage of Phase 3 consists of reconstructing the client's developmental history in an attempt to identify significant life events that will then be individually broken down into their corresponding scenes. Subsequently, the movieola technique will again be implemented. Accordingly, starting from the very earliest memories recalled, one proceeds to recall a thorough sample of affect-laden events, analyzing in succession the trend of the main maturational stages: infancy and preschool years (0–6 years), childhood (7–12 years), and adolescence and youth (13–21 years).

The developmental thread linking attachment and selfhood processes interdependently can be discerned by using a self-observational focus and going back and forth in the sequence of affect-laden scenes. More specifically, for each scene, one puts into focus both the objective sequence of interactions contained therein to reconstruct the attachment patterns in progress and the subjective experiences of the child at that time to reconstruct the sense of self that emerged in response to the world as appraised at that moment. In this way, the client is gradually able to reconstruct a developmental pathway at the base of his or her pattern of self-coherence while experimenting with and reordering his or her appraisal of the history.

In the example of the phobic client, the connecting thread of the whole history might consist of an inhibition of autonomy and exploratory behavior that was inadvertently actuated by the attentions and solicitations of parents who were, moreover, very much loved. It was precisely this indirectness that made it impossible from the very beginning for the client to associate the unsettling experiences with parental behavior and attitudes. Nor could he or she recognize and appraise the experiences as having emotional qualities inherent to his or her subjective experience. In this way, it slowly becomes evident to the client that the impossibility of referring perturbing feelings to parents' behavior forced the feeling to be experienced as localized in the physical aspects of the self and that this in turn gradually led to a sensorial decoding of their emotional modulation. Their psychological baptism in intersubjectivity, in other words, may have left them inclined to ignore, deny, or otherwise divert their focus from the dynamics of all-too-human affectivity and the underlying historical continuities that grant them the rights and responsibilities of being a participant in their own unfolding lives.

Making clients repeatedly recount their developmental history is a self-observational process that can potentially trigger the most important reordering of critical immediate experiences. This process, when optimally completed, results in a reframing of the memory of those events as well as an increased ability to distance and decenter from recurrent affective tonalities that are an integral part of ongoing patterns of self-perception. The emotional modulation continuously provided both by going back and forth through the past and by reframing processes triggers a parallel reordering of basic affective themes in which the increased distancing from critical emotional dimensions is matched by their recombination with the new tonalities of the feelings which have emerged by way of a third level of emotional restructuring.

One may therefore conclude that, at the developmental level, the change in the *me*'s appraisal of the *I* consists primarily in a shift from experiencing one's praxis of living as something "given" to appraising it as the basic, self-organizing process of creating coherence—a process that consistently orders past and present experiences in such a way that a recognizable continuity results. Hence, with the changes and reordering that come about during the first half of the second phase, emotional disturbances, rather than considered as given, are appraised as coproducts of one's way of experiencing affect. With the change that takes place at the end of the second half of this phase, the same thing happens for the affective style, the recognized coherence of which is increasingly experienced as the unfolding of one's personal meaning. With developmental analysis, what is no longer taken for granted is exactly that personal meaning that comes to be experienced as the lifelong process of scaffolding the coherence of one's being in the world.

REFERENCES

Clark, D. A., & Reis, H. T. (1988). Interpersonal processes in close relationships. *Annual Review of Psychology, 39,* 609–672.

Csikszentmihalyi, M., & Figurski, T. J. (1982). Self-awareness and aversive experience in everyday life. *Journal of Personality, 50,* 15–28.

Guidano, V. F. (1991). *The self in process.* New York: Guilford Press.

Miall, D. S. (1986). Emotions and the self: The context of remembering. *British Journal of Psychology, 77,* 389–397.

Ritter, W. (1979). Cognition and the brain. In H. Begleiter (Ed.), *Evoked brain potentials and behavior.* New York: Plenum.

Tulving, E. (1985). How many memory systems are there? *American Psychologist, 40,* 385–398.

9

A DIALECTICAL CONSTRUCTIVIST APPROACH TO EXPERIENTIAL CHANGE

LESLIE GREENBERG AND JUAN PASCUAL-LEONE

In this chapter, we first outline a dialectical constructivist epistemology and theory (Pascual-Leone, 1980, 1983, 1987, 1990b, 1990c, 1991; Pascual-Leone & Baillargeon, 1994; Pascual-Leone & Goodman, 1979; Stewart & Pascual-Leone, 1992) and then apply it to understanding experiential change processes in psychotherapy. Dialectics in its most essential form is rational analysis based on the splitting of a totality into its contradictory parts and the examination of the parts as they relate to each other (Lenin, 1915/1977). The totality of interest here is the dynamic system of a client's psychological processes. The contradictory parts are the different psychological processes that, when brought into contact, often interact to produce therapeutic transformations, self-development, or novelty through a dialectical synthesis of the components. Dialectical constructivism therefore explains human functioning and development in terms of the relations between parts.

The dialectic with which we are most concerned is that involved in the type of construction of meaning characteristic of life-engaged consciousness, a sort of consciousness that Pascual-Leone (1990b—after Ortega y Gasset, 1980) has called *vital reason*. This form of consciousness—the experiencing of oneself in one's world—is viewed by many psychotherapy theorists as a form of knowing that is wiser than knowing by intellect alone (Gendlin, 1981; Perls, Hefferline, & Goodman, 1951; Rogers, 1959). We argue that this form of consciousness involves an ongoing dialectic between two streams of consciousness: explanation and direct experience; that is, consciously mediated conceptualization, on the one hand, and automatic, immediate experiencing on the other (Gendlin, 1962, 1964, 1968; Greenberg, Rice, & Elliott, 1993; Greenberg & Safran, 1987; Guidano, 1991; Mahoney, 1991; Wexler & Rice, 1974). We see people as engaged continually in constructing conscious reality from the dialectical synthesis of various sources of information. This form of consciousness provides one's lived reflective experience. It is with this dialectic that therapists need to work if they are to produce enduring change.

A person's immediate experience of internal and external reality is fundamentally a construction of both self and world from constituents that originally appear as constraints in relation to the person's current structure and praxis. Meaning, we argue, is neither simply imposed on experience by language nor wholly contained in experience but, rather, is generated by a dialectical construction. This construction is continually guided by an implicit "felt sense" (Gendlin, 1964), which itself results from an automatic, dynamic synthesis of the individual's internal complexity (one's set of currently activated schemes). We use the term *internal complexity* as a phenomenological description of people's lived awareness of their own internal mental life, in the context of living. When attended to, this internal complexity can be symbolized in reflective awareness to create distinctions or experience that can then be further operated on by conceptual processing to generate new, vital explanations or meanings.

Tacit, or implicit, meaning and the accompanying bodily felt sense—which, when symbolized in awareness, is referred to by therapists as *experiencing* (Bohart, 1993; Gendlin, 1962, 1964)—results from the automatic activation by the situation and by the subject's own inner state (initial internal complexity) of information-processing components (schemes) in an individual's repertoire and from the synthesis of those schemes into a new representation of internal complexity. This experiential processing of patterns of emotional relevance into a holistic sense of things differs from the reflective (often sequential and propositional) level of conceptual processing of which humans are uniquely capable (Greenberg et al., 1993). The bodily felt sense constrains the possible conscious constructions that can satisfy it while eliminating many other possible meanings. A crucial part of the meaning-making process, however, is the making of linguistic distinctions to express this implicit bodily felt sense of meaning. Experience is not simply "in" us, fully formed; rather, we need to put words to our feelings to bring them to full awareness. Articulation, most often through language, is therefore crucial in the creation of new conscious experience and meaning.

Although constituted in part by the making of linguistic distinctions, experience is not totally determined by a linguistic order imposed on it from without, as certain radical constructivists, social constructionists, and deconstructionists have proposed (Derrida, 1981; Gergen, 1985; Spence, 1983; Watzlawick, 1984). Human nature has its own order and does not wait indifferently for order to be imposed on it from without by language and culture. People are guided by their own internal complexity in interaction with the particularities of a situation, and it is this that is experienced as a bodily felt sense of meaning (Gendlin, 1962, 1964, 1968). In this chapter, we attempt to illuminate the dialectical construction of meaning through a synthesis of bodily felt internal complexity with language-based explanations, by using the theory summarized below.

THEORY OF CONSTRUCTIVE OPERATORS (TCO)

Pascual-Leone (1969, 1970, 1980, 1987, 1990b; Pascual-Leone & Goodman, 1979) has proposed the TCO—a dialectical, causal-process theory suggesting that performance and experience are caused by the dialectical interaction among informational structures (schemes) and innate, general-purpose processing resources (hardware operators). According to this perspective, schemes carry domain-specific information about events, whereas hardware operators—such as mental attentional energy, attentional interruption (i.e., active inhibition), and the gestalt field factor (an attention "closure" operator)—are not informational but are truly meaning-free functions of the brain. A number of learning mechanisms that create new schemes from lived experience are also defined. The interactions of the different hardware operators and types of learning result in effortful, rapid, logical learning as well as in slow, effortless, detail-rich, and experiential learning. For further specification of these organismic factors, the learning mechanisms, and their dialectically constructive operation, see Pascual-Leone's research (1980, 1987, 1989, 1990b; Pascual-Leone & Goodman, 1979). All of these hardware operators are involved in such internal operations as activating, storing, combining, or integrating schemes. Experience is thus created by the dialectical interactions between hardware operators and schemes—not simply by schemes alone. This silent hardware process that modulates the functioning of schemes (by boosting or dampening activation levels and combining schemes to produce organized meaning) is one of the crucial dialectical processes in the TCO.

In dialectical constructivism, the psychological organism is seen as highly active and geared to praxis (intentional activity toward the world). Certain affective goals are innately determined and are progressively differentiated by experience. *Schemes* are highly active units seeking to apply and to assimilate situations to their structure, even under minimal conditions of satisfaction of degree of fit. Because of their assimilatory tendency, it is easy to explain the ability of schemes to generalize, but it is harder to explain why some fail to apply in certain situations and how a dynamic "choice" between mutually incompatible schemes takes place inside the organism. Pascual-Leone (1980, 1984, 1987, 1989, 1990b; Pascual-Leone & Goodman, 1979) showed that to explain how intelligent praxis is to occur despite the strong assimilatory tendencies of schemes, one must assume that a set of hardwired organismic operators exists to help explain the silent dynamic choices within the organism.

TCO's principle of schemes's overdetermination of performance (hereinafter, the *SOP principle*) is important for an understanding of complex human performance (Pascual-Leone, 1969, 1980; Pascual-Leone & Johnson, 1991). According to this principle, consciousness is overdetermined in the sense that often many schemes produce the same conscious result, even when just a subset of these schemes would suffice to produce the same final result (Pascual-Leone, 1980, 1987, 1990a, 1990b; Pascual-Leone & Johnson, 1991). This overdetermination is consistent with Freud's (1900) view of unconscious overdetermination and with Piaget's (1970a) view of the assimilatory tendency of schemes. As a consequence of this overdetermination, any overt performance (action or communication) may have more than one meaning—as many as there are semantically distinct schemes overdetermining the performance. Those performance-determining schemes, of which the subject is not aware, constitute his or her schematic unconscious—the only unconscious that there is.

The existence of this SOP principle implies that in misleading situations (situations that elicit task-irrelevant schemes with strong associative connections) subjects should never produce the desired performance—unless they can in a top-down (i.e., attentionally conscious) manner "choose" to reverse the misleading schemes' initial activation level by attending instead to task-relevant schemes. Because, under some circumstances, this is possible to do, a set of hardwired organismic operators must be assumed to exist that explain, by either boosting or interrupting schemes, these top-down dynamic choices within the organism (Pascual-Leone, 1980, 1984, 1987; Pascual-Leone & Baillargeon, 1994; Pascual-Leone & Goodman, 1979; Stewart & Pascual-Leone, 1992). In addition to the SOP principle, there are certain other principles, well illustrated by Piaget's intuitive notion of equilibration, that describe the organism as a dynamic system. According to these principles, structural change occurs in such a way as to (a) maximize internal consistency, (b) maximize adaptation, and (c) minimize internal complexity.

All of these processes (assimilation, overdetermination, and dynamic functioning) can easily be understood in the context of a rather uncontroversial neuropsychological interpretation of schemes as parts of the brain's neuronal network (Hunt, 1961; Pascual-Leone & Johnson, 1991)—notice that schemes are similarly defined in the literature of computer-connectionist networks (e.g., Smolensky, 1988). Under this interpretation, schemes appear as collections of neurons, often distributed over the brain, which are both coactivated (i.e., activated simultaneously or in a lawful sequence) and cofunctional (i.e., firing in coordination as a cell assembly, or as a sequence of cell assemblies, to cause performances that satisfy affective goals). Schemes are therefore modular parts of a neuronal network; they are defined functionally but "have a neuropsychological representation; and the nature of their content (e.g., whether they are cognitive—verbal, logical–conceptual, spatial—or affective) depends on where in the brain they are located (prefrontal, frontal, parietal, temporal, limbic regions, etc.)" (Pascual-Leone & Johnson, 1991, p. 156). But if schemes are just molar, functional descriptions of neuronal networks, they should be subject to the dynamic principles that Sherrington (1906, 1940) has long described for these networks: synaptic summation of activation (and inhibition) through the network, and the final common path principle (i.e., all interrelated activated neurons converge, in their transmission of firing through the network, onto the final output neurons that produce the performance). The molar, functional description of these summation and final common path principles over a collection of neurons (i.e., a scheme) corresponds to the SOP principle. And, thus, through the SOP principle, Piaget's assimilation and Freud's overdetermination principles appear equivalent, produced by the same dynamic activation–inhibition mechanisms.

This model allows organisms to go beyond simple learning through cue-generated responses (i.e., scheme activation) to generate truly novel performances. Indeed, in a process analysis, one must distinguish carefully among three different sorts of external or mental performances (Pascual-Leone, 1980, 1987, 1989; Pascual-Leone & Irwin, 1994). First, there are habitual or automatized performances or representations, which are already present as such—by way of a scheme module—in the subject's repertoire (or brain's network). Then there are novel performances or representations, which are not in the network (repertoire) but can be generated by it through dynamic coordination of available schemes.

Finally, there are truly novel performances or representations, which exhibit aspects that are not given by any set of scheme modules currently available in the brain's network; there is more structure in these performances than schemes in the repertoire can provide in any combination. Truly novel performances exist in humans. This is evidenced by human creativity and by the plasticity of human performance. People are capable, even in misleading situations, of synthesizing new dynamic totalities out of modified available schemes (Piaget's accommodation) when the structure of performance as a totality is nowhere represented in the repertoire. There is then a true enrichment in structure, content, or both. What gestalt psychologists have called "A-ha experiences" (i.e., major insights, whether in interpersonal exchanges, in dancing, or in one's self-knowledge) are dynamic syntheses of truly novel performances. These performances arise from dynamic interactions among schemes and mental attention (hardwired operators) and are synthesized by overdetermination by way of the gestaltist field factor (the so-called lateral inhibition in the brain's network) to bring about performance closure.

In the TCO model, affect is also seen as influencing performance. This occurs in three major ways. First, affective arousal is a basic, vital function that preserves life by providing organismic reactions. These reactions inform the organism of the organismic desirability or undesirability of events and bodily states as well as prepare the organism for action. Second, innate affective schemes (the roots of primary discrete emotions) are situation-bound organismic dispositions that set affective goals and affect the degree to which cognitive schemes are activated. All cognitive performances are motivated to some degree by affective schemes. Affective schemes influence the activation of cognitive schemes and monitor their direction; they are at the origin of an organism's emotions, index the value of an experience for the organism's well-being (Greenberg & Korman, 1993; Greenberg et al., 1993; Greenberg & Safran, 1987; Pascual-Leone, 1983, 1990a, 1990b), and boost the activation of congruent cognitive schemes. In this manner, affective schemes set goals and increase the salience of certain schemes and stimuli. Third, affect is involved in complex affective–cognitive structures that constitute personality biases or belief systems (Pascual-Leone, 1990a, 1990b, 1990c)—what we have elsewhere referred to as *complex emotion schemes* (Greenberg et al., 1993). These emotion schemes are structures resulting from the acquired coordination of cognition and affect in lived situations.

Finally, in the TCO model, all directed mental processes function under the monitoring control of executive structures (or cognitive goal systems), which determine what strategies are used. At each moment, a particular set of cognitive plans (executive schemes) is made dominant by currently dominant affective schemes, by personality biases, and by the cognitive appraisal of the situation; this executive scheme momentarily controls the course of conscious, effortful mental processing. Here, again, the significance of affective factors on cognition is apparent: Affect brings into play certain cognition-guiding executive schemes by activating them. The TCO model thus provides a variety of components and principles for explaining how an active agent constructs reality.

Dialectical Constructivism Versus Categorical Constructivism

At its roots, a dialectical constructivist perspective differs from simpler constructivist perspectives (a) in providing a greater role for experience of the external world, and conflict with it, in one's knowledge of the world and (b) in giving a greater role to internal experience and internal conflict in the construction of subjective meaning. A more traditional, purely constructivist position, what we refer to as *categorical constructivism*, relies on a categorical view of construction. This view emphasizes the existence of certain a priori fundamental principles, or categories, that often are kept shielded from empirical feedback and are not informed by, but rather inform, experience. Categorical constructivist perspectives are overly prescriptive (not dynamically open enough) about the nature of reality and of knowledge (e.g., Chomsky, 1965, 1987; Kant, 1965; Newell & Simon, 1972; the early Piaget, 1970a, 1970b; Spelke, 1991).[1] These perspectives assume the existence of predetermined ideal "logicomathematical" forms for categorizing reality (e.g., assuming as Kant, 1965, did that knowledge frameworks for space, time, substance, and causality, as such, exist a priori; or assuming that a universal grammar or repertoire of specific constraints is already written into the genetic code). Categorical constructivism has an idealist flavor, because it embraces the idea that certain content-bound ideal categories simply exist in the subject's head and precede experience. In addition, categorical constructivism ends up confounding concept (or construal) with raw (pure) experience and gives the former too great a role as a determiner of human conduct.

One of the major drawbacks of categorical constructivism is that it does not offer an easy explanation for emergence and change. In this

---

[1]Notice that early on, Piaget already had some dialectical aspects in his theorizing; he is much less a categorical constructivist than Kantians, Chomskian psycholinguists, or developmental neonativists. Piaget (1970b), as his book on structuralism made clear, did believe in the epigenetic dynamic construction of structures, and he thought that this construction was caused by such dynamic processes as "regulations," "accommodation/assimilation," and "equilibration." We classify the early and classic Piaget as *categorical* because his theory does not explicate these dynamic mechanisms but, instead, takes them for granted. The later Piaget was a dialectical constructivist, although his explication of mechanisms was incomplete.

view, at a particular point in time something is either totally A or totally not A; it is difficult to see how something in-between (partly A and partly not A) might exist, for example, something in actual evolution or semantic transition. Categorical constructivist theories, such as those of the classic Piaget (1970a) in developmental psychology or the classic Kelly (1955) in psychotherapy, propose that people construe reality through their own construct systems and, thereby, are the constructors of their reality. They do not, however, explicate the mechanisms by which raw reality enters the system. We agree that people construct their own reality but add that certain reality constraints are experienced directly in relation to one's actions in the world and are not, properly speaking, constructed. In this respect, Gibson (1979) and the ecological psychologists offered a healthy correction to constructivist idealism. Raw reality constraints do really exist out there in relation to individuals' structures and praxes, and veridical cognitions are constructions that successfully pick up this "information." What is needed in constructivist theorizing, in addition to the view that people construct their own realities, is a way of understanding three things: (a) how constructs are developed in the first place; (b) how constructs are involved in the generation of complex human performances that go beyond the transfer of learning; and, finally, (c) how change and novelty occur in human constructs.

A dialectical constructivist position, in contrast to categorical constructivism, relativizes all categories and sees basic psychological principles (other than those rooted in basic biological ones) as being open to change as a result of experience. Resistances to reality (e.g., Gibson's [1979] "affordances") naturally emerge in the context of intentional activity taken in one's environment. For this reason, goal-directed activity toward one's environment is seen as a crucial aspect of experience. In categorical constructivism, the paramount role of direct reality resistances is often replaced with domain-specific, innate constraints (e.g., an innate logic, archetypes, or grammar) that the organism imposes onto experience to structure it. A dialectical perspective, in contrast, minimizes the role of domain-specific, innate determinants, assuming instead that most innate mechanisms serve a general purpose and are domain-free (e.g., the mental attentional mechanism) and seeing only biology, experience, and culture as foundational. Ultimately, knowing is founded in evolution. We follow the evolutionary epistemological view that change occurs through (phylogenetic and ontogenetic) evolution, within a process of dialectical construction.

The External Dialectic

Dialectical constructivism helps to resolve the realist–idealist epistemological dichotomy of how one knows reality, in the following manner.

From a realist point of view, the organism picks up "facts" from an external world of existing objects. In this positivist–empiricist view, all that people can know is their sense impressions, thereby leaving the dilemma of how they can ever know what is actually "out there" objectively as distal objects in reality. Coming from an idealist point of view, categorical constructivism cannot resolve the problem of how people construct reality either. Although categorical constructivism posits that people construct what is out there, it does not clearly explain how this construction takes place or how change in existing constructs occurs— especially how change occurs that increases the validity of constructs with reference to their use in real-world affairs. Piaget's (1970a) principle of accommodation of schemes, which suggests that schemes change to adapt to reality, is an a priori principle—more the name for a problem than a solution. How accommodation (or change of internal structures) occurs is not explained. This is, however, crucial for understanding change. If humans construct or model reality, and yet accommodate to reality, then how do they know when to accommodate, or to change, to fit the constraints of reality? Within categorical constructivism, the criteria that determine when a model would improve its predictability by accommodating are not known, other than to say that goal-directed action—praxis—is involved.

How, then, does one explain what reality, as such, contributes to constructions? How does one gain access to information about what is out there beyond one's model? As we have suggested, idealist categorical constructivism often ultimately appeals to innateness to explain how people arrive at what is out there, whereas a radical empiricist view tends to resort to a type of realist, learning reductionism (i.e., you know it because you see it out there). This realist–empiricist view falls foul of the Kantian (1965) critique that one cannot see something unless one already has structures for seeing it. In addition, the empiricist explanation of learning falls into what Pascual-Leone (1980, 1987, 1991; Bereiter, 1985) has termed the *learning paradox*. The learning paradox results from the claim that complex performances are produced by schemes yet it is not explained how the schemes are acquired. Many human performances and judgments imply the existence of schemes that do not yet exist or whose existence has not been explained. The learning paradox essentially points to the difficulty of theories, such as learning theory and common information-processing theories, that deny the dynamic generation of truly novel performances. In other words, if all performance is based on past learning (or in prewired responses), then how does one explain the development of truly novel responses in misleading situations, where strong cues tend to evoke error performances based on past learning? For novel performance to be generated in this case, the misleadingness must be overcome to allow a new way to problem solve.

It is here that such hardwired operators as a mental attentional capacity (mental energy) and an interrupt capacity (i.e., a willful, active, central inhibition mechanism) are crucial in overcoming the salience of misleading situational cues, which cause performance errors in these situations. In a therapeutic context, for example, one might ask how a client overcomes habitual, overlearned, negative emotional responses—such as to authority or intimacy. It is only after overcoming these responses that the person will no longer react to situational cues of this type by reenacting the same old responses. When a problematic reaction is reevoked in therapy, clients—in the safety of the therapeutic situation—need to learn to interrupt their habitual reactions as well as to deploy increased attentional capacity to explore the problematic experience. In this manner, they discover the misleading cues and learn to overcome them (Greenberg et al., 1993; Rice, 1974).

A dialectical constructivist perspective attempts to account both for the genesis of whatever knowledge structures one has and for the dynamic generation of novel and truly novel performances through these structures. Dialectical constructivism explains the generation of current novel performance by the dynamic synthesis of some existing structures to construct a performance that fits the situation. The construction of reality, and of novelty in performance, is explained by means of a capacity of the human organism to tacitly (unconsciously) represent to itself the pattern of coactivation of its own processes, whether cued by external reality or by other processes currently activated by the organism (Pascual-Leone, 1970, 1978; Pascual-Leone & Goodman, 1979).

In this view, a person, at any one moment, possesses a repertoire of schemes that are activated by situations and apply to these and similar situations. As they apply their schemes, they organize certain perceptions of reality. Reality, in effect, selects which schemes will be evoked, by presenting resistances (caused by external features, or constraints) that function as potential cues and that are informational because they match or mismatch existing schemes to become actual cues. It is, in fact, the dependency relations among features of reality, in terms of the schemes activated by matching and mismatching these features, that constitute any real object as an object (Pascual-Leone, 1984; Pascual-Leone & Johnson, 1991).

At any moment, then, a person's knowing is dynamically derived from his or her repertoire of schemes, or "knowledge units." These units are activated by the situation and apply to configure—and at times, to synthesize—the particular state of affairs in the here and now. This occurs with the help of reality, which (through the subject's prior learned schemes, innate dispositions, or both) cues and selects from a person's repertoire the schemes that (in terms of the organism's or the species' past history) have releasing conditions that match features of reality. These schemes are then applied to dynamically configure or synthesize the reality in question. Schemes have built-in mechanisms (releasing conditions) for these matches or mismatches and also have built-in future expectations that may or may not be satisfied in the actual situation (Pascual-Leone & Johnson, 1991). Consequently, as one interacts in situations—the world of experience—the set of applicable schemes or dynamic syntheses (i.e., possibilities) narrows: Certain schemes apply and others do not, and this selection, by cues, of a subset of schemes is what establishes the semantic–pragmatic uniqueness of the situation, incorporating its "true" nature or lawfulness. Thus it is through the subject's own activities that a situation selects the relations of coexistence (or coactivation and coapplication) for schemes that best represent this concrete reality (Pascual-Leone & Goodman, 1979). It can therefore be said that reality offers resistances and that the person's own assimilation patterns (i.e., the patterns of coactivated schemes) in the situation epistemologically reflect these resistances and the dependency relations among them. To repeat: Dependency relations among these resistances (i.e., the cooccurrence of features) as defined by the schemes make up the infrastructure that serves to constitute the objects of experience in the form of more complex schemes. Each knowledge unit (scheme) thus comes from the subject (this is the idealist aspect), whereas the pattern of schemes' coexistence in the situation (pattern of coactivation and coapplication) comes from reality (the realist–empiricist aspect). Reality, then, is constructed; but schemes and hardware capacities that do the constructing are, in fact, driven by it—a dialectical circle that relates the encoded reality with raw reality.

The Internal Dialectic

Internal reality is similarly created by an internal dialectic in which people direct their knowing processes onto themselves. Cognition in external dialectics is about truth and knowledge. In the internal dialectic, there are cognitive schemes but there are also many emotionally based schemes that integrate affect with cognition, and emotion schemes are more concerned with value than with truth. In the internal dialectic, emotion schemes are particularly focused on evaluating the significance of situations to the person's well-being. Here, too, as in the construction of the external world of objects, the construction of self-experience is governed by the complex repertoire of schemes, but here the repertoire includes the emotionally toned self as well as self–other schemes. These emotion schemes are activated by internal or external events and are synthesized in a dynamic manner to continuously organize current experience. It is these dynamic syntheses of human internal complexity (i.e., of those schemes from one's repertoire that are currently activated) that create our internal, experiential, sense of what is relevant to our well-being.

In social and personal experience, there is not as clearly a set of reality constraints out there (with which to form the typical pattern of coexisting, scheme-activating features in the situation) as when one is constructing an object. Initially, however, the releasing conditions for emotion are out there in that they are in-wired, and these in-wired, emotion-releasing schemes become more and more differentiated with experience; they also become more coordinated with each other and with other, more cognitive schemes. With development, complex (psychologically and socially relevant) subjective cues develop that often become releasing emotional cues. These more idiosyncratic cues evoke patterns of schemes that configure a situation for a person. Internal experience is the synthesis of these activated internal structures.

Internal dialectics involves interactions among internal processes (some are schemes, others are hardware capacities or operators, such as mental attention or gestaltist field factors). Together, these organismic factors dynamically synthesize experience and performance. As happens in the case of external reality (where schemes that can apply in a particular situation will do so), in constructing internal reality within the organism, any elements that can apply and produce an effect will do so.

The construction in therapy of new "healing" schemes (one important form of therapeutic change) occurs by representing in the new scheme both the pattern of coactivation of schemes that produced the in-therapy performance and the subject's own reactions (cognitive, emotional, or affective) to this performance. When, for example, the components of a conflict are activated in therapy, the two opposing processes interact, and a new, higher level structure may be spontaneously synthesized (Greenberg et al., 1993). This new structure captures within itself the pattern of coactivation of the previously opposing schemes, as well as newly formulated material, thus forming a higher level structural totality. Internal contradictions (often of a multidimensional nature) are resolved by the tacit or explicit dialectical synthesis of opposing activated schemes, and this synthesis is a source of novel structures. This dialectical pattern of structural growth can be found already in infancy. For example, learning to walk involves coordinating the opposing structures of standing and falling (Pascual-Leone, 1993). Walking is, in essence, a dialectical process of synthesizing opposites into a novel integration. This simple example may illustrate how performance is produced through the dialectical syntheses of mutually contradictory processes. In a similar vein, novel internal experience (such as self-acceptance) is often the dialectical synthesis, into compassion and self-acceptance, of the opposing processes of self-contempt or negative self-evaluation and organismic feelings of sadness and the need for comfort (Greenberg et al., 1993; Greenberg & Safran, 1984). A new construction of this type is aided by increased mental attentional allocation to the present internal complexity—first, to boost previously neglected emotion schemes, and then, to create a new, higher order scheme by representing the current pattern of coactivated mental structures. Novelty of this type involves a true emergence of a new integrated way of being.

Another important form of therapeutic movement occurs through the symbolization of experience. Symbols arise in clients' consciousness when they synthesize and express internal patterns of experience with concepts or linguistic symbols—such as "feeling like a failure" or "feeling like a ship at sea"—thus bringing to consciousness distinctions that best capture the automatically synthesized internal complexity. The concepts often come from a set of linguistically based schemes, which exist at the conceptual-processing level to drive reflective thinking. Here, language is used to make distinctions that simultaneously discriminate and create experience. Once symbolized, this experience can be processed reflectively to help clients solve their problems. Thus, a client might say "if I feel like a ship at sea or a failure then I need to. . . ."

People thus both discover and create their experience through dynamic syntheses, and once experience is symbolized, they further operate on the chosen symbols as givens, to problem solve, explain, and create new meaning (Greenberg et al., 1993; Greenberg & Safran, 1987; Rice, 1974; Rice & Saperia, 1984; Watson & Rennie, 1994). In therapy then, at particular moments and after newly symbolizing experience, clients can think up new ways of coping or can think through something differently—but this is only after new symbols have arisen from a bodily felt sense of internal complexity (Watson & Rennie, 1994).

Although reflective processing (thinking) does play an important role in therapeutic change, it only does so later, in the process of reflexive meaning construction. The initial function of the therapist's interventions is to facilitate the construction of new meaning by minimizing the subject's own top-down conceptual processes; for, generally, it is the predominance of conceptual processing that prevents awareness of any new experiences that do not fit with the conceptualization (Greenberg & Safran, 1984, 1987). Most often, therapists facilitate change by helping clients focus their attention on suitable bottom-up cues, which can change existing conceptual structures, or by helping them elicit new (therapeutically desirable) schemes or structures to act as a source of new components for novel syntheses. The therapist guides the client's attention to activating new components by using process directives

(Greenberg et al., 1993), which range from empathic responses to feeling, through experientially focused questions, to dramatized enactments of the subject's internal processes (e.g., the "two-chair dialogue"). Propositional, reflective thinking generally is best encouraged after the emergence of new experiential material, to facilitate the conscious creation of new conceptual meaning from new elements.

Dialectical Constructivism in Therapy

In this view, we transcend the false dichotomy between reason and emotion while retaining a perspective on the difference (in nature and function) between emotion and cognition. It is clear that cognition is not inherently rational (Kahneman, Slovic, & Tversky, 1982), just as emotion is not inherently irrational (Frijda, 1986; Oatley & Jenkins, 1992). Instead, the two processes are intertwined in complex ways to enhance human functioning. Human beings thus need to use both their rapid action–emotion processes and their slower, cognitive knowing processes to best guide adaptive action in complex interpersonal environments. Rather than offering a model that dichotomizes thinking and feeling, we propose a model in which thinking and feeling encounter one another in a dialectical process that leads to their synthesis—integrating knowing, feeling, and acting into a repertoire of personal schemes and structures. It is these that become the personality structures that generate a unified sense of self and situation (Pascual-Leone, 1990b, 1990c; Stewart & Pascual-Leone, 1992).

Change in therapy, in our view, often comes about initially not by modifying cognitions, nor by intellectual insight, nor by catharsis, nor by "going with" one's feelings. Rather, change comes about through the construction of new personal meaning (i.e., affective and cognitive), which is based initially on the symbolization in awareness of truly novel dynamic syntheses occurring in the internal field of activation. In this process, the construction of new meaning is greatly facilitated by the vivid evocation in therapy of emotionally laden experience in order to bring emotional experience into contact with reflective processes. Dialectical syntheses of emotion and reflection are the key to therapeutic change, as opposed to catharsis or reasoning alone.

As we have said, novel experience emerges by a process in which aspects of different (and sometimes even opposing) schemes are synthesized into new, higher level schemes. These new schemes incorporate compatible coactivated features (not just the common features) of original schemes into new unified structures with new capabilities. It is therefore important that the felt experience be activated in therapy so that clients can use it in new constructions. Purely conceptual or rational constructions will not produce enduring therapeutic change because they do not involve a synthesis of emotional experience with other elements. Just like the baby who eventually synthesizes standing and falling into walking, so does the client in therapy need to eventually synthesize, for instance, tendencies to overeagerly approach (signaling the desire for closeness) and to fearfully withdraw from contact (signaling fear of rejection) into a sensible evaluation of the interest of the desired other. The two opposing tendencies need to be simultaneously evoked and attended to with increased attentional effort to create a new synthesis. This ability to attend and synthesize is greatly facilitated by the safety of an empathic and respectful therapeutic environment (Greenberg et al., 1993).

Attentional allocation is the central processing activity determining people's awareness of themselves. What is important for therapeutic purposes is that attention is under both deliberate and automatic control. By using different types of interventions at different times, therapists can orient, direct, and monitor clients' deliberate and automatic attention (Greenberg et al., 1993). In this way, attention provides a medium for change. People can use attention to alter their focus of awareness and to symbolize their inner experience. Personal change then can be achieved in many ways, including the following: (a) by attending to and symbolizing the internal complexity generated by automatic experience, (b) by bringing about a synthesis of new structures in therapy through coactivation of existing and newly formed schemes, (c) by generating vital explanations of currently symbolized experience, and (d) by restructuring emotional schemes by evoking them and exposing them to new input.

A dialectical constructivist perspective therefore yields a theory that recognizes the significance of the client's emotional experience as well as his or her capacity to construct meaning and develop concepts. This integration implies a view of human beings as multiple-level processors who use different types of propositional (symbolic–logical) information and affectively laden experiential (sensory, perceptual, imaginal, and representational) information. Human beings, in our view, construct representations of themselves and reality in a moment-by-moment fashion, all the while dynamically reacting to what they are attending to.

Thus, growth-promoting conscious experience derives from both deliberately controlled (often conscious, serial, and conceptual–representational) processing of information and automatic (often unconscious, parallel, and sensorimotor) processing of self-relevant information. Consequently, an adequate theory should recognize three major roots of experience: (a) a conscious, deliberate, reflexive, and conceptual process (thinking); (b) an automatic, direct emotional–experiential process (feeling); and (c) the constructive, dialectical–dynamic interactions between the two (Greenberg et al., 1993). Reflexive conceptual knowing processes provide explanations, whereas emotional schemes provide immediate reactions. The dialectical synthesis of these different sources of experience into a coherent, integrated whole (an integration of thought and emotion, or the "head" and the "heart") ultimately leads the person to enter the way of wisdom—psychological maturity (Pascual-Leone, 1983, 1990b, 1990c).

In therapy, this dialectical constructive process often involves exploring differences between actual immediate experience and prior conceptually held views of how that experience should be. Contradictions between one's reflexive or acquired concepts (explanations) about how things are, or ought to be, and one's immediate experience of how things actually are constitute a great source of emotional distress, and these need to be focused on to produce new syntheses that can provide a greater sense of personal coherence.

Emotion Schemes and the Construction of New Meaning

Emotion schemes function as automatic processors that generate people's emotionally toned responses; people's experience of these responses generates their holistic sense of who they are. These emotion schemes can be thought of as context-specific processors relevant to certain domains of experience. Emotion schemes are unique in that they incorporate innate as well as learned experience and provide crucial nonpropositional (sensory–perceptual as well as cognitive) information to guide the experience of life in consciousness. This stream of consciousness incorporates both cognition and affect, but it does not always involve reflective conceptual processing. Although emotion schemes are initially (and predominantly) sensorimotor in nature, they rapidly grow (with continued experience and learning) to represent a person's emotional history as well as the situations that generated these emotions. They also come to incorporate cognitive and propositional information about the self to form integrated cognitive–affective modules (Greenberg et al., 1993).

These schemes then come to be a rich combination of our biology, our experience, and our culture—providing high levels of integration in our vital-reason experiencing. They give us our "feeling" or "sense" of our self and of things ("felt sense"; Gendlin, 1981). They produce such global experiences as feeling worthwhile or worthless, as well as more specific senses of, for example, feeling "small" or "valued" in a particular situation. The dynamic syntheses of these emotion schemes generate complex internal emotional reactions and experiences. The outputs of these syntheses should not be confused with primitive passions; rather, they are complex, differentiated emotional responses. Experience of these complex emotional responses can be made available to consciousness when attended to, but at any given moment, such experience may or may not be symbolized or incorporated into a person's construction of reality. Rather than being denied to awareness, emotional states are often not attended to and processed and, thus, are not experienced in awareness. Once symbolized in awareness, they provide a basis for our subjective sense of reality and give us feedback about our automatic evaluation of the significance of events to us.

Dialectical Construction: Symbolizing and Explaining

Construction of personal meaning, therefore, involves two important moments. First, there is a moment of consciously symbolizing synthesized information to form a subjective reality. This is a process in which attention is directed to embodied felt experience and a particular current representation of reality is constructed. Second, there is a moment in which explanation of the symbolized experience is generated to produce a coherent narrative or identity. It is the combination of these two processes of symbolization and explanation that leads to the construction of new views of self and reality.

We not only live our lives, we also are compelled to evaluate and make meaning of our lives. To better understand ourselves, we continually explain ourselves to ourselves—forming a narrative of who we are. We thereby establish a stable identity. We are, however, strongly influenced in deciding who we are by the sources that we use in generating our identities, narratives, and self-evaluations. In addition to the automatically synthesized (bottom-up) bodily felt sense, there is the (top-down) conscious, meaning-making, and explaining process. This latter process depends highly on both attentional allocation and available symbolic, linguistic, and reflexive capacities. Within a healthy, vital-reason perspective, one's momentary conscious explaining of one's self is based predominantly on one's bodily felt sense—generated, bottom-up, through schematic and sensorimotor processing. Explaining, however, can also be based on more socially acquired schemes that were obtained from others or inferred from past experience. These have been referred to alternatively as "learned conditions of worth" (Rogers, 1951), "introjects" (Perls et al., 1951), or "faulty assumptions" (Beck, 1976). When one's identity is governed by these, one is not grounded in one's own primary experience, and dysfunction often results.

Both language and bodily experience thus play a critical role in constituting our identities. Our immediate experience both influences and is influenced by how we formulate it, putting language and experience in a circular causal relationship. Our identity is thus formed by dynamic syntheses of our direct experience with our learned views of self, in an ongoing process of construction. In addition to synthesizing representations of ourselves, we examine these representations, evaluate them, work out new possibilities, and select alternatives for action—this all, in turn, brings about new experiences.

Thus, for example, in constructing vital personal meaning, a person, guided in some situation by dynamic syntheses of emotion schemes, might react automatically to an experience as being one of threat and might pull back in fear. To construct meaning, the person will first have to attend to this response tendency, symbolizing the bodily felt sense as, for instance, "feeling afraid." The person then begins to explain this experience and to construct a complex situational meaning, such as "I'm feeling threatened because I'm feeling rejected." He or she evaluates whether or not this representation is fitting and, then, depending on the source of further higher order evaluations, may end up with a self-critical meaning of "I'm unlovable" or with an adaptive meaning that incorporates personal values and needs, such as "I want this person's affections and I will attempt to repair the breach." Then, he or she would generate a response. Obviously, this is a complex process, one that is ongoing and would involve progressive formulations and reformulations, not all of them fully conscious.

In a dialectical constructive view, a conscious cognitive explaining function draws on various sources of information in the construction of experience and constructs many different "selves" at different times, or even at the same time (Hermans, Kempen, & van Loon, 1992). Therefore, people are seen as being constantly engaged in actively representing themselves to themselves and to others in images, actions, and narratives. People continuously construct themselves in consciousness. A person is viewed as a multilevel, modularly organized, active processing organization that generates a unified stream of consciousness (Pascual-Leone, 1990b; Pascual-Leone & Irwin, 1994). Consciousness receives messages from a variety of different, lower level schematic structures (modules) that process information outside awareness and synthesizes them into a unified whole, working to explain these newly symbolized realities.

Vital reason is (or can become) the final arbiter of meaning by selecting what source or sources of information to attend to and what interpretation or interpretations to generate. This conscious selection and interpretation process involves components of will and choice, in that people can guide their attention at will, under the control of an internal, executivelike process. Consciousness is influenced by deliberate, controlled processing as well as by such features as the salience of certain external stimuli, the views and attitudes of others toward the self, and past responses of the self in similar situations, to mention only a few—consciousness is overdetermined by all of these and more. Consciousness is the arena for a final dialectical synthesis of the different sources of information about the self, as the person encounters and resolves felt contradictions between aspects of self and between self and the world.

Dialectical Constructivist Epistemology in Psychotherapy

A dialectical constructive view goes beyond a purely descriptive phenomenological approach. By claiming that experience is simply given, the phenomenological approaches leave unexplained the constructive process by which "what is" becomes conscious experience and is symbolized. A dialectical approach goes beyond radical constructivist approaches in recognizing the existence of reality constraints on mental constructions and constraints of the bodily felt sense on self-constructions, and it goes beyond categorical constructivism in explaining how constructs come into existence and change. In addition, a dialectical constructivist position does not usually presuppose the existence of theoretically specified, culturally invariant, psychic contents that predetermine experience, as do many psychodynamic approaches. Instead, it assumes only the operation of a certain set of processes that can generate forms and contents of experience through dynamic interactions between the existing repertoire of schemes, the hardware operators, and the constraints of the situation. This is in accord with the known active plasticity of human adaptability—the versatility of vital reason in adapting to life's circumstances. Using this approach, the therapist does not possess a priori assumptions about a set of psychic contents that need to be brought to the client's awareness for change to occur; rather, he or she is an expert in the process of facilitating attention to internal complexity and the construction of vital reason (Greenberg et al., 1993). This epistemological view results in an attitude of respect for clients as experts on the contents of their own experience. Finally, a dialectical constructivist position does not assume that behavior is lawfully governed by stimuli or by thought alone (as do behavioral and cognitive approaches) but, instead, assumes that both behavior and thought are determined by multiple dialectical syntheses.

In our view, therapeutic exploration and change are primarily generated by (a) the synthesis of concept and experience that requires active exploration of contradictions that arise and (b) the construction of new meanings through differentiation and integration of multiple experiential sources. Becoming aware is neither a purely passive process of simply perceiving sense experience nor a radical construction of experience (Greenberg et al., 1993; Greenberg & Safran, 1987). Thought and emotions both play a role in experience. New, growth-oriented experience and behavior result from the dialectical interplay of two streams of consciousness: the slow conceptual-reasoning system and the less deliberate, but rapidly adaptive, action–emotion system.

REFERENCES

Beck, A. T. (1976). *Cognitive therapy and the emotional disorders.* New York: International Universities Press.

Bereiter, C. (1985). Towards a solution of the learning paradox. *Review of Educational Research, 55,* 201–226.

Bohart, A. (1993). Experiencing: The basis of psychotherapy. *Journal of Psychotherapy Integration, 3,* 51–68.

Chomsky, N. (1965). *Aspects of the theory of syntax.* Cambridge, MA: MIT Press.

Chomsky, N. (1987). *Knowledge of language: Its nature, origin, and use.* New York: Praeger.

Derrida, J. (1981). *"Outwork": Disseminations.* Chicago: University of Chicago Press.

Freud, S. (1900). *The interpretation of dreams* (Standard eds. 4 & 5). London: Hogarth Press.

Frijda, N. H. (1986). *The emotions.* Cambridge, England: Cambridge University Press.

Gendlin, E. T. (1962). *Experiencing and the creation of meaning: A philosophical and psychological approach to the subjective.* New York: Free Press of Glencoe.

Gendlin, E. T. (1964). A theory of personality change. In J. T. Hart & T. M. Tomlinson (Eds.), *New directions in client-centered therapy* (pp. 129–173). Boston: Houghton Mifflin.

Gendlin, E. T. (1968). The experiential response. In E. Hammer (Ed.), *Use of interpretation in therapy* (pp. 208–227). New York: Grune & Stratton.

Gendlin, E. T. (1981). *Focusing* (2nd ed.). New York: Bantam Books.

Gergen, K. (1985). The social constructionist movement in modern psychology. *American Psychologist, 40,* 266–275.

Gibson, J. (1979). *The ecological approach to visual perception.* Boston: Houghton Mifflin.

Greenberg, L. S., & Korman, L. (1993). Assimilating emotion into psychotherapy integration. *Journal of Psychotherapy Integration, 3,* 249–265.

Greenberg, L. S., Rice, L. N., & Elliott, R. (1993). *Facilitating emotional change: The moment by moment process.* New York: Guilford Press.

Greenberg, L. S., & Safran, J. D. (1984). Integrating affect and cognition: A perspective on the process of therapeutic change. *Cognitive Therapy and Research, 8,* 559–578.

Greenberg, L. S., & Safran, J. D. (1987). *Emotion in psychotherapy: Affect, cognition, and the process of change.* New York: Guilford Press.

Guidano, V. (1991). *The self in process.* New York: Guilford Press.

Hermans, H. J. M., Kempen, H. J. G., & van Loon, R. J. P. (1992). The dialogical self: Beyond individualism and rationalism. *American Psychologist, 47,* 23–33.

Hunt, J. McV. (1961). *Intelligence and experience*. New York: Ronald Press.

Kahneman, D., Slovic, P., & Tversky, A. (1982). *Judgement under uncertainty: Heuristics and biases*. Cambridge, England: Cambridge University Press.

Kant, I. (1965). *Critique of pure reason*. (N. Kemp Smith, Trans.). New York: Macmillan.

Kelly, G. (1955). *The psychology of personal constructs*. New York: Norton.

Lenin, V. I. (1977). On the question of dialectics. In K. Marx, F. Engels, & V. I. Lenin (Eds.), *On dialectical materialism*. Moscow, Russia: Progress Publishers. (Original work published 1915)

Mahoney, M. (1991). *Human change processes: The scientific foundations of psychotherapy*. New York: Guilford Press.

Newell, A., & Simon, H. A. (1972). *Human problem solving*. Englewood Cliffs, NJ: Prentice Hall.

Oatley, K., & Jenkins, J. M. (1992). Human emotions: Function and dysfunction. *Annual Review of Psychology, 43*, 55–85.

Ortega y Gasset, J. (1980). *Sobre la razón histórica* [Understanding historical reason]. Madrid, Spain: Alianza Editorial.

Pascual-Leone, J. (1969). *Cognitive development and cognitive style: A general psychological integration*. Unpublished doctoral dissertation, University of Geneva, Switzerland.

Pascual-Leone, J. (1970). A mathematical model for the transition rule in Piaget's developmental stages. *Acta Psychologica, 32*, 301–345.

Pascual-Leone, J. (1978). Compounds, confounds and models in developmental information processing: A reply to Trabasso and Foellinger. *Journal of Experimental Child Psychology, 26*, 18–40.

Pascual-Leone, J. (1980). Constructive problems for constructive theories: The current relevance of Piaget's work and a critique of information-processing simulation psychology. In R. Kluwe & H. Spada (Eds.), *Developmental models of thinking* (pp. 263–296). San Diego, CA: Academic Press.

Pascual-Leone, J. (1983). Growing into human maturity: Toward a metasubjective theory of adulthood stages. In P. B. Baltes & O. G. Brim (Eds.), *Life-span development and behavior* (Vol. 5, pp. 117–156). San Diego, CA: Academic Press.

Pascual-Leone, J. (1984). Attentional, dialectic and mental effort: Towards an organismic theory of life stages. In M. L. Commons, F. A. Richards, & G. Armon (Eds.), *Beyond formal operations: Late adolescence and adult cognitive development* (pp. 182–215). New York: Praeger.

Pascual-Leone, J. (1987). Organismic processes for neo-Piagetian theories: A dialectical causal account of cognitive development. *International Journal of Psychology, 22*, 531–570.

Pascual-Leone, J. (1989). An organismic process model of Witkin's field-dependence–independence. In T. Globerson & T. Zelniker (Eds.), *Cognitive style and cognitive development* (pp. 36–70). Norwood, NJ: Ablex.

Pascual-Leone, J. (1990a). Emotions, development and psychotherapy: A dialectical constructivist perspective. In J. Safran & L. Greenberg (Eds.), *Emotion, psychotherapy and change* (pp. 302–335). New York: Guilford Press.

Pascual-Leone, J. (1990b). An essay on wisdom: Toward organismic processes that make it possible. In R. J. Sternberg (Ed.), *Wisdom: Its nature, origins, and development* (pp. 244–278). Cambridge, England: Cambridge University Press.

Pascual-Leone, J. (1990c). Reflections on life-span intelligence, consciousness and ego development. In C. Alexander & E. Langer (Eds.), *Higher stages of human development: Perspectives on adult growth* (pp. 258–285). New York: Oxford University Press.

Pascual-Leone, J. (1991). A commentary on Boom and Juckes' "On the learning paradox." *Human Development, 34,* 288–293.

Pascual-Leone, J. (1993, July). *Mental capacity constraints in infants' motor development.* Invited address given at a meeting of the Interamerican Psychological Association, Santiago, Chile.

Pascual-Leone, J., & Baillargeon, R. (1994). Developmental measurement of mental attention. *International Journal of Behavioral Development, 17,* 161–200.

Pascual-Leone, J., & Goodman, D. (1979). Intelligence and experience: A neo-Piagetian approach. *Instructional Science, 8,* 301–367.

Pascual-Leone, J., & Irwin, R. (1994). Noncognitive factors in high-road/low-road learning: I. Modes of abstraction in adulthood. *Journal of Adult Development, 1,* 73–89.

Pascual-Leone, J., & Johnson, J. (1991). The psychological unit and its role in task analysis. A reinterpretation of object permanence. In M. Chandler & M. Chapman (Eds.), *Criteria for competence: Controversies in the assessment of children's abilities* (pp. 153–187). Hillsdale, NJ: Erlbaum.

Perls, F., Hefferline, R., & Goodman, P. (1951). *Gestalt therapy.* New York: Dell.

Piaget, J. (1970a). Piaget's theory. In P. H. Mussen (Ed.), *Carmichael's manual of child psychology* (Vol. 1, 3rd ed., pp. 703–732). New York: Wiley.

Piaget, J. (1970b). *Structuralism.* New York: Harper & Row.

Rice, L. N. (1974). The evocative function of the therapist. In D. A. Wexler & L. N. Rice (Eds.), *Innovations in client-centered therapy* (pp. 289–311). New York: Wiley.

Rice, L. N., & Saperia, E. (1984). A task analysis of the resolution of problematic reactions. In L. Rice & L. S. Greenberg (Eds.), *Patterns of change: Intensive analysis of psychotherapeutic process* (pp. 29–66). New York: Guilford Press.

Rogers, C. R. (1951). *Client-centered therapy.* Boston: Houghton Mifflin.

Rogers, C. R. (1959). A theory of therapy, personality, and interpersonal relationships as developed in the client-centered framework. In S. Koch (Ed.), *Psychology: The study of a science* (Vol. 3, pp. 184–256). New York: McGraw-Hill.

Sherrington, C. (1906). *The integrative action of the nervous system*. New Haven, CT: Yale University Press.

Sherrington, C. (1940). *Man and his nature*. Cambridge, England: Cambridge University Press.

Smolensky, D. (1988). On the proper treatment of connectionism. *Behavioral and Brain Sciences, 11*, 1–74.

Spelke, E. (1991). Physical knowledge in infancy: Reflections on Piaget's theory. In S. Carey & R. Gelman (Eds.), *The epigenesis of mind: Essays on biology and cognition* (pp. 133–169). Hillsdale, NJ: Erlbaum.

Spence, D. (1983). *Narrative truth and historical truth*. New York: Basic Books.

Stewart, L., & Pascual-Leone, J. (1992). Mental capacity constraints and the development of moral reasoning. *Journal of Experimental Child Psychology, 54*, 251–287.

Watson, J., & Rennie, D. (1994). Qualitative analysis of clients' subjective experience of significant moments during the exploration of problematic reactions. *Journal of Counseling Psychology, 41*, 500–509.

Watzlawick, P. (Ed.). (1984). *The invented reality: Contributions to constructivism*. New York: Norton.

Wexler, D. A., & Rice, L. N. (1974). *Innovations in client-centered therapy*. New York: Wiley.

III

THE NARRATIVE TURN

10

HERMENEUTICS, CONSTRUCTIVISM, AND COGNITIVE–BEHAVIORAL THERAPIES: FROM THE OBJECT TO THE PROJECT

ÓSCAR F. GONÇALVES

When the great Rabbi Israel Baal Shem-Tov saw misfortune threatening the Jews, it was his custom to go into a certain part of the forest to meditate. There he would light a fire, say a special prayer, and the miracle would be accomplished and the misfortune averted.

Later, when his disciple, the celebrated Magid of Mezritch, had occasion to intercede with heaven for the same reason, he would go to the same place in the forest and say: "Master of the Universe, Listen! I do not know how to light the fire, but I am still able to say the prayer." And again the miracle would be accomplished.

Still later, Rabbi Moshe-Leib of Sasov, in order to save his people once more, would go into the forest and say: "I do not know how to light the fire and I do not know the prayer, but I know the place and this must be sufficient."

Then it fell to Rabbi Israel of Rizhyn to overcome misfortune. Sitting in his armchair, his head in his hands, he spoke to God: "I am unable to light the fire and I do not know the prayer; I cannot even find the place in the forest. All I can do is to tell the story, and this must be sufficient." And it was sufficient. God made men because He loves stories. (Robert Murphy, 1960, quoted in Kopp, 1972, pp. 20–21)

After a century of remarkable psychotherapeutic explorations, it is time for psychotherapists to overtly acknowledge that we are therapists because we love stories too. Can the theories of literary criticism, there-

Appreciations are expressed to Michael J. Mahoney, Daniel B. Fishman, Dianne B. Arnkoff, and Robert A. Neimeyer for their comments on an earlier version of this chapter.

fore, help us in our task of understanding and promoting human change (Landau, 1984)? I believe the answer is yes, and it is the nuances of this response that I try to address in this chapter.

I begin with the assertion that life is a narrative and human beings are inherent narrators, storytellers, and, of course, participants in their own emerging plots. I discuss therapy as a rehearsing scenario for the construction and deconstruction of stories. I then introduce hermeneutics as an alternative to a basic dialogic tension between the narrative and narrator, object and subject, knower and known. Finally, I contrast three paradigms from the cognitive–behavioral tradition—behavioral, cognitive, and constructivist—in terms of their notions of textuality, selfhood, and ontology and epistemology. I argue that the constructivist paradigm provides a hermeneutic alternative that allows the conceptualization of humans as neither objects nor subjects but as *projects*—that is, embodied metaphors whose eminent task is to exist through understanding and to understand through existence (Gadamer, 1960/1975).

LIFE AS A NARRATIVE

Life is a narrative, a story coconstructed through an intensive dialectical interchange between individuals and their ecological niches. It is, however, a unique kind of narrative. It is a narrative without a clear-cut beginning and end. The chapters that comprise the narrative are frequently elusive, and the characters and figures often remain loosely defined. The meaning and structure of this narrative keeps changing through a series of strange, recursive loops and creative cycles (Hofstadter, 1979; Varela, 1984). Overall, the narrative resembles a dance, a complex and aesthetic series of movements without any other objective than the dance itself:

> Whatever we do in every domain, whether concrete (walking) or abstract (philosophical reflection), involves us totally in the body, for it takes place through our structural dynamics and through our structural interaction. Everything we do is a structural dance in the choreography of coexistence. (Maturana & Varela, 1987, p. 248)

Another distinctive quality of the human narrative is that it subsists even beyond our physical permanence as authors. We never leave this world, even when we do not live anymore; we simply stop constructing (Fischer, 1987).

But it is not only human life that has the distinctive characteristic that allows its conceptualization as a narrative. The evolution of all species can be regarded as the unfolding of a narrative (Landau, 1984). Evolutionary epistemologists have promoted the interesting idea that all living systems are theories of their environments (Weimer, 1977).

However, it becomes obvious that, as used by these researchers and in this chapter, the meaning of the concept of "theories" differs dramatically from the logical–propositional sense traditionally attached to it. In this chapter, *theories* refers to stories and metaphors—to aesthetic representations of environments. Like any other kind of scientific theory, the stories that living creatures have to tell are metaphorical narratives of their coevolution with their environments (cf. Gonçalves, 1988, 1994a, 1994b; Gonçalves & Craine, 1990; Howard, 1989; Kalechofsky, 1987; Lakoff, 1987; Lakoff & Johnson, 1980; Polkinghorne, 1988; Sarbin, 1986).

What makes us distinctively human is not, however, the fact that our lives can be conceived as narratives, but the fact that we are creative storytellers. That is, we can decenter from our own narratives and tell our own tales, as Fischer (1987) has observed: "the ultimate evolutionary development of substance to brain led to its ability to tell stories to itself about itself, and do so in the first person narrative form" (p. 347). Mair (1988, 1989) recently elaborated on this idea, proposing the understanding of the storytelling process not only as the central task for psychologists but also as the central methodology of psychological inquiry: The psychologist should be "a storyteller with a profound concern for what is involved in the stories that we live and the stories that we tell" (Mair, 1988, p. 127).

This storytelling capacity conveys upon humans their distinctive qualities. In the process of human narration, the individual is simultaneously the writer, the written, and the literary critic. According to Fischer (1987), it is precisely the emergence of a third-level intentional system that allows the beginning of the narrative in human beings:

> In the Narcissus motif, Narcissus recognizes himself in the reflection of a pool as an object: "Iste ego sum," "I am the one," he exclaims when seeing the moving lips of his mirror image but does not hear any speech. In this very moment, Narcissus becomes an *observer*. Were he to hold up another mirror which reflects him as a *subject* that is looking into the pool which reflects him as an object, then he would evolve from an observer to a *narrator*. (Fischer, 1987, p. 344)

Thus, with human beings, there is more than a narrative. There is a definite narrator, someone who moves between the position of the subject and object of the story construction. In the process of writing their tales, humans skillfully elude the distinction between themselves as objects and themselves as subjects; they turn into "projects," that is, objects thrown forth into a process of continuous, endless, and somehow unpredictable movement.

THERAPY AS A NARRATIVE

The therapeutic hour is again the reenactment of Narcissus's encounter with his own image. As in Ovid's *Metamorphoses*, the client becomes simultaneously the observer, the observed, and the narrator. Not infrequently, however, clients get caught in each of these levels of intentionality: regarding themselves as objects (i.e., first-order intentional systems); regarding themselves as *subjects* (i.e., second-order intentional systems); or, ideally, transcending the subject–object distinction and regarding themselves as projects (third-order intentional systems).

As Sarbin (1984) aptly reminded us, clients as well as clinicians are inveterate story makers and storytellers. Our function as therapists then becomes that of literary critic—interpreting the narrative of the client while coconstructing with him or her yet another story.

The conceptualization of psychotherapy as a narrative was evident from the very first theoretical and practical advances in the late nineteenth century. In describing the therapeutic methodology devised for the treatment of Anna O., Freud (1895/1967) acknowledged Breuer's and his own astonishment in the face of the discovery that the hysterical symptoms disappeared once the client was able to recollect, reexperience, and verbalize the narrative of the traumatic event. That is, it was the client's reconstruction of the narrative (i.e., catharsis) that would create the necessary conditions for the therapeutic cure. In claiming that the "unconscious is structured like a language," another psychoanalyst, Jacques Lacan (1977), gave a new impetus for the conceptualization of the therapeutic process as a linguistic phenomenon. Particularly inspired by Saussure's (1959) linguistic structuralism, Lacan viewed the clinical phenomenon as a text obeying the rules of a structural interplay between signifiers and signifieds. However, it was undoubtedly the behavioral conceptualization of the therapeutic process that finally introduced the possibility for operationalizing the clinical process in terms of a verbal interchange (Skinner, 1957). As early as 1962, Joel Greenspoon claimed that verbal behavior represents an excellent meeting ground for both the experimental and the applied psychologist.

Somewhat paradoxically, it was Carl Rogers (1957) who helped open the doors for linguistic analyses of the therapeutic text. The facilitative conditions postulated by Rogers as necessary and sufficient for therapeutic change (i.e., genuineness, unconditional positive regard, and empathy) encouraged an enthusiasm for process research focused on the structure of the therapeutic narrative from the most disparate perspectives and frameworks: in terms of attitudes (Patterson, 1984); skills (Highlen & Hill, 1984); topic change (Friedlander, Thibodeau, & Ward, 1985); intentions (Hill & O'Grady, 1985); task analysis (Safran, Greenberg, & Rice, 1988); and, more recently, metaphor (Angus & Rennie, 1988).

From a phenomenological and cognitive perspective, Rennie (1992)—in an intensive recall process of several therapeutic experiences—has demonstrated that in the process of telling a story, a client accomplishes several important cognitive functions: addressing tension associated with past events; reexperiencing and understanding the real feeling; ventilating these feelings, generating ideas that could contribute to self-understanding; developing a sense of control; and examining the operation of private processes. Therapists, then, are in the presence of what Rennie (1992) has referred to as the "client's agency"; "the individual's ability to think about thinking and feeling, and to enact ensuing thinking and action in response to that monitoring" (p. 225). In other words, the client turns into a narrator who is able to be the tale, to tell the tale, and to reflect on and reconstruct the tale. The narrative nature of the therapeutic interaction is also evident from the growing interest of psychotherapists in the use of imaginative literature (e.g., Fuhriman, Barlow, & Wanlass, 1989) and metaphors (Evans, 1988; Gonçalves & Craine, 1990).

In summary, psychotherapy is a well-established scenario for storytelling and story making. Not unlike Narcissus, clients begin to recognize themselves in the mirror of their stories, becoming simultaneously objects, subjects, and projects of themselves. In the protection of the therapeutic niche, they seek to conquer the versatility of a text.

HERMENEUTICS OF THE THERAPEUTIC NARRATIVE

Hermeneutics is the discipline concerned with the interpretation of the narrative. In Greek mythology, Hermes, son of Zeus and Maia, was a skilled herdsman and musician, as well as the messenger of the gods. He traveled everywhere, coding and decoding the messages of the pantheon narrative. Hermes was the interpreter, and hermeneutics is the science of his action—the interpretation (Arciero & Mahoney, 1989).

Since the inception of contemporary hermeneutics, it is no longer the text that is the object of analysis. Instead, the process of understanding has become the central topic of hermeneutic inquiry. In this sense, psychology and hermeneutics become allied sciences for the meta-epistemic task of understanding human understanding (e.g., Messer, Sass, & Woolfolk, 1988).

The dichotomy between the written (object of the narrative) and the writer (subject of the narrative) is transcended by the act of writing—the ground where the client projects his or her understanding. As Derrida (1982) pointed out, "for the written to be the written, it must continue to 'act' and to be legible even if what is called the author of the writing no longer answers for what he has written" (p. 316).

The fact that every knowledge construction is inseparable from the act of human interpretation—that is, human projection—has been well illustrated and clarified by Heinz von Foerster (1984):

"out there" there is no light and no color, there are only electromagnetic waves; "out there" there is no sound and no music, there are only periodic variations of the air pressure; "out there" there is no heat or no cold; there are only moving molecules with more or less mean kinetic energy, and so on. Finally, for sure, "out there" there is no pain. (p. 46)

In other words, "everything said is said by someone. Every reflection brings forth a world" (Maturana & Varela, 1987, p. 26), or, more metaphorically, "if I don't see I am blind, I am blind; but if I see I am blind, I see" (von Foerster, 1984, p. 43).

There are few doubts about the power of interpretation as a tool of change for both client and therapist. For example, in an intensive analysis of the process and outcome of a single case, Hill, Carter, and O'Farrell (1983) identified interpretations as one of the central ingredients of change. Likewise, in an interesting dialogue between the multimodal therapist Arnold Lazarus and the psychodynamic therapist Stanley Messer about the same clinical case, both therapists agreed on the crucial importance of taking into account and interpreting clients' scripts at different therapeutic points; both were "interested in examining Ms. Davis's scripts and saw these as guiding fictions or core constructs that must be addressed in psychotherapy" (Lazarus & Messer, 1988, p. 69).

To change is to project another story through the understanding of the existing dynamics between the narrative written and the author of the narrative. Hermeneutics therefore becomes an essential tool for conceptualizing the therapeutic narrative.

FROM THE BASIC DIALOGIC TO THE HERMENEUTIC ALTERNATIVE

The human conceptual system—our personal epistemology—is largely metaphorical (Lakoff & Johnson, 1980). M. Johnson (1987), in his interesting book *The Body in the Mind*, claimed that our metaphors—guides of our thoughts and actions—are embodied; that is, they are deeply rooted in our body experience. According to M. Johnson (1987) and Lakoff (1987), one of the most central metaphors of our conceptual system derives directly from our body experience. They refer to this metaphor as the *containing scheme* or *containing metaphor*—"a scheme consisting of a *boundary* distinguishing an *interior* from an *exterior*. The container scheme defines the most basic distinction between the *in* and the *out*" (Lakoff, 1987, p. 271).

This containing metaphor is perhaps in the origin of our dialogical and dichotomic way of conceptualizing human experience. Since early work on dialectics, we have learned that there is no thesis without a correspondent antithesis. Things only exist in terms of their negation.

Psychotherapists' construction of reality has remained deeply rooted in an essential dialogical distinction between subject and object, observer and observed, mind and body, process and outcome, and an infinite set of other "black-and-white" contrasts. Different moments in the history of psychology have witnessed an alternative dominance of the *in* or the *out* sides of the containing epistemologies of therapists. Contemporary hermeneutics—in trying to overcome the distinction between the narrative and the narrator, the writer and the reader—provides, I believe, an alternative to this basic dialogic.

Let me clarify the hermeneutic alternative with the help of distinctions introduced by Karl Popper (Popper & Eccles, 1977) between three different types of worlds: World 1, World 2, and World 3. *World 1* refers to the world of physical objects and phenomena, including all animate or inanimate objects as well as such physical phenomena as tension, movement, and energy. *World 2* is the psychological world of human emotions and thought processes, both conscious and unconscious. Finally, *World 3* is the world of human productions, both intellectual and physical. Furthermore, World 3, which is based on human language, results from the interaction between what I have chosen to designate as the "world of objectivity" (World 1) and the "world of subjectivity" (World 2).

According to Popper (Popper & Eccles, 1977), the construction of reality results from the interaction between these different types of worlds: As we create, we create ourselves through the creation. It is in this sense that the hermeneutic focus on the creation process can represent an alternative to the basic dialogic discussed above.

Table 1 shows the essential tensions of the basic dialogic and their corresponding hermeneutic alternatives. The three essential tensions lie between the world of objectivity and the world of subjectivity and can be explained along three central parameters: (a) *textuality*, the vantage point of analysis of the human narrative; (b) *selfhood*, the role of the self in the inquiry process; and (c) *epistemology and ontology*, the underlying conceptions of knowledge and existence. For each of these parameters,

TABLE 1
Essential Tensions of Dialogical Distinctions Made in
Constructions of Reality

| Tension | Paradigm | | |
	Behavioral	Cognitive	Constructivist
Textuality	Written	Writer	Act of writing
Selfhood	Object	Subject	Project
Epistemology & ontology	Absolutism	Absolutism & relativism	Dialecticism

the essential tension between the world of objectivity and the world of subjectivity is transcended by a hermeneutic alternative emphasizing the continuous construction and deconstruction of human projects (World 3, or the world of projectivity).

Several researchers have addressed similar trichotomies in describing metatheoretical assumptions of broader psychological or cognitive–behavioral communities (cf. Fishman, 1988; Lyddon, 1989; Packer, 1985; Packer & Addison, 1989; Pepper, 1942; Woolfolk, 1988). The successive paradigmatic shifts of cognitive–behavioral therapies correspond, I believe, to the evolution from a basic dialogic to a hermeneutic alternative—that is, from a textuality based on the written and the writer to a textuality based on the act of writing; from a selfhood based on the subject–object distinction to a selfhood based on the project; and from epistemology and ontology based on absolutism and relativism to a dialectical alternative (see, e.g., Gonçalves, 1989; Gonçalves & Machado, 1989; Guidano, 1987, 1988; Joyce-Moniz, 1989; Liotti & Reda, 1981; Mahoney, 1988a, 1988b; Mahoney & Gabriel, 1990).

Next, I describe the evolution of the cognitive–behavioral ideologies, contrasting what I believe are the three major paradigms of the cognitive–behavioral tradition: the behavioral paradigm, the cognitive paradigm, and the emergent constructivist paradigm. I contrast each of these in terms of the three essential tensions presented above. I also discuss examples of the implications for research derived from the metapsychological assumptions of each paradigm.

THE BEHAVIORAL PARADIGM AND THE WORLD OF OBJECTIVITY

Behaviorism is the land of objectivity. In the opening statement of his behavioral manifesto, John Watson (1913) claimed that "psychology as the behaviorist views it is a purely objective experimental branch of natural science" (p. 158). In Popperian (Popper & Eccles, 1977) terms, the behavioral paradigm is primarily and almost exclusively focused on the material world of physical objects and phenomena. "The mind is what the body does," as B. F. Skinner (1987, p. 784) has claimed. As noted by Mahoney (1988b), and paraphrased below, three central theses underlie the objectivist conception of the behavioral paradigm:

1. An objective, separate "real world" lies beyond the organism and exists independently of being perceived;
2. True or valid knowledge about the world is ultimately rendered through sensory experience; and

3. Such knowledge can be totally separated from the individual knower.

As several surveys of American psychotherapists have repeatedly demonstrated, these objectivist assertions continue to orient a small but very active group of behaviorists (e.g., Mahoney, 1984; Mahoney & Gabriel, 1990). The objectivist conception of the behavioral paradigm has implications for the way the text of the human narrative is analyzed, the role of the self in this analysis, and the underlying conceptions of existence and knowledge.

Textuality

By *textuality*, I refer to the vantage point for an analysis of the human narrative. As discussed above, there are at least three important elements in human textuality: (a) the text, or the written; (b) the author, or the writer; and (c) the authoring process, or the act of writing. The behavioral approach to human textuality is similar to the objectivist approach to text analysis. Objectivists regard the text as finished—a physical entity separate from and independent of the writer. The objective of the literary critic then becomes that of an external and objective observer, aiming to classify and identify rules. Thus, from the objectivist position, the text is not an idiosyncratic phenomenon but an objective entity that can only be the object of a nomothetic inquiry. In other words, objectivists "treat a first-person report as a datum rather than as a report of a datum" (Zuriff, 1986, p. 697).

Again, Skinner (1974) has clearly illustrated the behavioral approach to human textuality:

> The words and sentences of which a language is composed are said to be tools used to express meanings, thoughts, ideas, propositions, emotions, needs, desires, and many other things in or on the speaker's mind. A much more productive view is that verbal behavior is behavior. (pp. 98–99)

Furthermore, the grammar of human narrative, ruled by the laws of operant conditioning, is disembodied from the writer. In summary, for the behavioral paradigm, the narrator is a mere epiphenomenon of the narrative. It exists by itself, independent from the author or the authoring process.

Selfhood

Selfhood refers to the dimension of the self that is the object of analysis: self as subject, self as object, or, alternatively, self as project. It was William James (1890) who, for the first time, identified two central dimensions of tension in this selfhood process: the self as object and as subject. The self as object refers to the *me*—the empirical self, or the observed, whereas the self as subject is the *I*—the knower or the active observer. The nature of the inseparable relationship between these two dimensions of selfhood generates a third and more viable alternative—the self as a project: "To reconcile 'I' with 'me', [I develop] the self as a text . . . that is simultaneously written and read. Reading parts from this text corresponds to 'me' and the writer of the text to 'I' " (Lehrer, 1988, p. 196).

Different resolutions of the essential tension between subject and object have been apparent throughout the development of psychology and, particularly, in the course of cognitive–behavioral history. Beginning with the inception of the behavioral paradigm, the self as subject was identified as an "enemy," whereas the self as object became an instrumental focus of analysis. In *Science and Human Behavior*, Skinner (1957) referred to the self as an artifact used to represent a system of responses that are functionally related. Therefore, it is the *me* side of selfhood, the objective side, that is the focus of analysis for the behavioral paradigm. Again, the words of Skinner (1974) are particularly clarifying:

> A person is not an originating agent; he is a locus, a point at which many genetic and environmental conditions come together in a joint effect. As such, he remains unquestionably unique. (p. 185)

Self-knowledge, then, shifts dramatically from the introspective approach to a so-called behavioral analysis of the particulars of behavior and its contingencies.

In summary, according to the behavioral paradigm, the self is regarded as an object, an empirical self—the *me*. It is real and material, it is clearly located outside, and its uniqueness and idiosyncratic nature can be externally approached.

Ontology and Epistemology

Whereas ontology is concerned with the nature of existence, epistemology concerns itself with the nature of knowledge. As has been recently demonstrated by several constructivists (e.g., Arciero & Mahoney, 1989), knowledge is inseparable from existence, and existence is inseparable from knowledge. Therefore, ontology and epistemology are two sides of the same coin.

The epistemological–ontological level of analysis is more or less equivalent to what Lakatos (1974) defined as the "metaphysical hard core"—the basic assumptions guiding the hypothesis-generation strategies of any research program. According to several developmental theorists, an essential tension can be identified between two opposite ontologies and epistemologies: absolutist versus relativist. An alternative synthesis to this dichotomous antithesis is represented by what is most commonly referred to as *dialectical* ontology and epistemology (see Basseches, 1984; Kitchner, 1983; Kramer, 1983; Riegel, 1973).

Broadly speaking, absolutist ontology assumes the existence of truth as universal, fixed, and unchanged; there is a natural order that can be apprehended objectively by the senses. Relativism, however, distrusts any search for order and knowledge; there is no objective reality, and there are as many truths as there are individuals. Finally, a dialectical position believes in the search for more appropriate forms of knowledge, keeping in mind that these forms should always be open to revision and replacement in the direction of never-ending, more complex models (Gonçalves & Machado, 1989; Kelly, 1955).

There seems to be little doubt that, at the ontological–epistemological level, the behavioral paradigm assumes the existence of a singular, stable, and external reality revealed through the senses—that is, that "there is an objective reality that is absolutely knowable and known" (Kitchner, 1983, p. 226). In fact, the extreme dualism set forth in the behavioral paradigm has imposed a pervasive conception of an absolute, or observer-free, knowledge (Mahoney, 1991).

Skinner (1987) complained about the shift of psychology from an objective science of behavior to a more relativist–subjective approach, blaming three major forces: humanist psychology, cognitive psychology, and psychotherapy. In a so-called reconstruction of behaviorism, Zuriff (1986) clearly summarized the absolutist nature of the paradigm:

> The first premise in the conceptual reconstruction of behaviorism is that psychology is a natural science. Two important corollaries are: (1) Science, and psychology in particular, must be empirically based; (2) Science, and psychology in particular, must be objective. (p. 687)

Research Implications

By rejecting the major assumption of internalism and subjectivism, behaviorists refuse to approach the research of therapeutic phenomena through the lens of any hypothetical construct. Aiming to bridge the gap between the consulting room and the laboratory, behaviorists have translated therapist and client responses into verbal and nonverbal operational microunits seen as obeying the same learning principles as any other response. The linear effects of different verbal and nonverbal skills and their use in the therapeutic process then became the major task for therapy-process research (Gonçalves, Ivey, & Langdell, 1988). This movement was largely prompted by Greenspoon's (1955) research on the differential effects of the sounds "mm-hmm" and "huh-uh" on the frequency of plural and nonplural nouns. Generally, the results showed that the "mm-hmm" increased the frequency of both plural and nonplural nouns, whereas "huh-uh" produced a decrease in the amount of plural responses. These results were partially replicated in a clinical setting when Ullman, Krasner, and Collins (1961) demonstrated how head nodding and verbal encouragement ("mmm-hum") to emotional messages produce greater improvement in clients in group therapy.

Research studies like these reflect the behavioral enthusiasm for operationalizing the therapeutic process in terms of stimulus–response conditions. The therapist is seen as providing certain discriminative stimuli for the client's responses, and vice-versa. In summary, the same principles of any other learning situation could be identified as ruling the therapeutic narrative.

From the research conducted within this paradigm, let me illustrate certain features of a behavioral approach with the intensive single-case study conducted by Hill, Carter, and O'Farrell (1983). To study the immediate effects of a therapist's verbal responses on client behavior, Hill et al. conducted a sequential analysis of 12 sessions with a female neurotic client. Only the two first "client units" following each therapist intervention were analyzed. The research showed that the client tended to respond more with description after closed questions were asked and was least likely to do so after direct guidance and interpretation. The client's experiencing (i.e., affective exploration of feelings, behaviors, or reactions about self or problems) most often followed silence and was least likely to occur after closed questions were asked. Insight, although rare in this case, most often followed the therapist's silence, open questions, or confrontation. However, Hill et al. recognized that these data, although confirming the hypothetical relationship advanced in the literature on skills training, added little or nothing to their understanding of the case.

Hill (1984), in a personal account of her evolution as a process researcher, disclosed her disappointment with and subsequent distancing from the behavioral paradigm:

> (a) there is no truth; rather there are multiple realities which are dependent on the vantage points, psychological filters, and predefined contours of the mind; (b) clinical phenomena are elusive and reactive; (c) clinical problems are often intractable; (d) human behavior should be studied holistically rather than in a piecemeal fashion; and (e) cause and effect relationships or linear causality concepts may be of limited utility at this point in our understanding of human behavior. (p. 105)

Hill's words illustrate the tension of the transition and the crises of the paradigmatic shift to cognition and the world of subjectivity.

THE COGNITIVE PARADIGM AND THE WORLD OF SUBJECTIVITY

If behaviorism represents the land of objectivity, then cognitivism typifies the world of subjectivity. More than 30 years have passed since the publication of George Miller's (1956) seminal article "The Magical Number Seven, Plus or Minus Two: Some Limits on Our Capacity for Processing Information." His article marked the first time that someone had reflected through rigorous analysis on the possibilities and limits of the subject as an information-processing system. It was part of a symposium on information processing held at the Massachusetts Institute of Technology in September 1956. Other presenters were Allen Newell, Herbert Simon, and Noam Chomsky. Scientists from different disciplines (i.e., psychology, computer science, linguistics, anthropology, and mathematics) were joining together to reflect on the inner world of the information processor. The concepts of the subject and his or her knowing processes were central to the birth of the cognitive sciences, triggering a "cognitive revolution" whose limits still cannot be fathomed (Gardner, 1987).

With the cognitive revolution, the focus of psychological inquiry shifted once more to the inner side of experience—the subjective experience. The cognitive revolution soon spread across several areas of psychology. However, a particularly fertile area for growth was in the clinical realm, especially in the so-called cognitive or cognitive–behavioral therapies. Recent surveys of American clinicians have illustrated the changing orientation of psychotherapy, and behavior therapy in particular, to this world of subjectivity. Below, I highlight some of the data recently obtained by Mahoney and colleagues (e.g., Mahoney & Craine, 1989; Mahoney & Gabriel, 1990; Mahoney, Norcross, Prochaska, & Missar, 1989) that are relevant to this discussion.

First, cognitive therapies are becoming increasingly popular approaches. Second, a differentiation within behaviorism and cognitivism has generated a cognitive–behavioral group, with an increasing tendency to acknowledge the agency and power of the organism. Third, there is strong consensus among clinicians from different theoretical orientations that significant change is closely associated with changes in an individual's self-system.

The emergence of self-control or self-management therapies was probably the first significant development of the increasing attention paid to the role of the self and personal agency. As acknowledged by Mahoney and Arnkoff (1978) in an early review of the cognitive revolution in therapy, "prior to this, the prevalent and explicit assumption of behaviorists was one of environmental determinism" (p. 690). From the unidirectional and even bidirectional notions of determinism, cognitivists advanced to a triadic or reciprocal alternative, according to which "behavior, cognitive and other individual factors, and environmental influences all operate as interlocking determinants that affect each other bidirectionally" (Bandura, 1985, p. 83).

The dramatic growth of the cognitive therapies during the past few decades has been such that it is difficult to approach the phenomenon with a well-established taxonomic coherence (Dobson & Block, 1988; Gonçalves, 1989; Mahoney & Lyddon, 1988). Nevertheless, four major groups currently illustrate the mainstream of what I refer to here as the *cognitive paradigm*: covert conditioning therapies (e.g., Cautela, 1967), self-control therapies, problem-solving therapies (e.g., D'Zurilla & Goldfried, 1971), and cognitive restructuring therapies (e.g., Beck, 1963; Ellis, 1962; Meichenbaum, 1969).

Despite their differences within the cognitive paradigm, all of these groups seem to align with the four central themes identified long ago by Mahoney (1977):

> (1) The human organism responds primarily to cognitive representations of its environments rather than to those environments per se; (2) These cognitive representations are functionally related to the process and parameters of learning; (3) Most human learning is cognitively mediated; (4) Thoughts, feelings and behaviors are causally interactive. (pp. 7–8)

Mahoney's assertions launched the field for a new reading of the therapeutic narrative in terms of textuality, selfhood, and ontology and epistemology.

Textuality

As stated above, three important elements can be identified in human textuality: the writer, the written, and the act of writing. In the behavioral paradigm, the focus of inquiry was on the written—a narrative separated from the writer. But in the cognitive paradigm, the narrative becomes a mere epiphenomenon, and the narrator becomes the central focus of inquiry. It is assumed that no text exists independently from the idiosyncratic and historical circumstances of the living theory that the narrator portrays. To read and understand a text is to decode the message of a narrator: his or her personal and scientific theories revealed through the metaphors of any chosen narrative style—romantic, realist, or surrealist. Each style more or less implicitly and potently reveals the narrator. The literary critic, then, becomes the authorized epistemological interpreter of the narrator's phenomenology, keeping in mind that he or she is a storyteller too.

Through storytelling, the narrator reveals his or her constructions of reality that are independent of, although sometimes correlated with, so-called objective reality. Much like the Stoic philosopher Epictetus, cognitivism assumes that "we are not disturbed by things, but by our views of things." The centrality of the narrator and his or her cognitive processes is apparent in the following observation made by Albert Ellis (1985):

> People largely bring their Beliefs to A (activating events); and they prejudicially view or experience As in the light of these biased Beliefs (expectations, evaluations) and also in the light of their emotional consequences (Cs) (desires, preferences, wishes, motivations, tastes, disturbances). Therefore, humans virtually never experience A without B and C, but they also rarely experience B and C without A. (p. 315)

In other words, any text holistically reveals the author's cognitions and emotional processes. No narrative can stand independently of the belief system of its author.

Through the storytelling process, the narrator reveals his or her models of reality, inner dialogue, cognitive filters, and distortions and beliefs. For the therapist, like the literary critic, the task is to correct the author's constructions to reestablish the rule and order of objectivity and functionality. In summary, in the cognitive paradigm, the narrator is always the central theme of the narrative. Every narrative is about a narrator and, as such, is extensively autobiographical.

Selfhood

I have argued that an essential tension can be identified between self as object and self as subject. This tension constitutes the basis of the dynamic interchange between personal and social constructions—"it is the tension between the social order and the individual existence that constitutes the real 'identity crises' " (Broughton, 1986, p. 159). Additionally, I have defended the idea that according to the behavioral paradigm the self is an object, something real and material that can be externally approached.

The cognitive revolution introduced a radical change in the conceptions of selfhood. The *I*, the self as subject, and the knower became the focus of attention. As was recognized by Broughton (1986) in an insightful analysis of the history, psychology, and ideology of self, more recent years have been characterized by a resurgence of what has been called *self psychology*. The cognitivist approach was central to this resurgence, and soon the literature was invaded by a multitude of concepts qualified by the *self* prefix (e.g., self-esteem, self-concept, self-efficacy, self-control, self-regulation, self-knowledge, self-awareness, or any other of the 250 *self* compound words that can be found in most dictionaries).

Continuity, distinctiveness, and volition (James, 1890) assure the existence of the self as an entity, whose autonomy, independence, and determinacy over the environment constitute its distinctive nature. The autonomy and power of an independent self, so treasured in the North American psychological tradition, is well illustrated in the Stoicist title that Albert Ellis (1988) chose for one of his recent books: *How to Stubbornly Refuse to Make Yourself Miserable About Anything, Yes Anything!* In his introduction, Ellis further clarified that "this book shows how to be an honest hedonist and individualist—to be true to thine own self first" (1988, pp. 11–12).

Because of its cognitive and symbolic capacities, the self becomes a powerful source of influence (an author) not only of the individual's own processes (behavioral, cognitive, and emotional), but also of the ecological niches that he or she continuously selects and constructs. The self is the central agency, the author legitimating the existence of disparate characters portrayed by several *mes*:

> Theories that seek to explain human behavior as solely the product of external rewards and punishments present a truncated image of human nature because people possess self-directive capabilities that enable them to exercise some control over their thoughts, feelings, and actions by the consequences they produce for themselves. (Bandura, 1985, p. 335)

Summing up, three central assumptions seem to underlie cognitive conceptions of selfhood. First, the self is a structural coherent whole composed by the generalizations that the individual draws about himself or herself. Second, the self is an autonomous and independent entity influencing both personal experiences and environmental circumstances. Finally, the self tends to remain fairly stable during adulthood. For the cognitive paradigm, the self is regarded as a subject—an active, cognitive, and information-processing structure—whose autonomy, independence, and stability are conditions for permanence and power of the individual in the evolutionary narrative.

Ontology and Epistemology

The metaphysical hard core of the behavioral paradigm was said to be characterized by an absolutist ontology and epistemology, assuming the existence of truth as universal, fixed, and unchanged as well as the existence of a natural order revealed to us by the senses. The position of cognitivism is particularly complex at this level. Cognitivism seems to alternate between the uncertainty of relativism and the security of absolutism. That is, cognitivists "sell" to their clients a relativist ontology and epistemology while endorsing for themselves an absolutist ideology. Generally speaking, cognitivists tend to subscribe to a relativist ontology and epistemology by claiming that individual perceptions, representations, and constructions are determinants over reality and that there are as many truths as there are individual information-processing systems.

Albert Ellis (1985), for instance, claimed that the central task of rational emotive therapy is to liberate clients from their innate tendencies to think absolutistically in the direction of more relativist ways of approaching reality. This is done by attacking and challenging all sorts of "musturbatory" beliefs expressed in the absolutist language of dogmatic "shoulds," "oughts," and "musts."

The aim of rational emotive therapy is the attainment of a mostly relativist conception of self-centered rationality. It is a means of helping people achieve their own goals and purposes:

> If the philosophy of musturbation is at the core of much psychological disturbance, then what philosophy is characteristic of psychological health? RET [rational emotive therapy] theory argues that a philosophy of relativism or "desiring" is a central feature of psychologically healthy humans. (Dryden & Ellis, 1988, p. 223)

The apparent solipsism of the cognitive paradigm brings cognitivists into a difficult situation. Not unlike adolescents attaining formal thought, cognitivists face what different authors have called the "plurality of solitudes" (Sartre, 1965), the "vertigo of relativity" (Berger & Luckman, 1966), or "epistemological loneliness"—"the initial recognition of this uncertainty principle is not . . . necessarily equivalent to its whole-hearted acceptance, nor is it all obvious how one is to cope with, let alone take pleasure in, the ultimate relativity" (Chandler, 1975, p. 172).

To cope with this epistemological loneliness, the cognitive paradigm shifted back to the regressive solution of an absolutist ontology and epistemology. Clients' constructions—labeled as unreal, irrational, and distorted—became the target for change according to the canons of objective reality portrayed in the therapeutic drama by the absolute authority of the therapist. Whether through an emphasis on rational thinking (e.g., Ellis, 1962), empirical testing (e.g., Beck, Rush, Shaw, & Emery, 1979), or repetition (e.g., Meichenbaum, 1977), cognitive therapists aim for a better match between clients' subjective constructions and objective reality (cf. Hollan & Beck, 1986).

Thus, like adolescents, cognitive therapists get caught in the epistemological trap of formal thought. The acknowledgment of the primacy of a thinking and individual self necessarily implies the relativist and subjective nature of existence and knowledge. The epistemological crises of loneliness of a potential solipsist attitude arouse a tendency to search for a better equilibrative structure. In cognitivism this equilibrium is maintained through a regressive movement into the lands of absolutism, where the authority figure of the therapist corrects the subjective views of the client from a more objective vantage point, by means of rational disputation, inner repetition, or empirical testing. Chandler's (1975) words about the potential dangers concerning the regressive movements of antirelativist maneuvers are enlightening:

> The difficulty with . . . familiar responses to the vertigo and isolation of relativism is that they all represent attempts to deal with the multiplicity of perspectives by denying their legitimacy out of hand. Whether through cliquishness and stereotype, religious or scientific intolerance, or simply by adopting a level of abstraction which syncretistically sacrifices important dimensions of difference, all these partial solutions appear essentially regressive and interfere with further growth and development. (p. 175)

Research Implications

Inspired by the impetus of the cognitive revolution, several researchers have attempted to decode and clarify the covert mechanisms of the therapeutic process. This movement has been illustrated in process research by studies on conceptual strategies (e.g., Strohmer & Chiodo, 1984), attitudes and beliefs (e.g., Stone & Kelly, 1983), perceptions (e.g., Elliott, Barker, Caskey, & Pistrang, 1982), and intentions (e.g., Hill & O'Grady, 1985). Among the voluminous research developed in this domain, the program of research developed by Jack Martin at the University of Western Ontario (Martin, 1984, 1985; Martin, Martin, Meyer, & Slemon, 1986) seems particularly illustrative. Martin and his colleagues have presented a cognitive mediational paradigm in which therapists' behaviors are not assumed to directly and linearly affect clients' behaviors. Instead, each therapist's actions are processed by each client's internal cognitive structures, and vice versa. Therapists' actions proceed from their intentions and are hypothesized to be products of their perceptions of clients' behaviors. These perceptions are themselves products of therapists' procedural and declarative knowledge structures as well as of their cognitive-processing mechanisms. In the same way, clients' intentions and actions result from the perceptions that result from their own declarative and procedural knowledge and from their cognitive-processing skills.

To test some of the model's underlying assumptions, Martin et al. (1986) carried out an intensive analysis of 10 counseling dyads engaged in time-limited therapy. Three times during the therapy process, data were collected on therapist and client behavior. Additionally, during the recall sessions the researchers gathered data on therapists' intentions, clients' perceptions of therapist's intentions, and clients' cognitive processing. The main objective of this research was to analyze the level of consistency at each point of the therapy chain: therapist intention and therapist behavior, client perception of therapist intention and behavior, and client cognitive processing and client behavior. Two main results are worth mentioning here. First, the level of consistency was lower for the interpersonal cognitive (i.e., therapist intention and client cognitive processing) than for the interpersonal behavior (i.e., therapist behavior and client behavior) or the intrapersonal cognitive behavior (i.e., client cognitive processing and client behavior). Second, therapists' ratings of therapy effectiveness were found to be significantly influenced by the level of consistency across different elements of the chain. In summary, this research illustrated the cognitive claim that a consistency between cognition and behaviors is fundamental for the coherence of the therapeutic process. Martin's research program showed how, to understand the dynamics of the therapeutic narrative, therapists need to shift toward the inner and subjective dimension of clients' experiencing by focusing on clients' perceptions, conceptualizations, hypothesis generation, and intentions.

Since the cognitive revolution, the therapeutic narrative has been thought to be incomplete without a detailed account of what is going on inside both epistemic subjects of the clinical enterprise—the client and the therapist. Recently, however, some advocates of the cognitive paradigm have claimed the need to move one step further in the inquiry by studying the personal epistemology underlying therapeutic cognitions and actions. Once more, Jack Martin (1988) portrayed this welcome and refreshing tendency in research on the relationship between therapists' and clients' scientific and personal theories:

> Inquiry into the personal theories of clients, counselors, and researchers of counseling may help to clarify existing relationships between scientific theories and practical wisdom in counseling. (p. 261)

It was this shift from an information-processing model to an epistemic model that marked the transition from the cognitive to the constructivist paradigm.

CONSTRUCTIVISM AND THE WORLD OF PROJECTIVITY

The existing tension between the material world of objectivity (portrayed by behaviorism) and the mental world of subjectivity (portrayed by cognitivism) is transcended by the "world of projectivity," which is outlined in the constructivist paradigm. By *projectivity* I refer to the world of human constructions, both intellectual and physical.

The dichotomy between mental and physical phenomena, subject and object, is overcome by "transcendent structures." As we have learned from physics, this transcendence is achieved by the entropic notion of energy, defining an unbounded and "potential" world (Pribram, 1986). That is, humans are potential sources of energy that constantly materialize and dematerialize into projects. Projects are energy thrown forth in the vacuum tubes of life scenarios. The materialization and dematerialization of energy accomplished through individual and social projects originates the world of projectivity. It is to this world of energy that the constructive spectacles are turned. Thus, for constructivists, the focus is on the potentiality, that is, the efficiency and functionality of human energy. As Pribram (1986) explained, "energy is not material, only transformable into matter. It is measured by the amount of work that can be accomplished by using it and the efficiency of its use depends on its organization as measured by its entropy" (p. 516).

More than 30 years have now passed since the beginnings of the cognitive revolution. There is currently some evidence that a constructivist revolution is under way in the cognitive sciences, and in cognitive therapy in particular (e.g., Mahoney, 1991). In this context, the term *constructivism* has been used to refer to "a family of theories that share the assertion that human knowledge and experience entail a (pro)active participation of the individual" (Mahoney, 1988b, p. 2).

Even though a considerable level of diversification is already apparent in the constructivist paradigm, four central assumptions can be identified as its major metatheoretical commonalities (e.g., Gonçalves, 1989, 1994a; Gonçalves & Craine, 1990; Gonçalves & Ivey, 1993; Guidano, 1987, 1991; Guidano & Liotti, 1983; Ivey, 1986; Ivey & Gonçalves, 1988; Ivey, Gonçalves, & Ivey, 1989; Joyce-Moniz, 1985; Kegan, 1982; Kelly, 1955; Liotti, 1986; Mahoney, 1980, 1988a, 1988b, 1991; G. J. Neimeyer & Neimeyer, 1987; R. A. Neimeyer, 1986):

1. Proactive cognition: Human knowledge processes entail an anticipatory construction. Reality is projected by the individual knower, and we construct reality through a process of embodied understanding.
2. Morphogenic nuclear organization: As stated above, energy is entropic (i.e., it has structure). That is, the potential free-floating energy of human projectivity originates a hierarchical structural organization with more explicit and tacit levels of knowing.
3. Humans are metaphors of the environment: Humans do not have theories of their environments; they are those theories. At least at the more tacit level of structural organization, human knowledge is an analogical embodiment—

"knowledge is basically an emotional and motor activity providing a global and immediate apprehension of reality" (Guidano, 1991). That is, humans are not scientists (in the traditional sense of the term); humans, as well as all living creatures, are artists—aesthetic representations of their environments.

4. Developmental nature: Knowledge entails a process of structural differentiation operating by a continuous assimilation and accommodation in the direction of more complex, integrated, and viable structures.

In summary, by emphasizing the energetic nature of human existence, constructivists aim for a therapy that is much more teleonomic than teleological, where the objective is to "throw forth" the client into a process of continuous and endless movement, opening her or him for more and more change rather than defining the limits of the change. As stated elsewhere, "the best metaphors are those that find their own way of construction and deconstruction inside our clients, like a kaleidoscope assuming new and ever growing meanings" (Gonçalves & Craine, 1990, p. 147). The constructive conceptualizations outlined above put into radical new terms the issues of textuality, selfhood, and ontology and epistemology.

Textuality

In terms of human textuality, I have shown that a fundamental tension exists between an emphasis on either the written or the writer. That is, whereas behaviorists approach the text as an entity separated from the writer, cognitivists are almost exclusively concerned with the writer. This essential tension can be transcended through a hermeneutic alternative of focusing simultaneously on the writer and the written by switching the emphasis to the common structure represented by the act of writing.

As stated above, constructivists perceive humans as theories of their environments; that is, individuals are embodied metaphors that exist through understanding. Alternatively, contemporary hermeneutics contends that "understanding is not something we chose to do, but instead our understanding is who and what we are" (E. A. Johnson, 1989). The act of writing is thus an act of projecting our own understanding. Understanding is not something that exists inside or outside an individual but, instead, is his or her own action. The individual understands the world through the dissemination of his or her own writing. The thematic narrative of his or her writing thus becomes the very condition of existence.

The centrality of action so akin to the constructive paradigm was also central to the developmental formulations of Jean Piaget (1975/1985), who claimed that to know an object is to act on it. By the same token then, change becomes the action of projecting—that is, of changing one's understanding through a new coordination of actions. As constructivists have repeatedly argued, human cognition is basically a motor rather than a sensory system: "Human brain activities involve powerful *feedforward mechanisms* that proactively orchestrate expectation/intention and action/experience" (Mahoney, 1988b, p. 6). For constructivists, human actions are processes of questioning (R. A. Neimeyer, 1988).

The concept of textuality focused on the act of writing is, I believe, central to modern European conceptualizations of superstructuralism and poststructuralism illustrated in the writings of, among others, Derrida, Foucault, Saussure, and Lyotard (cf. Dews, 1987; Harland, 1987). According to this tradition, "man is to be defined by his outward language rather than by his inward powers of mind" (Harland, 1987, p. 11). Derrida (1982), the key figure of deconstructivist philosophy, claimed that writing is a process by which the author disseminates the constantly changing nature of his or her understanding—constructing and deconstructing new meanings by transcending any fixed relationship between signifiers and signifieds. That is, by the act of writing, we continuously actualize new projects of existence and understanding.

Creation, change, and development are thus completely different from the contemplative Narcissistic strategies of self-reflection: "Narcissus has never been a narrator. Narrators do not keep on staring at their own reflection once they have pointed out: 'Isto ego sum' " (Bronnimann, 1987, p. 351). We change by changing the nature of our writing and by trying out new projects, new ways of understanding. We then face the continuous movement of the hermeneutic circle—understanding through writing and writing as a way of understanding, acknowledging "the positive necessity of prejudices," and striving to remain open both to seeing one's own prejudices and to trying on others' (E. A. Johnson, 1989).

In summary, the tension between the writer and the written can be transcended by a hermeneutic alternative of a circular movement in which the act of writing is seen simultaneously as a means of projecting our own understanding and as a way of trying out new ways of understanding. Therapy, then, becomes not a way of reading and telling stories but a setting in which new texts can be projected into individual and social existence. This central theme of the hermeneutic alternative in therapy has been well captured by Guidano (1987):

> A life theme is something dynamically constructed day by day and
> year by year. It is based upon the events by which the individual

has scaffolded his/her transitions, the way he/she has interpreted and dealt with them, and the consequences of this process. The results of these choices and actions, in turn, become events to be further synthesized in an even more comprehensive image of self and world, revealing to the individual with growing clearness how compulsory and unrepeatable is the trajectory of his/her past life. (p. 207)

Selfhood

The hermeneutic alternative to the traditional dualist tension between self as object and self as subject is provided by the notion of *self as project*—the potential world of entropic energy. Both the objective and subjective approaches to selfhood have been questioned by the neo-Darwinian and poststructuralist ideologies, which assert that subject and object are codependent and historically bounded by the social constructions of a given time and place. In this sense, the notion of self is inseparable from social constructions, and every self is a self in relationship. In fact, the looking-glass effect of social interaction is the origin of individual differentiation. Therefore, every self is a movement, an energetic interplay, between the individual and his or her cultural niche. The individual is inseparable from the individual project that he or she actualizes. In turn, this individual project is inseparable from the social constructions of his or her culture.

By questioning the notion of the self as an entity, the constructivist paradigm opens the door to understanding the elusive nature of structural organization (i.e., structures are energy in continuous transformation) and, necessarily, to the deconstruction of either an objective or subjective self. As has been stated elsewhere, the objective of the therapeutic enterprise thus becomes one of melting the boundaries between a self-sufficient self and the so-called objective reality by having people experience "more fully their basic oneness—their ontological and epistemological solidarity with the environment" (Ivey & Gonçalves, 1988, p. 412).

Constructivism firmly opposes the empiricist philosophy of objective reality and the idealism of subjective ideas. Both approaches labor on the common conceptual theme of equating reality with material things and the individual with mental processes (Harland, 1987). In the constructivist paradigm, the self can be equated with an authoring system that projects a character and infers the authorship from the character created. In the narrative of self-structure, there are characters in search of their author: "It's a mixing of the parts, according to which you who act your own part become the puppet of yourself" (Pirandello, quoted in Lehrer, 1988, p. 195).

Guidano (1987) clarified the constructive position by emphasizing two central elements in selfhood processes that are worth summarizing at this point. The first is that self-knowledge is inseparable from the knowledge of reality. All information about the world necessarily implies information about the self, and, as such, the conception of self is inseparable from our actions on reality. That is, we exist through the implementation of our projects, and we infer our sense of continuity through self-referential synthesis of these projects—the acting and experiencing *I* is always one step ahead of the current appraisal of the situation (Guidano, 1991). Second, the individual self is inseparable from a self in relationship. The self emerges through the looking-glass effect provided by the interpersonal nature of our existence. We learn how to become a self by the way that others react to the implementation of our own projects. An analogical self is thus continuously constructed and deconstructed on the basis of the emotionality experienced in the process of establishing, maintaining, and breaking these relationships. That is, the self is a transformational structure that is maintained through continuous "projective" actualizations in the interpersonal world of reality. Individuals no longer reflect metaphysically about themselves as objects. Instead, each individual sees himself or herself as a project: "When the person sees the horizon of his or her self, there is not only a piece of knowledge but also a task" (Hermans, 1987, p. 18).

By transcending the selfhood duality, constructivists are finally establishing a secure bridge between what I have elsewhere (Gonçalves, 1988) referred to as two of the most conflicting cultural, epistemological, and psychological traditions—the American dream of self and the European nightmare of its deconstruction.

Ontology and Epistemology

The nature of knowledge and existence has been approached in antithetical terms by adherents to the behaviorist and cognitivist paradigms. Recall that, whereas behaviorism subscribes to an absolutist attitude (i.e., assuming the existence of truth as universal, fixed, and unchanged), cognitivism balances between an absolutist and a relativist approach, assuming the centrality of human constructions (i.e., relativism) but still believing in the ultimate power of reality testing (i.e., absolutism).

I have stated above that the relativist attitude taken by some cognitivists is responsible for an ontological and epistemological crisis that several authors have alluded to as the plurality of solitudes, the vertigo of relativity, or epistemological loneliness. Cognitivists try to overcome this crisis at the expense of a regressive shift to an absolutist ontology and epistemology. However, constructivists once again propose a hermeneutic alternative to this crisis, claiming the need for a continuous search for more appropriate forms of knowledge while recognizing that these forms are always open to revision and replacement (i.e., Kelly's [1955] notion of constructive alternativism). In their view, "truth appears as the limit . . . toward which we tend without ever reaching it" (Guidano & Liotti, 1985, p. 102). Although ignorance is infinite, one's knowledge is always limited (Popper, 1972). Knowledge does not exist outside or inside the knower. Instead, knowledge is an ongoing critical movement between the knower and the known, an ever-evolving construction permanently bounded and constricted by the potentialities and limits of a biological and cultural time and space.

It is important, however, to distinguish between the solipsist attitude often adopted by radical constructivists and the more dialectical view shared by critical constructivists. Critical constructivists "are essentially 'realists' albeit 'hypothetical, critical, or representative realists'. They do not deny the existence of a real physical world, although they acknowledge our limitations in ever 'knowing' that world either directly or approximately" (Mahoney, 1988b, p. 4).

Cognitive–behavioral therapies have, in the course of their history, experienced a movement from an absolutist to a dialectical therapeutic ideology (Joyce-Moniz, 1985). There are at least two intertwined meanings for the translation of the dialectical ontology and epistemology in therapeutic practice. First, by acknowledging that knowledge is an ever-growing process of construction and deconstruction, constructive therapists plan with their clients the implementation of new projects of reality through a dialectical process of action, confrontation, and reflection (Gonçalves & Machado, 1989). That is, for constructivism, reality testing is a way of constructing characters and inferring models from them rather than a way of adjusting clients' perceptions to an immaculate reality (Gonçalves & Machado, 1989; Joyce-Moniz, 1989). In this sense, dialectics turns into a methodology—the independent variable of the therapeutic process. But a dialectical ontology and epistemology is also the dependent variable of constructivist intervention. Therapists aim to promote in their clients a basic dialectical attitude toward knowledge and existence by having them continuously face "ill-structured problems" or epistemological obstacles (Kitchner, 1983) to make them aware that understanding is a continuous process of evolving from contradictions to new syntheses in the direction of more encompassing ways of knowing—new orders that include what was previously excluded (Basseches, 1984). As Joyce-Moniz (1989) pointed out:

> nature, history or thought evolve dialectically, that is, from contradiction to synthesis, and from synthesis to contradiction. Ontology

and dialectics become themselves confounded and, thus, they assimilate the constant emergence of reality. (p. 51)

In summary, a dialectical ontology and epistemology represents a hermeneutic alternative to the more absolutist and relativist ideologies by assuming that understanding is an ever-changing process evolving through a process of continuous action, confrontation, and reflection, in the direction of stages of an encompassing but never definitive synthesis. To exist is, in this sense, to actualize the dialectical project of constant change.

Research Implications

The growing dissatisfaction with both the microanalytical behavioral and cognitive approaches to therapy process research is evident in (a) the recognition of the limitation of traditional extensive group designs, (b) the absence of consistent linear effects between therapist and client behavior, and (c) the limitations of verbal reports of cognitive processes. The complexities of the therapeutic process have forced researchers to move into single case designs (cf. Safran et al., 1988), the study of unconscious processes (e.g., Gonçalves & Ivey, 1987), and the exploration of the hermeneutics of the therapeutic narrative (e.g., Angus & Rennie, 1988).

One of the most promising fields of inquiry is, I believe, a hermeneutic approach to metaphor generation in psychotherapy. As stated above, humans are embodied metaphors. The study of metaphors can provide an account of the evolving deep understanding resulting from the therapeutic interaction (Gonçalves & Craine, 1990). Therefore, it represents a good way of operationalizing Martin's (1988) suggestion to inquire into the personal theories of therapeutic participants and into how those theories evolve throughout the therapeutic process.

Angus and Rennie (1988) have tried to hermeneutically approach the metaphoric exchange in therapy. They have aimed to unravel the metaphoric communicative interaction by exploring how clients and therapists construct, express, and apprehend metaphors. A single therapeutic session from four different therapeutic dyads was taped, and all the sequences that involved the repeated use of a particular metaphor were selected. Eleven metaphorical sequences were identified (5 were client produced, and 6 therapist produced). Separate recall interviews were conducted with the participants, in which the metaphors were presented and the subjects were instructed to recall their thoughts, images, emotions, and feelings associated with each metaphoric instance, both at the time it was presented and upon reflection. The characteristics of metaphorical experience for both the participants and the researcher were entered on an index card. A total of 676 cards were then sorted in terms of conceptualized, unifying themes. Finally, two global categories emerged out of these themes: (a) *metaphoric communication interaction* (i.e., conjunction and disjunction of meaning) and (b) *associated meaning context* (i.e., the components of participant's experiencing when saying or hearing a metaphor). Angus and Rennie only presented the results for the first global category—metaphoric communication interaction. Three results are worth mentioning. First, the extent to which mean conjunction or disjunction was produced in metaphoric communication depended on the collaborative nature of the therapeutic relationship. Second, collaborative relationship styles increased "meaning conjunction" (coconstruction of meaning; Angus & Rennie, 1988), involving both participants in a "free-play" of imaginative thought with a continous apprehension, articulation, and elaboration of inner association; that is, the narrative was expanded through the metaphoric elaboration. Finally, noncollaborative relationships were responsible for situations of meaning disjunction, in which participants were not able to articulate their covert and experiential responses, restricting and constricting the potential dissemination of the metaphor.

Angus and Rennie's (1988) study exemplifies how much insight can be gained by exploring the hermeneutics of the therapeutic narrative while concentrating on metaphoric coconstruction. Humans are indeed metaphors of their environments. Therapy researchers need to focus on the streaming process occurring between two embodied metaphorical beings—client and therapist. As Angus and Rennie insightfully concluded:

> Investigators who use client–therapist discourse as data are handicapped to the extent that verbal communication underrepresents subjective meaning. The qualitative analysis of tape-assisted recollection provides an entry into the covert worlds of therapy participants and thereby is a promising complement to a more conventional approach to psychotherapy process research. (1988, p. 559)

CONCLUDING REMARKS

Despite the apparent density of this presentation, I believe that the central underlying ideas remain quite simple and, indeed, can be summarized in four central statements:

1. Life is a narrative, and human beings are inherent narrators—that is, embodied metaphors whose eminent task is existing through understanding and understanding through existence.

2. Therapy is a rehearsing scenario for the construction and deconstruction of narratives. In the protection of the therapeutic niche, clients seek to conquer the versatility of a text.

3. Contemporary hermeneutics suggests that the action of the interpreter (i.e., interpretation) is an ontological projection of his or her understanding. Thus, the relationship between the interpreter and the understood is transcended by the act of understanding. Hermeneutics is therefore an alternative to the basic dialogical tension between the narrative and the narrator, the object and the subject, the knower and the known.

4. The successive paradigmatic shifts of cognitive–behavioral therapies correspond to the evolution from a basic dialogic to a hermeneutic alternative—from a textuality based on the written and the writer to a textuality based on the act of writing, from a selfhood based on the subject–object distinction to a selfhood based on the project, and from epistemology and ontology based on conflicting opposition between absolutism and relativism to a dialectical alternative.

In summary, the critical constructivism endorsed by some contemporary cognitive therapists is presented as a hermeneutic approach that transcends the traditional object–subject dichotomy by conceptualizing humans as projects—sources of energy continuously actualized in a process of dialectical construction and deconstruction of narratives. That is, we project (throw forth) a never-ending set of characters that, in turn, project us as authors.

Overall, the hermeneutic alternative endorsed by constructivists stimulates the revision of the mechanistic, computer, and scientific metaphors that have been ruling the narrative of cognitive–behavioral history. Humans are seen neither as computers nor scientists, but as artists simultaneously portraying the role of actors and directors. The narrative of human life is, however, very different from some of the well-structured novels of our daily reading. As suggested by novelist and literary critic David Lodge (1975), in an intriguing account of the relationship between the mutual dependence on changing places and changing narratives, the human narrative may more closely resemble a movie than a novel:

> Mentally you brace yourself for the ending of a novel. As you're reading, you are aware of the fact that there's only one page or two left in the book, and you get ready to close it. But with the film there's no way of telling, especially nowadays, when films are much more loosely structured, much more ambivalent, than they used to be. There's no way of telling which frame is going to be the last.

The film is going along, just as life goes along, people are behaving, doing things, drinking, talking, and we're watching them, and at any point the director chooses, without warning, without anything being resolved, or explained, or wound up, it can just . . . end. (1975, p. 25)

The only thing left is for us to tell the story.

REFERENCES

Angus, L. E., & Rennie, D. L. (1988). Therapist participation in metaphor generation: Collaborative and non-collaborative styles. *Psychotherapy, 25*, 552–560.

Arciero, G., & Mahoney, M. J. (1989). *Understanding and psychotherapy.* Unpublished manuscript, University of California, Santa Barbara.

Bandura, A. (1985). *Social foundations of thought and action: A social cognitive theory.* Englewood Cliffs, NJ: Prentice Hall.

Basseches, M. (1984). *Dialectical thinking and adult development.* Norwood, NJ: Ablex.

Beck, A. T. (1963). Thinking and depression: I. Idiosyncratic content and cognitive distortions. *Archives of General Psychiatry, 9*, 36–46.

Beck, A. T., Rush, A. J., Shaw, B. F., & Emery, G. (1979). *Cognitive therapy of depression.* New York: Guilford Press.

Berger, P., & Luckman, T. (1966). *The social construction of reality.* New York: Doubleday.

Bronnimann, W. (1987). Comment by Werner Bronnimann. *Journal of Social and Biological Structures, 10*, 343–351.

Broughton, J. M. (1986). The psychology, history and ideology of the self. In R. Harré (Ed.), *The social construction of emotions* (pp. 128–164). Oxford, England: Basil Blackwell.

Cautela, J. (1967). Covert sensitization. *Psychological Reports, 20*, 459–468.

Chandler, M. J. (1975). Relativism and the problem of epistemological loneliness. *Human Development, 18*, 171–180.

Derrida, J. (1982). *Margins of philosophy.* Chicago: University of Chicago Press.

Dews, P. (1987). *Logics of disintegration.* London: Verso.

Dobson, K. S., & Block, L. (1988). Historical and philosophical bases of the cognitive–behavioral therapies. In K. S. Dobson (Ed.), *Handbook of cognitive–behavioral therapies* (pp. 3–38). New York: Guilford Press.

Dryden, W., & Ellis, A. (1988). Rational-emotive therapy. In K. S. Dobson (Ed.), *Handbook of cognitive–behavioral therapies* (pp. 214–272). New York: Guilford Press.

D'Zurilla, T. J., & Goldfried, M. R. (1971). Problem solving and behavior modification. *Journal of Abnormal Psychology, 78*, 107–126.

Elliott, R., Barker, C. B., Caskey, N., & Pistrang, N. (1982). Differential helpfulness of counselor verbal response modes. *Journal of Counseling Psychology, 29,* 354–361.

Ellis, A. (1962). *Reason and emotion in psychotherapy.* New York: Stuart.

Ellis, A. (1985). Expanding the ABC's of rational-emotive therapy. In M. J. Mahoney & A. Freeman (Eds.), *Cognition and psychotherapy* (pp. 313-323). New York: Plenum.

Ellis, A. (1988). *How to stubbornly refuse to make yourself miserable about anything, yes anything!* Secaucus, NJ: Stuart.

Evans, M. (1988). The role of metaphor in psychotherapy and personality change: A theoretical reformulation. *Psychotherapy, 25,* 543–551.

Fischer, R. (1987). On fact and fiction—The structure of stories that the brain tells to itself about itself. *Journal of Social and Biological Structures, 10,* 343–351.

Fishman, D. B. (1988). Pragmatic behaviorism: Saving and nurturing the baby. In D. B. Fishman, F. Rotgers, & C. M. Franks (Eds.), *Paradigms in behavior therapy: Present and promise* (pp. 254–293). New York: Springer.

Freud, S. (1967). *Études sur l'histoire* [Studies about history]. Paris: Presses Universitaires de France. (Originally published 1895)

Friedlander, M. L., Thibodeau, J. R., & Ward, L. G. (1985). Discriminating the "good" from the "bad" therapy hour: A study of dyadic interaction. *Psychotherapy, 22,* 631–642.

Fuhriman, A., Barlow, S. H., & Wanlass, J. (1989). Words, imagination, meaning: Toward change. *Psychotherapy, 26,* 149–156.

Gadamer, H. G. (1975). *Truth and method.* New York: Seabury Press. (Originally published 1960)

Gardner, H. (1987). *The mind's new science.* New York: Basic Books.

Gonçalves, Ó. F. (1988, November). *Evolution and adaptation of the cognitive behavioral therapies: Between the American dream of self and the European nightmare of its deconstruction.* Paper presented at the 22nd Annual Convention of the Association for the Advancement of Behavior Therapy, New York.

Gonçalves, Ó. F. (1989). The constructive–developmental trend in cognitive therapies. In Ó. F. Gonçalves (Ed.), *Advances in the cognitive therapies: The constructive developmental approach* (pp. 11–31). Porto, Portugal: APPORT.

Gonçalves, Ó. F. (1994a). Cognitive narrative psychotherapy: The hermeneutic construction of alternative meanings. *Journal of Cognitive Psychotherapy, 8,* 105–126.

Gonçalves, Ó. F., (1994b). From epistemological truth to existential meaning in cognitive narrative psychotherapy. *Journal of Constructivist Psychology, 7,* 107–118.

Gonçalves, Ó. F., & Craine, M. (1990). The use of metaphors in cognitive therapy. *Journal of Cognitive Psychotherapy, 4,* 135–150.

Gonçalves, Ó. F., & Ivey, A. E. (1987). The effects of unconscious information on therapist conceptualizations, intentions and responses. *Journal of Clinical Psychology, 43*, 237–245.

Gonçalves, Ó. F., & Ivey, A. E. (1993). Developmental therapy: Clinical applications. In K. T. Kuehlwein & H. Rosen (Eds.), *Cognitive therapy in action: Evolving innovative practice* (pp. 326–352). San Francisco: Jossey-Bass.

Gonçalves, Ó. F., Ivey, A. E., & Langdell, S. (1988). The multilevel conception of intentionality: Implications for counseling training. *Counseling Psychology Quarterly, 1*, 377–386.

Gonçalves, Ó. F., & Machado, P. P. (1989). Cognitive therapies and psychological development: An introduction. In Ó. F. Gonçalves (Ed.), *Advances in the cognitive therapies: The constructive developmental approach* (pp. 1–9). Porto, Portugal: APPORT.

Greenspoon, J. (1955). The reinforcing effect of two spoken sounds on the frequency of two responses. *American Journal of Psychology, 68*, 409–416.

Greenspoon, J. (1962). Verbal conditioning and clinical psychology. In A. J. Bachrach (Ed.), *Experimental foundations of clinical psychology* (pp. 39-54). New York: Basic Books.

Guidano, V. F. (1987). *The complexity of self: A developmental approach to psychopathology and therapy.* New York: Guilford Press.

Guidano, V. F. (1988). A systems, process-oriented approach to cognitive therapy. In K. S. Dobson (Ed.), *Handbook of cognitive–behavioral therapies* (pp. 307–354). New York: Guilford Press.

Guidano, V. F. (1991). *The self in process: Toward a post-rationalist cognitive therapy.* New York: Guilford Press.

Guidano, V. F., & Liotti, G. (1983). *Cognitive processes and emotional disorders.* New York: Guilford Press.

Guidano, V. F., & Liotti, G. (1985). A constructivist foundation for cognitive therapy. In M. J. Mahoney & A. Freeman (Eds.), *Cognition and psychotherapy* (pp. 101–142). New York: Plenum.

Harland, R. (1987). *Superstructuralism: The philosophy of structuralism and post-structuralism.* London: Methuen.

Hermans, H. J. (1987). Self as an organized system of valuations: Toward a dialogue with the person. *Journal of Counseling Psychology, 34*, 10–19.

Highlen, P. S., & Hill, C. E. (1984). Factors affecting client change in individual counseling: Current status and theoretical speculations. In S. D. Brown & R. W. Lent (Eds.), *Handbook of counseling psychology* (pp. 285–315). New York: Wiley.

Hill, C. E. (1984). A personal account of the process of becoming a counseling process researcher. *The Counseling Psychologist, 12*, 99–109.

Hill, C. E., Carter, J. A., & O'Farrell, M. K. (1983). A case study of the process and outcome of time limited counseling. *Journal of Counseling Psychology, 24*, 92–97.

Hill, C. E., & O'Grady, K. E. (1985). List of therapist intentions illustrated in a case study and with therapists of different theoretical orientations. *Journal of Counseling Psychology, 32,* 3–22.

Hofstadter, D. R. (1979). *Godel, Escher, Bach: An eternal golden braid.* New York: Vintage Books.

Hollan, S. D., & Beck, A. T. (1986). Cognitive and cognitive–behavioral therapies. In S. L. Garfield & A. E. Bergin (Eds.), *Handbook of psychotherapy and behavior change* (3rd ed., pp. 443–482). New York: Wiley.

Howard, G. S. (1989). *A tale of two stories: Excursions into a narrative approach to psychology.* San Diego, CA: Academic Press.

Ivey, A. E. (1986). *Developmental therapy.* San Francisco: Jossey-Bass.

Ivey, A. E., & Gonçalves, Ó. F. (1988). Developmental therapy: Integrating developmental processes into the clinical practice. *Journal of Counseling and Development, 66,* 406–413.

Ivey, A. E., Gonçalves, Ó. F., & Ivey, M. (1989). Developmental therapy: Theory and practice. In Ó. F. Gonçalves (Ed.), *Advances in the cognitive therapies: The constructive developmental approach* (pp. 91–110). Porto, Portugal: APPORT.

James, W. (1890). *The principles of psychology.* New York: Holt.

Johnson, E. A. (1989, August). *Beyond objectivity: Prejudice and process in understanding.* Paper presented at the 97th Annual Convention of the American Psychological Association, New Orleans, LA.

Johnson, M. (1987). *The body in the mind: The bodily basis of meaning, imagination, and reason.* Chicago: University of Chicago Press.

Joyce-Moniz, L. (1985). Epistemological therapy and constructivism. In M. J. Mahoney & A. Freeman (Eds.), *Cognition and psychotherapy* (pp. 143–179). New York: Plenum.

Joyce-Moniz, L. (1989). Structures, dialectics and regulation in applied constructivism: From developmental psychopathology to individual drama therapy. In Ó. F. Gonçalves (Ed.), *Advances in the cognitive therapies: The constructive developmental approach* (pp. 45–89). Porto, Portugal: APPORT.

Kalechofsky, R. (1987). *The persistence of error: Essays in developmental epistemology.* New York: University Press of America.

Kegan, R. (1982). *The evolving self: Problem and process in human development.* Cambridge, MA: Harvard University Press.

Kelly, G. A. (1955). *The psychology of personal constructs* (Vols. 1 & 2). New York: Norton.

Kitchner, K. S. (1983). Cognition, metacognition and epistemic cognition: A three-level model of cognitive processing. *Human Development, 26,* 222–232.

Kopp, S. B. (1972). *If you meet Buddha on the road, kill him!* New York: Bantam Books.

Kramer, D. A. (1983). Post-formal operations? A need for further conceptualization. *Human Development, 26,* 91–105.

Lacan, J. (1977). *Écrits: A selection.* London: Tavistock.

Lakatos, I. (1974). Falsification and the methodology of scientific research programs. In I. Lakatos & A. Musgrave (Eds.), *Criticism and the growth of knowledge* (pp. 91–196). Cambridge, England: Cambridge University Press.

Lakoff, G. (1987). *Women, fire and dangerous things: What categories reveal about the mind.* Chicago: University of Chicago Press.

Lakoff, G., & Johnson, M. (1980). *Metaphors we live by.* Chicago: University of Chicago Press.

Landau, M. (1984). Human evolution as a narrative. *American Scientist, 72,* 262–267.

Lazarus, A. A., & Messer, S. B. (1988). Clinical choice points: Behavioral versus psychoanalytic interventions. *Psychotherapy, 25,* 59–70.

Lehrer, R. (1988). Characters in search of an author: The self as a narrative structure. In J. C. Mancuso & M. L. G. Shaw (Eds.), *Cognition and personal structure: Computer access and analysis* (pp. 195–228). New York: Praeger.

Liotti, G. (1986). Structural cognitive therapy. In W. Dryden & W. L. Golden (Eds.), *Cognitive–behavioral approaches to psychotherapy* (pp. 92–128). New York: Harper & Row.

Liotti, G., & Reda, M. (1981). Some epistemological remarks on behavior therapy, cognitive therapy and psychoanalysis. *Cognitive Therapy and Research, 5,* 231–236.

Lodge, D. (1975). *Changing places.* Middlesex, England: Penguin Books.

Lyddon, W. J. (1989). Root metaphor theory: A philosophical framework for counseling and psychotherapy. *Journal of Counseling and Development, 67,* 442–448.

Mahoney, M. J. (1977). Reflections on the cognitive-learning trend in psychotherapy. *American Psychologist, 32,* 5–13.

Mahoney, M. J. (1980). Psychotherapy and the structure of personal revolutions. In M. J. Mahoney (Ed.), *Psychotherapy processes* (pp. 157–180). New York: Plenum.

Mahoney, M. J. (1984). Behaviorism, cognitivism and human change processes. In M. A. Reda & M. J. Mahoney (Eds.), *Cognitive psychotherapies* (pp. 3–30). Cambridge, MA: Ballinger.

Mahoney, M. J. (1988a). The cognitive sciences and psychotherapy: Patterns in a developing relationship. In K. S. Dobson (Ed.), *Handbook of cognitive–behavioral therapies* (pp. 357–386). New York: Guilford Press.

Mahoney, M. J. (1988b). Constructive metatheory: I. Basic features and historical foundations. *International Journal of Personal Construct Psychology, 1,* 1–35.

Mahoney, M. J. (1991). *Human change processes.* New York: Basic Books.

Mahoney, M. J., & Arnkoff, D. (1978). Cognitive and self-control therapies. In S. L. Garfield & A. E. Bergin (Eds.), *Handbook of psychotherapy and behavior change* (pp. 689–722). New York: Wiley.

Mahoney, M. J., & Craine, M. (1989). [Psychotherapists: Their views on human development, psychotherapy, and their change over time.] Unpublished data, University of California, Santa Barbara.

Mahoney, M. J., & Gabriel, T. (1990). Essential tensions in psychology: Longitudinal data on cognitive and behavioral ideologies. *Journal of Cognitive Psychotherapy, 4,* 5–22.

Mahoney, M. J., & Lyddon, W. J. (1988). Recent developments in cognitive approaches to counseling and psychotherapy. *Counseling Psychologist, 16,* 190–234.

Mahoney, M. J., Norcross, J. C., Prochaska, J. O., & Missar, C. D. (Eds.). (1989). Psychological development and optimal psychotherapy: Converging perpectives among clinical psychologists. *Journal of Integrative and Eclectic Psychotherapy, 8,* 251–263.

Mair, M. (1988). Psychology as storytelling. *International Journal of Personal Construct Psychology, 1,* 125–137.

Mair, M. (1989). Kelly, Bannister and a storytelling psychology. *International Journal of Personal Construct Psychology, 2,* 1–14.

Martin, J. (1984). The cognitive mediational paradigm for research on counseling. *Journal of Counseling Psychology, 31,* 558–571.

Martin, J. (1985). Measuring clients' cognitive competence in research on counseling. *Journal of Counseling and Development, 63,* 556–560.

Martin, J. (1988). A proposal for researching possible relationships between scientific theories and personal theories of counselors and clients. *Journal of Counseling and Development, 66,* 261–265.

Martin, J., Martin, W., Meyer, M., & Slemon, A. (1986). An empirical investigation of the cognitive mediational paradigm for research on counseling. *Journal of Counseling Psychology, 33,* 115–123.

Maturana, H. R., & Varela, F. J. (1987). *The tree of knowledge: The biological roots of human understanding.* Boston: New Science.

Meichenbaum, D. (1969). The effects of instructions and reinforcement on thinking and language behaviors of schizophrenics. *Behavior Research and Therapy, 7,* 105–114.

Meichenbaum, D. (1977). *Cognitive behavior modification.* New York: Plenum.

Messer, S. B., Sass, A. L., & Woolfolk, L. R. (Eds.). (1988). *Hermeneutics and psychological theory.* Rutgers, NJ: Rutgers University Press.

Miller, G. A. (1956). The magical number seven, plus or minus two: Some limits of our capacity for processing information. *Psychological Review, 63,* 81–97.

Neimeyer, G. J., & Neimeyer, R. A. (Eds.). (1987). *Personal construct therapy casebook.* New York: Springer.

Neimeyer, R. A. (1986). Personal construct therapy. In W. Dryden & W. Golden (Eds.), *Cognitive–behavioral approaches to psychotherapy* (pp. 224–260). New York: Harper & Row.

Neimeyer, R. A. (1988). The origin of questions in the clinical context. *Questioning Exchange, 2*, 75–80.

Packer, M. J. (1985). Hermeneutic inquiry in the study of human conduct. *American Psychologist, 40*, 1081–1093.

Packer, M. J., & Addison, R. B. (Eds.). (1989). *Entering the circle: Hermeneutic investigation in psychology.* Albany: State University of New York Press.

Patterson, C. H. (1984). Empathy, warmth and genuineness in psychotherapy: A review of reviews. *Psychotherapy, 21*, 431–438.

Pepper, S. C. (1942). *World hypotheses: A study in avoidance.* Berkeley: University of California Press.

Piaget, J. (1985). *The equilibration of cognitive structures.* Chicago: University Press of Chicago. (Originally published 1975)

Polkinghorne, D. E. (1988). *Narrative psychology.* Albany: State University of New York Press.

Popper, K. R. (1972). *Objective knowledge: An evolutionary approach.* Oxford, England: Clarendon.

Popper, K. R., & Eccles, J. C. (1977). *The self and its brain.* Berlin: Springer-Verlag.

Pribram, K. H. (1986). The cognitive revolution and mind/brain issues. *American Psychologist, 41*, 507–520.

Rennie, D. L. (1992). Qualitative analysis of the client's experience of psychotherapy: The unfolding of reflexivity. In S. G. Toukmanian & D. L. Rennie (Eds.), *Psychotherapy process research: Paradigmatic and narrative approaches* (pp. 211–233). Newbury Park, CA: Sage.

Riegel, K. F. (1973). Dialectical operations: The final period of cognitive development. *Human Development, 16*, 371–381.

Rogers, C. R. (1957). The necessary and sufficient conditions of therapeutic personality change. *Journal of Consulting Psychology, 21*, 95–103.

Safran, J. D., Greenberg, L., & Rice, L. N. (1988). Integrating psychotherapy research and practice: Modeling the change process. *Psychotherapy, 25*, 1–17.

Sarbin, T. R. (1984, August). *Clinical prediction: Calling forty years later.* Paper presented at the 92nd Annual Convention of the American Psychological Association, Toronto, Ontario, Canada.

Sarbin, T. R. (Ed.). (1986). *Narrative psychology: The storied nature of human conduct.* New York: Praeger.

Sartre, J. P. (1965). *Being and nothingness.* New York: Philosophical Library.

Saussure, F. (1959). *Course in general linguistics.* New York: Philosophical Library.

Skinner, B. F. (1957). *Verbal behavior.* New York: Appleton-Century-Crofts.

Skinner, B. F. (1974). *About behaviorism*. New York: Vintage Books.

Skinner, B. F. (1987). What happened to psychology as the science of behavior? *American Psychologist, 42*, 780–786.

Stone, G. L., & Kelly, K. R. (1983). Effects of helping skills on the attitudes toward psychological counseling. *Counselor Education and Supervision, 22*, 207–214.

Strohmer, D. C., & Chiodo, A. L. (1984). Counselor hypothesis testing strategies: The role of initial impressions and self-schema. *Journal of Counseling Psychology, 31*, 410–419.

Ullmann, L. P., Krasner, L., & Collins, B. J. (1961). Modification of behavior through verbal conditioning: Effects in group therapy. *Journal of Abnormal and Social Psychology, 62*, 128–132.

Varela, F. J. (1984). The creative cycle: Sketches on the natural history of circularity. In P. Watzlawick (Ed.), *The invented reality* (pp. 309–323). New York: Norton.

von Foerster, H. (1984). On constructing reality. In P. Watzlawick (Ed.), *The invented reality* (pp. 41–61). New York: Norton.

Watson, J. (1913). Psychology as the behaviorist views it. *Psychological Review, 20*, 158–177.

Weimer, W. B. (1977). A conceptual framework for cognitive psychology: Motor theories of the mind. In R. Shaw & J. Bransford (Eds.), *Perceiving, acting, and knowing* (pp. 267–311). Hillsdale, NJ: Erlbaum.

Woolfolk, R. L. (1988). The self in cognitive behavior therapy. In D. B. Fishman, F. Rotgers, & C. M. Franks (Eds.), *Paradigms in behavior therapy: Present and promise* (pp. 168–184). New York: Springer.

Zuriff, G. E. (1986). Precis of behaviorism: A conceptual reconstruction. *Behavioral and Brain Sciences, 9*, 687–723.

11

CLIENT-GENERATED NARRATIVES IN PSYCHOTHERAPY

ROBERT A. NEIMEYER

If we take seriously the proposition that each of us is in some sense the "author" of our experience, then the narrative form in which we organize or structure that experience becomes a central concern of psychotherapy. In particular, I suggest that insufficient attention has been paid to even the most literal forms of such narrative activity on the part of clients in therapy—namely, those diaries, personal journals, or other forms of reflective writing that many clients pursue spontaneously and that therapists might more consciously cultivate. In this chapter, I reflect on the role of such client-generated narratives and suggest that they serve vital intrapersonal, as well as interpersonal, functions in psychotherapy, as illustrated by the entries extracted from one client's personal therapeutic journal. I follow with a discussion of the defining features of narratives in both their historical and anticipatory dimensions and conclude by noting the range of procedures developed by constructivist therapists for fostering therapeutic reconstruction.

FINDING ONE'S VOICE

Consider the following reflections of a young woman, "Mandy," excerpted from an entry in her personal journal:

> The results of my reptest . . . I am disappointed. Reflected is my superficial public self; I could not tap my inner core. As I write this I sense an enmeshment with that inner being . . . the self I have much to learn from. In public, I am separated from it . . . I hide from myself. As I completed the grid in group my inner self begged for more time . . . for a safe place to think and feel . . . . I had none at that moment. I am left with what I know; the grid reflected only what I fed it. I contemplate the separateness of my being. What does it feel like to be whole? (something in this line has moved me to tears).

Mandy's statement can be understood at several levels. In one sense, it could be considered a commentary on the group environment in which she completed the repertory grid—a quantitative assessment device aimed at elucidating the structures behind the respondent's way of construing (Fransella & Bannister, 1977; R. A. Neimeyer, 1993a). In a more accepting, less structured environment, could the grid have functioned as intended—that is, as a technical means to promote self-exploration? In a more general sense, Mandy's remarks also embody a critique of repertory grid technique that has been voiced more formally by Mair (in R. A. Neimeyer, 1985) and by Yorke (1989), among others. Perhaps, as Yorke (1989) contended, "it is difficult for meanings to pass through the linguistic constrictions of the grid matrix" (p. 65), even when the "subject" and "psychologist" are one in the same person. But it is a third level of implication in Mandy's entry that I would like to emphasize here: her feeling of constraint in reflecting herself and her struggles in the decontextualized antonyms of the repertory grid. In stark contrast, she not only identified these limitations, but also surmounted them in the narrative flow of her continuing journal entry. Associating to her sense of separation between her "inner self" and her "public persona," she recalled a thematically related incident:

> Dina's wedding. Larry and I wrote the words for the service . . . I read them aloud to all in the church. I cried. I feel. And feel. Grandma approached me outside the church. She introduced me to distant relatives by stating, "And this is the cry baby". . . . A hand from the past slapped my face till my cheeks felt raw; all that I felt were the tears racing to the edge of my face. "Be truthful, Mandy . . . you didn't cry (Lia did) . . . you smiled at her greeting. The bitch . . . you didn't dare hurt her by being honest."

In this passage, Mandy linked the sense of inner separation she experienced on the rep grid to a poignant recent memory, construed here, as elsewhere throughout her journal, in terms of the schism between "Mandy," the young woman known to others, and "Lia," the voice of her suppressed emotionality. Reflecting further on this distinction, she observed: "the smile is automatic; it separates me from what I feel. It protects me from the 'something bad' that could happen. It prevents me from being honest with my inner self. I cry for that self whose voice I have stolen; she whispers though, and I hear her."

Finally, Mandy completed the entry with another, more distant, autobiographical memory:

> In the bathtub this morning I began to cry . . . an embrace with old pain. I remember my father's cigarette-stenched fingers running through my hairs as he lifted them away from my head. . . . Inevitably a snarl caught but he continued to pull despite my angry cries to stop. His response: "You're just a cry baby . . . it doesn't hurt." I learned to quiet my protests; I continue to respond as a victim. . . . Something bad will happen if I react honestly. I remain divided from the very self I love. Verbalizing is the key to integration. . . . I am fearfully aphasic.

In the narrative flow of her journal, Mandy was anything but aphasic. She found a voice, a strong and searching one, as she continued her quest for coherence and wholeness in a personal world of discontinuities and extremes.

Although Mandy's narrative is uniquely her own, her choice of a narrative form to formulate and reformulate her account of herself is nearly universal. My goal in this chapter is to reflect briefly on the therapeutic functions of this universal form and to illustrate its use by clients in the context of their self-reconstruction.

STORIES THAT YEARN FOR COHERENCE

What is, or might be, the function of therapeutic narratives, as told or written from the client's point of view? Clearly, there is no single answer to such a question. In the interpersonal context of the therapeutic relationship, client stories can be told to instruct, entertain, impress, implore, test, admonish, invite, or distance the therapist; occasionally, several of these intents may be compressed into a single storytelling. But I believe that client stories also have a vital *intra*personal function— namely, *to establish continuity of meaning in the client's lived experience.* Kelly (1969) once defined *symptoms* as "urgent questions, behaviorally expressed, which had somehow lost the threads that lead either to answers or to better questions" (p. 19). If we accept this provisional definition, then a client's storytelling can be seen as a means of "voicing," rather than mutely enacting, such questions and of exploring a series of deeply personal answers. When first uttered in the therapeutic dialogue or recorded in other formats, such as a personal journal, these attempts at sense-making may be as vague, intense, fragmentary, or apparently incoherent as the symptomatic behaviors they articulate. But across time, if such narrative inquiries are nurtured rather than suppressed or glibly answered by the therapist, then they often become an important vehicle that carries the client toward greater degrees of integration and sensitivity—in a word, toward greater self-development.[1]

ONE CLIENT'S JOURNEY

Carol was referred to me by another therapist who was "burned out" after working with her for 3 years, during which she was repeatedly hospitalized for self-injurious behavior. The most serious of these episodes followed an abortion for an unplanned pregancy, which triggered massive guilt and depression and led her to ingest a potentially fatal dose of barbiturates. Found at the point of death by a friend, Carol was immediately taken to an intensive care facility. There, contemptuous physicians brutally resuscitated her, only to curse her later for "failing" in her attempt to end her life, thereby distracting them from their mission to save the lives of more worthy patients. On her release from the medical facility, Carol was informed that her therapist would no longer be available to see her, feeling that he had exhausted his own attempts to help her.

---

[1]Of course, this leaves open the question of *how* the therapist nurtures such narrative activity on the part of the client. Certainly, one key to such nurturance is the demonstration of real interest in clients' initial (often spontaneous, sometimes assigned) excursions into reflective writing, whether it is in the form of informal notes to themselves of topics to discuss further with the therapist in the next session or more elaborate written "dialogues" with other persons, aspects of themselves, or a source of "inner wisdom," as in the highly evolved "intensive journal" methods refined by Progoff (1975). What seems critical is developing an attitude of attunement to the "subtext" of the client's writing (What themes cut across the various entries? Do subsequent entries represent unexpected elaborations of earlier ones, or speak from a different or conflicting aspect of the client's experience? What features of the client's lived experience are symbolized or "explained" by this journal entry?), rather than literally following only the events or "surface structure" captured by the writing. By "nurturing" a client's narrative activity I also mean to imply encouraging him or her to write deeply and honestly, even to the point that words begin to fail to adequately convey the meanings, issues, and feelings at stake. I would contrast such narrative nurturance with the posture of therapist disputation, challenge, and "reality testing" that characterizes some traditional therapies that also make use of written client "self-monitoring" techniques, such as the cognitive approaches of Beck (Beck, Rush, Shaw, & Emery, 1979) or Ellis (1979). Later in this chapter I note several alternative constructivist approaches that encourage a narrative impulse in clients, although I suspect that more sustained attention to this area would lead to creative forms of intervention that are only partially foreshadowed in our current work.

Abused and abandoned by these previous "caregivers," Carol skeptically came to see me in outpatient psychotherapy. In the early weeks of our contact, she was disheveled and almost mute, frequently withdrawing into an impenetrable silence accompanied by tears and self-injury in the form of banging her arms against the wooden arms of her chair. These silences were often punctuated by angry outbursts at people in her life, including myself, during which she took on a wild, half-crazed appearance. Her behavior between sessions was equally unpredictable and included frequent self-mutilation, usually marked by cutting her wrists, thighs, and breasts at times when her subjective pain became unbearable.

As Carol gradually began to express her distress in the accepting, invitational atmosphere of therapy, she spoke of her confusion, anguish, self-hatred, and general powerlessness, especially in relation to the "voices" within her that fought among themselves and impelled her toward acts of self-punishment. These voices or selves sometimes "dominated" Carol, as when "Kayla" enacted rage toward a therapist or demanded Carol's death or when a vulnerable and nameless self left her feeling mute and disconnected. Carol herself cried out desperately for help in the face of this fragmentation, sometimes literally in our sessions, sometimes metaphorically between contacts. In a particularly poignant expression of her despair, she described "carving messages to me in her flesh" during one episode of self-mutilation. My response was to encourage her to substitute a pen for the knife and to bring in the resulting communications for discussion in our therapy sessions.

What ensued was a remarkable journal, at first scribbled on torn scraps or pages of loose-leaf paper and later penned in more durable and sequential "logbooks" of her personal journey. In both form and content, these narrative entries reflected her inner struggle. An early entry, printed initially in block letters, expressed her shifting and fragmentary sense of self:

> I feel very scattered now. Pills—I have all sorts of pills now. I'm very close to doing something. I don't know if you will be of help or not. Carol looks through a shadowy, dark fog—nothing is clear to her. She hurts. I can't stop the pain and I don't know if you can either. . . . She wants to cut herself now. The pills in the a.m. Puzzles are often hard to put together. . . .

Then, in a small, uncertain cursive hand, she continued,

> She wants to live. She cries. She wants to live but it seems impossible. What can you do? What can anyone do? Cut herself. See the blood flow, feel the pain. Take the pills and stop her breathing, stop her heart beat. Then no longer a problem to you or anyone. Please help me. Please help me be happy again.

Carol concluded the entry in a larger, looser, and more uneven writing with five words: "I didn't do it. Death."

This and similar entries—with their shifting narrative style (from first to third person and back again), changing penmanship (from strident, to plaintive, to disorganized), and graphic violence—sometimes set the stage for an act of self-injury (such as the cutting that preceded the "I didn't do it" of the entry above) and sometimes took the place of this more primitive response to her despair. By validating rather than challenging the experiential realities of which she wrote (cf. Leitner, 1988), Carol and I were gradually, over a course of months, able to articulate these shifts more metaphorically, enabling her to symbolically express rather than symptomatically enact her inner drama. During this period, I encouraged her to pursue her journal work in tandem with our ongoing dialogue, using it to elaborate, extend, or personalize the conversation of therapy outside the session per se. From time to time, she responded to my standing invitation to share an important passage by reading it aloud to me in session (or, when the text was particularly painful or inexpressible, allowing me to do so). These poignant moments provided me as a listener and Carol as an author a sense of immediacy and connectedness with the evolving narrative of her life and allowed us to search together for a vocabulary of imagery adequate to the contours of her experience. The use of Mair's (1977) metaphor of the "community of selves" was particularly useful, as she identified and began to write of the "cast of characters" who made up her self-system.

> Kayla dances freely around in my mind. How can she be controlled? The feathery blackness of her frightens me. Her power grows. Are we back to Carol and her parts? Will we ever get any further than this? We have in the past—why not now? Why not now? She has power, in a subtle sort of way. Stop her. To stop her you must hurt yourself, Carol. [Then, in a more insistent hand] To stop her you must HURT. [Again, a shift toward a looser scrawl] Remember when you were a small child—you were all alone and you still are—a child, all alone. I want something different! I want something different. I want to change, dammit, but I can't. I can. I can. I will. I am so weary.

As her journal entries became more searching, so did our therapeutic dialogues. In fragmentary and exquisitely painful flashes, Carol began to recover images of a distant, almost surreal childhood, in which she suffered at the hands of a cruel and rejecting mother and retreated into an incestuous relationship with her father. Her immersion in a reclusive and sexually abusive religious cult in her teen years did nothing to give her a more coherent sense of self, instead, reinforcing her conviction of her own sinfulness and isolation. But in the face of this often traumatic self-exploration, Carol's narrative began to take on a clearly poetic quality, with emerging hints that she could envision an alternative future.

> Days fade into weeks and weeks into months
> Time passes by much too quickly
> I cry for it to stop, to slow
> It ignores me as it rips through my mind
> Leaving it torn, twisted, bleeding.
> I fear
> They fear
> Is it Carol
> Or her parts
> Are not her parts
> Her?
> No, I don't want them there.
> Fear—I want to run.
> I want to run.
> Then who fears—Carol or her parts.
> Relapse. If you do everyone walks out on you.
> Is it worth hiding your feelings?
> It eats away inside like a cancer—
> Goes into remission and then shows its ugly
> Self again—for more pain and fear.
> For God hath not given us the spirit of fear
> But of power, and of love, and a sound mind.
> Remission—is that the best I can ever expect?
> Why should it be?

Although Carol's quest to become more whole was punctuated by both major and minor setbacks across time, she gradually consolidated her narrative stance and became attuned to new murmurings of hope within her, to which she gave voice in her journal. Significantly, she began signing and dating these entries for the first time, suggesting that she was beginning to view herself as the author of her own experience:

> As the sun rises
> The birds awaken.
> In the silence and stillness of the moment
> You can hear their songs.
>
> As the sun rises on my life
> I begin to sing.
> In the silent stillness of the moment
> My song can be heard.

As Carol shifted her gaze toward the horizon of her life, she was also able to adopt a new perspective on the earlier chapters of her biography:

> I cried.
> I felt anger.

Depression was a way of life.
My thoughts were scattered.
My impulsiveness left me cut, bleeding.
Drugs were my shadowy hiding place.
Hopelessness dominated my future.
I sat stagnant in misery.
Was that not yesterday?

The personal victories symbolized in Carol's poems were accompanied by more visible public accomplishments: the decision to end an abusive love relationship; stability in her work; and then, commendation and promotion in a new career, and a growing circle of friends, who valued her for her insightfulness and warmth and who tolerated her occasional lapses into anger and despair. Her artistic dimension found further expression in a new pastime of photography, in which she displayed a gift for capturing images that engendered a self-reflective mood in the viewer. These photographs, accompanied by some of her poetic verse, began to find a broader audience, eventually being featured in two public exhibitions of her work. Throughout this period of impressive growth, Carol began accepting and exploring the ambiguities of the new and uncertain world that she had begun to inhabit.

Somewhere between here and there,
Between the good and the bad,
Between the positive and the negative,
Somewhere between the realities of life
Lies an unsure ground.
A ray here and a ray there
Teases us, entices us
To hope for more. . . .
To reach for more.
What lies beyond that smokey screen
That blocks my view?
I see the light bursting through.
I feel the warmth as the rays touch me.
I sense the healing that must lie beyond.
I hope for more.
I reach for more.

Finally, 4 years after our work together had begun, Carol penned an extended poetic self-statement entitled "I am Me," parts of which are reproduced here:

In all the world, there is no one else exactly like me.
There are persons who have some parts like me,
But no one adds up exactly like me.
Therefore, everything that comes out of me
Is authentically mine because I alone chose it.

I own everything about me—
My body, including everything it does;
My mind, including all its thoughts and ideas;
My eyes, including all the images they behold;
My feelings, whatever they may be—
Anger, joy, frustration, love, disappointment, excitement;
My voice, loud or soft,
And all my actions, whether they be to others or to myself. . . .

Because I own all of me, I can become
Intimately acquainted with me.
By so doing I can love me and be friendly with me
In all my parts. . . .

However I look and sound, whatever I say and do,
And whatever I think and feel at a given moment
Is me.
This is authentic
And represents where I am at that moment in time.
When I review later how I looked and sounded,
What I said and did,
And how I thought and felt,
Some parts may turn out to be unfitting.

I can discard that which is unfitting,
And keep that which proved to be fitting,
And invent something new for that which I discarded.

I can see, hear, feel, think, say, and do.
I have the tools to survive,
To be close to others,
To be productive,
And to make sense and order out of the world
Of people and things outside of me.
I own me,
And therefore I can engineer me.
I am me
And I am okay.

NARRATION IN PSYCHOTHERAPY

What do client-generated narratives like those of Mandy and Carol teach about the role of such devices in therapy? This is a difficult question to answer, partly because of the generality of the narrative concept and partly because of the particularity of the narratives produced by actual clients in actual therapy contexts. For this reason, it is useful first to focus the definition of *narrative* by considering what it is and is not and, then, to instantiate this definition by reflecting on some of its various forms and functions in the process of psychotherapy.

Narrative Versus Nonnarrative Activities in Psychotherapy

In the view of some authors (e.g., Howard, 1991), *narrative* is virtually synonymous with human mentation and human culture. In such an extended meaning of the term, one might search in vain for any nonnarrative processes in therapy or in any other domain with which psychologists are concerned, for that matter. But it strikes me, as it did Kelly (1955), that any meaningful concept must have a contrast, and therapeutic narratives are no exception. Russell and Lucariello (1992) pointed out that "most definitions of narrative require a protagonist inspirited with intentionality, undertaking some action, physical or mental, real or imagined, within the story itself" (p. 671). Similarly, if narratives are viewed as intentional pursuits whose goal is to construct meaning (Gonçalves, 1994, p. 110), then they must establish implicit or explicit end points and marshal events that are relevant to these projected conclusions (Gergen & Gergen, 1986). In this sense, narrative has both a historical dimension (in the sense of selectively recruiting past events, whether real or imagined) and an anticipatory thrust (in the sense of reaching toward a conclusion or end point that is posited with more or less clarity and conviction). The (attempted) integration of material in light of the author's intentionality imparts a narrative structure to human experience.

If we accept this provisional definition, then much that transpires in psychotherapy—information gathering, coaching in communication skills, advice giving, problem solving, and most psychological testing— involves nonnarrative processes, although they may, in some more abstract sense, be part of a "script" or cultural tale of what constitutes therapy or helping. Moreover, one can easily identify acts of human mentation that are nonnarrative. For example, mathematical and logical processing lack the plot structure that defines narrative, and even important feeling states are not necessarily "stories," although they may be triggered or conveyed by a story. Even Kellian construing, viewed in its irreducible essentials of simultaneously positing a dimension of comparison and contrast, is not narrative in this sense, though it may be a precondition for constructing narratives that weave together the events and thematic constructs an individual construes. Thus, I believe it is conceptually possible to identify reasonably distinct storytelling episodes or processes in counseling and to study or use their impact on therapy outcome.

Ultimately, of course, all definitions (of narrative or any other concept) are working fictions that classify or punctuate the ambiguity of experience in more or less useful ways, as judged from the standpoint of the person or language community adopting that definition. I am simply suggesting here that a relatively concrete definition of client- or therapist-generated accounts can be useful in sensitizing us to the role of narrative in therapeutic change, both at the level of general change strategies and at the level of specific therapeutic techniques.

Functions of Narration

Attempting to specify the particular value of client-generated narratives in therapy runs up against a second obstacle as well—namely, the uniqueness of each client's narrative production. Even in the two examples cited above, of Mandy and Carol, which dealt with a similar thematic issue (i.e., a sense of inner separation, or fragmentation) in a similar format (a personal journal), each was unique in its style and function. Earlier I suggested that one function of such narratives is the implicit or explicit goal of establishing continuity of meaning in the client's lived experience, and the yearning for coherence that characterized the writing of both women supports this view. Of course, I have read and heard many client narratives that told apparently different stories—of abuse, indignation, loneliness, dejection, and, sometimes, joy and love—but even these can be viewed as quests for (or celebrations of) a growing sense of coherence and adequacy in one's system of meaning. The difficulty is that each client's story may also serve other goals or have other intents that may be therapeutic (or countertherapeutic) in their own right. Is the story offered for primarily expressive purposes, to lighten the client's burden of secrecy? Is it used to buttress a shaky but deeply held conviction—that is, in Kelly's (1955) terms, "to extort validational evidence in favor of a type of social prediction that has already been recognized as a failure" (p. 565)? Is it a way of placing a set of confusing experiences on the table of public discourse, so that they can be sorted out in new and, perhaps, more functional ways? Or is it, as often happens in client journals, a dialogue between one's sensed or possible selves, sometimes sharpening and sometimes blunting the hard edges of one's inner contradictions? Unfortunately, at present, we lack even an adequate taxonomy of such questions, much less a complete set of tools for helping clients accomplish the aims that their stories might or could embody.

In general, however, the functions of client-generated narratives can be as varied as clients' writings themselves, which may historicize their struggles, reach into the past, or project into the future, consolidating a sense of oneself over time and suggesting new choices or life directions. The active experimentation with different voices, perspectives, and literary styles (e.g., writing a description of oneself or one's family in the third-, rather than first-, person form; R. A. Neimeyer, 1993a) offers new and sometimes surprising glimpses of the facets of one's selfhood and their potential integration. Concretely, clients use these forms of self-exploration to confront important choices in work and relationships; place past traumas in a more contemporary frame of reference; and give voice to concerns, insights, and new hopes that they may be reluctant to verbalize to another, even to an accepting therapist. Thus, to be effective, a therapist's encouragement of a client to use a journal to deepen and personalize the work of therapy should be coupled with the reassurance that he or she may "edit" disclosures of the journal's content in later therapeutic discussion, rather than baring its pages for the scrutiny of the therapist or other readers.

At a more abstract level, the very act of writing about oneself tends to promote both an awareness of the limits of one's self-observation and a sense of gradually transcending these limits, as one struggles to articulate the dimensions of a problem or issue in emotionally vivid terms. In this more "process-oriented" view, journal work, self-reflective poetic excursions, and the like can represent literary means of attending to and symbolizing the "internal complexity" of experience, in the words of Greenberg and Pascual-Leone (1995). The articulation of the often "opposing schemes" represented in these entries sets the stage for their "dialectical synthesis," allowing for the emergence of novel self-constructions. The further therapeutic processing of these emergent constructions (whether with the therapist or in further written form) promotes the tightening of these new schemes through their verbal articulation and permits them to be used to construct new narrative explanations of one's experience and its projection into alternative futures. From this perspective, the content of a client's journal becomes secondary to the act of authoring it and, with it, achieving a greater sense of authorship of one's own life.

Illustrative Narrative Techniques

Both current and enduring contributions to a narrative psychology offer some intriguing leads regarding the use of storied accounts in therapy, and I believe that these deserve greater attention from constructivists. Kelly's (1955) original self-characterization technique and the development of fixed-role enactment sketches are quintessential narrative techniques (R. A. Neimeyer, 1993a), as are related methods used in individual (Fransella, 1981), couples (Kremsdorf, 1985), and family therapies (Alexander & Neimeyer, 1989). By inviting the client to first formulate an account of himself or herself "as if" from the standpoint of a hypothethical other and then collaborate with the therapist in conjuring an "orthogonal" identity or role that is enacted for a fixed period of time, such methods mitigate the threat of personal change (G. J. Neimeyer, 1995). Personal journals, such as those of Mandy and Carol, can be powerful and flexible tools for inner dialogue and self-development (Mahoney, 1991), whether these take a more structured (Progoff, 1975) or open-ended form (Rainer, 1978). Plotting one's personal struggles or quests according to the mythic structures of one's own experience (Feinstein & Krippner, 1988) or the great cultural tales of humankind (Jung, 1964) offers further possibilities for framing and reframing elusive subjective realities. All of these methods have in common a relatively nondirective, invitational quality, encouraging the client to cultivate the personal poetic sensitivities needed to "speak into being" new worlds of possibility (Mair, 1989), with only the minimal prompting of the therapist or journal format to provide guidance. They therefore place inflection on the client's own role in formulating the content of the narrative and its specific purposes in that individual's therapy or life.

Therapist-generated stories are equally relevant to the therapy process. These have perhaps been developed most artfully by therapists working within the Eriksonian tradition, using metaphorically relevant narratives in part to circumvent the usual rational counterarguments that clients tend to mount against change (Zeig, 1985). White and Epston (1990) have further developed "narrative means to therapeutic ends," by making clever use of therapist commentaries, letters to clients, "declarations of independence" from target problems, and other forms of documentation to help clients first externalize, and then conquer, the difficulties that brought them to therapy. Epston and White (1995) have extended these methods to include public documentation of the client's "rite of passage" so that it can be socially validated and can powerfully reinforce therapeutic change. My own experimentation with writing change-affirming progress notes that are then shared with clients has had a similar intent (R. A. Neimeyer, 1993b). If offered as respectful reflections on a shared journey rather than as authoritative professional pronouncements, such therapist-generated narratives may interweave with the client's own, to help validate and consolidate the changes fostered by their joint contact.

Finally, explicitly collaborative work in eliciting and restructuring narratives has been pursued by some constructivist therapists. By articulating and deepening the sensorial metaphors embedded in a client's account, therapists such as Woolum have helped clients bring forth the organizing themes of their experience.[2] In a similar vein, Gonçalves

---

[2]Readers interested in the work of Woolum, Efran, Mahoney, Feixas, and other narrative constructivist therapists can contact PsychoEducational Resources, P.O. Box 2196, Keystone Heights, Florida, 32656, for a listing of studio-produced training videotapes suitable for professional continuing education or classroom use.

(1994) has developed a form of cognitive narrative psychotherapy whose aim is to help clients *recall*, *objectify* (amplify the sensory detail), *subjectify* (amplify the inner experience), *metaphorize* (symbolize core themes), and *project* life narratives (by developing possible overarching metaphors). Finally, Forster (1991) has developed an interactive protocol for eliciting and validating durable qualities or constructs of the client that he or she engages in the production of "good experiences." This "dependable strengths articulation process" involves both journallike entries and the facilitation of their disclosure in the context of small group interaction. Rather than representing competing approaches to therapy, the broad range of narrative methods can be selectively combined (e.g., the "deep structure" of a client's personal journal can be systematically explored through therapist inquiry or metaphoric elaboration or can be sharpened and validated through written therapist or client documentation).

In summary, although I believe that narrative documentation and reconstruction is but one of many processes that facilitate psychotherapy (and human change more generally), it is one that holds considerable promise for constructivist therapists. I hope that other therapists concerned with the exploration and elaboration of their client's personal stories will accept the invitation to participate in the further extension of these methods.

REFERENCES

Alexander, P. C., & Neimeyer, G. J. (1989). Constructivism and family therapy. *International Journal of Personal Construct Psychology, 2,* 111–122.

Beck, A. T., Rush, J., Shaw, B., & Emery, G. (1979). *Cognitive therapy of depression.* New York: Guilford Press.

Ellis, A. (1979). Toward a new theory of personality. In A. Ellis & J. M. Whitely (Eds.), *Theoretical and empirical foundations of rational-emotive therapy* (pp. 7–32). Monterey, CA: Brooks/Cole.

Epston, D., & White, M. (1995). Termination as a rite of passage: Questioning strategies for a therapy of inclusion. In R. A. Neimeyer & M. J. Mahoney (Eds.), *Constructivism in psychotherapy* (pp. 339–356). Washington, DC: American Psychological Association.

Feinstein, D., & Krippner, S. (1988). *Personal mythology.* Los Angeles: Tarcher.

Forster, J. R. (1991). Facilitating positive changes in self-constructions. *International Journal of Personal Construct Psychology, 4,* 281–292.

Fransella, F. (1981). Nature babbling to herself: The self-characterization as a therapeutic tool. In H. Bonarius, R. Holland, & S. Rosenberg (Eds.), *Personal construct psychology* (pp. 219–230). London: Macmillan.

Fransella, F., & Bannister, D. (1977). *A manual for repertory grid technique.* San Diego, CA: Academic Press.

Gergen, K. J., & Gergen, M. M. (1986). Narrative form and the construction of psychological science. In T. R. Sarbin (Ed.), *Narrative psychology* (pp. 22–44). New York: Praeger.

Gonçalves, Ó. F. (1994). From epistemological truth to existential meaning in cognitive narrative psychotherapy. *Journal of Constructivist Psychology, 7,* 107–118.

Greenberg, L., & Pascual-Leone, J. (1995). A dialectical constructivist approach to experiential change. In R. A. Neimeyer & M. J. Mahoney (Eds.), *Constructivism in psychotherapy* (pp. 169–191). Washington, DC: American Psychological Association.

Howard, G. S. (1991). Culture tales: A narrative approach to thinking, cross-cultural psychology, and psychotherapy. *American Psychologist, 46,* 187–197.

Jung, C. G. (1964). *Man and his symbols.* Garden City, NY: Doubleday.

Kelly, G. A. (1955). *The psychology of personal constructs.* New York: Norton.

Kelly, G. A. (1969). Ontological acceleration. In B. Maher (Ed.), *Clinical psychology and personality* (pp. 7–45). New York: Wiley.

Kremsdorf, R. (1985). An extension of fixed-role therapy with a couple. In F. Epting & A. W. Landfield (Eds.), *Anticipating personal construct psychology* (pp. 216–224). Lincoln: University of Nebraska Press.

Leitner, L. M. (1988). Terror, risk, and reverence: Experiential personal construct psychotherapy. *International Journal of Personal Construct Psychology, 1,* 251–263.

Mahoney, M. (1991). *Human change processes.* New York: Basic Books.

Mair, J. M. M. (1977). The community of self. In D. Bannister (Ed.), *New perspectives in personal construct theory* (pp. 125–149). San Diego, CA: Academic Press.

Mair, M. (1989). *Between psychology and psychotherapy: A poetics of practice.* London: Routledge & Kegan Paul.

Neimeyer, G. J. (1995). The challenge of change. In R. A. Neimeyer & M. J. Mahoney (Eds.), *Constructivism in psychotherapy* (pp. 111–126). Washington, DC: American Psychological Association.

Neimeyer, R. A. (1985). *The development of personal construct psychology.* Lincoln: University of Nebraska Press.

Neimeyer, R. A. (1993a). Constructivist approaches to the measurement of meaning. In G. J. Neimeyer (Ed.), *Casebook of constructivist assessment* (pp. 58–103). Newbury Park, CA: Sage.

Neimeyer, R. A. (1993b). Constructivist psychotherapy. In K. T. Kuehlwein & H. Rosen (Eds.), *Cognitive therapy in action: Evolving innovative practice* (pp. 268–300). San Francisco: Jossey-Bass.

Progoff, I. (1975). *A journal workshop.* New York: Dialogue House Library.

Rainer, T. (1978). *The new diary.* Los Angeles: Tarcher.

Russell, R. L., & Lucariello, J. (1992). Narrative, yes: Narrative ad infinitum, no! *American Psychologist, 47,* 671–673.

White, M., & Epston, D. (1990). *Narrative means to therapeutic ends.* New York: Norton.

Yorke, M. (1989). The intolerable wrestle: Words, numbers, and meanings. *International Journal of Personal Construct Psychology, 2,* 65–76.

Zeig, J. (1985). *Experiencing Erikson.* New York: Brunner/Mazel.

12

FROM ASSESSMENT TO CHANGE: THE PERSONAL MEANING OF CLINICAL PROBLEMS IN THE CONTEXT OF THE SELF-NARRATIVE

HUBERT J. M. HERMANS

We see it as the ultimate objective of the clinical-psychology enterprise . . . *the psychological reconstruction of life*. We even considered using the term *reconstruction* instead of *therapy*. If it had not been such a mouth-filling word we might have gone ahead with the idea. Perhaps later we may! (Kelly, 1955, p. 187)

The main thesis put forward in this chapter is twofold. First, the personal meaning of clinical problems can be understood by placing them in the context of the client's self-narrative; and second, as part of an intelligible story, the client's problem is shared with the psychotherapist in such a way that, in the process of telling and retelling, the personal meaning of the problem changes in the course of time. This process of telling and retelling represents a gradual transition between assessment and change.

Initially, I present a theoretical framework—valuation theory—showing how personal meanings emerge from people's self-narratives. Next, I describe a method of self-investigation as a concrete tool for

I thank Els Hermans-Jansen, who was the psychotherapist in the three case studies reported and who placed the data of the self-investigations at my disposal.

247

assessing and changing these personal meanings. I then present three idiographic studies reflecting how clinical problems, as integrative parts of the client's self-narrative, change their meaning: one client with a persistent tendency to avoid conflict situations, another with a disturbing fear of death, and a third with an incomprehensible psychosomatic complaint. Finally, I broaden the scope of the chapter to discuss the root metaphor of contextualism and the role of the client–subject as coinvestigator for assessment and change.

VALUATION THEORY: PERSONAL MEANINGS ORGANIZED IN A SELF-NARRATIVE

Valuation theory (Hermans, 1987a, 1987b, 1988, 1989; Hermans, Fiddelaers, De Groot, & Nauta, 1990) was originally developed for studying individual experiences, their ordering into a narrative structure, and their development over time. The theory's view of the person was inspired by the philosophical thinking of James (1890) and Merleau-Ponty (1945/1962). Within the theory, the self is conceived of as an organized process of valuation. The *process* aspect refers to the historical nature of personal experience and implies a specific spatiotemporal orientation: The embodied person lives in the present and is therefore oriented toward the past and the future from a specific point or position in time and space. The *organizational* aspect emphasizes that the person, through the process of self-reflection, creates a composite whole containing divergent experiences associated with different positions in time and space. In this composite whole, the experiences are ordered into a coherent and intelligible self-narrative.

The theory's central concept, *valuation*, is an active process of meaning construction. As such, it is an open concept referring to anything that a person finds to be important when telling his or her life story. A valuation is any unit of meaning that has a positive (pleasant), negative (unpleasant), or ambivalent (both pleasant and unpleasant) value in the eyes of the individual. It includes a broad range of phenomena: a precious memory, an impressive event or series of events, a difficult problem, a psychological or psychosomatic complaint, an unreachable goal, the anticipated death of a significant other, and so forth. Through the process of self-reflection, valuations get organized into a system, and, depending on the changes in the person–situation interaction, different valuations may emerge.

James's (1890) I and Me and Sarbin's (1986) Narrative Translation

The concept of valuation as an active process of self-reflection is based on the difference between the *I* and the *me*, which was originally conceived of by James (1890) and was characterized by Rosenberg (1979) as a classic distinction in the psychology of the self. Recently, Sarbin (1986) dwelled on this distinction in an attempt to phrase the self in narrative terms. James, Mead, Freud, and others, Sarbin argued, have all emphasized the distinction between the *I* and the *me* and between their equivalents in other European languages to give meaning to that vague but indispensable construct: the self. The uttered pronoun *I* stands for the author, whereas *me* represents the actor, or narrative character. That is, the self as author, the *I*, can imaginatively construct a story in which the *me* is the protagonist. According to this view, the self as author can imagine the future and reconstruct the past, describing himself or herself as an actor (see also Crites, 1986). Such a narrative construction, more-over, is a means for organizing episodes, actions, and the significance of one's actions; in this construction, different facts and fantasies are brought together that may be spread across both time and space (Sarbin, 1986, p. 9).

Valuation and Affect

An important assumption in the present theory is that each valuation has an affective connotation; that is, each valuation implies a specific pattern of affect, or an affective modality. When one knows which types of affect are implied by a particular valuation, one also knows something about the valuation itself. The affective quality of a valuation as a unit of meaning in a self-narrative is in agreement with the general notion that affect plays an essential role in the organization of one's self-narrative (Bamberg, 1991; McAdams, 1985a). In other words, people are inclined to select and tell those experiences that have, for example, a positive or negative affective quality. This implies that a great number of experiences that have no particular affective appeal are not selected for the process of telling.

The affective domain of the valuation system has been further explored by the introduction of the latent–manifest distinction. It is assumed that a small set of basic motives is represented latently in the affective component of a valuation and that these motives play an important role in organizing the self-narrative. These basic motives are assumed to be similar across individuals and to be continuously active within each individual moving through time and space. It is supposed that the basic motives have an organizing influence on the great variety of valuations on the manifest level. At the manifest level, valuations vary phenomenologically, not only across individuals but also within a single individual across time and space.

Basic Duality of Human Motivation

So far, researchers have identified two motives as central to the affective component of the valuation system: (a) the striving for self-enhancement, or S *motive* (i.e., self-maintenance and self-expansion) and (b) the longing for contact and union with the other, or O *motive* (i.e., contact with other people and the surrounding world). This distinction resulted from a review of a number of researchers' conceptions of the basic duality of human experience. For example, in his treatise on the duality of human existence, Bakan (1966) viewed agency (self-mainte-nance and self-expansion) and communion as basic dynamic principles. For Angyal (1965), the difference between healthy and neurotic develop-ment depended on the balance between two mutually complementing forces—autonomy (self-determination) and homonomy (self-surrender). Loevinger (1976) described the reconciliation of autonomy and interde-pendence at the highest (i.e., autonomous and integrated) stages of ego development. Klages (1948) considered *Bindung* (solidification) and *Lösung* (dissolution) to be two dynamic forces in human character. In a clinical–developmental study, Gutmann (1980) observed a blending of masculinity and femininity after midlife. In a study of mystic and medita-tive experiences, Deikman (1971, 1976) distinguished between an action mode and a receptive mode of consciousness. Fowler (1981) described the rapprochement of the rational and the ecstatic at the highest stage of human faith. More recently, McAdams (1985b) has identified the distinction between power and intimacy within a narrative context, again suggesting the basic character of the S and O motives. It should be noted, however, that it is not necessarily my intention to exclude other theoretically well-founded motives that could also be incorporated into valuation theory.

In summary, when a person values something, he or she always feels something about it, and in these feelings, basic motives are reflected. When a valuation represents a gratification of the S motive (e.g., "I passed a difficult examination"), the person experiences a feeling of strength and pride in connection with the valuation. In a similar way, a valuation can function as a gratification of the O motive (e.g., "I enjoy my son playing his instrument"). Feelings of tenderness and intimacy experienced in connection with the specific valuation are indicators of this particular motive. The affective rating of individual valuations can be seen as a representation of the latent motivational base.

The model of the self presented above provides a conceptual base for the study of the personal meaning of clinical problems. A clinical problem is conceived of as a personal valuation that functions in the context of the valuation system as a whole. From the perspective of the manifest level, the problem may develop over time in close relation to changes in the situation. From the perspective of the latent level, a clinical problem may have a basic motivational function, as I show in the idiographic studies presented later in this chapter.

THE SELF-CONFRONTATION METHOD: TELLING AND RETELLING ONE'S SELF-NARRATIVE

The self-confrontation method is an idiographic assessment procedure based on valuation theory. For a proper understanding of the method, one must be aware that it not only lends itself to the study of individual narratives but may also be used to arrive at nomothetic types of generalizations about people (see Epstein, 1983; Hermans, 1988; Lamiell, 1987; Pervin, 1984; Thomae, 1968—who have argued, often in different ways or with different emphases, for a combination of idiographic and nomothetic approaches and their integration).

The method of self-confrontation is designed to study the relation between valuations and types of affect as well as the way in which these variables get organized into a structured whole (Hermans & Hermans-Jansen, in press). The procedure involves eliciting a set of valuations and then associating these valuations with a standardized set of affect terms. The result is an individualized matrix in which each cell represents the extent to which a specific affect is characteristic of a specific valuation (see Table 1).

Construction of Valuations

The valuations (i.e., rows in the matrix of Table 1) are elicited by the therapist with a series of open-ended questions. The main questions, outlined in the Appendix, are intended to evoke important units of meaning from the client's past, present, and future. The questions—read aloud by the psychotherapist while sitting next to the client—are used in such a way that clients feel free to mention those concerns that are most relevant from the perspective of their present situation. Clients are encouraged to phrase valuations in their own terms so that the formulations agree as much as possible with their intended meaning. Clients typically express valuations in sentence form. However, when it is difficult or impossible for a client to formulate a valuation as a sentence, he or she is permitted to express it in just a few words or even a single word. A quick response is not required, and there is no one-to-one relation between question and answer; that is, typically, each question leads to more than one valuation. The aim of this part of the self-investigation is to arrive at a survey of the experiences relevant to the individual from

TABLE 1
Matrix of Valuation × Affect: Raw Ratings of a Subject

Valuation No.	Affect Term															
	1	2	3	4	5	6	7	8	9	10	11	12	13	14	15	16
1	4	3	1	2	1	0	4	5	0	0	1	3	0	1	1	0
2	0	3	0	0	0	0	0	0	3	0	0	0	2	0	2	1
3	3	4	2	0	4	0	3	0	0	0	3	1	0	3	0	3
4	0	0	0	2	0	0	0	0	3	0	0	0	2	0	0	0
5	4	4	4	0	2	0	3	4	1	3	3	2	0	0	1	5
6	0	0	0	0	0	0	0	1	3	0	1	1	1	0	3	0
7	5	3	4	0	2	5	0	0	0	2	4	1	0	2	0	5
8	4	4	4	1	4	4	3	2	0	2	1	0	1	3	1	5
9	0	0	0	3	0	0	0	0	3	0	0	0	2	0	4	0
10	1	3	1	0	0	1	2	3	1	2	3	3	0	1	1	1
.	.	.	.	.	.	.	.	.	.	.	.	.	.	.	.	.
.	.	.	.	.	.	.	.	.	.	.	.	.	.	.	.	.
.	.	.	.	.	.	.	.	.	.	.	.	.	.	.	.	.

Note. Rows represent valuations and columns represent affect terms used for the indexes S, O, P, and N, where S = affect referring to self-enhancement, O = affect referring to contact with the other, P = positive affect, and N = negative affect. 1 = joy (P); 2 = self-esteem (S); 3 = happiness (P); 4 = worry (N); 5 = strength (S); 6 = enjoyment (P); 7 = caring (O); 8 = love (O); 9 = unhappiness (N); 10 = tenderness (O); 11 = self-confidence (O); 12 = intimacy (O); 13 = despondency (N); 14 = pride (S); 15 = disappointment (N); 16 = inner calm (P). Dots indicate that there could be more than 10 rows.

his or her present perspective. At the end of the interview, clients are asked whether the survey contains all of the experiences they want to include. If something is missing, they can add it. At the end of the procedure, the number of valuations greatly varies; but in most cases, a client expresses between 20 and 40 valuations.

Combining Valuation and Affect

In the second part of the investigation, the therapist provides the client with a standard list of affect terms (see Table 1). Concentrating on the first valuation, the client indicates the extent to which he or she experiences each affect in relation to each valuation on a scale ranging from 0 (*not at all*) to 5 (*very much*). The client, working alone, rates each valuation with the same list of affect terms, and the different valuations can then be compared according to their affective profiles. The list of affect terms found in Table 1 is the condensed form of a more extended list (see Hermans, 1987a) and provides a maximum amount of affective information with a minimum number of terms. The indexes relevant for the present study are summarized below.

1. *Index S* is the sum of the scores for the four affect terms expressing self-enhancement (2, 5, 11, and 14 of Table 1).
2. *Index O* is the sum of the scores for the four affect terms expressing contact and union with the other (7, 8, 10, and 12). For each valuation, the S–O difference can be determined. When the experience of self-enhancement is stronger than the experience of contact with the other, S > O. When the feeling of contact with the other prevails, O > S. When both kinds of experiences coexist, S = O.
3. *Index P* is the sum of the scores for the four positive affect terms (1, 3, 6, and 16).
4. *Index N* is the sum of the scores for the four negative affect terms (4, 9, 13, and 15). For each valuation, again, the P–N difference can be studied. This indicates the degree of well-being that a person experiences in relation to a specific valuation. Well-being is positive when P > N, negative when N > P, and ambivalent when P = N.[1]
5. *Index r* represents the correspondence between the affective profiles for two valuations, that is, the correlation between any two rows in the matrix. This correlation indicates the extent of similarity between the affective meanings associ-

---

[1]The scores for Indexes S, O, P, and N range from 0 to 20 for each valuation.

ated with two valuations as far as the shape of the two affective profiles is concerned. The correlation often shows that valuations referring to quite different experiences (e.g., "being at a party" and "being lost in a big city") have highly similar affective profiles in the particular world of an individual. For the present purposes, Index *r* may be helpful when the affective profile associated with a clinical problem is compared with the affective profiles of the other valuations of the system. Indexes S, O, P, and N can be used to compare the valuation corresponding to the clinical problem with the contextual valuation in more detail.

These theoretically derived indexes have been psychometrically analyzed with a group of 43 students (20 men and 23 women) and a group of 40 clients (20 men and 20 women who had identity problems and problems in social relationships). In the student group, the reliabilities (coefficient alpha) of the S, O, P, and N indexes were .83, .86, .85, and .88, respectively. The correlation between Indexes S and O was .27, and the correlation between Indexes P and N was −.79. In the client group, the reliabilities of the S, O, P, and N indexes were .83, .89, .93, and .91, respectively. The correlation between Indexes S and O was .64, and the correlation between Indexes P and N was −.70. When the groups were compared, the client group showed lower scores for Index S ($p < .001$), lower scores for Index O ($p < .001$), lower scores for Index P ($p < .001$), and higher scores for Index N ($p < .001$) than did the student group. (For psychometric properties of Index *r*, see Hermans, 1987a, pp. 169–171.)

The following example shows how a person's self-narrative is organized in terms of valuations.

		Index			
		S	O	P	N
Past:	"Last year I lost my wife in an accident."	2	16	0	18
Present:	"I am now involved in a project that absorbs all of my attention."	14	5	15	8
Future:	"In the future, I hope to find a mutually stimulating relation with a partner."	16	17	19	2

Although on the manifest level valuations are temporally ordered as an intelligible story, on the latent level they may have a very different motivational structure. In this example, the O motive is predominant in the experience of the past, the S motive is reigning in the present situation, and the future is colored by the integration of these two motives. In other words, the latent motivational structure is represented by a specific affective profile associated with a particular valuation.

Second Self-Investigation

Usually, a second self-investigation is performed after several weeks or months to document any changes in the client's valuation system as the result of extended self-reflection. However, clients do not start from scratch. Instead, they are confronted with the statements they constructed in their first session. The psychotherapist reads the original question and then produces the statements formulated in the first session. The clients are instructed to consider, for each statement separately, whether they still agree with it: Would they still come up with the same response to the question? If not, there are various options available: An old valuation may be reformulated (modification), replaced (substitution), or discarded altogether (elimination), or a completely new statement may be added (supplementation). In this way, clients have considerable freedom and can point to both the constant and the changing parts of their valuation systems.

The valuation system is studied quantitatively through the use of the indexes described above and qualitatively through a content analysis of the individual formulations. The two types of analyses often give complementary information, and together they contribute to an overall understanding of the person's self-narrative in general and the clinical problem in particular. Take, for example, two valuations, one referring to a client's persistent headaches and another referring to the troubles this client has with his father. Even when the client does not see any relationship between the content of these two valuations, they may be associated with highly similar affective profiles. In this similarity (e.g., low S, low O, low P, and high N) a basic commonality is reflected suggesting that the two valuations have a highly similar meaning from the perspective of the latent level. The two valuations may be studied, in turn, in the context of the valuation system as a whole. Moreover, the valuations and their affective profiles may be followed in successive self-investigations. The content (formulation) of the valuations reveals how the person tells and retells his or her story over time; inspection of the indexes reveals how the valuation system gets organized and reorganized from the perspective of the person's latent level of functioning.

THE CHANGING MEANING OF CLINICAL PROBLEMS

In this section, I present three different clinical problems to demonstrate how the meaning of a problem can be assessed as part of the client's self-narrative as well as how self-investigation can be used in the psychotherapist–client collaboration to change this meaning.

Client 1: Avoidance of Conflict

Ann, a 40-year-old married woman with two adolescent children, contacted a psychotherapist during a period in which she was having serious difficulties with her work. In the school where she taught, she had become involved in a conflict between the administration and her colleagues. She was friends with the managing couple of the school and, therefore, became an "in-between" person who was often approached both by the administration and by colleagues in attempts to solve the conflicts. This situation reactualized her problematic home situation in the past, in which, being the oldest child, she had to play a mitigating role in frequent conflicts between her parents. She had to make the difficult decision of whether to stay in a nonsupportive job situation or give up her job.

Ann performed two self-investigations, with 9 months intervening. In the intervening period, she had regular sessions with the psychotherapist once a week. In her first self-investigation, Ann formulated 24 valuations in response to the questions referring to past, present, and future. Some of the valuations that were most relevant to her problem—the fearful avoidance of conflict situations—are presented in Table 2.

A general feature of Ann's valuation system was the low level of self-enhancement for almost all her valuations (see the low level of S in Table 2). More specifically, Ann tells in Valuation 1 that she learned to avoid conflict situations from her early family experience, and, as part of the same unit of meaning, she explains that this tendency is closely related to her fear of losing people. In the conflicts between her parents, she felt "between two fires," and, in reaction, used to close herself off (Valuation 2). The experience of being between two fires was reactualized in her current work situation, in which a conflict arose that was interpreted by Ann as highly similar to the conflicts in her early family experience (Valuation 3; see also the similarity among the affective indexes for Valuations 3 and 2). Although Valuations 1–3 are relevant for understanding Ann's reaction to her work conflict, they do not offer much assistance in solving her problem. This is not true for Valuation 4: Here, she expresses that she feels more strength and clarity "on the inside" than she expresses "on the outside." Although this valuation was formulated as an ideal ("I'd like"), it was associated with more negative than positive affect and with a low degree of affect referring to self-enhancement. This suggests that, in this period of her development, Ann felt unable to express those capacities that, in her experience, were closed off from the outside (see the term *close off* in Valuation 2). In spite of the negative

TABLE 2

Valuations Referring to Conflict Avoidance at Time 1 and Development of Corresponding Valuations at Time 2

Valuation Referring to Conflict Avoidance at Time 1	Index				Developing Valuation at Time 2	Index			
	S	O	P	N		S	O	P	N
1. I've always had a fear of losing people (my parents' marriage was not good; there was always tension); whenever possible I try to avoid conflict situations.	6	15	3	17	1. I feel more sure of myself and accepted by others being that way; I don't avoid conflict as much.	11	13	16	5
2. I wanted to close myself off from the outside world whenever I was approached by my father or mother and didn't know what to do (between two fires).	0	5	0	20	2. I fight more for my own interests.	13	9	16	3
3. In the conflict at school I feel like a buffer between two clashing parties.	0	0	0	17	3. I'll quit my job; giving up my financial independence is less bad than going back to the old work environment where nothing is discussed.	18	10	14	1
4. I'd like to appear on the outside as the person that I am on the inside, but have never let anyone see (above all stronger and clearer).	1	4	1	15	4. I am in the process of coming out as the person that I am on the inside but simply haven't let anyone see (above all stronger and clearer).	13	2	16	4
5. —[a]					5. I've stopped being what other people want me to be (new).	16	0	17	0

Note. S = affect referring to self-enhancement; O = affect referring to contact with the other; P = positive affect; N = negative affect.
[a] A fifth valuation was not measured at Time 1.

affective quality of Valuation 4, the psychotherapist decided (after discussing the system as a whole with Ann) to take this valuation as a starting point for developing the system in the direction of a higher level of self-enhancement.

After a period of concentrating on the nature of Valuation 4 in the context of the other valuations of the system, Ann began to train herself in taking new initiatives, beginning with easy ones and gradually moving to more difficult ones. These initiatives, discussed with the therapist in weekly sessions, typically related to the assessed gap in her system: the low level of self-enhancement. For example, when there was a misunderstanding at her daughter's school, she decided to write a letter to clarify things, although previously she would have left this to her husband. Or, when she heard that a neighbor had accused her of potential dishonesty, she got in touch with this neighbor to explain her view, although she previously had avoided conflict at all costs.

Nine months after the initial self-investigation, Ann and the psychotherapist felt that so much had changed in Ann's view of herself and the world that they should perform a second self-investigation. The changes in Ann's original valuations are presented on the right side of Table 2. A most conspicuous change was that Ann's modified valuations had a higher level of self-enhancement (S) and, at the same time, a higher degree of positive (P) than negative (N) affect. Perhaps it is important to note that the increased level of self-enhancement was not at the cost of the experience of contact and union (O). The reason is exemplified in Valuation 1 at Time 2: Ann not only felt more sure of herself but also felt accepted by others in "being that way" (i.e., by her friends, husband, children, and the psychotherapist). In that atmosphere, it was also possible for her to make the difficult decision to quit her job (Valuation 3 at Time 2). This decision was not to be understood as another way to avoid a conflict situation. On the contrary, she made this decision after she had made several serious attempts to discuss the communication problems among the people at work; however, she had little success.

The main strategy that Ann followed to change her position in life is indicated by Valuation 4 at Time 2: She brought to the outside what she felt was present somewhere on the inside. This is an example of one of the central notions in valuation theory: the gradual transition from assessment to change. The therapist decided to give Ann an opportunity to express all "meaning units" (valuations) that she experienced as relevant in her life situation. The assessment of the valuation system and associated affective connotation provided a base for therapist and client to explore "entrances for change." The valuation system as a whole functioned as a common plane for a thorough investigation and discussion of the structure of the client's self-narrative in order to start a process of change. The direction of this change process was more specifically indicated by Valuation 4, after client and therapist had examined the various implications of this valuation by placing it in the context of the valuation system as a whole.

Client 2: Fear of Death

The second client is Sandra, an artistically gifted, 18-year-old woman who contacted a psychotherapist in a period of identity problems. In the first self-investigation, she expressed her feeling of being an outsider, described a number of disappointing friendships, and wondered what the meaning of her life would have been in the event that she were to die. For the present purposes only, I selected two valuations (see Table 3) from her total valuation system that refer to her experience of death to show how the meaning of death changed for her in the course of time.

The first valuation in Table 3 describes how Sandra feels threatened by dead people. In her fantasy, she imagines all the dead watching, criticizing, and ridiculing her. At the same time, she is strongly occupied with her grandmother who recently died and whom she loved very much (Valuation 2). The two valuations—although both representing negative experiences—contrast the feeling of contact and union. Valuation 2 reveals a specific pattern of low S, high O, low P, and high N. This pattern has been found to typically indicate a so-called *fugit amor* experience—that is, a loving orientation to a person or object that is or has become unreachable (Hermans, Hermans-Jansen, & Van Gilst, 1987). This loving orientation is entirely absent in Valuation 1, which evokes no feelings of contact and union at all. In fact, the two valuations are incompatible: The lovable grandmother belongs to the group of dead people by whom Sandra feels threatened.

Sandra was very active in exploring her experiences and in taking new initiatives. She became more and more involved in artistic perception and expression of the great variety of her experiences and in the theme of death in particular. For example, she became interested in a variety of processes in nature related to the cycle of life and death: the change of color in plants, the process of rotting and decay, and the blossoming of flowers in spring. She read the work of several poets who focused on the theme of death, and she wrote poems herself, in which her relation with significant others played a central role. In the meantime, there were a limited number of sessions (about one in every 3 weeks) with the psychotherapist, with whom Sandra discussed her daily experiences and sometimes read her poems.

TABLE 3
Valuations Referring to Death at Time 1 and Development of Corresponding Valuations at Time 2

Valuation Referring to Death at Time 1	Index				Developing Valuation at Time 2	Index			
	S	O	P	N		S	O	P	N
1. I think that all the dead are watching me.	0	1	0	15	I enjoy the succession of the seasons: I've surrendered myself to life; I don't resist it any longer.	11	16	18	4
2. I didn't want to cry about the death of my grandma.	3	16	0	15	My grandma: Her death blossomed in my deepest / and nourished itself in my heart.	10	19	13	10

Note. S = affect referring to self-enhancement; O = affect referring to contact with the other; P = positive affect; N = negative affect.

In one of the next self-investigations, almost 2 years after the first, Sandra reformulated the two original valuations in a more positive direction. In the reformulation of the first valuation, she expressed her enjoyment of the succession of seasons—representing the eternal cycle of life and death—and emphasized that she had "surrendered" herself to this natural process. This change is associated with an increase not only in feelings of contact and union but also, to some degree, in self-enhancement (she no longer felt a victim of the dead). A similar tendency toward self-surrender was revealed by the change in the second valuation: She was very impressed by a verse of one of her favorite poets and incorporated this in her valuation of the death of her grandmother.

There are two important differences between the cases of Ann and Sandra. First, Ann showed a remarkable increase in self-enhancement, whereas Sandra developed more in the direction of self-surrender (as far as her relation with death was concerned). Second, Ann moved from the inside to the outside (expressing strength and clarity), whereas, in Sandra's case, the change was more from the outside to the inside. That is, Sandra opened herself up, so that the deeper personal meaning of an important event (the death of her loved grandmother) could enter her heart. However different the changes in the two cases may have been, there was an important commonality: Both Ann and Sandra told their self-narratives in such a way that their specific problems became meaningful once they were actively related to contextual valuations. They did this in such a way that the meaning of their problems changed both on the manifest level (reformulation of the problem) and on the latent level (change in motivational characteristics).

Client 3: A Psychosomatic Problem as a Signal of Stress

In the last example, I describe how a psychosomatic problem that was initially experienced by a client as entirely meaningless was later understood as a signal of stress related to specific circumstances in her life.

Alice, a 54-year-old woman, performed a self-investigation during a period of serious difficulties with her husband. Their marriage problems worsened when her husband, a playwright, published a play in which Alice could be recognized as one of the main characters. Both Alice and her husband decided to perform self-investigations as a basis for a number of sessions in which they would discuss their respective problems and contrasting views under the guidance of the psychotherapist. One of Alice's valuations referred to "a pain in my neck and back of my head" (see Table 4).

Before discussing the results of Alice's self-investigation, I need to make a more general observation. Over the course of time, I have studied a variety of psychosomatic complaints as parts of an organized valuation

TABLE 4
Psychosomatic Complaint and Highest Correlating Valuation at Times 1 and 2

Time	Psychosomatic Complaint	Index S	O	P	N	r	Highest Correlating Valuation	Index S	O	P	N
1	Pain in my neck and back of my head	1	2	0	10	.98	My father: He avoided problems and used his children in his struggle against my mother; he always conformed with her authority and so he enforced our powerlessness as children	1	2	0	12
						.92	In my husband's play, I don't recognize myself in the way he depicts me	3	0	0	14
2	Pain in my neck and back of my head	2	0	0	17	.91	I regret that my husband has disclosed our problems in public before we had a chance to discuss them privately	4	1	0	15

Note. S = affect referring to self-enhancement; O = affect referring to contact with the other; P = positive affect; N = negative affect; r = product-moment correlation between two affective patterns.

system. From a clinical perspective, a typical finding has been that many clients have no idea about the psychological significance or origin of their complaints. The therapist's answer to this ignorance has been to develop a strategy for integrating the psychosomatic complaints as part of the self by proposing that the client include the complaint as a separate valuation. In most cases, clients then simply mention the existence of these problems (e.g., "my headache" or even shorter "headache"), or they describe it in a short sentence that does not reveal more than the frequency or degree of seriousness of the problem (e.g., "I often have pain in my heart" or "I suffer from terrible pain in my stomach"). In the next stage, the valuation referring to the psychosomatic complaint is studied in the context of the other valuations to explore meaningful relationships. In other words, an initially isolated valuation is integrated as part of the system by being actively linked to other parts of the system.

To study the psychosomatic complaint in close relation with other parts of the system, the therapist should correlate the complaint as a separate valuation successively with all the other valuations of the system. In such an analysis (called *modality analysis*), one supposes that the highest correlating valuations are of particular significance, because they have affective profiles similar to the complaint and, therefore, share a similar affective meaning (for a discussion of the validity of the highest correlations, see Hermans, 1987a, pp. 169–171). By taking these highest correlating valuations into account, the therapist can enlarge the personal meaning of a psychosomatic complaint (or any clinical problem). In Alice's first self-investigation, two valuations showed very high correlations with the psychosomatic problem (see the right side of Table 4). Although correlations may not be interpreted in terms of a causal relation, they indicate that there is a common meaning in the pain, on the one hand, and the problematic relation with her father and her husband, on the other hand. In a second self-investigation, 8 months after the first, a high correlation was found again between the same psychosomatic complaint and the modified valuation referring to the relation of Alice with her husband. (Note that the valuation referring to her father was eliminated from the system at Time 2 and that Alice's objections were more directly formulated against the play). It was at the end of the second investigation that Alice and the psychotherapist decided to focus on the meaning of the complaint in a more explicit way. This was done by concentrating on the highest correlating valuations at Time 1 and Time 2 and was meant to invite Alice to phrase in her own terms the common meaning of the psychosomatic problem and the valuations with the highest correlations. This resulted in the following formulation:

> My pain may be suppressed anger or resistance (the basic pattern
> of my behavior). I express my dissatisfaction in an indirect and,

therefore, powerless manner. This means that a more direct resistance may relieve my pain.

A peculiar feature of this interpretation is that Alice not only interpreted the affective commonality between her pain and the relation with her husband but also formulated the direction in which to change her behavior. In this way, she gradually moved from assessment to change.

No follow-up data were available for Alice because she and her husband ended contact with the psychotherapist after the second investigation. But even the case material at hand may serve as an example of the procedure that can be followed if one aims to broaden the personal meaning of a clinical problem that would otherwise function as an isolated phenomenon.

FROM ASSESSMENT TO CHANGE: CONTEXTUALISM AND THE THERAPEUTIC RELATIONSHIP

In this final section, I argue that contextualism as a root metaphor for psychology provides a basis for a dialogical relationship between psychotherapist and client. Moreover, I show how a dialogical relationship contributes to a client's active exploration of his or her own situation and leads to a gradual transition from assessment to change.

Contextualism as a Root Metaphor and the Nature of Causes

Contextualism as a basic metaphor of viewing the world was originally formulated by Pepper (1942) and has more recently been elaborated in terms of a narrative psychology by Sarbin (1986). The central element of contextualism is the historical event, which can only be properly understood when located in the context of time and space. Contextualism presupposes an ongoing texture of multiple events, each being influenced by collateral episodes and by the efforts of agents who engage in actions. Contained in the metaphor is the idea of constant change in the structure of situations. Sarbin argued that the historical act and the narrative have approximately the same semantic structure. History is not to be viewed simply as a collection of records of past or present events. Rather, annals and chronicles are used by professional historians as raw materials for the construction of narratives. Both the historian and the novelist are narrativists, although their emphases are different. The novelist writes about fictive characters in a context of real world settings or combines elements from reality in such a way that fiction results. The historian writes about presumably actual events, populated by reconstructed people, and in this process of reconstruction, imagination is indispensable. Both novelistic literature and history make use of fact and fiction.

Personal meaning conceived as an active process of valuation should also be understood as a combination of fact and fiction. For example, Client 2, who was confronted with the death of her beloved grandmother, felt this fact to be particularly threatening because of her fantasy of being watched by all the dead. However, in a later period, she reinterpreted the same event in a poetic manner ("her death blossomed . . . and nourished itself in my heart"), so that the same event finally received a positive meaning. In this process of revaluation, imagination played a central role in determining the positive or negative connotion of her self-narrative.

Apparently, personal meaning is determined not by "brute facts," as Anscombe (1957–1958) has called them, but by their interpretation. At this point, a sharp distinction must be made between contextualism and mechanicism—two root metaphors originally discussed by Pepper (1942). The mechanistic metamodel derives its constructs from the concept of a machine. As Pepper has noted, the mechanistic view considers the human organism as reactive from a basic state of rest and activity as a result of external stimulation. Complex phenomena, such as affect and problem solving, are considered to ultimately be reducible to simple phenomena governed by efficient causes (i.e., causes affect subsequent behavior). A mechanistic model of development typically focuses on the role of events as antecedents to various response outcomes. In contextual models, however, events exist neither as facts themselves nor in association with fixed meanings. On the contrary, contextualism supposes that the meaning of a fact or event results from an interpretion of events in relation to other events. Therefore, there is much sense in Cohler's (1988) conclusion that collection of brute facts is impossible when one is studying meanings embedded in stories or narratives.

An important implication of the contextual model is that meaning changes with its context. That is, a particular event or fact, embedded in a developing story or narrative, may have different or even contrasting meanings in the course of time. This observation indicates that the meaning of events comes from the top down rather than from the bottom up. A story as an organized whole represents a text in which sentences form parts of a discourse. And the meaning of a sentence comes down from the top level of discourse, just like words derive their meaning in the context of a sentence. Therefore, new events, or any change in the situation, typically give rise to a retelling of the story as a whole (e.g., an event in the present may alter one's story of the present, but it may also alter one's story about the future and even the past). Moreover, events never determine a change in the story in terms of a straight cause–effect relationship. Even if one considered a new event to cause a change in the narrative, one would have to be aware that the term *cause* may be used in vastly different ways.

Three Kinds of Causes

A classic distinction, originally made by Aristotle and recently summarized by Rychlak (1988), may clarify the issue of causation. Three kinds of causes are relevant for the present discussion: efficient cause, formal cause, and final cause. The *efficient cause* concerns the impetus for events. The usual phrasing indicates that some antecedent event is assumed to invariably and necessarily cause a consequence, called an *effect*. Rychlak explained that most people think of this meaning for the term *cause* because of natural science and its zest for experimentation. A *formal cause* refers to a pattern, shape, outline, or recognizable organization in the flow of events. Communication with words combined into sentences and texts along with theory construction involve such formal patterning. *Final cause* can best be defined as that for the sake of which something happens or comes about: There is a final reason, purpose, or intention for the sake of which something happens. If so, the event is called *telic* or the account *teleological*, from the Greek word *telos*, meaning "end."

There is a clear affinity between the distinction of different causes, on the one hand, and the distinction between the root metaphors of mechanicism and contextualism on the other hand. Mechanistic models favor efficient cause relationships, whereas it is in the nature of contextualism to conceptualize changes in terms of formal and final relationships. An example of a mechanistic view is Holmes and Rahe's (1967) research, in which particular events (e.g., death of a spouse) are defined as more stressful than other events (e.g., trouble with the boss). Of course, there is no reasoning against ordering events according to their stressful influence, but one must realize that such a model supposes that it is because of the nature of the event itself that a certain degree of strain results. A contextual view, however, supposes that the meaning of an event results from a formal cause, in that as part of a text, the event is part of a patterned whole. For example, the first word in a text is not to be conceived as the efficient cause of the next word, because the second word does not necessarily follow the first word (and a second sentence does not necessarily follow from the first one). However, in combination, the several words and sentences form an organized pattern in which the several elements constitute meaning in their interrelationships. When the text has the character of a narrative, the meaning of the specific events have their formal cause in the story as an organized whole. Depending on this organized whole, the death of a significant other, for example, may be a positive or a negative experience for the same person at different moments in time or from different perspectives.

The narrative metaphor also has an affinity with the final cause. A person telling a narrative intends to explain something, to share something, or to make a point. The telling of a story implies at least two elements: (a) there is an actual or imagined listener who costructures the content and form of the story (e.g., one tells a story differently to a young child than to an adult) and (b) there is a purpose for which one tells it (e.g., one wants to persuade, explain, or express one's emotions). Both factors—the listener and the purpose of telling—have their repercussions for the content and structure of a narrative.

Valuation theory and the self-confrontation method are based on the contextual root metaphor and on the workings of formal and final causes. The organized valuation system should be conceived as a structured story that a client tells to a listening psychotherapist for the purpose of sharing this story and cooperating in changing it so that it "makes more sense." Basically, such a relationship is of a dialogical nature (Hermans & Kempen, 1993; Hermans, Kempen, & Van Loon, 1992). In the next section, I examine the methodological implications of this relationship.

Client as Coinvestigator in the Therapeutic Relationship

The present approach is based on the notion that the psychotherapist who listens to the stories clients tell about their lives may actively contribute to the storytelling by helping them organize and reorganize their stories. This is done by offering clients a relational and semistructured procedure that enables them to express the main topics in their past, present, and future. Once these topics are formulated, clients confront themselves with the question of whether or not they want to continue to live in correspondence with their present valuations. At this point, the collaboration between therapist and client is decisive. The trusting and communicative relationship between therapist and client is necessary not only for the formulation and examination of the self-narrative but also for its rethinking and retelling. The self-confrontation method is devised as a relational procedure in which therapist and client collaborate, not only to investigate the content and structure of the narrative but also to create a new perspective as it emerges from the process of the investigation itself. The process of telling one's story and the structure and overview of valuations may stimulate the seeing of new relationships, thus leading to a retelling that deepens the self-narrative and completes it with new meanings (e.g., see Table 2: The client added a new valuation at Time 2 to emphasize a specific aspect of her recent development).

Self-Investigation as a Collaborative Enterprise

When one takes into account the arguments outlined above, one cannot simply label the presented method a standardized test or a traditional form of psychotherapy or counseling. The self-confrontation method is better described as a form of theory-based self-investigation in which the client functions as coinvestigator to the psychotherapist. Arguments for such a position can be found in recent developments in personality psychology. In an extensive review of current research methods, Hermans and Bonarius (1991) argued that personality psychology is well on its way to recognizing the individual as an expert on his or her own self and situation. Clients are increasingly asked to take an active role in personality research and are invited to contribute to this research from their own perspectives and on the basis of their own expertise. The study of personal meaning in particular represents an area where the construing and interpretative capacities of a client are indispensable sources of information. In the method I have described, the specific contribution of clients as coinvestigators is stimulated by inviting them to intensively self-reflect and to formulate their personal meanings in the form of valuations. The specific contribution of the psychotherapist is to offer the client a structured way of realizing this reflection, with the basic motives serving as organizing principles, useful for the analysis of the individual's self-narrative. This cooperative and dialogical effort between the two parties represents a form of investigation in which "reality" is not simply discovered by an "objective" assessment instrument. Rather, reality is construed as resulting from a cooperative effort: It is not a given but an "emergent." From this perspective, one may conclude that the concept of valuation is, in Mahoney's (1988) terms, to be understood as a form of "proactive cognition" and, thus, provides a conceptual tool that stimulates psychotherapist and client to proceed as cocreators of the realities to which they respond.

A specific argument for placing the client in the position of self-investigator and coinvestigator is apparent from the notion of "irreducibility of meaning," as has recently been discussed by Bruner (1986). Meanings, Bruner stated, cannot be studied according to a criterion of correspondence. In other words, there is no criterion that provides a means to determine if a meaning is correct or incorrect. Meanings are in no way copies of some kind of reality; therefore, they do not conform to any objectivist criterion of truth. If meanings, and personal meanings in particular, are principally irreducible, then there is no external position from which a researcher or a psychotherapist can determine if any person is right or not right in attributing a particular meaning to reality. Therefore, it must be concluded that any person—subject or client—has the inalienable capacity to create meaning or to re-create existing meanings that are part of the consensus of his or her culture. This human capacity to construct and reconstruct reality is reason enough to approach any individual as "an expert of meaning." On the methodological level, this view implies that subjects in research, and clients in psychotherapy, must be approached not so much as suppliers of data, but as creators of insights. Along this line, Kelly's (1955) advice should be remembered: When you want to know something about a person, ask it; he or she may tell you.

Bridging the Scientist–Practitioner Gap

In accordance with the arguments presented above, it is my thesis that the position of coinvestigator for the subject in psychological research is also applicable to the client in a psychotherapeutic relationship. To put it straightforwardly: There is no essential difference between a subject as a self-expert contributing to the research situation and a client as a self-knowledgeable individual coworking with the psychotherapist. Both are thoroughly examining, in cooperation with a professional, their own situations. And in this collaborative enterprise, clients may deepen their self-knowledge in such a way that they find their own direction in the process of change. In other words, the position of the client as coinvestigator is essential for his or her gradual transition between assessment and change. Moreover, this position may contribute to the further exploration of one of the most difficult and challenging problems psychologists are faced with in the history of their discipline: the gap between science and practice. Further exploration of the position of the individual as coinvestigator in research and practice requires a rethinking of the nature of the theoretical concepts underlying psychology. I expect that such a position will be promising only if psychologists are prepared to more greatly emphasize the organization and coherence of personality as a system, greater openness and sensitivity to the particular world of the individual, and an even more dynamic conception of individuality than is currently found in psychological assessment and research.

I have presented a theoretical perspective in which the personal meaning of clinical problems can be understood in the context of the self-narrative. From a methodological point of view, this form of self-investigation may help a client realize a gradual transition from assessment to change of this meaning. For a proper understanding of the nature of this self-investigation, use of the root metaphor of contextualism and positioning of the person as coinvestigator are crucial.

REFERENCES

Angyal, A. (1965). *Neurosis and treatment: A holistic theory.* New York: Wiley.

Anscombe, G. E. M. (1957–1958). On brute facts. *Analysis, 18,* 69–72.

Bakan, D. (1966). *The duality of human existence*. Chicago: Rand McNally.

Bamberg, M. (1991). Conceptualization via narrative: A discussion of Donald E. Polkinghorne's "Narrative and self-concept." *Journal of Narrative and Life Story, 1,* 155–167.

Bruner, J. S. (1986). *Actual minds, possible worlds*. Cambridge, MA: Harvard University Press.

Cohler, B. J. (1988, December). The human studies and the life history: The *Social Service Review* lecture. *Social Service Review,* 552–575.

Crites, S. (1986). Storytime: Recollecting the past and projecting the future. In T. R. Sarbin (Ed.), *Narrative psychology: The storied nature of human conduct* (pp. 152–173). New York: Praeger.

Deikman, A. J. (1971). Bimodal consciousness. *Archives of General Psychiatry, 25,* 481–489.

Deikman, A. J. (1976). Bimodal consciousness and the mystic experience. In Ph. R. Lee, R. E. Ornstein, D. Galin, A. Deikman, & Ch. T. Tart (Eds.), *Symposium on consciousness* (pp. 67–88). New York: Viking Press.

Epstein, S. (1983). Aggregation and beyond: Some basic issues on the prediction of behavior. *Journal of Personality, 51,* 360–392.

Fowler, J. (1981). *Stages of faith*. New York: Harper & Row.

Gutmann, D. L. (1980). The post-parental years: Clinical problems and developmental possibilities. In W. H. Norman & T. J. Scaramella (Eds.), *Mid-life: Developmental and clinical issues* (pp. 38–52). New York: Brunner/Mazel.

Hermans, H. J. M. (1987a). The dream in the process of valuation: A method of interpretation. *Journal of Personality and Social Psychology, 53,* 163–175.

Hermans, H. J. M. (1987b). Self as organized system of valuations: Toward a dialogue with the person. *Journal of Counseling Psychology, 34,* 10–19.

Hermans, H. J. M. (1988). On the integration of idiographic and nomothetic research method in the study of personal meaning. *Journal of Personality, 56,* 785–812.

Hermans, H. J. M. (1989). The meaning of life as an organized process. *Psychotherapy, 26,* 11–22.

Hermans, H. J. M., & Bonarius, H. (1991). The person as co-investigator in personality research. *European Journal of Personality, 5,* 199–216.

Hermans, H. J. M., Fiddelaers, R., De Groot, R., & Nauta, J. (1990). Self-confrontation as a method for assessment and intervention in counseling. *Journal of Counseling and Development, 69,* 156–162.

Hermans, H. J. M., & Hermans-Jansen, E. (in press). *Self-narratives: The emergence of meaning*. New York: Guilford Press.

Hermans, H. J. M., Hermans-Jansen, E., & Van Gilst, W. (1987). The *fugit amor* experience in the process of valuation: A self-confrontation with an unreachable other. *British Journal of Psychology, 78,* 465–481.

Hermans, H. J. M., & Kempen, H. J. G. (1993). *The dialogical self: Meaning as movement*. San Diego, CA: Academic Press.

Hermans, H. J. M., Kempen, H. J. G., & Van Loon, R. J. P. (1992). The dialogical self: Beyond individualism and rationalism. *American Psychologist, 47*, 23–33.

Holmes, T. H., & Rahe, R. H. (1967). The social readjustment rating scale. *Journal of Psychosomatic Research, 11*, 213–218.

James, W. (1890). *The principles of psychology* (Vol. 1). London: Macmillan.

Kelly, G. A. (1955). *The psychology of personal constructs, Volume 1: A theory of personality*. New York: Norton.

Klages, L. (1948). *Charakterkunde* [Characterology]. Zürich, Switzerland: Hirzel.

Lamiell, J. T. (1987). *The psychology of personality: An epistemological inquiry*. New York: Columbia University Press.

Loevinger, J. (1976). *Ego development*. San Francisco: Jossey-Bass.

Mahoney, M. J. (1988). Constructive metatheory: 1. Basic features and historical foundations. *International Journal of Personal Construct Psychology, 1*, 1–35.

McAdams, D. P. (1985a). The "imago": A key narrative component of identity. In P. Shaver (Ed.), *Self, situations, and social behavior. Review of Personality and Social Psychology, 6* (pp. 115–141). Beverly Hills, CA: Sage.

McAdams, D. P. (1985b). *Power, intimacy, and the life story: Personological inquiries into identity*. New York: Guilford Press.

Merleau-Ponty, M. (1962). *Phenomenology of perception* (Colin Smith, Trans.). London: Routledge & Kegan Paul. (Original work published 1945)

Pepper, S. (1942). *World hypotheses*. Berkeley: University of California Press.

Pervin, L. A. (1984). *Personality* (4th ed.). New York: Wiley.

Rosenberg, M. (1979). *Conceiving the self*. New York: Basic Books.

Rychlak, J. F. (1988). *The psychology of rigorous humanism* (2nd ed.). New York: New York University Press.

Sarbin, T. R. (1986). The narrative as a root metaphor for psychology. In T. R. Sarbin (Ed.), *Narrative psychology: The storied nature of human conduct* (pp. 3–21). New York: Praeger.

Thomae, H. (1968). *Das Individuum und seine Welt* [The individual and his world]. Göttingen, Germany: Hogrefe.

Appendix follows on next page

APPENDIX

QUESTIONS USED TO ELICIT VALUATIONS IN THE SELF-CONFRONTATION METHOD

Set 1: The Past

These questions are intended to guide you to some aspect of your past that is of great importance to you:

- Was there something in your past that has been of major importance or significance for your life and that still plays an important part today?
- Was there, in the past, a person, an experience, or circumstance that greatly influenced your life and still appreciably affects your present existence?

(You are free to go back into the past as far as you like.)

Set 2: The Present

This set is also composed of two questions that will lead you, after a certain amount of contemplation, to formulate a response:

- Is there in your present life something that is of major importance for, or exerts a great influence on, your existence?
- Is there in your present life a person or circumstance that exerts a significant influence on you?

Set 3: The Future

The following questions will again be found to guide you to a response:

- Do you foresee something that will be of great importance for, or of major influence on, your future life?
- Do you feel that a certain person or circumstances will exert a great influence on your future life?
- Is there a goal or object that you expect to play an important role in your future life?

(You are free to look as far ahead as you wish.)

IV

SOCIAL SYSTEMIC
PERSPECTIVES

13

RADICAL CONSTRUCTIVISM: QUESTIONS AND ANSWERS

JAY S. EFRAN AND ROBERT L. FAUBER

Radical constructivism has generally been good for the field of psychotherapy. It has reawakened interest in the larger issues and seems to hold the key for resolving some of the field's most perplexing dilemmas. However, a conspicuous number of practitioners who have "bumped" into constructivist thinking have found the experience jarring rather than helpful. They have heard that conceptual treasure is buried somewhere deep in constructivist territory, but they are at a loss about how to dig it out or make practical use of it. Some practitioners have concluded, perhaps too hastily, that constructivism is just another of those abstract, academic exercises—much ado about very little of pragmatic importance. As one therapist put it, "It shook my confidence in my old beliefs and methods, without replacing them with anything concrete or workable." Another psychologist described her introduction to constructivism as being akin to stepping into quicksand—there seemed to be nothing to

We wish to thank Etiony Aldarondo, Elsa R. Efran, Richard J. Leffel, and Salvatore Libretto for their assistance in the preparation of this chapter.

hold on to and no way out. For such individuals, constructivism has churned up a cloud of ambiguity and confusion, raising vexing questions without providing clear answers.

Maturana and Varela (1987) noted that unanswered questions are system "perturbations." Radical constructivism has indeed perturbed many, especially because it challenges the objectivist worldview in which most people have grown up and that grounds their daily living. The sophisticated epistemologist may regard objectivism as naive and anti-quated, but everyone else still relies on it to get through breakfast. Tamer variants of constructivism, such as critical constructivism (Mahoney, 1991), permit objectivists a certain amount of elbow room, but radical constructivism does not—it insists on an all-out epistemological battle, with no prisoners taken.[1]

To aid those who are intrigued but perplexed by the issues that radical constructivism raises, we offer responses to some of the questions that therapists ask us most frequently. In the process of replying to these questions, we clarify aspects of our own point of view and offer several illustrations of how we work with clients.

LANGUAGE, EMOTION, AND ACTION

Question: Why do radical constructivists make such a fuss over language? Isn't it better to urge clients to get out and behave differently in the real world instead of sitting around and gabbing about it?

Answer: Language is indeed a central concern of constructivist therapists, but different interpretations of the term have led to misunder-standings about what this emphasis means. For example, the phrasing of the above question implies a sharp dichotomy between language and action—a distinction that radical constructivists reject as false and misleading. Language is a particular form of action, not a substitute for it. To understand the implications of this, one must first appreciate that language, as constructivists define it, encompasses the use of symbols as well as words and includes both verbal and nonverbal modes of expres-sion. Thus, a person who points to the left to help someone find Room 322 is using language and so is the individual who rolls his or her eyes in disdain at the mention of a disliked person. The separation of the

---

[1]The major distinction between radical and critical constructivism concerns their respective assumptions about an underlying reality. Critical constructivists tend to be realists who assume that there is a definite reality that people increasingly approximate in their constructs, even though they may never be able to "access" it completely. In contrast, radical constructivists are idealists who do not concern themselves with the ultimate nature of a reality beyond the human experience.

verbal from the nonverbal, perhaps convenient for certain investigative purposes, perpetuates the unfortunate notion that words and symbols are abstractions that carry meanings apart from the social contexts in which they occur. However, to the constructivist, the meaning of a linguistic interchange always hinges on an amalgam of situational, contextual, and postural markers. Words and symbols lose their identity in a social vacuum.

Therapists intuitively recognize this when they object to discussing sensitive issues over the telephone. Even if phone lines permit a pin drop to be heard, they do not transmit the full range of interpersonal cues. The same thinning of cues can, however, be an advantage to people initiating a difficult or embarrassing confrontation. In this case, the phone can protect the individual from being thrown off stride by the intensity of the other person's reactions and can limit the leakage of cues that he or she might want to keep private (Goffman, 1971).

Thus, language is not separate from action, and meanings are fully dependent on the contexts in which words and symbols are used. Expressions such as "actions speak louder than words" and "talk is cheap" imply that language is an inconsequential or subsidiary form of activity. It is not. Furthermore, language is not simply a product of the intellect or a separate cognitive process. Rather, it is a form of communal choreography—a specialized way to coordinate activity in a social domain.[2] That is why Maturana (1988) insisted that the so-called higher cortical functions take place in the space of the community, not in the head or in the nervous system. Of course, one needs a nervous system to be able to participate in the social games that language comprises, but words and phrases are societal negotiations, not disembodied sounds or private cognitions stored in file cabinets of the brain.

Many language activities that are typically considered solitary and insignificant are, in fact, thoroughly communal and consequential. Consider a man lying in bed, daydreaming. He is engaged in linguistic social action, using the words and symbols given to him by his community. This is true despite the fact that no one else happens to be in his bedroom at the time and his feet happen to be resting on a mattress instead of on the pavement. Daydreams, and other forms of conversation with oneself, are crucial links in social processes that launch careers, generate projects, and galvanize social movements.

A momentary thought at the meal table can unsettle the status quo as readily as an automobile accident, an extramarital affair, or a business bankruptcy. Because people so automatically reify thoughts and

[2]Following Maturana (1988), language can be defined as a second-order coordination—a coordination of coordinations, if you will.

actions into separate categories, they have a tendency to view the pulling of a handgun trigger as somehow more real than the hatching of the homicidal or suicidal plot that preceded it. However, although a person's quiet resolve may not get as much press as an actual physical assault, each phase of a human dance is essential to its overall identity and potentially crucial to its outcome.

Question: If language is a form of action, as radical constructivists maintain, then why do constructivists describe therapy as "conversation" rather than activity? Do they ever assign clients actual tasks?

Answer: Constructivists have perhaps made matters worse rather than better by choosing the term *conversation* to describe their therapeutic approach. For many people, that term conjures up an image of a fireside chat and a therapist who is relatively passive and inactive. To set the record straight, constructivist therapists are using the term *conversation* quite broadly. Under that rubric, they are allowed to give homework assignments, to engage in role playing, and, in fact, to use the full range of so-called action techniques. When rational emotive therapist Albert Ellis prescribes one of his famous "shame-attacking exercises" (Ellis & Dryden, 1987)—such as having the client go to a department store and announce, town-crier fashion, "It's 3 p.m. and all's well"—he could be said to be advancing a particular conversational theme. (He is arguing that people in this culture have more latitude in the social world than they might have suspected.) Thus, constructivists consider Ellis's bombastic exercises to be compatible with a designation of therapy as *conversation*. Incidentally, Ellis's procedures also exemplify another conception with which constructivists can readily identify: the view of therapy as a process of inquiry.

Years ago, George Kelly (1955) noted that people are inveterate investigators: They continually devise—and test out for themselves—hypotheses about how the world works. Kelly attempted to understand and characterize these individual quests. He saw that some people's hypotheses, being well formed and forward-leaning, served to expand their range of life alternatives. These inquiries led, in turn, to still more intriguing questions and adventures. Alternatively, others, by focusing on questions that were trivial or poorly framed, got bogged down in life's side passageways and blind alleys. Following Kelly's analysis, constructivists view the therapist's primary job to be helping clients frame their personal questions more effectively, so that they can produce, for themselves, more satisfying answers and get on with the business of living. (Kelly used the metaphor of "therapist as research consultant," which constructivists find perfectly suited to their own purposes.)

As we have indicated, clients bring certain questions to therapy, and, of course, they develop other concerns while they are there. Sometimes their search for answers can be handled through armchair discussion. At other times, as in the case of the rational emotive therapy exercise cited above, fancier fieldwork is required. Constructivists regard it as limiting to define therapeutic interaction in terms of set formats or techniques. As therapists, our attention is on clarifying the question being asked, elucidating the context from which it sprang, and making sure it gets answered—that is, ensuring that the questioner experiences "completion" on that point. As in other research endeavors, the methods used to investigate a particular issue need to be tailored to the requirements of the problem, and some may have to be invented on the spot. Constructivist therapy, like life itself, is an adventure.

Although constructivists by no means primarily limit therapy to verbal interaction, we hasten to add that there are many times when a frank dialogue between client and therapist is all that is needed. Consider the power of such films as *My Dinner With André*, which manages to be highly evocative by using footage of people quietly talking rather than riding horses, brandishing swords, or making arrests. As everyone knows, a few whispered words can be as sexually provocative as explicit erotic photographs, and a fantasized image can lead to a complete change in point of view. As demonstrated once again by the reaction to the publication of Salman Rushdie's book *The Satanic Verses*, language, in its simplest and most straightforward forms, can be serious business.

Question: It is still not clear why language is so important to constructivists, especially because you have redefined it as a subcategory of action. What is so special about that form of action?

Answer: Language is where people live (Packer, 1985). It allows people to have names, to "know" who they are, and to carve separable things out of the interconnected flux that they take to be the universe. One can manage to play baseball without a shortstop, but not without the words and symbols that differentiate first base from home plate. Without language, it would not be possible for a person to engage in self-conscious thought, to keep an appointment book, or to have problems (Jaynes, 1990). Problems are not just sets of circumstances, as objectivists would have everyone believe. They are appraisals—in words and symbols—of what should and should not be, what might or might not happen, what is fair or unfair, lucky or unlucky, malleable or fixed.

Paradoxically, without language, it would be impossible for objectivists to form a class called *actual circumstances* and consider its contents discriminably different from the contents of other categories, such as figments of the imagination, individual perceptions, plans for the future, and so on. It is with language that all such considering about what belongs where takes place. A mental health problem is created by a series of layered considerations—a person (or group of people) first determines that something is a circumstance and then considers what to make of it. Facts and circumstances are the products of human ponderings, but facts do not, by themselves, constitute problems or coerce conclusions. There has to be an additional step: Somebody, in language, has to decide what a set of facts means with regard to a purpose or an importance. If a person simply tells you that it is raining out, it is not yet clear whether he or she is alluding to a curse or a blessing. (That would depend on whether the issue that has captured the group's attention is a nearly depleted reservoir or an already bloated river.) If an individual announces that his or her marriage is at an end, it will take more discussion to establish whether condolences or congratulations are in order.

Because it is in the domain of language that problems are created and sustained, it is in that domain that they must be solved. Language, therefore, is the medium of all psychotherapy, regardless of the school of thought to which the therapist belongs. Moreover, the problem-solving conversation that takes place between a client and a therapist never occurs in isolation. It resonates with themes that are afoot in the larger community, and it reflects the progress that the community has made in terms of figuring out how people ought to live together. In other words, the problems that arise in a local venue have parallels in the broader social order; they are regional manifestations of a civilization's unfinished business—the debris of unresolved boundary disputes. For example, therapist's offices were recently deluged with calls from women concerned about spousal abuse in the wake of publicity about the O. J. Simpson case. Clearly, the culture is further refining its options in these matters, both on the national scene and in individual families and crisis centers across the land.

A problem might also be usefully thought of as a linguistic *maybe* afloat in a sea of *yeses* and *nos*. The average client does not worry whether he or she will be asked to run for the presidency, to fly to work without an airplane, or to eat soup with a fork. For most people, those issues are settled and therefore out of mind. What keeps people up nights, and sometimes propels them to the therapist's door, are their personal *mights* and *might nots*. In a nutshell, language—a form of action that coordinates other forms of action—is important to the therapist because it is the medium in which people's *maybes* reside.

Question: You characterize problems as unresolved quandaries. Are you also implying that they are not exactly real, the way floods or earthquakes are real?

Answer: Not at all. Problems are absolutely real, and they hurt. However, the word *real* means something different to the radical constructivist than it does to the objectivist or the naive realist. To the constructivist, floods owe their existence not merely to the presence of a large quantity of water but to a conception, built in language, that includes ideas about where the excess water comes from, why it is overflowing riverbanks, when it might stop, what to do about it, and so on. Moreover, such ideas are agreements between people—agreements that constitute plans of action and the apportionment of responsibilities. Floods are all that and more.

Years ago, dentists did not offer their patients Novocain, because it had not been invented. Moreover, the drills being used at the time were not today's water-cooled, high-speed wonders, but were instead those slow, vibrating, belt-driven models that have now become museum curiosities. Nevertheless, going to the dentist in those days was not viewed as a heroic act; it was routine. What is more, it is doubtful that there were more (or fewer) cases of dental phobia then than there are now. People accepted the conditions that existed because nothing else was known—no vexing maybes were involved. Today, asking a patient to do without Novocain (or to endure a slow-speed drill) might create a significant maybe. Furthermore, the person is likely to suffer more—to experience more pain and discomfort—than people would have suffered in past decades under equivalent circumstances. It is not that dental patients have become "soft" or are now constitutionally inferior. Rather, once a problem has been created in language, it constitutes a context that affects the entire complexion of events, and it cannot be easily ignored or rationalized away. The experiences that a problem generates are absolutely real for those involved. Furthermore, reminding the person that the old context was different—for example, that small children used to regularly face dental work without anesthesia—is usually insufficient to set the modern patient's mind at ease about returning to such practices.

In Peru and Ecuador, people enjoy eating toasted leaf-cutter ants as a snack at movie theaters—the equivalent of the popcorn tradition in Western theaters. In Zambia and Zimbabwe, caterpillars are considered a delicacy, and in Mexico, agave worms are consumed with gusto. Knowing these things is not likely to obliterate the discomforts that an average American would experience when asked to try these foods. Again, problems are language dependent, but not imaginary or insubstantial.

Question: You described aversions to strange foods in terms of language. This is a bit odd, because most people consider such reactions to be emotional responses rather than language issues. In fact, in your discussion thus far, you have omitted any reference to the term *emotion* or to the notion that people suffer from emotional problems or need help learning to express their feelings. What is the role of emotion in your version of radical constructivism?

Answer: We have pointed to the disadvantages of taking the verbal–nonverbal dichotomy seriously, and we have also argued against reifying the language–action split. However, a still more mischievous scheme that grips people's lives is the Aristotelian insistence that experience should be divided into feelings, thoughts, and behaviors. It is an arbitrary cleavage "that confuses everything and clarifies nothing" (Kelly, 1969, p. 91). This mythology insists that people dualistically locate talking (and thinking) "in the head" and feelings somewhere down below. It has resulted in no end of trouble in the culture, including the enormous amount of time investigators have wasted attempting to establish the primacy of one of the three presumed subsystems—feelings, thoughts, and behaviors—over the other two. Brands of therapy have also been differentiated and labeled on the basis of whichever category workers choose to consider primary: Behavior therapists emphasize performances, cognitive therapists attack beliefs, and humanists focus on the exploration and expression of feelings. Each group assumes that by changing one of these elements, the others will eventually follow suit. Also, they assume some degree of independence among these postulated subsystems, even if they are willing to talk of linkages and interactions.

Obviously, a vast array of schools has been created by mixing and matching these fundamental approaches to problems, and the popularity of particular intervention points has waxed and waned over time. The 1960s were the heyday of the primal scream and the encounter group, but the expression of raw emotion was upstaged in the 1970s and 1980s by a direct emphasis on behavior change and, later, on cognitive manipulation and modification. Ironically, there now seems to be a revival of interest in emotion and techniques for encouraging emotional expression.

However, the constructivists' use of the term *emotion* differs significantly from the usages implied by the Aristotelian trichotomy. Aristotelians generally think of emotions as those wild frenzies, vengeful rages, joyful enthusiasms, and mournful depressions that command so much attention. In our brand of constructivism, *emotion* refers more broadly to the particular bodily postures required by any form of human activity, including the most ordinary and humdrum; emotions are not separate neural or hormonal processes that kick in only on special occasions. Emotional states, including shifts and adjustments in hormonal levels, are continuous support factors that affect all human performance. Thus, rational deliberation and serious contemplation have specific emotional requirements, just as attacking, escaping, and affiliating do. In this culture of rational supremacists (see Mahoney, 1991), people are not used to considering rationality as a mood that can come and go much like anger, disappointment, or frustration can. Instead, they think of rationality as a steady state—a neutral backdrop against which emotions may then be superimposed. Children sometimes think of vanilla ice cream in the same way, assuming erroneously that it is the natural state in which ice cream occurs and to which distinct flavors, such as strawberry and chocolate, are later added. But, of course, vanilla is itself a flavor. Similarly, rationality is a strong system preference, not simply a baseline against which other modes of operation are to be assessed.

Bodily postures, including those that poeple label *rationality*, either facilitate or interfere with what individuals do. Reverie is facilitated by lying down and closing one's eyes; standing under a shower spray seems to be a catalyst for operatic vocalizing; and relaxing with wine, music, and candlelight is the traditional route to romance. Notice that the relaxed, affiliative mood of a candlelight dinner will not suffice for a tax audit, which requires instead that one maintain vigilance and be prepared to protect one's turf. Sexual encounters tend to interfere with divorce mediation, because the principal participants are attempting two incompatible postures—coming and going. It is hard to think straight in the midst of a public humiliation and difficult to maintain a tough stance while being flattered. A parent's angry thoughts may unexpectedly dissolve because a child does something cute or tells a joke at just the right moment. (Some of us, in growing up, were able to save our hides many times over by developing this last-minute joke-telling strategy into an art form.) As comedian Victor Borge put it, "No one ever fights 'smilingly'—and wins."

The point is that people are not free-floating "heads" that can think whatever they like or collections of feelings that well up from unknown depths to cause mischief. Action is embodied; lines of thought are context dependent and are always propped up by environmental and bodily supports (Krüll, Luhmann, & Maturana, 1988; Maturana, 1988; Varela, Thompson, & Rosch, 1991). In this purview, conflicts are not fights between thoughts and feelings. Instead, they are contradictions between opposing programs of action, each of which aims to satisfy the real or imagined demands of a constituency that exists in the person's experience (Akillas & Efran, 1989; Mendez, Coddou, & Maturana, 1988).

Question: Can you give an example of how your view of emotions, which is so different from the typical perspective, can be of use to a therapist struggling to understand his or her clients?

Answer: Sure. In the calm of a therapist's office, an airplane phobic can afford to be rational. In that setting, he or she may easily understand that flying is less risky than driving or taking a bus. However, the ironclad logic of that argument can be expected to fall apart when boarding time approaches. In the office, the client and therapist have the luxury of being able to please the voice of reason. At the airport, however, survival fear takes precedence and energizes an entirely different set of preferences and activities. One set of emotional demands tends to wipe out the other. As one of our clients recently reported, "In here, it all seemed so obvious and sensible, but when the time came, I couldn't remember a single thing we had talked about." The experience that the client becomes another person as the context shifts is understandable in terms of the theory of emotion we have been explicating. These shifts are commonplace and do not represent either duplicitous motives or a failure of learned generalization.

The resolve of the most ardent dieter can suddenly fade into the background when he or she comes face to face with a favorite dessert. Later, with the moment gone, the person may be perplexed about why he or she succumbed so completely to a transient desire. It is at that point that the individual usually casts about for fancy explanations. Unfortunately, such explanations are all too readily available on every talk show and in most therapists' offices. The individual may be told that he or she is engaged in "self-defeating behavior," has a "deep-seated need to rescue the family," is "an addictive personality," and so on. Yet the observed inconsistencies in behavior, being ordinary, do not require elaborate explanation. Almost no one's actions, if closely scrutinized, would appear logical or consistent. In life, there are too many interest groups to please and too many competing preferences to enact for people's behavior to be consistent from moment to moment or from one setting to another. Fortunately, humans' sense of continuity is preserved because we construct, and manage to believe in, a relatively smooth narrative of events, the major purpose of which is to convince ourselves (and each other) that we are operating sensibly. Our friends are either too polite or too preoccupied with their own narratives to call attention to obvious discrepancies in our performances. Civilized living obligates all people to be armed with reasonable-sounding accounts of their behavior and to accept at face value the accounts of their associates. Everyone hates to be caught with their reasons down, and it is an embarrassment to catch others in that state of linguistic nudity (Goffman, 1959).

Therapists who do not take into account the embodied and ever-changing nature of human performances can become fixated, along with their clients, on cumbersome, reified explanations. These create unnecessary diversions and distract attention from issues of context. To the radical constructivist, discontinuities in action are to be expected at every level of social living, from the individual to the communal. Each of the many contexts in which people live elicits and supports different conversational elements. For the most part, people's lives neither are driven by rational considerations nor are a function of uncontrollable inner urges—they are socially situated creations. Problems arise when contexts clash.

Therapists who trichotomize emotions, thoughts, and actions often feel obliged to urge clients to get in touch with their feelings or learn to better express their emotions. In saying such things, therapists are unwittingly taking sides in a dispute between people in a person's life. Take the simple example of a young boy who practices the violin but would rather be out skateboarding with his friends. If he rebels by refusing to take lessons, his mother will be upset and disappointed. If he practices too much, his friends will tease him for being under his mother's thumb. Again, this is not a struggle between presumed system components, such as thoughts and feelings or feelings and actions. It is a conflict between two courses of action, each of which has costs and payoffs. The therapist who urges the boy to express his feelings is siding with the skateboarding forces and potentially "inciting" him to revolt against his mother's wishes. What is insidious in such a scenario is that the therapist is apt to deny having taken a position or having any sort of stake in the direction of the outcomes that follow. Ostensibly, the therapist is only making a statement about feelings, not about the politics of the situation. However, there are no feelings to be expressed apart from those related to each participant's performance preferences, and all statements made support the values of one subgroup over another. Neutrality is an objectivist chimera. Therapy is never value-free or apolitical. The advantage of radical constructivism is that it acknowledges that this must indeed be so. In this view, it is not a sin for therapists to have opinions or even to give explicit suggestions about how members of natural groups might best get along with one another. What is objectionable is to mask such value operations with antiseptic-sounding professional jargon. The warfare of life is not between emotions and cognitions but between social constituencies, each of which wants its own way. A therapist who recognizes that basic fact of social living is better positioned to be helpful and effective with clients.

THE REALITY OF CONSTRUCTIONS

Question: Because you have mentioned social forces, perhaps this is a good place to ask how radical constructivists view the harsh realities of life, such as poverty, racial intolerance, and terminal illness.

Answer: Salvador Minuchin (1991), in a recent article criticizing the constructivist viewpoint, described a woman living in poverty. He made the point that her reality "is *not* [italics added] a construct; it is a stubbornly concrete world" (p. 50). From the constructivist perspective, Minuchin is missing the point. Again, he seems to want to establish a firm dividing line between circumstances and interpretations of circumstance and to argue that this woman is suffering from the former rather than the latter. He regards circumstances—the hard realities themselves—as being somehow outside the province of constructivism and takes it as axiomatic that the difficulty in modifying such circumstances illustrates a flaw in constructivist thinking. Hidden in that argument is the subtle implication that constructivists have made a promise to "vanish" any and all difficult conditions through some sort of verbal magic or manipulation and that any failure to do so constitutes reneging on that agreement.

However, radical constructivists have not promised to change anything. Radical constructivism is an approach to understanding how the world people think they know comes into existence. That does not mean that it is easy to change. In fact, many aspects of the world are next to impossible to modify, including some elements that are clearly products of people's opinions or belief systems. As human beings, we live our beliefs and take them very seriously. The witches of Salem were created sheerly on the basis of attitude and belief, but they were hung nevertheless, and with real rope! It took quite a while for such practices to cease, and they did not stop until a constellation of economic and social forces shifted the social consensus in the right directions. It is doubtful that a constructivist, operating in Salem in those times, could have talked anybody into or out of conducting witch trials. In fact, it would have been highly dangerous to try.

In any event, radical constructivism is a mode of analysis, not a guarantee that poverty will instantly disappear, that cancer will be cured, or that life will become a breeze. Constructivists, perhaps even more than objectivists, respect the labels that society has assigned to various phenomena. The reason certain diseases are called *terminal* is to acknowledge the current relative ineffectiveness that humans have to influence their course. If constructivists, or anyone else, had a surefire means of arresting the bodily deterioration that such conditions cause, people would rather quickly reassign these diseases to a less lethal category, as has already been done with a variety of disorders. When constructivists maintain that we humans, in language, create our world, the implication is not that we should therefore ignore or trivialize that which we have just gone to the trouble to create. In other words, when the sign says "Thin Ice," it is probably a good idea to skate elsewhere, regardless of epistemological orientation.

Although no therapies, including those of the constructivist ilk, have been set up to eliminate poverty and redistribute the nation's wealth, it seems clear that the condition labeled *poverty* is sustained by elements of the social order, as transacted in language, and that these elements are certainly susceptible to a constructivist analysis. Some of them are hard to shift, and others are surprisingly malleable. Recently there was a precipitous drop in the price of an automotive stock simply because the company's CEO announced that he would soon be issuing a message of importance to employees. In the prevailing climate, that statement was greeted with considerable alarm. As it turned out, all the CEO intended to do was wish his employees "Merry Christmas and Happy New Year." However, by the time his message was released, the company's stock had decreased in value and a number of his workers, expecting the worst, had already made plans to leave the company in favor of more stable employment elsewhere. In this particular instance, a single mistimed language pronouncement rearranged career plans and investment opportunities.

Alternatively, radical constructivists understand full well how ruthlessly limiting certain aspects of the social consensus can be. Denying the truth of that reality or of other elements in one's personal experience is the antithesis of constructivism. Radical constructivists also understand something that objectivists sometimes miss—that social conditions, no matter how harsh and unyielding, do not automatically and inevitably produce a single, invariant set of experiences in all who are exposed to them. Everyone's positioning is a little different, and each person couples with elements of the social and natural environment in unique ways. People living in essentially the same community, and with similar income levels, will have very different experiences of themselves and of the world. Thus, there are as many different poverties as there are individuals who consider themselves poor. Even in the meanest of ghettos, it would not take long to find people who are deeply fulfilled, lead meaningful lives, and have a clear vision for their children and for the future. Alternatively, a visit to an affluent community will quickly turn up many lost souls, leading "lives of quiet desperation" amid an overabundance of creature comforts and venture capital.

The objectivist who becomes overly wedded to just the basic facts risks overlooking the important subtleties of individual experience. He or she may actually be handicapped in working with disadvantaged populations because of the perception that little can be done until or unless major circumstances improve. In contrast, constructivists understand that no group has a monopoly on personal satisfaction and that ghetto dwellers as well as suburbanites can profit from increased clarity about life goals and purposes. Even a person faced with severe shortages of food and heat still lives in terms of his or her personal dreams for the future (Efran, 1991). It is patronizing to assume that the only service meaningful to a disadvantaged individual is the replacement of a missing welfare check, the provision of additional child care, or an increase in food stamps. Access to social services is surely important, but it is not the whole story, as influential leaders such as Martin Luther King and Malcolm X were quick to recognize. Constructivist therapy is certainly not a substitute for medical research, political action, or a steady job. However, on another level, it can be quite useful to the terminally ill as well as to the unemployed and those living in shelters for the homeless. The therapist can help such individuals clarify their goals and their concerns about the meaning of life.

INDIVIDUAL CHOICES AND ECOLOGICAL IMPERATIVES

Question: Radical constructivists seem to consider free will and individual choice just observer illusions. If it is the system or the ecology that ultimately controls what people think and do, what is the point of visiting a therapist or working to improve oneself?

Answer: Concepts such as free will and individual choice generate great consternation and perplexity in Western culture. Cultural arrangements force people to change their minds on this issue several times a week—in some instances, several times a day. Sometimes individuals will maintain that upbringing determines a person's behavior, particularly if he or she has a background involving sexual abuse or child abuse, but at other times they will want to hold the person individually responsible for his or her choices, regardless of family environment or genetic endowment. On the one hand, people believe that the mass murderer should be punished, even though his father beat him as a youngster, because he "knew what he was doing," and it was wrong. On the other hand, people are willing to excuse a child's failing grades on the grounds that these are the unfortunate outcome of having been raised in an enmeshed family system. If a boy or girl is more highly reinforced for playing baseball than for completing a mathematics assignment, is the child to be faulted for his or her personal preferences? What if the person's genetic structure makes it relatively easy for him or her to excel on the athletic field but hard to do better than average in classroom pursuits? To what extent does the spotlight of blame then shift to the teacher, the coach, the parents, the peer group, or society as a whole? Therapy clients often want individual credit for "choosing" to do something about their problems, but then they immediately switch gears and expect that the therapist can trace the origin of their undesirable behaviors to factors beyond their control, such as having an alcoholic father or an overprotective mother (Efran, Heffner, & Lukens, 1987). If they make progress in therapy, they again want to change the ground rules and take credit for their willingness to change, their personal courage in facing up to problems, their persistence, and so on. No one is fully consistent in assigning blame, attributing cause, or establishing responsibility. Ironically, people often have unwarranted—sometimes unshakable—confidence in the inconsistent and illogical explanatory judgments they establish for themselves.

When one buys a household appliance that proves to be defective, one could—with equal justification—rail against the salesperson who sold it, the company that marketed it, the factory workers who assembled it, the advertisers who misrepresented it, the stock market manipulators who drove quality companies out of business, a work ethic that tolerates shoddy workmanship, the political leadership that has mismanaged trade agreements, and so on. All such complaints would be legitimate, and yet none would be definitive. Although this is not the place to launch into an extended philosophical debate on issues of free will and determinism, we should note that confusion in people's attempts to attribute blame and responsibility arise largely because of the human propensity for applying a "logic of parts" to phenomena that might better be analyzed in more holistic terms. The human desire to give each thing (as created in language) a discrete beginning and end generates, as in the classic chicken-and-egg problem, a virtually endless supply of explanatory paradoxes. The process loops in which people live do not necessarily have identifiable, objective beginnings and ends, nor can exact, lineal cause–effect sequences be defined. Typically, the logic of parts leads to an infinite regression of explanatory fictions. As in a playground fight, it may be difficult, and useless, to try to decide once and for all who started it or who is to blame. All one will ever know for certain is that fighting broke out, one is in the thick of it, and one wants peace to be restored. Life is a continuous drift in which all elements count and no form of analysis captures the complete picture. Radical constructivist therapy is not about coming up with that final explanation that takes precedence over all others. Such explanations are inevitably partial explanations or pseudoexplanations. That is why constructivist therapists have less interest than some others in the detective work of pinning down past precedents for current dilemmas. Their focus is on future options rather than on past influences. Philosophy aside, the discussion that constitutes therapy has to take place between individuals who are willing to assert responsibility for who and what they are. Responsibility and blame are not the same. People are responsible not because they personally selected their genetic structures, their parents, or their organismic preferences, but because they are located right in the middle of their experiential world. As the existentialists say, we are our choices. No matter how we got here, if we do not act as if the job of living our lives is ours, it is not going to be reassigned to someone else. Moreover, although our lives are lived within communal structures, those structures only change when the people that constitute them behave differently. You can only fix a car by modifying it one component at a time. There is no way to repair the car "as a whole." Alternatively, every part that is replaced or adjusted affects the entire car's operation. Similarly, as an individual interacts with a therapist, there are ripple effects throughout the person's ecology, which then loop back to affect the individual.

In group or family therapy, several conversations—again, between pairs of individuals—may take place at roughly the same time and in the same place, and each conversation forms the relationship context in which the others occur. However, constructive therapists contend that, although there are linkages, it is best to view these conversations as separate, individual undertakings, each with its own pitfalls and potentials. Each person in a family session entertains questions that have precedence for him or her. Family members participate in the general proceedings to find answers to their particular questions, and that determines the way they process what is being said in the room. In other words, although there are many people in the room, each person is operating in a somewhat different and unique framework of meaning (Efran, Lukens, & Lukens, 1990).

Constructivists do not subscribe to the view of some family or group therapists that a therapist can work with a group or speak to a family. Only individuals speak and listen. The therapist negotiates with individuals, perhaps speaking to several at the same time. The therapist may even look directly at one individual, intending that, at the same time, what is being said will be overheard by others and will play a role in advancing the conversations in which they are involved. Remember, communal consensus evolves through people's participation in it, not despite that participation. In politics, a single voter rarely determines the outcome, yet an election victory is the summation of individual acts of lever pulling—many bits of conversation pooled together produce a general outcome. The individual counts, but the meaning of his or her actions can only be understood through reference to the social network.

Question: Did radical constructivists choose that point of view as the position to believe in and espouse?

Answer: Had they been different people or had they grown up in another time or place, radical constructivists undoubtedly would have found some other point of view more appealing. The same can be said for advocates of any other approach, including objectivism. Furthermore, how a theorist or a therapist happened to adopt a particular point of view says almost nothing about that viewpoint's validity or viability. Alfred Adler (1968) presumably emphasized birth order and sibling rivalry because he was the third child in a large family and was always in competition with his older brother. It is also said that his invention of such concepts as the inferiority complex and striving for superiority grew out of his experience of being short and having had serious bouts of rickets and pneumonia at an early age (Rychlak, 1981). However, the value to others of these theoretical inventions must be assessed independently of the historical accidents of birth and stature that led Adler to devise them.

THE IMPORTANCE OF TELLING THE TRUTH

Question: Your earlier statement about "verbal magic" apparently places you in sharp disagreement with some brief, strategic, and family therapists, who rely on reframing and other techniques of verbal reinterpretation to which radical constructivists seem to object. Isn't what you dismissed as verbal magic a crucial aspect of constructivist practice?

Answer: In our view, some workers have stretched the meaning of such terms as *reframing* and *positive connotation* (see Nichols & Schwartz, 1995, for definitions) to the breaking point. They underestimate the solidity of a constructed reality and assume that because something is language dependent, it is insubstantial and can be easily modified by relabeling problems willy-nilly. They feel free to portray faults as virtues, failures as successes, and selfishness as altruism. Some therapists will say almost anything for strategic effect. Critics have attacked such ad hoc conceptualizations as superficial and manipulative—an uncomfortable melding of the roles of therapist and con artist (Bogdan, 1984, 1986; Johnson, 1986; Ridley & Tan, 1986). We tend to agree.

For example, in a case involving chronic pain (following an automobile accident), a client who objected to the suggestion that his problems might have a psychological genesis was told by his therapist, "Perhaps you are trying too hard; you really ought to be in bed . . . in the hospital" (Shutty & Sheras, 1991, p. 638). The therapist assumed that this idea would be rejected by the client because of his distaste for being under the control of others. The therapist's suggestion, presented as a professional opinion, was not based on an actual assessment of the patient's need for bed rest or institutional care but, instead, was calculated to provoke a rebellion. In fact, the client did not rebel; he checked into a hospital. Despite this unexpected turn of events, Shutty and Sheras considered the ploy a success because the client later arranged to be discharged and eventually began a home exercise and rehabilitation program.

Even if this strategic—but patently deceitful—therapeutic recommendation was useful in the long run (and in situations of this complexity, it is almost impossible to tell), the costs are high in terms of lost client confidence, not to mention the unnecessary hospital expenses. From the perspective of the client and the hospital staff, the hospitalization did not work out and was an inappropriate suggestion on the part of the therapist. Experiences of this sort not only erode a client's faith in the pronouncements of particular mental health professionals but also create a serious credibility gap for those who wish to espouse constructivism without being branded as used-car dealers. In point of fact, radical constructivism neither authorizes nor requires the abandonment of the conventional distinctions between accurate reporting and deliberate fabrication. Recall that language is socially embedded activity and that cultures, for good and sufficient reasons, have established categories of discourse and guidelines for linguistic performances. Breaking language agreements or purposely confusing language categories can be hazardous, and flouting such rules routinely is a surefire prescription for social censure and invalidation. There are certainly times when it may be appropriate to violate communal codes—to test their limits and to push for reform. However, those instances need to be carefully weighed exceptions, because they rapidly use up a field's "idiosyncrasy credits." For most therapeutic purposes, honesty is still the best policy. Good therapy, constructivist or otherwise, is not verbal sleight of hand. It should be built on a bedrock of trust, solid reliability, and conceptual clarity. Constructivists may have a special interest in investigating the origin and epistemological status of such language categories as fact, opinion, and fantasy, but—understanding the potency of words and symbols—they use them with special care and respect.

Question: But then, what is invented in an "invented reality," to use Watzlawick's (1984) phrase?

Answer: One does not make something so just by saying it is so. One cannot fly without wings by saying so, although one may be able to invent the airplane, as the Wright brothers did, by speaking of it as a possibility. Language is, in this sense, both free and constrained, both cause and effect. A novelist creates a new story by putting her or his imaginings on paper, but in doing so she or he is obliged to use mainly words and meanings that have already been created; otherwise, no one will understand what the novelist is talking about, and finding a publisher will be difficult. Even innovation must take into account current idioms and conventions. As Doherty (1991) put it, "A new movement can only breathe the air available at its birth" (p. 39). The story may be new, but it is created within historically determined constraints of form and substance—it draws on the accumulated background of meanings.

Similarly, clients and therapists will evolve new truths for themselves, but only by beginning with the current truth of their experience. Although constructivism holds that human beings do not have privileged access to ultimate objective truths, this does not prevent them from sharing their personal and social perspectives with one another. In fact, that is exactly the process that makes the constructivist world go around. For example, one woman may go to a therapist because she is overweight and unhappy about it. Although today's body standards are not sacrosanct, and no one is obligated to lead a long life, she will probably need to lose a few pounds if she is to be happy. She is operating in a particular time and place—a social context—and she has made promises to herself, in that context, that she has not been keeping. She is suffering because of it. Those promises are in language—not fatty tissue—and they are tied to larger social issues. However, satisfaction in living requires being in alignment with oneself, that is, being true to one's word or agreeing to change it.

As we intimated above, in a constructivist world, all one really has is one's word, so it had better be kept in good shape. Objectivists have the luxury of claiming that what they do is dictated by external authority, but radical constructivists recognize that they themselves are the final authorities. If a person says that he or she should be thinner, then that word becomes law in his or her universe, until or unless revoked by a later proclamation. There is no right or wrong way to live—the universe simply does not care, one way or another. The sets of values that count are those that people themselves devise and agree to enact. When they are untrue to their own standards, they suffer personal consequences, which can be severe. Many who have committed suicide did so because they had disappointed themselves. American writer Christopher Morley claimed that "there is only one success—to be able to spend your life in your own way," and, although people may wonder what the neighbors will think, they project onto those neighbors the standards that they themselves take seriously.

A person who wants to be thinner may trade in any number of excuses and rationalizations, such as claiming that being overweight is the result of having been neglected as a child. Such rhetorical devices— and they are rhetorical devices, even if true—do not yield personal satisfaction. At best, they take the heat off temporarily. Excuses may actually prolong a person's agony, making him or her feel weaker rather than more potent. According to a French proverb, "He who excuses himself, accuses himself," and, as Szasz (1990) stated, "A person who speaks in the language of excuses . . . has lost half the battle for self-esteem before he has begun to fight it" (p. 61).

In life, people are satisfied exactly to the extent that they are able to accomplish their goals, as defined in the language that they use. Those definitions shift and change as people develop (e.g., most adults no longer truly aspire to be firefighters, as they dreamed in grade school), but active quests that remain unfulfilled are a major source of distress and disorientation in life (Cummings, 1979). From this vantage point, such symptoms as anxiety and depression might best be considered the sequelae of "lost dreams" (Efran, Germer, & Lukens, 1986). When a personal goal is in a state of disrepair, the connective tissue that unites events is weakened or broken. (For similar notions, see Bergner, 1988, and Marris, 1974.)

Part of the function of the constructivist therapist is to provide a forum in which clients can recall and articulate their dreams and goals as well as find forms in which they can be appropriately pursued and realized. They are also invited to identify more sharply the price they pay when they trivialize, postpone, or abandon such pursuits. Visions change and transmigrate of their own accord, but ignoring preferences that are still active or inventing ones that do not match experience are costly alternatives. Sometimes clients, like the woman described above, come to therapy looking for a quick fix. They want to be thinner without having to work at it, or they want an unassailable excuse for postponing the work that needs to be done. However, underneath those desires, they are often hoping someone will remind them, in no uncertain terms, of the obligations they set for themselves. Life is so full of distractions that people need to be reminded periodically of what they said they wanted, so that they can either revise those goals or consummate them. As everyone knows, incomplete projects are draining, and completions satisfy. Thus, there are cases in which some no-nonsense advice, such as "eat less, exercise more, or stop bothering us with your complaints," can be more supportive and reassuring than a plethora of feel-good positive connotations or reframings. Confronting a person with the bold truth of his or her experience is a therapeutic strategy with which constructivist therapists can readily identify.

SOCIAL RETICENCE

Question: Can you give another example of how the approach of a radical constructivist to a problem might differ from other approaches with which people are familiar?

Answer: Let us consider the problem of social reticence (Phillips, 1991), because we have been doing some research on this topic recently. Objectivist approaches in this arena have usually consisted of training shy clients to mimic the outward behaviors and appearances of assertive individuals and of having them repeat the kinds of self-statements that outgoing people presumably use.[3]

A recent treatment manual lists conversational topics that a shy person might try, as well as connective phrases—such as "of course," "in the second place," "accordingly," and "also"—that he or she can practice to improve conversational flow. This approach attempts to build social assertion from the ground up, or—if you prefer a different metaphor—from the outside in. The assumption is that by teaching a person how

---

[3]It is not entirely clear what self-assured individuals do say to themselves, especially when they are not being asked for a specific report on the matter. We suspect that it is not anything like the kind of self-bolstering statements that shy individuals are asked to rehearse. The assured person has little focus on self, but is apt to be more invested in what is going on around him or her.

an assertive individual acts, one can create assertion itself. Yet, in our experience, it is difficult if not impossible to cure shyness through such programs of cognitive and behavioral rehearsal. Words, gestures, and beliefs cannot be transplanted intact from one person to another. Meanings are socially situated and are not readily transferable. Behaving and speaking like an outgoing person does not yield the experience of being outgoing, any more than feigning an upper-class English accent makes a person either upper class or English. An Englishman speaks the way he does because of how his life has been lived, but the actor or impostor who emulates his sounds and mannerisms does not thereby inherit a similar point of view, set of experiences, or genetic endowment.

Indeed, if self-assurance could be produced simply through the powers of imitation, then accomplished actors and actresses would rarely show up at a psychotherapist's office complaining of shyness and insecurity; yet they do, and in droves. Sir Lawrence Olivier, one of the most accomplished and acclaimed actors of the modern era, reported developing abject terror about facing live audiences. Late in his career, he had to take special precautions to avoid looking directly at another actor, lest he give in to the temptation to flee into the wings and run for his life (see, e.g., Holden, 1988).

On the other side of the equation, it should be noted that even excruciatingly shy individuals may become tigers under the proper circumstances, such as when dealing with their younger brothers and sisters, disciplining their own children, or championing a just cause in which they are invested. In those settings, such individuals manifest a surfeit of the very skills—verbal and expressive—that leaders of assertive training groups are usually working so assiduously to teach them. They speak in fluid sentences even without consulting a crib sheet of connective phrases. Such glaring inconsistencies in performance between settings or occasions are, as we indicated earlier, taken for granted within the constructivist framework. Moreover, they appear to have more to do with changes in context and meaning than with the generalizability or transfer of social or verbal skills.

In the world of acting, a performance that is composed of theatrical posturing without underlying meaning is sometimes called *indicating*. Even when done skillfully, it results in what one author (Marowitz, 1961) has called "the splendid shallows." Similarly, in computer programming, so-called expert systems, based on a parroting of the decisions that experienced professionals make, can only bring novices up to a relatively rudimentary level of performance. After that, imitation alone cannot take the place of internalized experience.

Motivated individuals, working hard, can polish their presentations through exposure to cognitive–behavioral regimes. Sadly, however, they rarely seem to cross that invisible threshold that separates them from the truly self-assured. In fact, they sometimes feel more edgy after the training than before because they are pretending to be someone they are not. We recall an individual who had practiced and practiced, but as assertive training progressed, he seemed more reluctant than ever to go up to someone at a lunch table and say "hello." The leader told him that he should not be so frightened of failing. The individual replied that he was not frightened of failing, he was frightened of succeeding. Now that he had perfected his introductory routine (with appropriate opening phrases and conversational gambits), someone might mistake him for a truly facile individual. He knew he could never make good on that promissory note. Furthermore, any positive responses he received would serve only to validate the performance he had been trained to give, not the person within. As we hinted earlier, self-satisfaction is not just a matter of receiving outside applause or pleasing others. It involves satisfaction with self—a far different requirement. Although, in the words of German philosopher Arthur Schopenhauer, "we forfeit three-fourths of ourselves to be like other people," the prize we seek—self-satisfaction— remains elusive.

In the constructivist view, socially reticent individuals who seek treatment have burning questions. They want to know something about who they are and what life is about. Unfortunately, not many of the relevant answers can be found by training the person to imitate someone else. Reticent clients have already done too much pretending—they pretend to enjoy themselves at a party, to be sick on the day of the class report, and to be more interested in computers than in getting a date for Saturday night. They do not need to add still more layers of pretense on top of those that have already been installed.

A very different approach, more in keeping with the constructivist mandate and yet bearing some superficial similarities to the behavioral techniques we have been criticizing, is George Kelly's (1955) "fixed-role therapy." In this format, individuals are invited to play the role of another character for short periods of time. However, this is not behavioral rehearsal, skill training, or cognitive modification. The function of the exercise is to further a process of personal inquiry. The person is being given a tool for exploring social questions from an alternative vantage point—producing the advantages of what Bateson (1979) called "double description." Kelly was careful to develop characterizations that people could enact without significant role strain (Neimeyer & Feixas, 1990). Thus, he did not ask quiet individuals to become boisterous. Instead, he might have suggested that they consider themselves "thoughtful" rather than hesitant or fearful. Furthermore, the pretense was time limited, private, and accurately labeled. When the experiment was over, the person was under no obligation whatsoever to change his or her behavior or system of beliefs.

The constructivist approach to helping reticent individuals is to provide them with opportunities to establish, in their own conversation, the social rights and privileges to which they feel entitled. Genuine social confidence comes from being clear about one's entitlements, not from practicing add-on gimmicks. For example, one client found herself unable to confront her mother around the issue of family visits (and a variety of other family obligations). She was continually experiencing guilt and apologizing for not visiting more often. It puzzled her that her behavior was continually criticized, even though she was more attentive to her mother's needs than was her sister, who rarely did anything for the family.

In discussions with her therapist, she finally made explicit to herself what had been implicit in her performances—that she had adopted the role of "good child," defining her job in life as pleasing her mother, no matter what. Moreover, she had more or less automatically assumed that in doing so she was complying with her mother's wishes and expectations and was therefore entitled to her mother's approbation. Yet her mother had never insisted that she be good, did not seem to reward her when she was, and showed just as much approval (or more) to the sister who was "negligent."

Out of her discussions with her constructivist therapist, the client concluded that she—not her mother—had arranged that she be the good child, and that although she could certainly continue in that role, no one owed her anything for it. She was operating on her own recognizance, so to speak. She could also carve out other roles for herself, because neither her mother nor anyone else in the world could dictate the right way to be in her family. Furthermore, to be criticized while trying to be good was neither fair nor unfair. To a constructivist, the world is never fair. Fairness is a concept that we humans invoke to win sympathy, establish territories, gain support for our causes, and punish those who oppose us. In that sense, it is always a political gimmick.

These discussions clarified, for the client, where everyone stood. By recognizing her own involvement with the decision to be good, she felt more powerful, freed of the burden to construe herself as a hapless victim of her mother's desires. That context change took the horror out of her relationship with her mother. It opened up a new realm of possibilities, including that she might take "vacations" from attending family events, even if others disapproved. It also made family visits more enjoyable, because only in knowing that one is authorized to say no does one truly acquire the ability to say yes and mean it (Szasz, 1990).

Conversing is for human beings what grooming behavior is for chimps—it validates a person's role in the social order and, at the same time, contributes to the maintenance of that order. In therapy, itself a form of grooming, a person has an opportunity to take a close look at the role ambiguities with which he or she has been plagued and to understand the way in which interpersonal snares have been generated. The therapist assists the client by listening carefully to the person's language declarations and feeding them back to the client. Let us take a miniexample:

A client states that he is not sure whether he is satisfied with his current job. The therapist says, "I can tell you that you aren't satisfied."

"How do you know?"

"You just said so."

"I said 'I wasn't sure.' "

"Well—are you satisfied?"

"No! But my problem is I don't know what else I would like any better if I dropped this job."

"That's an entirely different issue."

Even in this short piece of dialogue, something important has happened: One question has disappeared (been cleared up) and another, more challenging question has taken its place. Later, in that same session, the client and therapist agreed that it is often possible to know what "is not it," even in the absence of certainty about what is. An artist can usually tell you that his canvas is not yet finished, although he may not yet know what the finished product will look like or how long it will take to complete it. Of course, it is frightening to contemplate a career change without being sure about what might come next, especially if one has a family to support. Furthermore, when people are fearful, they like to slow down events by "becoming confused." However, it is possible to be clear, to be fearful, and to postpone taking costly or precipitous action. That is the responsible stance, because all factors are taken into consideration and given their proper due. Clear language and personal responsibility invariably go together, hand in glove.

Question: How do constructivist therapists know when to work on snippets of dialogue, as in the preceding example, or on larger issues and patterns?

Answer: Actually, constructivists usually connect conversational glimpses to the larger issues they elucidate. Any ambiguity in the moment reflects a larger unresolved question. But let us look at the more complex case that follows and focus this time on the overall picture rather than on a small slice of dialogue.

A wife complained that her husband, from whom she was separated, was wasting time at their joint therapy session. Instead of detailing the week's events, she thought, he ought to be talking about how he intended to improve their relationship. The husband, who desperately wanted his wife to return home, attempted to comply by reviewing the personal reforms he had planned. The wife was not impressed; in fact, she seemed even grumpier as he continued, although he was obviously trying hard to be accommodating. Paradoxically, as the therapist later pointed out, had he refused to meet her request, her mood might have brightened dramatically. In fact, she could not avoid smiling at the therapist's suggestion that he was being "too compliant."

One of her major disappointments in their union was that the "strong" husband she had thought she was marrying, and on whom she had hoped to rely, turned into Caspar Milquetoast shortly after their marriage was consummated. He had been a business whiz at an early age, which was one of the factors that attracted her to him. However, he had since decided to return to school for an advanced degree, trading the boardroom for the classroom. Moreover, he was quite deferent to her at home, letting it be known how deeply he loved her and how much he needed her in order to be happy. For instance, when she was away on a trip to her family, he had become quite depressed and had placed repeated lengthy phone calls to her.

Ironically, the more he tried to please, the more strained their relationship became. During their courtship, she had a secret (and unacknowledged) hankering to be his "daughter." However, after they were married, she found herself increasingly cast in the role of being his mother. Instead of her being able to depend on him, he seemed utterly dependent on her. As her attraction for him decreased, he became still needier and more suppliant, perpetuating a vicious cycle.

For this wife, as for many people, love and need are experienced as incompatible postures: Love denotes sufficiency and openness, whereas neediness is associated with possessiveness and entrapment. In terms of these experiences, a person cannot love (or be loved by) that which he or she needs. Moreover, the more grasping and needy a person becomes, the fewer occasions there are when love can put in a spontaneous appearance (Smothermon, 1979). Few people would find it attractive to be with a person who keeps threatening to collapse the moment they move a few feet away.

In cases such as this one, changing partners is not usually the answer, because each individual is apt to select another mate of the same breed and end up right back in the same predicament. What has to be addressed is the issue of self-sufficiency. An adult has to discover a way to be satisfied with himself or herself, before he or she can expect to share much genuine pleasure with another. A marriage based on a need for security is not likely to be very nourishing to the participants. The goal of the constructivist therapist in a case of this sort is to help the partners discover that the relationship context in which they have been operating is unworkable and must be supplanted by a more inclusive framework of meaning—one in which satisfaction with self becomes possible.

Contexts are all-important to the work of the constructivist. A woman once called to ask if we "worked with addicts." There are many possible replies to that sort of inquiry. In this instance, the therapist responded, "No, I work with people—some of whom think of themselves as being addicted to something." This was the beginning of a negotiation in which a potentially disadvantageous reification was being held up to scrutiny rather than automatically accepted. Clients handicap themselves by buying into a series of reifications that make living more difficult. It is advisable that therapists take steps to point out the traps such reifications create and avoid endorsing them as operating principles. An addiction might be thought of as involving the easy repetition of a solution that has previously saved one's hide. In that sense, everyone is an "addict" (Maturana & Varela, 1987). A person only "drinks too much" in someone else's opinion (Efran & Heffner, 1991; Efran et al., 1987). Of course, the person himself or herself may hold the same opinion the morning after, because by then there has been a shift in context. However, addiction does not necessarily imply broken organismic machinery in need of repair. To the constructivist, the organism's solutions to the perplexities it confronts are perfectly legitimate, even if costly from some other perspectives. To take a related example, we were talking recently with a person who thought of himself as having a severe gambling addiction. He was concerned that he was throwing his money away. He thought that gambling was a peculiar activity, indicating something objectively defective about his system. We reminded him that gambling was the essence of living. A person who crosses the street gambles, as does the person who changes jobs or orders a Caesar salad in a restaurant. Gambling is not a process invented by gaming establishments and confined to the roulette table. On the other hand, both inside and outside the casino, it is always useful to inspect the odds. Some games are costlier than others, and the payoffs are too few and far between. This brings us full circle to the kind of personal projects that radical constructivist therapists are most comfortable tackling—helping individuals shape up and clarify their life questions, so that these can be satisfactorily answered with a minimum of fuss and interpersonal travail.

RECAPITULATION

Question: Perhaps it would be useful to review some of the major points about the radical constructivist stance that have emerged in this discussion. What are the major notions that set this approach to therapy apart from others?

Answer: First, language is clearly central to psychotherapy because it is the domain in which problems are created and in which they reside. However, language is not to be misinterpreted as "just talk." It is a form of communal coordination, made possible by the body's emotional support apparatus and the circumstances in which people live together. Constructivist therapy is certainly a form of conversation, but it is not restricted to the purely verbal or hypothetical domains—it involves consequential action.

Second, people's worlds may be constructed in language, but those language constructions include such harsh social realities as poverty and abuse, illness and inequality. Nature does not care what people do with their lives—but people do. In consultation with one another, people jointly determine their own criteria for success and failure, happiness and despair. Psychotherapy was not designed to fix the economy or to find a cure for cancer, but it is a forum for attaining clarity about one's place in the social ecology and discovering ways to be an effective family member, a useful citizen, and a satisfied individual.

To say that problems exist in language arrangements is not to brand them as trivial or imaginary. In life, satisfaction requires that one speak clearly about who one is and what one stands for. Hypocrisy in such matters can be expedient, but it hurts in the realm of self-fulfillment. Even when you can fool others, you cannot fool yourself. In this respect, certain con artists lead quite contented lives because they are absolutely clear about the lies they tell and the risks they take. They take full responsibility for the path they are following. That is more than some people can say about the life experiences they have created for themselves. To the constructivist, personal satisfaction is a function of keeping one's word, not necessarily practicing a conventional morality or living in objectively enviable circumstances.

Radical constructivists do not maintain that their point of view is objectively correct, nor do they maintain that they choose it, in the usual sense of that term. They know that constructivism appeals to them because of who they are and the milieu in which they developed. Like every other point of view (including objectivism), constructivism has evolved out of the patterning of interactions at this time in history. Having worked its way into one's awareness, radical constructivism becomes a legitimate and potentially useful scheme, even if it was selected for historical reasons rather than on the basis of free will or a process of rational choosing.

People do not unilaterally control their destinies; they are social beings immersed in both a natural ecology and a social community. They cannot think or do anything they please; their behavior is a reflection of a broader evolving conversation. However, the community develops through the participation of individuals, not despite it. Everyone, including a therapist, is entitled to have preferences and to work for the establishment of particular values and points of view. In a world without objective truths, all people have is each other, and it is the social inventions that people are able to enact together that count.

Problems arise through collective acts of distinction, but once distinguished, they cannot necessarily be made to vanish overnight through verbal sleight of hand. Radical constructivists are not interested in getting clients to feel better by giving them formulaic and glossy reinterpretations of their concerns. They are more interested in helping clients clear up the ambiguities of living and the conflicting role demands that derive from multiple community memberships. As constructive therapists, we invite them to settle territorial disputes to their own satisfaction.

We provide clients with a context for inquiry, not a technology for retraining particular behaviors or for modifying discrete cognitions. Constructivism is not an argument for or against particular methods or strategies. It provides a framework in which to note that people are truly responsible for answering their own questions and that a meaningful existence cannot be obtained in any other way.

REFERENCES

Adler, A. (1968). *The practice and theory of individual psychology.* Totowa, NJ: Littlefield, Adams.

Akillas, E., & Efran, J. S. (1989). Internal conflict, language and metaphor: Implications for psychotherapy. *Journal of Contemporary Psychotherapy, 19,* 149–159.

Bateson, G. (1979). *Mind and nature.* New York: E. P. Dutton.

Bergner, R. M. (1988). Status of dynamic psychotherapy with depressed individuals. *Psychotherapy, 25,* 266–272.

Bogdan, J. (1984). Doctor Pangloss as family therapist. *The Family Therapy Networker, 8*(2), 19–20.

Bogdan, J. (1986). Do families really need problems? *The Family Therapy Networker, 10*(4), 30–35, 67–69.

Cummings, N. A. (1979). Turning bread into stones: Our modern antimiracle. *American Psychologist, 34,* 1119–1129.

Doherty, W. J. (1991). Family therapy goes postmodern: Deconstructing clinical objectivity. *The Family Therapy Networker, 15*(5), 36–42.

Efran, J. S. (1991). Constructivism in the inner city. *The Family Therapy Networker, 15*(5), 51–52.

Efran, J. S., Germer, C., & Lukens, M. D. (1986). Context and psychotherapy. In R. Rosnow & M. Georgoudi (Eds.), *Contextualism and understanding in behavioral science: Implications for research and theory* (pp. 169–186). New York: Praeger.

Efran, J. S., & Heffner, K. P. (1991). Change the name and you change the game. *Journal of Strategic and Family Therapy, 10,* 50–65.

Efran, J. S., Heffner, K. P., & Lukens, R. J. (1987). Alcoholism as an opinion: Structure determinism applied to drinking. *Alcoholism Treatment Quarterly, 4,* 67–85.

Efran, J. S., Lukens, M. D., & Lukens, R. J. (1990). *Language, structure, and change: Frameworks of meaning in psychotherapy.* New York: Norton.

Ellis, A., & Dryden, W. (1987). *The practice of rational-emotive therapy.* New York: Springer.

Goffman, E. (1959). *The presentation of self in everyday life.* Garden City, NY: Doubleday.

Goffman, E. (1971). *Relations in public: Microstudies of the public order.* New York: Basic Books.

Holden, A. (1988). *Olivier.* London: Weidenfeld and Nicholson.

Jaynes, J. (1990). *The origins of consciousness in the breakdown of the bicameral mind.* Boston: Houghton Mifflin.

Johnson, M. (1986). Paradoxical interventions: From repugnance to cautious curiosity. *The Counseling Psychologist, 14,* 297–302.

Kelly, G. A. (1955). *The psychology of personal constructs.* New York: Norton.

Kelly, G. A. (1969). *Clinical psychology and personality: The selected papers of George Kelly* (B. Maher, Ed.). New York: Wiley.

Krüll, M., Luhmann, N., & Maturana, H. R. (1988). Basic concepts of the theory of autopoietic systems. In J. Hargens (Ed.), *Systemic therapy: A European perspective* (pp. 79–104). Broadstairs, Kent, United Kingdom: Borgmann.

Mahoney, M. J. (1991). *Human change processes: The scientific foundations of psychotherapy.* New York: Basic Books.

Marowitz, C. (1961). *Stanislavsky and the method.* New York: Citadel Press.

Marris, P. (1974). *Loss and change.* New York: Pantheon Books.

Maturana, H. R. (1988). Reality: The search for objectivity or the quest for a compelling argument. *Irish Journal of Psychology, 9,* 25–82.

Maturana, H. R., & Varela, F. J. (1987). *The tree of knowledge: The biological roots of human understanding.* Boston: Shambhala Publications.

Mendez, C. L., Coddou, F., & Maturana, H. (1988). The bringing forth of pathology. *Irish Journal of Psychology, 9,* 144–172.

Minuchin, S. (1991). The seductions of constructivism: Renaming power won't make it disappear. *The Family Therapy Networker, 15*(5), 47–50.

Neimeyer, R. A., & Feixas, G. (1990). Constructivist contributions to psychotherapy integration. *Journal of Integrative and Eclectic Psychotherapy, 9,* 4–20.

Nichols, M. P., & Schwartz, R. C. (1995). *Family therapy: Concepts and methods* (3rd ed.). Boston: Allyn & Bacon.

Packer, M. J. (1985). Hermeneutic inquiry in the study of human conduct. *American Psychologist, 40,* 1081–1093.

Phillips, G. M. (1991). *Communication incompetencies: A theory of training oral performance behavior.* Carbondale: Southern Illinois University Press.

Ridley, C. R., & Tan, S. Y. (1986). Unintentional paradoxes and potential pitfalls in paradoxical psychotherapy. *The Counseling Psychologist, 14,* 303–308.

Rychlak, J. F. (1981). *Personality and psychotherapy: A theory-construction approach* (2nd ed.). Boston: Houghton Mifflin.

Shutty, M. S., Jr., & Sheras, P. (1991). Brief strategic psychotherapy with chronic pain patients: Reframing and problem resolution. *Psychotherapy, 28,* 636–642.

Smothermon, R. (1979). *Winning through enlightenment.* San Francisco: Context Publications.

Szasz, T. (1990). *The untamed tongue: A dissenting dictionary.* La Salle, IL: Open Court.

Varela, F. J., Thompson, E., & Rosch, E. (1991). *The embodied mind: Cognitive science and human experience.* Cambridge, MA: MIT Press.

Watzlawick, P. (Ed.). (1984). *The invented reality: How do we know what we believe we know? Contributions to constructivism.* New York: Norton.

14

PERSONAL CONSTRUCTS IN SYSTEMIC PRACTICE

GUILLEM FEIXAS

Life provides man with no scientific footholds on reality, suggests
to him no narrative plots, offers no rhythmic metaphor to confirm
the moving resonance of a human theme. If he chooses to write
tragedy, then tragedy it will be; if comedy, then that is what will
come of it; and if burlesque, he, the sole reader, must learn to laugh
at its misanthropic caricatures of the only person he knows—himself.
(Kelly, 1969d, p. 24)

Kelly's (1955) personal construct theory (PCT) and the systems
approach are, at least at first sight, two different traditions in approaching
the therapeutic endeavor. Originally, PCT emphasized the processes of
construction of a single individual (e.g., Bannister & Fransella, 1986),
and it has only gradually been expanded in focus to include couples (e.g.,
G. Neimeyer, 1985; Ryle, 1975). Therefore, its therapeutic approach was
mainly intrapsychic or dyadic. Conversely, the conceptualization of a
problem from a systemic perspective always included the family context.
In that context, individual behavior was primarily understood as a func-

This chapter was partially written while I occupied a postdoctoral position at Memphis State
University, Department of Psychology, with the assistance of a grant to the Center for Applied
Psychological Research through the State of Tennessee's Centers of Excellence Program. I also
received support from the Departament de Personalitat, Avaluació i Tractaments Psicológics,
Universitat de Barcelona.
   I gratefully acknowledge the helpful comments of Robert Neimeyer, Harry Procter, Pamela
Alexander, and Kat Bagley.

tion of the larger family system. As a consequence, systemic treatment focused on family groups, thereby deemphasizing individual therapy.

Recently, some important changes have taken place. On the one hand, the systemic movement has become much more flexible, both in acknowledging the necessity of paying more attention to the individual (even to the point of treating only individuals or dyads instead of the entire family; e.g., Fisch, Weakland, & Segal, 1982) and in adopting a constructivist epistemological position (e.g., Efran, Lukens, & Lukens, 1988; Hoffman, 1988a). On the other hand, some personal construct therapists have elaborated a construct approach to systemic interventions (Feixas, Cunillera, & Villegas, 1987; Procter, 1978, 1981, 1985a) that establishes a basis for a convergence of both approaches.

Although the similarities between current systemic therapies and Kelly's (1955) PCT have been described elsewhere (Feixas, 1990b), they can be summarized in the following way. First, PCT and the systemic therapies share a common epistemological stance: constructivism. Even though there are notable differences among the various systemic therapies, they share the view that knowledge results from a construing process rather than from a direct representation of reality. Second, PCT can be described as a systemic theory. It contains the properties of totality, equifinality, feedback, and a tendency to constant states that are postulated by systemic theorists about open systems. Finally, PCT and the systemic therapies take similar positions on several relevant clinical issues, such as the influence of labeling in pathology, the central role of anticipation, the view of "resistance" as a coherent movement of the system, the use of the client's language and metaphors, the exploration of intended solutions, the potential use of prescriptions, and the view of therapy as a reconstructive process.

In this chapter, I explore the clinical usefulness of incorporating personal construct concepts and methods into systemic practice. As an initial step, I begin with an analysis of Kelly's constructivism in the context of other constructivist positions that continue to inspire many systemic developments. I then outline a model of change that has applicability to both individual and systemic therapies and introduce the concept of the family construct system as a means of bridging these two distinct therapeutic traditions. I next illustrate the application of some of these concepts and methods in the context of a brief clinical case study and outline some of the issues entailed in strategizing about both content and process in the practice of family therapy. Finally, I conclude with some implications for research and an expression of optimism regarding the mutual enrichment of individual and family-based constructivist perspectives.

PCT AND SYSTEMIC CONSTRUCTIVISM

As I have mentioned, PCT and the systemic therapies share the common epistemological stance of constructivism. Even though there are notable differences among the various systemic therapies (Anderson & Goolishian, 1988; Feixas, 1990b; Kenny & Gardner, 1988), they agree in viewing knowledge as resulting from a construing process rather than from a direct representation of reality. Because knowledge of the external world is actively construed by the subject (observer) in a given social context, the idea of having a "true" knowledge about reality vanishes. Thus, Kelly's (1955) assertion that reality can be interpreted in a variety of ways is shared by many constructivist thinkers (e.g., Bateson, 1979; Kenny & Gardner, 1988; Mahoney, 1988; Maturana & Varela, 1987; von Foerster, 1981; Watzlawick, 1984). This view contrasts with the traditional one, objectivism, which holds that reality is directly represented in the subject's mind, which passively receives the stimuli from the environment.

In chapter 2 of this volume, Robert A. Neimeyer offers a summary of the main distinctive assertions of constructivism and objectivism. The core epistemological issue, the nature of knowledge, has already been pointed out in the previous paragraph. The notion of knowledge as invention (e.g., von Glasersfeld, 1984) contrasts with the objectivist belief in discovering an already existing truth. The evolutionary nature of knowledge has been described by Popper (1972), Campbell (1974), and others. Rejecting the justificationist assumption of knowledge as a true belief, Popper (1959) asserted that data are conceptual and that hypotheses have only the status of conjectures (Popper, 1963) as long as they are not falsified. In short, human organisms are "theories of their environments," and human knowledge structures are adaptations to that environment that are subject to selective processes through refutation or invalidation.

The problem of a constructivist position has to do with the question of how people assign validity to their knowledge. If human perceptions are not to be taken for granted, then what criteria can one use to decide whether to incorporate or refuse a bit of knowledge according to one's system, either at the level of single individuals or at the level of science itself? Again, an evolutionary response is appropriate. A hypothesis is regarded as (provisionally) valid as long as it fits with the context and seems to be viable (von Glasersfeld, 1984). It should also, to a certain extent, be consistent with previous acquired knowledge (e.g., Kelly, 1955) to be integrated into one's system. Proponents of the social constructionist movement (e.g., Berger & Luckman, 1966; Gergen, 1985) and contemporary philosophers of science (e.g., Kuhn, 1962) have emphasized the social nature of knowledge. Knowledge arises in the context of a social interaction influenced by language, culture, and family environments, and the very process of determining its validity is a social process in itself.

Both Kelly (1955) and Bateson (1979) have viewed the creation of knowledge as a process of grasping differences rather than one of concept formation, which has been proposed in the information-processing paradigm put forth by the objectivists. Kelly further emphasized the organization of knowledge (constructs) in a hierarchical, self-organized system, much as Maturana and Varela (e.g., 1987), at a more abstract level, described living organisms as autonomous, autopoietic systems that create their own structure. As an extension of this notion, Chilean biologists Maturana and Varela conceived of the interaction between living organisms not as a direct transmission of information (interactive instruction), but as a complex process of coupling two autonomous self-organized structures.

Despite these points of agreement on their epistemological preference for constructivism, PCT and the systemic therapies reached constructivism through quite different paths and encompass some distinctive assumptions. I therefore present the epistemological evolution of Kelly's (1955) approach first, give a brief account of systemic constructivism, and conclude this section by elucidating some of their contrasts as well as similarities.

Kelly's Constructive Alternativism

George A. Kelly (1955), along with Bartlett, and Piaget (1937), was among the earliest constructivist thinkers in psychology and pioneered the constructivist therapies (Feixas & Villegas, 1990; Mahoney & Gabriel, 1987). His approach to psychology and psychotherapy (Kelly, 1955) has been one of the few that reveals its epistemological bases. Furthermore, although Kelly was influenced by philosophers Vaihinger and Dewey, he reached his epistemological position chiefly through his own clinical practice. He started his clinical and academic career during the 1930s in a college that drew students from a wide rural area. Because he was one of three faculty members and the only clinical psychologist in the department, he had few resources with which to accomplish the clinical and educational responsibilities his position entailed. Moreover, psychology—and especially psychotherapy—was very immature, offering few alternatives to the practitioner. Kelly soon rejected the stimulus–response paradigm because of its simplicity and inability to solve the clinical problems he was facing; however, he was not convinced by the obvious alternative—psychoanalysis.

> So I began fabricating "insights." I deliberately offered "preposterous interpretations" to my clients. Some of them were as un-Freudian

as I could make them. . . . My *only criteria were that the explanation account for the crucial facts as the client saw them and that it carry implications for approaching the future in a different way* [italics added].

What happened? Well, many of my preposterous explanations worked, some of them surprisingly well. To be sure, the wilder ones fell flat, but a reexamination of the interviews often suggested where the client's difficulty with them lay. (Kelly, 1969a, p. 52)

Thus, through clinical experimentation, Kelly realized the central role of the (re)construction of the client's experience (in terms of generating more viable alternatives). As set forth above, the main criterion was not the truth value of the reinterpretation but (a) its relevance to account for what the client considered crucial and (b) its potential for the generation of an alternative way of facing the future. Kelly's (1955) main emphasis lay on the possibility of generating new alternative constructions for any given event: "No one needs to paint himself into a corner; no one needs to be completely hemmed by circumstances; no one needs to be victim of his biography" (p. 15).

Because of this emphasis on the generation of alternatives, Kelly (1969c) labeled his epistemological principle *constructive alternativism*, saying that "reality is subject to many alternative constructions, some of which may prove to be more fruitful than others" (p. 96). These "fruitful" constructions would be viable and fit with a person's previous system of construing.

One of the most interesting features of Kelly's constructivism is not only that it has been developed through clinical practice but that the entire corpus of personal construct psychology (a psychological theory, a clinical theory, assessment methods, strategies for intervention, and therapeutic techniques) was coherently derived from Kelly's constructivist assumptions. Such a consistency among these different levels of theory and practice is rare in psychology, particularly in psychotherapy (Feixas & Villegas, 1990; R. Neimeyer, 1988).

In his fundamental postulate, Kelly (1955) asserted that "a person's processes are psychologically channelized by the ways in which he anticipates events" (p. 46). As Bruner (1956) noted, the anticipation of the future seems to be the main motivational principle of PCT. Thus, the way a person anticipates, for Kelly, is his or her most relevant characteristic. Such an outlook results in the conceptualization of human beings as proactive, goal directed, and purposive. In this way, Kelly's constructivism was developed through his psychological theory and practice instead of only being an armchair reflection expressed in the epistemological chapter of his 1955 work. I describe some of these constructivist issues later in a discussion of the personal construct model of change.

Systemic Constructivism

In earlier systemic formulations still regarded as central for many family therapists (e.g., Haley, 1963; Watzlawick, Beavin, & Jackson, 1967), the presenting problem was considered in the context of a behavior sequence of the family members in which the symptom had a homeostatic function related to the whole system. Either it was related to trigenerational coalitions (e.g., Haley, 1963; Minuchin, 1974), or the solution attempted by the family to solve the problem was considered a key segment of the behavioral pattern perpetuating the problem (Watzlawick, Weakland, & Fisch, 1974). However, in the past decade, increasing numbers of systemic therapists have adopted a constructivist-oriented stance.

Gregory Bateson, one of the precursors of the systemic family movement, elaborated his epistemological thoughts (e.g., 1972, 1979) in a way that has greatly influenced the sensitivity of many systemic therapists to the importance of the process of knowing and its relevance for clinical practice. As a result, subsequent constructivist authors—such as von Glasersfeld (1984), von Foerster (1981), and Maturana and Varela (1987), along with Bateson—are among the most quoted sources of theoretical and clinical inspiration in the systemic literature of the past decade.

Hoffman (1985, 1988a) is perhaps the author who has most clearly narrated the evolution of the systemic movement toward constructivism. Its initial focus on behavior sequences shifted to the investigation of meanings, that is, of how behaviors are construed by different family members. Problems are currently explained in terms of family myths, premises, or shared belief systems that are coherent with symptomatic behaviors. Thus, the new systemic techniques (e.g., circular questioning) are devised to make explicit and challenge those family premises. A paradigmatic example of this constructivist–systemic approach is represented by the Milan team formed by Boscolo and Cecchin (Boscolo, Cecchin, Hoffman, & Penn, 1987). Other relevant examples are Watzlawick's (1984) edited book, Keeney's (1983) conceptualization of change, Goolishian's (e.g., Goolishian & Winderman, 1988) notion of problem-determined systems, and other derived clinical applications. A sign of its influence in the field was the appearance of a special 1988 issue on constructivism in *The Family Therapy Networker*, in which Efran, Lukens, and Lukens (1988) and others presented constructivism, its clinical implications, and its relation with Kelly's epistemology and clinical position.

Humberto Maturana has been regarded as an epistemologist who has inspired a great deal of systemic epistemological thinking, and his position has been considered more radical than Kelly's. Below, I compare the ideologies of these two authors to further reveal the epistemological relationship between PCT and the systemic therapies.

Kelly and Maturana: An Ontological Contrast

Because they share more assumptions than not, I first briefly point to some similarities between the thinking of Kelly and Maturana. As explained earlier, both authors hold a common constructivist position at the epistemological level. Likewise, both deny the possibility of a true and objective knowledge of reality. As noted by R. Neimeyer and Feixas (1990b), Maturana's (Maturana & Varela, 1980) concept of autopoiesis— the view of living systems as self-organized and as determining their own evolution—has its parallel in PCT in the choice corollary. According to the latter, every system makes choices that increase its predictive power, that is, choices that contribute the most to a greater elaboration of the system. Sometimes a person's choice can even include a "symptom" in order to increase the scope or precision of his or her anticipatory structures. In this sense, there is no right direction of elaboration to be defined by an arbitrary observer: "It is the system itself that regulates the direction and extent of change" (R. Neimeyer & Feixas, 1990b, p. 78). Therefore, as Maturana (Maturana & Varela, 1987) maintained, fluctuations in the environment can, at most, trigger change in the living system. This leads to the ideas of *structural determinism* and *operational closure* (Maturana & Varela, 1980), which suggest that changes that occur in any living system are determined by the characteristics of its structure rather than by external reality. Similarly, Kelly (1955), in his modulation corollary, stated that "the variation in a person's construction system is limited by the permeability of [its superordinate] constructs" (p. 77). This means that a given system does not allow for just *any* change, but for only a limited range of alternatives. The range of existing possibilities within the system depends on the degree to which its superordinate structure allows for the inclusion of new axes of construction—the system's permeability.

Another parallelism can be found in Maturana's aphorism "anything said is said by an observer" (Maturana & Varela, 1980, p. 8), intended to convey the idea that when someone makes a statement about reality that person is talking about his or her view of reality. Attention must therefore be directed to the observer rather than to that reality. Similarly, Kelly (1969b) asserted the following:

> When I say Professor Lindzey's left shoe is an "introvert," everyone looks at his shoe as if this were something his shoe was responsible for. Or if I say that Professor Cattell's head is "discursive," everyone looks over at him, as if the proposition had popped out of his head instead of out of mine. Don't look at his head! Don't look at that

shoe! Look at me; I'm the one who is responsible for the statement. (p. 72)

Despite their epistemological similarities, Maturana and Kelly disagree in their belief about the existence of reality. For the former "nothing exists outside language" and reality is only "an explanatory proposition" (Maturana, 1988, p. 80). Although Kelly would agree, in that the only criterion for the validation of one's hypotheses is the internal correlation between anticipations (superordinate constructs) and low-order sensory discriminations (subordinate constructs), he has unambiguously stated his presumption about the existence of reality: "We presume that the universe is really existing and that [humans are] gradually coming to understand it" (Kelly, 1955, p. 6). This straightforward disagreement is not, however, epistemological, but ontological. Both agree that human beings cannot come to know reality directly (an epistemological position), but they disagree in their beliefs about whether or not reality exists independently of an observer (an ontological position). Kelly presumes the existence of reality (a position traditionally related to realism or materialism), and Maturana asserts that reality does not exist (a position traditionally related to idealism and solipsism).

In looking at this divergence, if one takes as rigorous a point of view as did Held and Pols (1985, 1987), one realizes that it is a logical inconsistency to make any kind of statement about the existence of reality—that is, any kind of ontological statement:

> A considerable part of the family therapy field adopts an epistemology ... NR [meaning "no independent reality attainable" (p. 456)], and if one adopts an epistemology of that kind, a contradiction will arise if one also adopts a metaphysics/ontology—any metaphysics/ontology. (Held & Pols, 1987, p. 457)

Now that this logical inconsistency is recognized, let me tentatively pursue this ontological controversy for a moment. To assert the metaphysical and ontological existence of reality presents several advantages (despite the already acknowledged disadvantage of logical inconsistency). It accounts for a number of phenomena that most people see intuitively as "bits of reality": abuse, violence, physical illness, and death. These phenomena are frequently raised as objections to constructivism (e.g., Taggart, 1985). To share a personal example, I recently had the experience of a minor car accident. Even if it was not serious, I, as a living system, received a distressing perturbation from the environment. There was something "out there" influencing me. Of course, my structure (body constitution, position, and psychological state) determined the damage that the impact produced on my body as well as on my cognitive construction of the event. But some bit of reality triggered (only triggered) some changes in my physical and psychological state. Perhaps it was not an "interactive instruction," but something out there was structurally coupling my body in a way that my autopoietic and autonomous system had not chosen.

On the other hand, other relevant thinkers have more or less explicitly expressed this logically inconsistent (though at another level, intuitively reasonable) position. Max Planck (1932), considered the forerunner of quantum physics, asserted simultaneously that "(1) there is a real outer world which exists independently of our act of knowing [and] (2) the real outer world is not directly knowable" (p. 32). Prigogine (Prigogine & Stengers, 1984), along with quantum physicists and many other constructivists, proposed a view of matter (reality) that depended to some extent on the observer, such that reality is not a "passive substance" described by a "mechanistic world view." Therefore, matter, although not passive, exists. This could be deduced even from von Glasersfeld's (1984) writings: "The only aspect of that 'real' world that actually enters into the realm of experience is its constraints" (p. 24). Although Kelly's position is logically inconsistent with epistemological constructivism, one could take this position and assert that the universe really exists even though it cannot enter the human "realm of experience" except through "its constraints."

This ontological divergence between Kelly and Maturana had been previously suspected by Mahoney (1988) and by Kenny and Gardner (1988). In consequence, the latter did not consider Maturana as a constructivist but as the creator of the alternative "bring forth paradigm" (Kenny & Gardner, 1988, p. 9). As noted earlier, my position is different; I consider Maturana one of the more relevant contributors to contemporary constructivism, despite his ontological claim for the inexistence of reality.

Mahoney (1988), on the other hand, has distinguished critical constructivists—those who "acknowledge the existence of a 'real' external world"—from radical constructivists[1]—"an approach that is basically

---

[1] Mahoney (1988) borrowed the term *radical* from von Glasersfeld (1984). Ironically, however, I have not been able to find any statement by von Glasersfeld denying the existence of reality. Nor does the text quoted by Mahoney (1988, p. 4):

> Radical constructivism, thus, is *radical* because it breaks with convention and develops a theory of knowledge in which knowledge does not reflect an "objective" ontological reality, but exclusively an ordering and organization of a world constituted by experience. The radical constructivist has relinquished "metaphysical realism" once and for all. (von Glasersfeld, 1984, p. 24)

In fact, this definition of radical constructivism fits very well with epistemological constructivism as defined here. Furthermore, the only thing that von Glasersfeld (1984) mentions about "metaphysical realism" is that the radical constructivist has "relinquished" it. It is perfectly consistent with epistemological constructivism to relinquish any kind of metaphysical and ontological assumption. Moreover, in the same chapter, von Glasersfeld (1984) stated clearly, in concordance with Held and Pols (1985, 1987), the impossibility of making a "right" or "true" judgment about reality, saying that "the question is unanswerable" (von Glasersfeld, 1984, p. 26).

indistinguishable from 'idealism' " (Mahoney, 1988, p. 4). I find this solution elegant though not completely accurate. To distinguish among constructivist thinkers, Mahoney used not an epistemological but an ontological criterion.

In the end, however, this issue becomes a matter of classifying thinkers and written thoughts—a matter of labeling. But one of the clinical points of constructivism is precisely the importance of the labels applied to behaviors, thoughts, and feelings. Because labels and "languaging" have a prominent (perhaps exclusive) role in social domains, it becomes important to point out the distinctions that relevant thinkers make because they inspire, to some extent, the clinical practice of a number of therapists.

A MODEL OF CHANGE: THE CONSTRUCTIVIST "PREJUDICE"

In a critical article, Golann (1987) noted how the adoption of cybernetic and constructivist perspectives in the family therapy field "has resulted in an unnecessary devaluation of representational description of family interaction" (p. 331). Because from a "second-order,"[2] cybernetic perspective any description tells more about the observer than about the observed event, it seems that description has little place within a constructivist framework. However, I completely agree with Golann's assertion that suggesting that "attempts at verifiable description of family interaction are not valuable in understanding the family, is to throw out the baby with the bath water" (1987, p. 332). Certainly, Kelly's (1955) commitment to constructivism did not curb his interest in conceptualizing the functioning of the construing systems. Moreover, he derived his psychological theory[3] in congruence with his epistemological conviction.

Actually, the assertion that constructivism implies that therapists avoid conceptualizing, attaching labels, and creating a "road map" about the client's system can be seen as incoherent. Although descriptions of a family interaction are not representational descriptions, but constructions, therapists—just like any other human beings—need to construe

---

[2]The distinction between second-order and first-order cybernetics was introduced by von Foerster (1981) and adopted for family systems therapy by Hoffman (1985) and Keeney (1983). Although first-order cybernetics was based on the premise of studying an external reality, without reference to the cognitive activity that makes that study possible, second-order cybernetics (also known as "cybernetics of observing systems" and as "cybernetics of cybernetics") focuses on the role of the observer in construing the observed reality. Because I consider this an epistemological constructivist position, as described earlier in this chapter, I hereinafter use *constructivism* and *second-order cybernetics* as interchangeable terms.
[3]As Bogdan (1987) has noted, to elaborate how belief systems (*constructs* in Kelly's terms) are organized and change is not "to do" epistemology but, rather, to do psychological theory.

the events they are dealing with. Kelly (1955) postulated that therapists should have a professional subsystem of construing (which would undoubtedly bear a relationship with their personal construct systems) to possess the skills to discriminate among clinical events they face in their everyday practice. This professional system should be comprehensive and elaborated in such a way as to acquire the greater predictive power. Of course, this subsystem would be furnished with the concepts of the therapist's particular orientation. Once Kelly recognized the impossibility of acting without a model, he tried to elaborate a personal construct model coherent with the constructivist position. Thus, as long as we, as therapists, cannot operate without a "prejudice," let us at least have a constructivist prejudice.

A model of human processes and change should have the following characteristics to be considered coherent with constructivist epistemology: (a) It should be centered in the process of construing rather than the reality construed (content); (b) it should be *contextualist*[4]—that is, it should account for the way that broader systems of construing interact with narrower ones; and (c) it should be *reflexive*—that is, it should account for the construing processes of both the observer and the observed. I believe that PCT can provide such a constructivist model.

Next, I outline the personal construct model of human functioning. Because, for PCT, life is continuous movement, this is also a model of change. PCT is organized in 11 corollaries that develop a fundamental postulate (mentioned above). A formal presentation of these corollaries can be found in other works (e.g., Bannister & Fransella, 1986; Kelly, 1963; R. Neimeyer, 1987a). To take a more informal stand, I focus on the cycle of experience, also proposed by Kelly (1970) and elaborated by later construct theorists (Feixas & Villegas, 1990; R. Neimeyer, 1985).

PCT as a Process-Centered Model

From a constructivist view, experience plays a crucial and exclusive role in the generation of knowledge. For Kelly (1955), the process of experience was an intrinsic part of being human, and, therefore, he was not concerned with explaining its causes and motives—the *why*. Rather, he proposed to consider this very process as the most fundamental mechanism of change and evolution. He thought that a deep understanding

[4]The term *contextualism* has been used in social sciences by Pepper (1942) as one of the four root metaphors (viz., formism, mechanism, contextualism, and organicism). Contextualism here holds both that (a) all knowledge is provisional, conjectural, and not leading to a conclusive "truth" and (b) knowledge is framed by contextual (relational) factors imbedded in a sociohistorical and cultural context of meanings and relationships (see Efran, Germer, & Lukens, 1986, for therapeutic implications). Therefore, the term *contextualism* meets my intentions here both in common sense and in Pepper's sense.

of this mechanism, as a continuous circular process, would enable us to better comprehend human action instead of just original causes and impulses. Because the universe itself is constantly transforming, this "invites the person to place new constructions upon [events] whenever something unexpected happens" (Kelly, 1955, p. 72).

Kelly (1955) proposed the metaphor "man the scientist" to describe the *cycle of experience*. He compared everyday human activity with that of the scientist. The first stage of this cycle, which emerges from previous cycles, refers to the anticipatory nature of human existence as well as to the predictive aspiration of science. The anticipations (constructs) or hypotheses are hierarchically organized in a system that serves both for understanding events and for anticipating the future. As scientific hypotheses, anticipations are linked to a whole theory: the personal construct system.

This comparison between the average person and the scientist does not imply that most people are aware of having hypotheses (and theories) in the same way that scientists are. Even though we are unaware of it, at any single moment of our existence we are involved in this process of anticipation. For example, in selecting a key out of a set to open a closed door, one anticipates making the right selection. There is enough investment to act according to this anticipation and to take the key and try to open the door, that is, to encounter the event. The outcome of this behavior provides a confirmation or disconfirmation of the anticipation, which in turn leads one to carry out a constructive revision. In case of validation of the hypothesis, the distinction that made that choice possible is consolidated in the system. In case of invalidation, new distinctions (constructs) should evolve to guide the subsequent behavior. A crucial question at this stage is how an anticipation becomes validated or invalidated. For Kelly (1955), it is not reality that provides (in)validation. Instead, (in)validation is "subjectively construed" (p. 158). That is, the hypothesis involves its own criteria, in terms of low-order sensory constructs, for (in)validation. As noted elsewhere (Feixas, 1990b), the cycle of experience can be summarized as a feedback loop in which behavior (represented by the encounter stage) and anticipation influence each other in a circular way.

More attention must be paid here to the nature of people's anticipations—their personal constructs. They are reports of a difference, in Batesonian terms (see Foley, 1988, and Feixas, 1990b, for a comparison between Kelly and Bateson), and evolve every time people make a distinction. Constructs are the way in which people perceive things or others as either similar to or different from each other. In this sense, constructs are dichotomous, for, as Kelly (1955) asserted, "much of our language . . . implies a contrast which it does not explicitly state. Our speech would be meaningless otherwise" (pp. 62–63). Certainly, meaning is constructed through contrasting differences. Moreover, meaning arises from the way that two or more constructs are related. The construct religious–atheist can bear different relationships with the construct good–bad. In some families, *religious* is linked with *good* and *atheist* with *bad*, whereas in others this relationship is reversed or nonimplicative (to be religious is considered neither bad nor good). PCT has elaborated models to account for the different possible relationships among constructs (a summary of one of these models is presented in Feixas, 1990b). In addition, PCT inspires more precise models for specific areas, such as that proposed by Viney, Benjamin, and Preston (1988) for the elderly.

PCT as a Contextualist Model

Although this description of the construing process can be seen as highly individualistic (as the idea of "personal construct" suggests),[5] this model has been adapted by Procter (1978, 1981, 1985a) and, subsequently, by Feixas (1990a) to describe family construct systems (for a review, see Feixas, 1992). In fact, what Kelly (1955) proposed was a model of functioning for construing systems, but because validation of a personal construct system is mainly provided in an interpersonal domain—the family in one's early years, and wider systems later (Procter & Parry, 1978)—this model allows itself to be extended to wider systems of construing. According to Procter (1981), this extension had "simply not yet been elaborated" (p. 354). Feixas (1990a) has tentatively proposed an adaptation of PCT corollaries to describe family and other multipersonal construct systems.

Procter (1978) has added two new corollaries, related to groups and families, to PCT as a foundation for his theory of the family construct system (FCS). In this approach, families negotiate a common reality, the FCS, that "provides the members with alternative 'slots' so they do not necessarily have to be in agreement" (Procter, 1981, p. 355).[6]

---

[5]Feixas (1990a) made a distinction among atomistic (intrapsychic), molecular (relational), and molar (systemic) foci of interest of therapeutic approaches. Kelly's (1955) original personal construct theory (PCT) is seen as basically atomistic and, thanks to the sociality corollary, molecular as well. However, with the idea of the family construct system, PCT acquires a molar level of conceptualization, understanding, and treatment of human phenomena.

[6]This approach bears some similarities to Reiss's (1981) "family paradigms," Penn's (1985) "family premises," and Bogdan's (1984) elaboration of Bateson's (1972) "ecology of ideas." Although these "shared-idea" models are potentially useful, Bogdan (1987) himself noted a problem that emerges: "Typically, family members come in to therapy with very different ideas about the problem" (p. 32). Within the family construct system model this can be explained, because constructs—unlike premises, concepts, or beliefs—are bipolar dimensions of meaning that can be either verbal or preverbal. Thus, a father who holds a biological view of a problem and a mother who defines it as psychological can both be using the same avenue of movement, even though they are construing the problem from opposite poles. To share a construct does not mean to be in agreement. In fact, it may mean just the opposite.

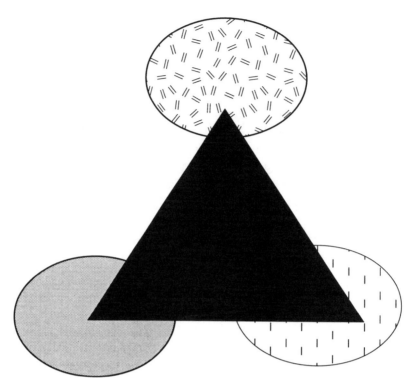

Figure 1. The overlap among the family construct system and some personal construct systems. Circles represent different people or "personal construct systems"; the triangle represents the family construct system.

One of the main advantages of PCT as extended by Procter (1978) is that it uses the same model to describe the construing processes of personal systems and those of family or wider systems (see Feixas, 1990a). Furthermore, it can provide a framework for explaining interaction in families. Using this model in previous research, my colleagues and I (Feixas et al., 1987) graphically presented this overlap among personal construct systems and FCS (see Figure 1). One can see that different personal construct systems have a different degree of overlap with the FCS. The construing system of the members represented as having a major degree of overlap is mainly centered in the FCS. Their hierarchically superordinate constructs are embedded in the FCS, meaning that their main source of validation lies in the perceived meanings and attitudes of other family members. Conversely, those members who are represented as having a minor degree of overlap receive their major validation from other sources. Their more superordinate constructs (core constructs) are not tied to the FCS, even though some of their views are (see Harter, Neimeyer, & Alexander, 1989, for some empirical evidence about these points).

One could build a developmental story within this model. For example, children's systems of construing are mainly directed through the avenues of movement of their FCSs. As children grow and achieve more individuation (Stierlin, 1987) as well as a more external life, their core constructs can become more independent of the FCS. Of course, this process could lead to many different developments. For example, young adults could also identify their thinking with that of the FCS in such a way that leaves them little space for individuation. For these people, to leave the family would be almost out of the range of available alternatives in their systems of construing. Many others, even though they leave their family of origin, often carry the same FCS when developing a new family.

The idea of an FCS goes beyond Kelly's (1955) emphasis on the individual construct system. In his writings, Procter (1978, 1981, 1985a) depicted a system of construing that has a life of its own. The FCS comprises a set of shared constructs of the family members that results from the partner's implicit negotiation and from the evolution of the system through the family life cycle. The FCS also includes the meta-perspectives (Laing, Phillipson, & Lee, 1966) of the family members.[7] In PCT, the mutual anticipation that one member has of the construction processes of the others (e.g., the way a father thinks his son views his mother) is termed a *role relationship*. Thus, family (and other social) relationships can be viewed as role relationships in which every member anticipates the others' thinking and behavior. Although such an anticipation is both necessary and desirable, when one member behaves unexpectedly this can invalidate the others' role constructs. Because such innovative pathways are inherent to personal growth and development, the efforts made by other members to enforce conformity to older patterns are potential sources of conflict in family development. In these conflicts, one member often has to make a choice between personal growth and adapting to others' expectations. Symptoms of distress are often compromise solutions to that conflict. Notwithstanding these considerations, the FCS does not provide a model of "functional families" or the ideal "family life cycle" but, rather, a comprehensive model to understand those very different evolutionary paths that families undertake.

PCT as a Reflexive Model

Several personal construct authors (e.g., Bannister, 1966) have emphasized the reflexive nature of Kelly's (1955) theory. In describing the process of construing, the personal construct model accounts for the

---

[7]Several construct researchers (e.g., Feixas, Cunillera, & Villegas, 1987; Harter, Neimeyer, & Alexander, 1989; Procter, 1985b) have adapted Kelly's (1955) repertory grid technique in their studies to incorporate family members' metaperspectives (for a review, see Feixas, 1992).

very activity of describing the model; that is, it is able to account for the observer as well as for the observed. PCT is a way of construing how people construe. Family members, thus, can be viewed as family theorists who elaborate theories (constructs) to anticipate and predict each others' behavior. Equally, PCT, as Kelly (1969b) recognized, is in itself a construction and, as such, will be reconstrued: "our theory is frankly designed to contribute effectively to its own eventual overthrow and displacement" (p. 66).

Reflexivity was also developed in Procter's (e.g., 1985a) extension of PCT. He postulated that every family member takes a position in the FCS. As I discuss in the next section, the notion of position entails two levels: the level of construction and the level of action. When a problem arises, every person or institution related to the problem takes a position. I have found the idea of problem-determined systems to be useful here (e.g., Anderson, Goolishian, & Winderman, 1986). According to this, the system to be considered includes not only family members but also the professionals "who are languaging about the problem" (Anderson et al., p. 9). In this sense, it would be more accurate to talk about problem-construct systems.

Procter (1985a) suggested including the views of these other professionals when investigating presented problems as well as the therapist's own perspective. This would lead to the construction of therapeutic road maps or schema, as described in the following section. To conclude, one can assert that PCT—with the inclusion of Procter's FCS conceptualization—can be considered a process-oriented, contextualist, and reflexive model of human processes. Therefore, it provides a coherent and consistent prejudice for constructivist therapists.

FROM BEHAVIORS TO MEANINGS, AND VICE VERSA

Hoffman (1985) viewed the development of the family therapy field as pendular. Family therapy started with a great emphasis on behaviors, in part as a reaction against excessively intrapsychic approaches. Now, the constructivist orientation has swung the pendulum the other way: "ideas, beliefs, attitudes, feelings, premises, values and myths have been declared central again" (Hoffman, 1985, p. 390). Furthermore, Hoffman (1988a) considered "a shift in focus from behaviors to ideas" as one of the commonalities of "a general style of systemic therapy . . . influenced by a constructivist approach," and she clearly stated that "problems do exist but only in the realm of meanings" (p. 124).

Although I would basically agree with this new shift, I have always thought that pendular movements were unbalanced and dangerous. I would prefer that the contribution of constructivism to the therapeutic arena be comprehensive and holistic enough to also include some of the advances produced by family therapy's prior emphasis on behavior. However, I think that in the context of the previous evolution of the family therapy movement it may have been difficult to suggest an alternative to the pendulum movement. Perhaps the issue of the central relevance of meaning is difficult to present without conveying the image of a therapist doing nothing but conversing. The new constructivist therapist can appear to be a weak practitioner, especially when prescriptions, rituals, and other active interventions used by traditional family therapists have proven to be so clinically useful. I like the idea of a conversational model for therapy (it brings new and fresh air into the therapy room), but this idea needs more elaboration, because the word *conversation* might also connote a lack of clinical resources. Consequently, a constructivist model of change should include behaviors as well as meanings and should allow the therapist to act on both of these levels of experience.

In my view, the personal construct model of change offers a comprehensive framework that allows the therapist to consider behaviors as well as ideas as a focus, both at the moment of gathering information and when intervening. I think this would also fit with Hoffman's (1988b) suggestion of a "both/and position" instead of an "either/or stance" (p. 67) as well as with Keeney's (1982) view. In fact, Keeney and Ross (1985), who also derived their approach from constructivism, have taken a similar stance in considering two different frames of reference: the semantic (related to meanings) and the political (related to patterns and sequences of behaviors). In his integrative model of intervention, Linares (personal communication, 1988) also proposed a model with two orthogonal dimensions. One of them, the epistemic versus pragmatic dimension, corresponds with this comprehensive emphasis on considering meanings as well as behaviors.

Procter's (1985a) notion of *position*, defined as the integrated stance that each member of a system takes, entails two levels: the construction level and the action level. Taking into account the experience cycle (described in the previous section), Procter suggested that the position that one member takes involves his or her construction of himself or herself, the construction of the others' thinking, and several levels of metaperspectives. The actions of this member are derived in accordance with those constructions. These actions are ways to test his or her hypotheses. At the same time, other members' actions are (in)validational evidence for further cycles of construing. In fact, the FCS is the interconnection of the family members' different positions in such a way that each one provides (in)validational evidence for the other. This is not only a conceptual device; several implications can be derived from this framework for clinical assessment and intervention.

Position as a Framework for Clinical Assessment

Keeping the notion of position in mind, a therapist may start at any given point, either with a specific behavior (perhaps the one labeled as "the problem") or with an idea expressed by some family member. The therapist should then proceed to investigate concurrent behaviors and meanings of other problem-related members. To explain this with a case example, I introduce the Pérez family (an alias). José requested that he and his wife, Rosa, be seen for help with marital problems. The couple were in their early 50s and had an 18-year-old daughter, Lucia, who was profoundly retarded. Rosa's own family had emigrated in her adolescence to Barcelona from Andalucia, a southern area of Spain characterized by emotional and expressive people living in harmony with its warm climate. Alternatively, José was born in Aragón, a dry area where people seldom tend to express feelings. He had moved to Barcelona in his mid-20s, met Rosa, and married her a few months later. Rosa began the description of their lack of marital satisfaction by claiming that José was not providing all the love and affection she needed, whereas she appeared to be a sensitive lover. She was talkative and generous in providing examples of José's lack of a caring attitude toward her as well as of his eagerness to take overprotective care of their daughter. The thought of caring for Lucia was especially painful for Rosa because she was losing her sight and planned to retire from her job as cleaning assistant in a hospital. She was becoming very depressed with the prospect of retiring and having such a calloused husband, who was available only for their retarded girl. While she was describing this problem, José looked ashamed and concentrated his efforts on disputing minor details of his wife's description of his disregard toward her.

After the initial problem is presented, the process of gathering further information about the members' positions on the problem can be carried out in several ways. In this case, I investigated José's view of the problem—that is, his construction of his wife's criticism and nagging. José resented that Rosa would not trust in the love he had proven through 20 years of marriage, but he was particularly struck by her lack of understanding that Lucia was completely dependent on their care. He further insinuated that if he did not provide such care their daughter would be left unattended (which led Rosa to respond energetically with the numerous things she did for Lucia). It appeared that the major conflict occurred when the three of them were together and José assumed an exclusive role in looking after the girl. This provided evidence for Rosa that he preferred Lucia to her, which was consistent with her slightly more distant attitude toward the girl. That attitude, in turn, confirmed for José that he should take care of their daughter. Procter (1985a) has called this process of the mutual confirmation of undesirable anticipations the "bow tie" of the problem. The bow tie is illustrated for this case in Figure 2.

Of course, this schema could be complemented with various levels of metaperspectives for Rosa and José and also with the views of other people involved in the problem, including the therapist and other professionals (aspects that usually emerge with the help of circular questions). To simplify, I reduced the issue to its bow tie. The point here is that the therapist, in using this framework, guides the interview in a way that goes from meanings to behaviors, and vice versa throughout all the problem-related members. Procter (1985a) described this way of interviewing as a "zig-zag." Although the therapist does not have a straight list of questions, he or she has two levels of investigation in mind (meaning and action) and has a process-oriented hypothesis according to which each level (construing or acting) is related to other members' meanings and behaviors.

Position as a Framework for Intervention

Sometimes the conversation about the bow tie of the problem that arises in this kind of interview provides a different kind of (in)validational evidence that generates some form of constructive revision (fifth stage of the cycle of experience) in the members' personal construct system or in the FCS. However, in many other situations, the therapist has to intervene at some point of the cycle of family construing to trigger an alternative construction. Although every therapeutic orientation is usually committed to a definite number of techniques, many others can

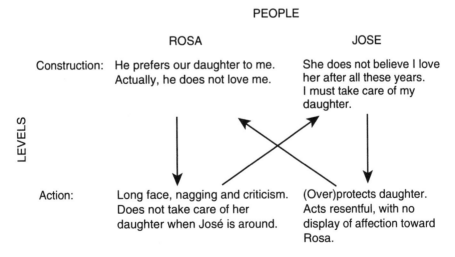

Figure 2. A diagram for the positions of Rosa and José in their marital conflict.

be available to a therapist. In this sense, PCT is technically eclectic but theoretically consistent (Feixas & Villegas, 1990; R. Neimeyer, 1988; R. Neimeyer & Feixas, 1990a). Therefore, what characteristically defines the approach I am presenting is not the option that a therapist will pursue on a technical level but, instead, his or her therapeutic stance and conceptualization. For example, one could try to reframe one of the family member's actions by attaching a different meaning to a behavior—one more congruent with the existing FCS. This, then, leaves open the possibility of an alternative construction. On the other hand, one could try to bring into focus some kind of alternative behavior, either by emphasizing an existing behavior or prescribing one, to provide evidence for (in)validation of a hypothesis of the family.

These therapeutic implications per se are not new to most family systemic therapists. These therapists have been reframing and prescribing (with different emphases, depending on their particular orientations) in this way for a long time. However, I have presented some therapeutic implications to illustrate the flexible framework that PCT can provide, by incorporating Procter's (1978, 1981, 1985a) ideas of the FCS and the notion of position. As an example of this flexibility, Feixas, Cunillera, and Mateu (1990) have presented a case in which dream interpretation was used in the context of systemic family therapy. Besides offering additional clinical flexibility, such a proposal allows the therapist to incorporate some personal construct techniques—such as hypothesis testing, fixed-role, and family characterization sketch techniques—which I briefly summarize in the following paragraphs.

The first of these techniques, hypothesis testing, needs some theoretical elaboration before it is described. It is derived from the model of change presented in the experience cycle. From the fresh perspective that this cycle offers, Kelly (1970), in his article entitled *Behavior Is an Experiment*, presented a new view of behavior. From the circular model provided by this experience cycle, behavior can be viewed as both the antecedent and the consequence of a (re)construction. Behavior is an encounter (third stage of the cycle) with an event. That encounter will provide the evidence to validate or invalidate an implied anticipation. In this sense, behavior is a form of inquiry, a "way of posing a question" (Kelly, 1969d, p. 13). Although many forms of therapy (i.e., behavior therapy) consider behavior the dependent variable to be changed through treatment, Kelly (1970) proposed that behavior can be the independent variable. That is, the therapist can prescribe ("manipulate" in the experimental metaphor) behavior to trigger a revision of the construing system. Thus "the psychotherapist helps the client design and implement experiments. He pays attention to controls. He helps the client define hypotheses" (Kelly, 1955, p. 941). This is expressed within the personal scientist metaphor; therefore, these terms must be interpreted within an experimental analogy. "Implement experiments" means putting into practice some of the clients' anticipations or hypotheses to watch how they work and to help clients define what kind of evidence ("controls") will serve to validate their hypotheses. In other words, hypothesis testing involves an agreement between therapist and client to carry out some tasks outside the therapy room. These tasks may sometimes take the form of a therapist's prescription. In further sessions, this technique involves a revision of the task and of some of the (in)validational and (re)constructive implications that it carries. As I have already outlined (Feixas, 1990b), this technique bears some similarities to the prescription of tasks and rituals commonly used by many systemic therapists, although its rationale is presented in a somewhat different form.

In the case of the Pérez family, I proposed a hypothesis-testing experiment in the form of a reenactment. Before the exercise, I posed the following general reframing:

> I have noticed how much you love each other, beyond the fact that you express your affection in different ways. I also have to express my sincere admiration for the excellent care both of you have given all these years to your daughter. I am impressed by the great deal of sacrifice you both are devoting to the difficult task of raising Lucia, although you carry out such efforts in different ways.

They listened with attention—thus breaking their previous, mutually interruptive pattern—and some tears appeared in José's eyes. Then I suggested that I would take care of their daughter for the rest of the session (they brought Lucia to the session because they did not trust anybody else to look after her), and I proposed an exercise for both of them. While seated beside Lucia, I invited them to turn their chairs and look into each other's faces. I then asked Rosa directly:

> Do you agree with what I said, that you truly love your husband?
> *Rosa:* Yes!!
> *Me:* Well, why don't you tell *him*?
> *Rosa:* Yes I love him, indeed. [looking at me]
> *Me:* Don't tell it to me. He is the one who needs to hear it! Please, tell him looking straight at his eyes.

At this point she was seemingly embarrassed but had the courage to say "I love you José," with tears in her eyes. I repeated this process with José, who also showed evident difficulties in expressing his love directly to Rosa and appeared touched too.

This intervention, as I said before, could be carried out by practitioners of various therapy orientations. The purpose here, however, is to show its theoretical relevance according to the notion of position. The reframing and the subsequent exercise were intended to provide striking evidence for the invalidation of the hypotheses they held that one did not love the other. Moreover, this intervention provided a balanced picture of both spouses as having problems expressing feelings (both showed difficulties in expressing their love in the enactment) and as being responsible and active in raising their daughter (a reformulation that was mutually accepted). Therefore, by invalidating some of their constructions, the intervention implicitly proposed an alteration of the bow tie of the problem, implying the possibility of alternative actions, which would in turn validate alternative constructions. The course of therapy that followed enabled both partners to commit themselves in negotiated steps toward satisfying their mutual needs—negotiation that framed the subsequent therapy sessions.

Kelly's (1955) fixed-role technique has been presented in many textbooks as a behavioral technique. However, in my opinion this procedure derives directly from a constructivist stance. In the context of individual therapy, the therapist asks the client to write a *self-characterization*—a minimally structured self-description of relevant aspects of the client's view about herself or himself from the standpoint of a hypothetical friend who is neither unrealistically critical nor complimentary. Then, the therapist, preferably with the help of a small team of colleagues, elaborates an alternative description according to a set of simple, formal rules (Kelly, 1955). This alternative sketch is presented to the client to be enacted full time in his or her real life for a 2–week period. During this time, therapist and client meet approximately three times each week to ensure the goal of an accurate enactment of the prescribed new role. In these sessions, the therapist supports the client, and they both role-play those situations that are especially difficult for the client to enact. Once the intensive 2–week period is over, the therapist helps the client to contrast the distinct implications that the client's initial view and the prescribed sketch carry for some of the problems the client faces. This process leads clients to elaborate their own alternative perspective. The core of this procedure involves a forced generation of an alternative view in the clients' construing systems. Once clients are capable of holding two different views of the events they face everyday, they will be able to generate other alternatives without the therapist's directions. The remainder of therapy is devoted to providing clients with an appropriate context in which to elaborate their own alternatives. Thus, the essence of this technique is to generate a fully experienced alternative (as opposed to a verbal reframing or suggestion) in order to open the system of construing to new ways of construing. This procedure, of course, requires a more complete explanation (for more detailed accounts see, e.g., Epting & Nazario, 1987; Kelly, 1955; R. Neimeyer, 1993). Kremsdorf (1985) has presented an interesting example of the use of this technique in the context of couples therapy.

Alexander and Neimeyer (1989) have presented the *family characterization sketch,* an interesting adaptation for family practice of Kelly's (1955) self-characterization technique. This is presented as a pencil-and-paper task to be done individually by every member in the therapy room. Instructions for this task are as follows:

> Write a brief character sketch of this family. Write it from the perspective of someone who knows the family intimately and sympathetically, perhaps better than anyone really knows the family. You should write it in third person. For example, begin by saying, "I know the Smith family." (Alexander & Neimeyer, 1989, p. 113)

The resulting individual commentaries can provide a good glimpse of areas of convergence and divergence in terms of members' family constructs. This is a way to enable the family members to make explicit their (usually implicit) view of themselves as a family group through their own writings and comments, with moderate participation of the therapist.

In conclusion, PCT, with the integration of Procter's (1978, 1981, 1985a) FCS and position notions, can provide a comprehensive and flexible model at both the theoretical and clinical levels. It articulates behaviors and meanings in a way that provides the therapist with a framework for mapping the system's interaction as well as for implementing a variety of interventions. Moreover, a number of the personal construct techniques can be incorporated into the family therapist's set of tools. Several case examples in which this approach has been used can be found in studies by Procter (1987), by Feixas et al. (1990), and by Brennan and Williams (1988). Feixas, Procter, and Neimeyer (1993) offer a comprehensive review of these procedures.

STRATEGIZING ABOUT CONTENT AND PROCESS

The controversial issue of whether or not, and to what extent, the therapist should be directive has been debated by psychotherapists for many years. In the history of the family therapy movement, this debate has taken the form of a discussion about the therapist's power. The notion of power (and related ideas, such as "one-up," "one-down," and "control of the therapeutic relationship") has been broadly adopted and used by many family therapists, despite Bateson's (1972) reservations. More recently, Hoffman (1988a) has taken a position similar to Bateson's in this debate, suggesting "a relative absence of hierarchy" (p. 125) and "a tendency to inhibit intentionality" (p. 127) as characteristics of a constructivist position for family therapy. She recommended that "it may be necessary to build into therapy ... provision for less deliberate procedures. ... In other words, it may be important to minimize the consciousness of the therapist in pushing for, or strategising for, change" (Hoffman, 1988a, p. 119).

In an article that has initiated some discussion, Golann (1988) noted that Tomm's (e.g., 1987) emphasis on strategizing, intention, and deliberation "may have reintroduced therapist power and control into systemic work in a way that corrupts Hoffman's aspirations for a second-order practice" (Golann, 1988, p. 62). Despite this, both Hoffman and Tomm seem to have been influenced by the same constructivist authors. Essentially, the issue here is whether or not elaborating strategies in therapy is a legitimate position for a constructivist-oriented therapist. Obviously, one could apply constructivism reflexively, thereby raising the idea that there may be several different interpretations of constructivism. This would lead one to examine which interpretation is more viable and consistent with constructivist assumptions or, alternatively, would lead one to search for a social consensus on it. However, the point here is to present Kelly's position on this controversial issue.

Whereas the Rogerian (1977) approach considers the therapist-client relationship in a person-to-person way, PCT construes an expert-to-expert relationship with the client. Clients are experts in the content of their lives; nobody knows more about their lives than they do. However, therapists are experts in the processes of construction, in the way role relationships develop, and, in particular, in the therapeutic process. The personal construct model of experience enables the therapist to be an expert about the process of construing. The content of the anticipations and the kinds of events the person faces in light of these anticipations lie within the client's domain of expertise. Therapists cannot assume knowledge of all these content issues but have to learn them from every client. Furthermore, this learning about the client's content should be neutral, that is, not biased by judgment. The aim of this approach is to enable the client to become a better scientist by developing more viable hypotheses and controls, regardless of their content. This idea of therapy as a "research paradigm" has the advantage of limiting the power of both client and therapist to circumscribed areas of expertise. Because society, and thus most clients, invests the therapist with certain power, personal construct therapists do not find themselves in the paradoxical position of (a) being perceived as powerful social agents of change but (b) seeking no change and showing no exercise of power. PCT enables therapists to work in a responsible way for acquiring certain process changes, regardless of the normative content of these changes. Content is the client's responsibility. This parallels Hoffman's (1988a) ideas of "reciprocal" power and "shedding" power (p. 126). Also within this model and in concordance with Hoffman (1985), when the therapist is required to control content issues and acquire certain normative changes (usually in certain cases involving violence and abuse), he or she is acting as an agent of social control instead of a constructivist therapist.

This distinction between issues of process and content parallels Bateson's (1972) distinction between Learning I and Learning II and can also be compared with the distinction between Change I and Change II (Watzlawick et al., 1974). PCT is not a model about what kind of normative learning a system must acquire but about the process of learning. Neither Bateson nor Kelly used learning in the conventional sense. Both viewed learning as the very process of experience and its construction. "Learning to learn" thus refers to the process by which humans construe their experience, and this cannot be instructed. The only thing a therapist can do is generate alternative (in)validational experiences oriented to trigger a constructive revision of the system of construing—to create a new "context" for learning (Bateson, 1972).

From a PCT perspective, it makes sense to talk about *strategy* and intentionality. In fact, any human action can be seen as intentional because it is invested with anticipations. However, I am talking here of strategizing about the process instead of the usual connotation of the word. Its use in the latter sense can lead to controlling the direction of a client's life. Actually, Kelly (1969e) suggested, and other construct theorists (Feixas & Villegas, 1990; R. Neimeyer, 1987b) have developed, theoretically grounded process strategies for change. In summary, the basic distinction between process and content used in PCT sheds a different light on inconsistencies about the issues of power, intentionality, and strategizing pointed out by Golann (1988).

SOME IMPLICATIONS FOR RESEARCH

The emergence of the epistemological debate in family therapy, represented by the March 1982 issue of *Family Process*, threw into question the legitimacy of psychotherapy research. Later elaborations (e.g., Gurman, 1983) have challenged the presumed incompatibility between the new epistemologies and psychotherapy research. The question of what kind of directions for research arise from a constructivist position is, however, still open.

Unlike many constructivist positions, PCT has prompted a great deal of empirical research. R. Neimeyer, Baker, and Neimeyer (1990) reported approximately 1,700 published accounts in which personal construct concepts and methods were used, 65% of which were research articles. Kelly's (1955) position about measurement and research was not directed toward assessing "reality" but toward viewing the kind of constructions people create through personal experience. The direction of research in PCT goes not only from the researcher to the layperson but also from the layperson to the researcher. The latter suggests a format or context (process) in which the individual (or any observed system) can express his or her personal meanings (content). Thus, the assessment results from a cocreation of a unique device for that specific client or family. Moreover, in PCT there are no hidden content rules with which to evaluate or classify the client in preestablished psychopathological categories. Instead, this clear assessment provides some characteristics of the structural noncontent qualities of the construing system. This is known as Kelly's (1955) *credulous approach* to assessment: "If you don't know what is wrong with a person, ask him; he may tell you" (p. 322). Paradigmatic examples of this approach are the self-characterization technique (presented above as an adaptation to families; see also Kelly, 1955, chap. 7) and the repertory grid technique. The latter is a kind of semistructured interview in which the therapist elicits relevant elements (usually, family members and other significant figures outside the family, but events, places, and so forth may also be elements) and some dimensions of meaning (constructs) that are used to draw distinctions among those events. The client then rates the constructs as they apply to each element. The therapist can then perform a statistical analysis of this rating matrix that provides an organizational map of the client's construct system (for a detailed description and applications, see, e.g., Beail, 1985; G. Neimeyer & Neimeyer, 1981; R. Neimeyer, 1993). Assessment with a grid has proved to be a powerful method that generates theory-relevant findings as well as clinical guidelines for conducting therapy. Grid methods have already been successfully used in several types of family research (e.g., Feixas et al., 1987; Harter et al., 1989; Procter, 1985b; Vetere & Gale, 1987) and family therapy training (Zaken-Greenberg & Neimeyer, 1986). (See G. Neimeyer, 1993, for a comprehensive and updated presentation of available constructivist methods for psychological assessment.)

Hampson (1982) distinguished two major orientations for psychological research and assessment. The first is centered in the investigator. In this orientation, researchers propose a set of dimensions relevant to their theoretical assumptions (e.g., extroversion–introversion), devise instruments to measure the concepts they have invented, and apply those instruments to people to classify them according to their theory-derived categories. The second orientation, centered on the client's lay perspective, focuses on devising procedures to study categories that people use when classifying other people and events (e.g., what kind of theories people construct to understand their world). Simply put, researchers in this latter approach are interested in eliciting meanings instead of superimposing their own meanings on the client. PCT, along with implicit theories of personality, fits very well with this second orientation. Of course, this approach is somewhat less developed (and less academically accepted within an objectivist paradigm) than its counterpart centered in the investigator. However, I think this orientation, which leads one to investigate the theories (constructs, myths, and stories) that families cocreate, is more relevant to systemic practice.

CONCLUSIONS

PCT is a constructivist approach to the understanding of human experience and to clinical practice. Kelly evolved into a constructivist through clinical practice, and his approach to explanation, assessment, and intervention of human processes was coherently derived from his epistemological position. Because of this experience in viewing the therapeutic endeavor from a constructivist point of view, PCT is an interesting approach for systemic therapists to have in mind when trying to think in constructivist terms about therapy. This is especially true if one considers the extension of PCT presented by Procter (1981, 1985a). His notions of position and FCS allow family processes to be conceptualized in terms of constructions and actions tied to one another in interactional sequences. Moreover, this model enables the therapist to use any technique at hand to generate an alternative (re)construction. Therapists can also be included in the model. They provide (in)validational evidence that may be construed by the family in terms of their family constructs, in the same way that the family has interpreted previous views of the problem given by other professionals or relatives.

Current controversial issues—such as the role of power, strategies, and control in therapy—can be reviewed in light of the distinction used in PCT between content and process. In approaching the therapeutic relationship on an expert-to-expert basis, PCT attributes expertise to the client in terms of the content of his or her constructions while still regarding the therapist as an expert (as is somewhat expected by society) in the form and the process of how constructs are organized and applied to events and relationships. The same distinction can be applied to research, in which an emphasis on content approaches directs researchers to set forth standards to evaluate people whereas a focus on process leads researchers to set up a context in which people may express their unique content and meanings. The latter is much more relevant for a practitioner in terms of guidelines for therapy, and it is more appropriate for a constructivist approach to systemic family therapy. Thus, the integration of PCT and systemic therapies is an interesting but complex issue. There is no doubt, however, that an exchange of ideas and perspectives developed under the same epistemological assumption—constructivism—may lead to mutual enrichment of these approaches.

REFERENCES

Alexander, P., & Neimeyer, G. (1989). Constructivism and family therapy. *International Journal of Personal Construct Psychology, 2,* 111–121.

Anderson, H., & Goolishian, H. (1988). Human systems as linguistic systems: Preliminary and evolving ideas about the implications for clinical theory. *Family Process, 27,* 371–393.

Anderson, H., Goolishian, H., & Winderman, L. (1986). Problem determined systems: Toward transformation in family therapy. *Journal of Strategic and Systemic Therapies, 5,* 1–14.

Bannister, D. (1966). Psychology as an exercise in paradox. *Bulletin of the British Psychological Society, 19,* 21–26.

Bannister, D., & Fransella, F. (1986). *Inquiring man: The psychology of personal constructs* (3rd ed.). London: Routledge & Kegan Paul.

Bateson, G. (1972). *Steps to an ecology of mind.* New York: Ballantine Books.

Bateson, G. (1979). *Mind and nature: A necessary unity.* New York: Dutton.

Beail, N. (Ed.). (1985). *Repertory grid technique and personal constructs.* London: Croom Helm.

Berger, P., & Luckman, T. (1966). *The social construction of reality.* Garden City, NY: Doubleday.

Bogdan, J. (1984). Family organization as an ecology of ideas: An alternative to the reification of family systems. *Family Process, 23,* 375–388.

Bogdan, J. (1987). "Epistemology" as a semantic pollutant. *Journal of Marital and Family Therapy, 13,* 27–35.

Boscolo, L., Cecchin, G., Hoffman, L., & Penn, P. (1987). *Milan systemic family therapy: Conversations in theory and practice.* New York: Basic Books.

Brennan, J., & Williams, A. (1988). Clint and the black sheep. *Journal of Strategic and Systemic Therapies, 7,* 15–24.

Bruner, J. (1956). You are your constructs. [Review of the book *The psychology of personal constructs*]. *Contemporary Psychology, 1,* 355–357.

Campbell, D. T. (1974). Evolutionary epistemology. In P. A. Schilpp (Ed.), *The philosophy of Karl Popper* (Vol. 14, Pts. 1 and 2, pp. 413–463). LaSalle, IL: Open Court.

Efran, J., Germer, C. K., & Lukens, M. D. (1986). Contextualism and psychotherapy. In R. L. Rosnow & M. Georgourdi (Eds.), *Contextualism and understanding in the behavioral sciences: Implications for research and theory* (pp. 169–186). New York: Praeger.

Efran, J., Lukens, R., & Lukens, M. (1988, September–October). Constructivism: What's in it for you? *The Family Therapy Networker,* 27–35.

Epting, F. R., & Nazario, A. (1987). Designing fixed-role therapy: Issues, techniques, and modifications. In R. Neimeyer & G. Neimeyer (Eds.), *Personal construct therapy casebook* (pp. 277–289). New York: Springer.

Feixas, G. (1990a). Approaching the individual, approaching the system: A constructivist model for integrative psychotherapy. *Journal of Family Psychology, 4,* 4–35.

Feixas, G. (1990b). Personal construct theory and the systemic therapies: Parallel or convergent trends? *Journal of Marital and Family Therapy, 16,* 1–20.

Feixas, G. (1992). Personal construct approaches to family therapy. In G. J. Neimeyer & R. A. Neimeyer (Eds.), *Advances in personal construct psychology* (Vol. 2, pp. 215–255). Greenwich, CT: JAI Press.

Feixas, G., Cunillera, C., & Mateu, C. (1990). Dream analysis in a systemic therapy case: A constructivist approach. *Journal of Strategic and Systemic Therapies, 9,* 55–65.

Feixas, G., Cunillera, C., & Villegas, M. (1987, August). *Personal construct theory and the systems approach: A theoretical and methodological proposal for integration.* Paper presented at the Seventh International Congress on Personal Construct Psychology, Memphis, TN.

Feixas, G., Procter, H., & Neimeyer, G. (1993). Convergent lines of assessment: Systemic and constructivist contributions. In G. J. Neimeyer (Ed.), *Casebook in constructivist assessment* (pp. 143–178). Newbury Park, CA: Sage.

Feixas, G., & Villegas, M. (1990). *Constructivismo y psicoterapia* [Constructivism and psychotherapy]. Barcelona, Spain: Promociónes y Publicaciónes Universitarias.

Fisch, R., Weakland, J., & Segal, L. (1982). *The tactics of change: Doing therapy briefly.* San Francisco: Jossey-Bass.

Foley, R. (1988). Kelly and Bateson: Antithesis or synthesis. In F. Fransella & L. Thomas (Eds.), *Experimenting with personal construct psychology* (pp. 57–68). London: Routledge & Kegan Paul.

Gergen, K. (1985). The social constructionist movement in modern psychology. *American Psychologist, 40,* 266–275.

Golann, S. (1987). On description of family therapy. *Family Process, 26,* 331–340.

Golann, S. (1988). On second-order family therapy. *Family Process, 27,* 51–65.

Goolishian, H., & Winderman, L. (1988). Constructivism, autopoiesis and problem determined systems. *Irish Journal of Psychology, 9,* 130–143.

Gurman, A. (1983). Family therapy research and the "new epistemology." *Journal of Marital and Family Therapy, 9,* 227–234.

Haley, J. (1963). *Strategies of psychotherapy.* New York: Grune & Stratton.

Hampson, S. (1982). *The construction of personality.* London: Routledge & Kegan Paul.

Harter, S., Neimeyer, R., & Alexander, P. (1989). Personal construction of family relationships: The relation of commonality and sociality to family satisfaction for parents and adolescents. *International Journal of Personal Construct Psychology, 2,* 123–142.

Held, B., & Pols, E. (1985). The confusion about epistemology and "epistemology"— And what to do about it. *Family Process*, *24*, 509–524.

Held, B., & Pols, E. (1987). Dell on Maturana: A real foundation for family therapy? *Psychotherapy*, *24*, 455–461.

Hoffman, L. (1985). Beyond power and control: Toward a "second-order" family systems therapy. *Family Systems Medicine*, *3*, 381–396.

Hoffman, L. (1988a). A constructivist position for family therapy. *Irish Journal of Psychology*, *9*, 110–129.

Hoffman, L. (1988b). Reply to Stuart Golann. *Family Process*, *27*, 65–68.

Keeney, B. (1982). Not pragmatics, not aesthetics. *Family Process*, *21*, 429–434.

Keeney, B. (1983). *The aesthetics of change*. New York: Guilford Press.

Keeney, B., & Ross, J. (1985). *Mind in therapy: Constructing systemic family therapies*. New York: Basic Books.

Kelly, G. A. (1955). *The psychology of personal constructs* (2 vols.). New York: Norton.

Kelly, G. A. (1963). *A theory of personality*. New York: Norton.

Kelly, G. A. (1969a). The autobiography of a theory. In B. Maher (Ed.), *Clinical psychology and personality: The selected papers of George Kelly* (pp. 46–65). New York: Wiley.

Kelly, G. A. (1969b). Man's construction of his alternatives. In B. Maher (Ed.), *Clinical psychology and personality: The selected papers of George Kelly* (pp. 66–93). New York: Wiley.

Kelly, G. A. (1969c). A mathematical approach to psychology. In B. Maher (Ed.), *Clinical psychology and personality: The selected papers of George Kelly* (pp. 94–113). New York: Wiley.

Kelly, G. A. (1969d). Ontological acceleration. In B. Maher (Ed.), *Clinical psychology and personality: The selected papers of George Kelly* (pp. 7–45). New York: Wiley.

Kelly, G. A. (1969e). Personal construct theory and the psychotherapeutic interview. In B. Maher (Ed.), *Clinical psychology and personality: The selected papers of George Kelly* (pp. 224–264). New York: Wiley.

Kelly, G. A. (1970). Behavior is an experiment. In D. Bannister (Ed.), *Perspectives in personal construct psychology* (pp. 255–270). San Diego, CA: Academic Press.

Kenny, V., & Gardner, G. (1988). Constructions of self-organising systems. *Irish Journal of Psychology*, *9*, 1–24.

Kremsdorf, R. (1985). An extension of fixed-role therapy with a couple. In F. Epting & A. Landfield (Eds.), *Anticipating personal construct psychology* (pp. 216–224). Lincoln: University of Nebraska Press.

Kuhn, T. (1962). *The structure of scientific revolutions*. Chicago: University of Chicago Press.

Laing, R., Phillipson, H., & Lee, A. (1966). *Interpersonal perception: A theory and method of research*. London: Tavistock.

Mahoney, M. J. (1988). Constructive metatheory: I. Basic features and historical foundations. *International Journal of Personal Construct Psychology, 1,* 1–35.

Mahoney, M., & Gabriel, T. (1987). Psychotherapy and the cognitive sciences: An evolving alliance. *Journal of Cognitive Psychotherapy, 1,* 39–59.

Maturana, H. (1988). Reality: The search for objectivity or the quest for a compelling argument. *Irish Journal of Psychology, 9,* 25–82.

Maturana, H., & Varela, F. (1980). *Autopoiesis and cognition.* Boston: Reidel.

Maturana, H., & Varela, F. (1987). *The tree of knowledge.* Boston: New Science Library.

Minuchin, S. (1974). *Families and family therapy.* Cambridge, MA: Harvard University Press.

Neimeyer, G. J. (1985). Personal constructs and the counseling of couples. In F. Epting & A. Landfield (Eds.), *Anticipating personal construct psychology* (pp. 201–215). Lincoln: University of Nebraska Press.

Neimeyer, G. J. (Ed.). (1993). *Casebook in constructivist assessment.* Newbury Park, CA: Sage.

Neimeyer, G. J., & Neimeyer, R. (1981). Personal construct perspectives on cognitive assessment. In T. Merluzzi, C. Glass, & M. Genest (Eds.), *Cognitive assessment* (pp. 188–251). New York: Guilford Press.

Neimeyer, R. (1985). Personal constructs in clinical practice. In P. C. Kendall (Ed.), *Advances in cognitive–behavioral research and therapy* (Vol. 4, pp. 275–329). San Diego, CA: Academic Press.

Neimeyer, R. (1987a). An orientation to personal construct therapy. In R. Neimeyer & G. Neimeyer (Eds.), *Personal construct therapy casebook* (pp. 3–19). New York: Springer.

Neimeyer, R. (1987b). Personal construct therapy. In W. Dryden & W. Golden (Eds.), *Cognitive–behavioral approaches to psychotherapy* (pp. 224–260). New York: Harper & Row.

Neimeyer, R. (1988). Integrative directions in personal construct therapy. *International Journal of Personal Construct Psychology, 1,* 283–297.

Neimeyer, R. (1993). Constructivist approaches to the measurement of meaning. In G. J. Neimeyer (Ed.), *Constructivist assessment: A casebook* (pp. 58–103). Newbury Park, CA: Sage.

Neimeyer, R., Baker, K., & Neimeyer, G. (1990). The current status of personal construct theory: Some scientometric data. In G. J. Neimeyer & R. A. Neimeyer (Eds.), *Advances in personal construct theory* (Vol. 1, pp. 3–24). Greenwich, CT: JAI Press.

Neimeyer, R., & Feixas, G. (1990a). Constructivist contributions to psychotherapy integration. *Journal of Eclectic and Integrative Psychotherapy, 9,* 4–20.

Neimeyer, R., & Feixas, G. (1990b). Disturbi di costruzione. In F. Mancini & A. Semerari (Eds.), *Le teorie cognitive dei disturbi emotivi* [A cognitive theory of emotional disorders] (pp. 77–92). Rome, Italy: Nuova Italia Scientifica.

Penn, P. (1985). Feed-forward: Future questions, future maps. *Family Process, 24,* 299–310.

Pepper, S. C. (1942). *World hypotheses.* Berkeley: University of California Press.

Piaget, J. (1937). *La construction du réal chez l'enfant* [The construction of reality in the child]. Neuchatel, France: Delachaux et Niestle.

Planck, M. (1932). *Where is science going?* New York: Norton.

Popper, K. R. (1959). *The logic of scientific discovery.* New York: Harper.

Popper, K. R. (1963). *Conjectures and refutations.* London: Routledge & Kegan Paul.

Popper, K. R. (1972). *Objective knowledge: An evolutionary approach.* Oxford, England: Clarendon Press.

Prigogine, I., & Stengers, I. (1984). *Order out of chaos: Man's new dialogue with nature.* New York: Bantam Books.

Procter, H. (1978). *Personal construct theory and the family: A theoretical and methodological study.* Unpublished doctoral dissertation, University of Bristol, England.

Procter, H. (1981). Family construct psychology: An approach to understanding and treating families. In S. Walrond–Skinner (Ed.), *Developments in family therapy: Theories and applications since 1948* (pp. 350–366). London: Routledge & Kegan Paul.

Procter, H. G. (1985a). A personal construct approach to family therapy and systems intervention. In E. Button (Ed.), *Personal construct theory and mental health* (pp. 327–350). London: Croom Helm.

Procter, H. G. (1985b). Repertory grids in family therapy and research. In N. Beail (Ed.), *Repertory grid techniques and personal constructs: Applications in clinical and educational settings* (pp. 218–239). London: Croom Helm.

Procter, H. G. (1987). Change in the family construct system: Therapy of a mute and withdrawn schizophrenic patient. In R. A. Neimeyer & G. J. Neimeyer (Eds.), *Personal construct therapy casebook* (pp. 157–170). New York: Springer.

Procter, H., & Parry, G. (1978). Constraint and freedom: The social origin of personal constructs. In F. Fransella (Ed.), *Personal construct psychology, 1977* (pp. 157–170). San Diego, CA: Academic Press.

Reiss, D. (1981). *The family's construction of reality.* Cambridge, MA: Harvard University Press.

Ryle, A. (1975). *Frames and cages: The repertory grid approach to human understanding.* London: University of Sussex Press.

Stierlin, H. (1987). Coevolution and coindividuation. In H. Stierlin, F. Simon, & G. Schmidt (Eds.), *Familiar realities: The Heidelberg conference* (pp. 99–108). New York: Brunner/Mazel.

Taggart, M. (1985). The feminist critique in epistemological perspective: Questions of context in family therapy. *Journal of Marital and Family Therapy, 11,* 113–126.

Tomm, K. (1987). Interventive interviewing: Part I. Strategizing as a fourth guideline for the therapist. *Family Process, 26,* 3–13.

Vetere, A., & Gale, A. (1987). *Ecological studies of family life.* New York: Wiley.

Viney, L., Benjamin, Y., & Preston, C. (1988). Constructivist family therapy with the elderly. *Journal of Family Psychology, 2,* 241–258.

von Foerster, H. (1981). *Observing systems.* Seaside, CA: Intersystems.

von Glasersfeld, E. (1984). On radical constructivism. In P. Watzlawick (Ed.), *The invented reality* (pp. 17–40). New York: Norton.

Watzlawick, P. (1984). Self-fulfilling prophecies. In P. Watzlawick (Ed.), *The invented reality* (pp. 95–116). New York: Norton.

Watzlawick, P., Beavin, J., & Jackson, D. (1967). *Pragmatics of human communication.* New York: Norton.

Watzlawick, P., Weakland, J., & Fisch, R. (1974). *Change: Principles of problem formation and problem resolution.* New York: Norton.

Zaken-Greenberg, F., & Neimeyer, G. (1986). The impact of structural family therapy training on conceptual and executive therapy skills. *Family Process, 25,* 599–608.

15

TERMINATION AS A RITE OF PASSAGE: QUESTIONING STRATEGIES FOR A THERAPY OF INCLUSION

DAVID EPSTON AND MICHAEL WHITE

Traditional models and metaphors for psychotherapy suffer from many limitations. One of these is the emphasis on "termination as loss," the position that the discontinuation of therapy inevitably is experienced as the painful relinquishment of a therapeutic relationship on which the "patient" has come to be dependent. Although we acknowledge that the transition from "patienthood" to full-fledged personhood is indeed an important one, we believe that the preoccupation of therapists with the loss metaphor subtly reinforces the dependency of the person seeking

This chapter is a revised version of the article "Consulting Your Consultants: The Documentation of Alternative Knowledges," by D. Epston and M. White, 1990, *Dulwich Centre Newsletter, 4*, pp. 1–11. Copyright 1990 by Dulwich Centre Publications. Adapted with permission. The originally published article was reprinted in *Experience, Contradiction, Narrative and Imagination* (pp. 11–26), edited by D. Epston and M. White, 1992, Adelaide, South Australia: Dulwich Centre Publications. Copyright 1992 by Dulwich Centre Publications.

assistance on the "expert knowledge" of the therapist. More important, we believe that this dominant metaphor fails to legitimize the person's own role in freeing himself or herself from the problem-saturated identity that brought him or her to therapy in the first place. In contrast with the practices informed by the termination-as-loss metaphor, in this chapter we outline a model of the final stage of therapy as a rite of passage from one identity status to another. Importantly, this passage centers around the person joining with others in a familiar social world and encourages the recruitment of others in the celebration and acknowledgment of the person's arrival at a preferred destination or status in life. We refer to those therapies that are informed by these practices as *therapies of inclusion*.[1]

We describe a therapeutic practice that encourages clients to document the ways in which they have resisted and surmounted the dominant stories of their lives—stories organized around their problems, symptoms, and socially ascribed pathologies (White & Epston, 1990). In describing our therapeutic practices, we have found it helpful to view the concept of "knowledge" as a plural noun and to formulate questioning strategies that elicit from the clients we work with the "solution knowledges" and the "alternative knowledges" about their lives and relationships that have been resurrected or generated in therapy. These knowledges then become more available for clients to redeploy when necessary and for others to consult as aids to their own self-development.

We begin by reviewing some of the limitations of the dominant termination-as-loss metaphor and then suggest an alternative rite-of-passage analogy that provides an organizing conceptual frame for our own work. Placing this transition in the broader systemic context of the client's world, we go on to outline a protocol for establishing clients as consultants to themselves and to others. In doing so, we present and categorize an array of questions that assist clients in engaging in an archaeology of their alternative knowledges, in a way that makes such knowledges more available for future use.

THE TERMINATION-AS-LOSS METAPHOR

Of all aspects of the transformative process called *therapy*, the concluding stage has been among the most inadequately understood. We believe that this is because the termination-as-loss metaphor has long

---

[1]In "Confession: Studies in Deviance in Religion," B. Turner and Hepworth (1982) distinguished between two major classes of ritual: those that include people in social groups and those that exclude people from them.

dominated the literature on this stage of therapy, blinding therapists to more fruitful ways of viewing and facilitating the termination process.

The dominance of the termination-as-loss metaphor is premised on a particular orientation to therapy. This is an orientation that privileges the therapeutic microworld above all others.[2] It represents the final stage of therapy as one that is dominated by the loss of this microworld and its central and, supposedly, all-important relationship as well as by the requirement for an adjustment to "going it on your own."

We believe that this orientation to therapy—one that constructs an entirely separate and private stage for clients' lives—is in turn premised on certain cultural conceptions and practices. These include the dominant individualizing conception of personhood in Western culture—the idea that the person is the source of all meaning—and the modern practices of the objectification of people and their bodies that are common to the "disciplines" (Foucault, 1973). Commenting on this individualizing conception of personhood, Geertz (1976) observed that

> the Western conception of the person as a bounded, unique cognitive universe, a dynamic centre of awareness, emotion, judgment and action organized into a distinctive whole is, however incorrigible it may seem to us, a rather peculiar idea within the concept of the world's cultures. (p. 225)

Because they separate the self from social context, we refer to those therapies that are informed by these cultural conceptions and practices as *therapies of isolation*. Within this highly individualized conception, it follows that the termination of therapeutic relationships deepens clients' sense of isolation and, in so doing, accentuates their sense of loss.

AN ALTERNATIVE METAPHOR: TERMINATION AS RITE OF PASSAGE

We believe that the class of rituals referred to by van Gennep (1960) as "rites of passage" has a great deal to offer as a metaphor for the process of therapy. Essentially, van Gennep asserted that the rite of passage is a universal phenomenon for facilitating transitions in social life, from one status or identity to another. He proposed a processual

---

[2]In challenging this privileging of the therapeutic microworld, we are not proposing that all aspects of therapy be undertaken in some public domain. We believe that clients should have access to a private place in which they can feel safe and secure and can have their desire for confidentiality honored. However, we consider it inappropriate to place this world above all other worlds, and we believe that all knowledges that arise in therapy that are preferred knowledges for clients should be made available for circulation in larger communities. We prefer to construe the concluding stages of therapy as being about new beginnings.

model of this rite, consisting of the stages of separation, liminality, and reincorporation. In traditional cultures, the initiation of each of these stages is marked by ceremony. At the *separation stage*, people are detached from familiar roles, statuses, and locations, and they enter an unfamiliar social world in which most of the taken-for-granted ways of going about life are suspended—a liminal space. This liminal space, which constitutes the second stage of a rite of passage, is betwixt and between known worlds and is characterized by experiences of disorganization and confusion, by a spirit of exploration, and by a heightened sense of possibility. The third stage, *reincorporation*, brings closure to the ritual passage and assists people in relocating themselves in the social order of their familiar world, but at a different position. This new position is characteristically accompanied by new roles, responsibilities, and freedoms. Traditionally, the arrival at this point is augmented by claims and declarations that the person has successfully negotiated a transition, and this is legitimated by acknowledgment within the person's own community.

We have found that the rite-of-passage metaphor provides a useful map for orienting therapists to the process of therapy and for assisting those people who seek therapy while in transit from problematic statuses to unproblematic ones (Epston 1985, 1987). Our interpretation of this metaphor structures a therapy that encourages people to negotiate the passage from novice to veteran and from client to consultant. Rather than instituting a dependency on the "expert knowledge" presented by the therapist and other authorities, this therapy enables clients to arrive at a point where they can have recourse to more liberating alternative and special knowledges that they have resurrected or generated during therapy.

In therapy, the separation stage can be invoked through a range of interventions, including those encouraging clients to distinguish themselves from their problems by engaging in "externalizing discourses" in relation to these problems (White & Epston, 1990). That is, therapy enables them to see their problem (e.g., depression, bed-wetting, or anorexia) as something outside of themselves that can be resisted rather than as an essential feature of themselves. This dislodges clients from certain familiar and taken-for-granted notions about problems and from the dominant internalizing (and self-blaming) discourses that guide their lives. It initiates the experience of liminality.

It is in this liminal space that new possibilities emerge and alternative knowledges can be resurrected or generated. It is also in this space that clients' experiential worlds are "subjunctivized," that is, treated as hypothetical and malleable rather than as real and fixed. Thus, V. Turner (1986) has spoken of "the liminal phase being dominantly in the subjunctive mood of culture, the mood of maybe, might be, as if, hypothesis, fantasy, conjecture, desire—depending on which of the trinity of cognition, affect, and conation is situationally dominant" (p. 42). It is the "as if" nature of the therapeutic reconceptualization of their problems that enables clients to begin to envision an alternative self-identity or alternative life story.

Therapists can best gauge the extent of their participation in the liminal stage by the degree to which they lose track of time and are unable to estimate the length of the session as well as by the degree to which they experience a sense of *communitas* with those who seek therapy. Individual, family, and group therapists and clients operating in this way resemble the traditional liminal groups described by V. Turner (1967): "a community of comrades and not a structure of hierarchically arrayed positions. This comradeship transcends distinctions of rank, age, kinship position, and, in some kinds of cultic groups, even of sex" (p. 100).

The final stage, reincorporation, brings therapy to its conclusion. It is through reincorporation that the alternative knowledges that have been resurrected or generated in therapy become authenticated in the presence of others. It is through reincorporation into the larger family and community system that the possibilities for a renewed identity can be realized.

OVERCOMING OBSTACLES TO REINCORPORATION

However, despite the possibilities that accompany the reincorporation metaphor, there are some obstacles to therapeutic practice that are suggested by it. For example, Kobak and Waters (1984), who have also referred to the rite-of-passage metaphor, have drawn attention to the practical difficulties of linking the microworld of therapy to the world at large:

> In relation to his more "primitive" tribal counterpart, who manages a publicly recognized rite of passage, the family therapist is at a relative disadvantage in creating long-lasting, second-order change. The most apparent disadvantage is that the family therapist does not have the ties to the family's community and community norms that reinforce the changes that occur during the rite of passage once the participants return to ordinary life. . . . Such participation of the community in the change process serves to stabilize second-order changes that occur during the liminal rites. By operating without knowledge of community norms, the family therapist may create liminal change that is not sustained in the reaggregation phase. (p. 99)[3]

---

[3] In the translation of van Gennep's text, we prefer the term *reincorporation* over *reaggregation*.

A developmental view of family problems may assist the therapist, yet the relative isolation of the therapist from the family's community remains a problem. Potential solutions to this dilemma have emerged in the form of involving the family "network" or, less extensively, by activating the family kin system. The rite-of-passage analogy suggests that such efforts should be further explored.

For a number of years, we have been experimenting, in various ways, with overcoming the sort of obstacles referred to above. The feedback that we have received in response to this experimentation has convinced us (a) of the pertinence of the rite-of-passage metaphor and the appropriateness of considering the concluding stage of therapy as reincorporation and (b) of the inappropriateness of strongly emphasizing the termination-as-loss metaphor for this stage of therapy.

Because we have preferred to construe the concluding stage of therapy as reincorporation, we have had cause for celebration with clients who have sought therapy, rather than for commiseration. We have been able to challenge the conception of therapy as an exclusive and esoteric social space or individual stage, necessarily bound by rigid rules of privacy and exclusion. We have helped people explore various ways and means by which to counter the practices that have arisen from this conception—to protest the limitations of this privacy. Along with our clients, we have participated in publicizing and circulating the alternative and preferred knowledges that have been resurrected or generated in therapy. We have joined them in their attempts to identify and recruit audiences to the performance of these alternative knowledges in their day-to-day lives. And we have worked with clients in their efforts to document these knowledges in popular discourses and forms.

On reviewing our exploration of practices of reincorporation, we have classified various approaches that clients have found helpful. All of these approaches include the identification and recruitment of audiences for the authentication of change and the legitimation of alternative knowledges. The ritual approaches include (a) celebrations, prize givings, and awards, with significant people in attendance, including those who may not have attended therapy (White, 1986); (b) purposeful "news releases" whereby pertinent information about the person's arrival at a new status is made available to various significant people and agencies; (c) personal declarations and letters of reference; and (d) consultation with clients, in a formal sense, concerning the solution knowledges that have enabled them to free their lives and in regard to the alternative and preferred knowledges about their lives and relationships.

We addressed the first three approaches mentioned here in our book *Narrative Means to Therapeutic Ends* (White & Epston, 1990). In this chapter, we restrict our discussion to the fourth of these approaches, presenting a protocol for what we refer to as "consulting your consultants."

When people are established as consultants to themselves, to others, and to the therapist, they experience themselves as more of an authority on their own lives, their problems, and the solutions to these problems. This authority takes the form of a kind of knowledge and expertise that is recorded in a popular medium so that it is accessible to the consultant, therapist, and potential others.

Throughout, the relative inequality of "therapist as helper" and "client as helped" is redressed. The gift of therapy is balanced by the gift of consultancy. We consider this reciprocity to be of vital importance in reducing the risk of indebtedness and replacing it by a sense of fair exchange. In his book *The Gift*, Mauss (1954) eloquently drew attention to the hazards inherent in such inequality, noting that to accept without returning or repaying more is to face subordination, to become a client and subservient. To receive something is dangerous not only because it is illicit to do so, but also because it comes morally, physically, and spiritually from a person. Thus, we view the rite of passage at the point of "graduation" from therapy as the time for both restoring and enhancing clients' self-respect by providing an opportunity to inform the therapist and his or her community as well as future clients seeking assistance with similar problems.

Protocol for Documenting Alternative Knowledges

We conclude therapy by inviting clients to attend a special meeting with the therapist so that the knowledges that they have resurrected or generated in therapy can be documented. These will include those alternative and preferred knowledges about self, others, and relationships and those knowledges of problem solving that have enabled clients to liberate their lives. They consist of the person or family's own constructions of their strengths, resources, and helpful patterns of relating that permitted them to transcend or resist the destructive influence of their problem and to begin to author a new and more hopeful chapter in their life narrative.

In anticipation of the termination interview or interviews, clients are told that special attention will be given to an exploration of how they arrived at these useful knowledges and how they made these knowledges work for them. This gives clients advanced notice that they will be invited to provide some historical account of the struggle with their problems and the discoveries that made it possible for them to free their lives. Our intention is to emphasize that these knowledges are significant and that preserving them through documentation is warranted.

Various means can be used to substantiate and document knowledges. Clients can choose to express themselves in a variety of formats, including videotapes, audiotapes, autobiographical accounts, diaries, interview transcripts, and the like. If clients are concerned that they might have difficulty recalling relevant details, a sample of orienting questions can be supplied beforehand for them to reflect on. This usually helps them prepare for the consulting-your-consultants interview.

On convening the meeting, the therapist runs through a prologue to further orient clients to its purpose. During this prologue, future audiences (e.g., other therapists and clients with similar histories or problems) are presupposed and explicitly referred to. The therapist then asks clients to recount their transition from a problematic status to a resolved one, asking questions that encourage them to locate significant events and steps in time in a sequential fashion. Alternatively, the therapist can provide her or his account of the client's transition and invite the client to comment on it, elaborate on it, alter it, and contribute his or her reflections in ways that dramatically bring the account to life.

As an example, we present below a small sample of the sort of questions that have been helpful in encouraging clients to articulate these knowledges. Readers will note that these questions are constructed in a "grammar of agency" rather than of passivity and determinism; that is, in responding to these questions, clients achieve a sense of personal agency. This is the experience of being able to play an active role in shaping one's own life—of possessing the capacity to influence developments in one's life to bring about preferred outcomes.

Encouraging clients to respond to questions in a grammar of agency—or, as Douglas (1982) might have put it, in the "active voice"—effectively counters their tendency to solely impute the therapist's actions as critical to the emergence of solutions and is essential to the constitution of self-knowledge. As Harré (1983) has observed, "self-knowledge requires the identification of agentive and knowing selves as acting within hierarchies of reasons. It follows that this kind of self-knowledge is, or at least makes available the possibility of, autobiography" (p. 260).

We have grouped the questions we use to prompt this process in several categories. Some of these categories have been discussed elsewhere (e.g., White, 1988a); they are offered to readers here as an aid to the organization of this work. They should not be limiting to the reader's imagination, nor should they interfere with the expression of the reader's experience. Because of space considerations, the questions appear here in a single form. However, they can be easily modified or simplified according to the background and age of the person seeking therapy.

Orientation Questions

These questions are used to orient clients to the consulting-your-consultants interview, calling attention to the importance of (a) rendering a client's steps in the development of solution knowledge visible so that she or he might be clearer about the foundations for future problem solving in her or his own life; (b) establishing details about what personal resources and knowledges clients have relied on to make solutions work for them; and (c) making these discoveries and knowledges available to others who might be experiencing similar plights.

- When reviewing your problem-solving capabilities, which of these do you think you could depend on most in the future? Would it be helpful to keep your knowledge of these capabilities alive and well? How could this be done?
- Let's assume that you decided to preserve this know-how about dismissing problems from your life. If at any time in the future you needed to take a "leaf out of your own book," what advice would be written on it?
- Understanding the steps that you took in solving this problem is half of the story. If we could work out how you made this approach work for you, we would understand the other half. What personal and relationship qualities were essential in achieving what you have achieved?
- Just imagine that I was meeting with a person or family experiencing a problem like you used to have. From what you know, what advice do you think I could give that person or family?
- Let's suppose that someone found out that you were a veteran of this sort of problem and that you had freed your life from it. If they were to consult you, how would you help them?
- Most of what therapists know that is useful they learn from working with people who seek their help. Would you be prepared to support my efforts to preserve knowledges about solving problems so that these might be available to others in the future?

The purpose of these questions is therefore to accentuate the client's own role in generating alternative knowledges that could be useful to both self and others in the future.

Unique Account Questions

Unique account questions encourage clients (a) to develop an account of the nature of their *solution knowledges*—their hard won know-how about how to resolve the kinds of problems that brought them into therapy—and (b) to plot the steps that they took in developing their problem-solving knowledges, as they unfolded through time. Articulating and naming these knowledges contributes to their survival and accessibility, and the experience of the unfolding of preferred developments in one's life, through history, appears vital to a positive sense of future.

- Alright, you have given me a summary of what you did. However, this is quite general, and I would be interested in some of the specifics. Would you be prepared to give me a step-by-step description of how you arrived at this?
- So what led up to this breakthrough? Tell me about your preparation for this. What advice were you giving to yourself? What did you witness yourself doing that might have been the first step? Did anyone else notice this, and if so, what part did they play?
- I now have a reasonable idea of what you did that worked for you. I doubt that this just came out of the blue. What foundation is this approach based on, and how did you develop it?
- What could you tell me about your history that would help me understand the development of your problem-solving abilities?
- What would I have witnessed in your life, at an earlier time, that would have enabled me to conclude that you would break free of the problem at this point?[4]

By "historicizing" the development of solutions to the client's problem and grounding it in preexisting features of the client or family's outlook, one creates a story that gives the client's solution knowledge a sense of durability and substance for redeployment should he or she face similar challenges in the future.

Unique Redescription Questions

These questions encourage clients to reflect on the alternative knowledges of self, others, and relationships that were resurrected or generated during therapy. The therapist directs attention to the conclusions reached, and realizations had, about the capabilities and competencies of people and relationships and about how these capabilities and competencies are reflected in the solution know-how that was used to deal with the problem.

---

[4]These can also be constructed as "experience of experience" questions (White, 1988b). For example, "What would [a historically significant person] have noticed that would have told him or her that you would have been able to achieve this at this point in time?" Daphne Hewson (1990) has proposed similar questions from a cognitive social psychology orientation.

- As you review the meetings that we have had together, what occur to you as important realizations about who you are as a person and about the qualities in your relationships?
- Over the time that we have been meeting, what have you become clearer about in terms of who you are as a person and about your preferred way of relating to others? What do you now know about what kind of a life suits your sort of person and what does not?
- Let's consider the steps that you took to achieve this break-through. What personal and relationship qualities do you think you were relying on to see this through? Which personal and relationship qualities were most supportive of these steps?
- What do these achievements reflect about your life and relationships that is important for you to know?
- What would you conclude about a person who achieved what you have achieved in challenging the problem's influence in your life?
- Having witnessed yourself taking this action, what conclusions have you been able to reach about yourself and your relationships—conclusions that were not available to you before? What do you now know about yourself as a person that you would not have known otherwise?
- Who, from all of those people who have known your past, would have been most likely to have reached similar conclusions about you? What might they have observed about you as a younger person that could have led them to these conclusions?
- What do these achievements reflect about the sort of person you are that is important for you to know? Are you the first person to know this about yourself, or have others known this about you in the past? If others have known this, what told them?

As much as possible, these questions also historicize these alternative knowledges, organizing them sequentially as they emerged over the process of therapy. In addition, they place personal change in the context of family and more extended relationships, both present and past, that help legitimize a new form of self-knowledge.

Unique Possibility Questions

These questions encourage clients to speculate about the various options and possibilities that might accompany a knowledgeable life.

They bring forth a discussion of new destinations and futures and of the specific steps that might be taken to realize these. In general, the questions are future-oriented, and "future-oriented, backward-looking" questions are strongly featured. Future-oriented, backward-looking questions are those that ask clients to imagine themselves arriving at some valued destination in life and, then, to look back to the present to determine (a) which of the steps they are taking are most relevant or important to achieving that destination and (b) what subsequent steps would be most helpful in achieving that end.

- Knowing what you now know about yourself and your preferred way of living, how will this knowledge affect your next step? When you witness yourself taking this step, how do you expect that to influence how you feel? And how do you think this will further influence your view of yourself as a person?
- Would you mind if we speculate about what sort of new possibilities accompany these new realizations?
- I am becoming aware of a history that is different, in some respects, from the one that you previously had—or at least the one that you thought you had. Would you mind if I ask some questions about the sort of future that it might be bringing with it? How might this new future be different from the future of the other past?
- I would like you to imagine that you are now further up the road of life, at some valued destination, and looking back to the present. With the benefit of hindsight, what stand out as the most significant steps that you are taking at the moment, and where did those steps lead to next?
- From that vantage point in your future, what new directions were made possible by what you have recently discovered about yourself? How did these realizations and conclusions make it possible for you to intervene in your future, and in what way?

Thus, these questions help a client gain perspective on the larger horizon of his or her life, considering the reciprocal implications of present developments for bringing into being a hoped-for future, and vice versa.

Circulation Questions

Circulation questions assist clients in identifying and recruiting appropriate audiences for the performance of solution knowledges and the alternative knowledges of lives and of relationships. Such audiences play a very significant part in authenticating the preferred claims that accompany these knowledges. At this time, the therapist can ascertain the extent to which clients are prepared to make their knowledges accessible to others who might be experiencing similar problems and can determine the conditions under which this material could be made available to these people.

- Now that you have reached this point in life, who else should know about it? What difference do you think it would make to their attitude toward you if they had this news?
- What would be the best way of introducing them to this news?
- Do you think it would be helpful to catch others up on these developments? If so, how could you engage their interest? What would be most important for them to know?
- Because it is important to put others in the know, what might give people a reasonable familiarity with the new realizations and conclusions that you have recently arrived at?
- I guess there are a number of people who have an outdated view of who you are as a person. What ideas do you have for updating these views? What would be most newsworthy?
- Would it be helpful to go along with others in the illusion that everything is just the same in your life? If not, how could you arrange for others to join you in celebrating your achievement?
- If other people seek therapy for the same reasons that you did, can I share with them any of the important discoveries that you have made? If so, to what extent can I do this, and under what circumstances?

Questions of this type help the client envision ways of "circulating" news of his or her therapeutic accomplishments and changed status to relevant audiences in the family or larger social world. The recruitment of social legitimation for this new knowledge of self and solutions is centrally important to consolidating the changes the person and therapist have worked hard to bring about, and completes the "reincorporation" phase suggested by the rite-of-passage metaphor.

OWNERSHIP AND USAGE OF DOCUMENTS

We acknowledge that therapeutic productions are cocreated, but we consider people who seek therapy to be the senior partners in the ownership of this property. Thus, such clients have the power to veto the use of any documents (including videotapes) produced by their consultancy. Clients are informed that these documents, which we refer to as *archives*, are considered to be on loan to the therapist for specific purposes and for specific periods of time and that this loan can be retracted at any time. Despite this, many clients wish to deed these archives to the therapist to use at his or her discretion.

The therapist may suggest that clients consult the knowledges expressed in their own documents at certain points in time or may request that these documents be made available, with discretion, to others who are experiencing problems or for teaching purposes, with an understanding that the responses of others will be recorded and made available.

Recording the responses of participants in teaching contexts (e.g., seminars, training programs, and workshops) with the explicit goal of providing feedback to those whose documents are being presented encourages participants in these training settings to more fully appreciate and respect the nature of their privileged position. This is a position in which participants are privy to the lives and relationships of those clients who have been willing to contribute to the development of "therapeutic knowledge." This recording of responses engages participants more fully in an understanding of the experiences of people and mitigates against those responses that result from a position of detachment that is so easily arrived at by participants in teaching contexts.

Clients are almost invariably enthusiastic about receiving feedback from others about their therapeutic productions. At times, this feedback provokes ongoing and productive correspondences between these clients and others who are experiencing similar problems, or between these clients and workshop participants when these participants have appended an address to their comments.

CONCLUSION

In this chapter, we have described a process that we sometimes refer to as an *archaeology of therapy*. In this process, the solution knowledges that have been resurrected or generated in the context of therapy and the history of, or conditions that made the production of these knowledges possible, become known. By using the rite of passage signaled by therapy termination to explicitly attend to and document the hard-won know-how that helped free them from bondage to their problems, clients become knowledge makers, and knowledge makers become knowledgeable. Both their knowledge-making capabilities and their knowledge-ableness are authenticated, not only in the presence of the therapist, but in the presence of other relevant present and future audiences as well.

The practices outlined in this chapter encourage clients to deploy their knowledges more knowingly, increase their own authority in matters of their concern, and decrease their dependency on so-called expert knowledges. We believe that such personal solution knowledges can be more viable, enduring, and efficient than "imported" expert knowledges, which too often disable those that therapists seek to help and induce in them a stupefying "patienthood." Viewed in this perspective, the artful use of therapeutic questions can help transform the experience of therapy termination from one marked only by loss and diminishment to one offering the prospect of genuine gain and fuller authorship of the story of one's life.

REFERENCES

Douglas, M. (1982). *In the active voice*. London: Routledge & Kegan Paul.

Epston, D. (1985). An interview with David Epston. *Family Therapy Association of South Australia Newsletter,* 11–14.

Epston, D. (1987, Summer). A reflexion. *Dulwich Centre Newsletter,* 16–17.

Foucault, M. (1973). *The birth of the clinic: An archaeology of medical perception.* London: Tavistock.

Geertz, C. (1976). From the natives' point of view: On the nature of anthropological understanding. In K. Basso & H. Shelby (Eds.), *Meaning in anthropology.* Albuquerque: University of New Mexico Press.

Harré, R. (1983). *Personal being: A theory for individual psychology.* Oxford, England: Basil Blackwell.

Hewson, D. (1990). *From laboratory to therapy room.* Unpublished manuscript, Macquarie University.

Kobak, R., & Waters, D. (1984). Family therapy as a rite of passage: The play's the thing. *Family Process, 23,* 89–100.

Mauss, M. (1954). *The gift: Forms and function in archaic societies.* London: Cohen & West.

Rogers, C. R. (1977). *Rogers on personal power.* New York: Delacourt Press.

Turner, B., & Hepworth, M. (1982). *Confession: Studies in deviance in religion.* London: Routledge & Kegan Paul.

Turner, V. (1967). *The forest of symbols: Aspects of Ndembu ritual.* Ithaca, NY: Cornell University Press.

Turner, V. (1986). Dewey, Dilthy, and drama. In V. Turner & E. Bruner (Eds.), *The anthropology of experience* (pp. 33–44). Chicago: University of Illinois Press.

van Gennep, A. (1960). *The rite of passage.* Chicago: Chicago University Press.

White, M. (1986, Spring). Awards and their contribution to change. *Dulwich Centre Newsletter,* 1–5.

White, M. (1988a, Winter). The process of questioning: A therapy of literary merit. *Dulwich Centre Newsletter*, 37–46.

White, M. (1988b, Spring). Saying hullo again: The incorporation of the lost relationship in the resolution of grief. *Dulwich Centre Newsletter*, 29–36.

White, M., & Epston, D. (1990). *Narrative means to therapeutic ends*. New York: Norton.

V

THE CHALLENGE OF CONSTRUCTIVIST PSYCHOTHERAPY

16

OPTIMAL THERAPEUTIC DISTANCE: A THERAPIST'S EXPERIENCE OF PERSONAL CONSTRUCT PSYCHOTHERAPY

LARRY M. LEITNER

Personal construct psychology (Kelly, 1955) recently has become increasingly applied to the broad area of psychotherapy. Epting (1984), for example, has written a useful basic overview of some personal construct approaches to therapy. Dunnett (1988) has edited a volume in which contributors from many professions wrote about the usefulness of personal construct psychology in their professional lives. Button (1985) edited a work on personal construct approaches to mental health, and Mair (1989) has written a highly moving personal volume in this broad area. These and other scholars, practitioners, and theoreticians have established a solid foundation for theorizing about the potential of personal construct

In all clinical examples, names and identifying information have been altered to protect confidentiality. I thank April Faidley, Chris Meshot, David Pfenninger, Teresa Dill-Standiford, and, especially, Andrew Garrison for comments on drafts of this chapter.

psychology for the field of psychotherapy. In particular, there has been an increasing emphasis on personal experience in these writings. I hope to follow up on that tradition in this chapter.

Psychotherapy forms an integral part of my personal and professional life. In particular, I have been interested in elaborating the implications of Kelly's (1955) sociality and choice corollaries for psychotherapy. These thoughts have proven to be stimulating (at least for me) and have evolved into a view of psychotherapy that I call (at least for now) *experiential personal construct psychotherapy* (Leitner, 1988). (Although the term *experiential* may seem redundant when applied to personal construct psychotherapy, I use it to differentiate this approach to personal construct therapy from more cognitive–behavioral ones.) In this chapter, I discuss the concept of optimal therapeutic distance—a position blending profound experiential closeness to and a professional understanding of the client. I contrast this position with "therapeutic" strangers and "therapeutic" unity, positions that are not helpful to our clients' growth. Before doing so, I review briefly what I mean by experiential personal construct psychotherapy.

EXPERIENTIAL PERSONAL CONSTRUCT PSYCHOTHERAPY

I have elaborated this view of experiential personal construct psychotherapy on the basis of my interactions with therapy clients over the years. These people typically are highly verbal, yet extremely disturbed, adults. Although I will focus on examples based on these cases, I believe that my views can be extended to other client populations.

The sociality corollary is as follows: "To the extent that one person construes the construction process of another, he [or she] may play a role in a social process involving the other person" (Kelly, 1955, p. 95). (Hereinafter, I use the term *role* when referring to Kelly's definition of interpersonal action based on an understanding of another. In previous publications, this has appeared as ROLE to emphasize my particular use of this term.) The first words in the corollary ("to the extent") clearly imply that individuals vary in the extent of knowledge they have about others. These words also clearly imply that we can never know each other "totally." Thus, in many ways, we are mysteries to each other (Mair, 1977). Although this mysteriousness often is an attractive feature of relationships, it also may lead to interpersonal predictive failures. Thus, it leaves us open to invalidation—the source of many disconcerting (and potentially devastating) experiences. The fact that there will always be aspects of my construction process that you will never know is intimately linked, then, to both the attraction and the danger of role relationships (i.e., a relationship characterized by the sharing of core role constructs—the most central determinants of who we are as people).

A role relationship involves more than the construing of constructs. Kelly (1955) defined role relationships in terms of the construing of the construction "process." In other words, the process of our construing (not just the content of our constructs) is the critical focus of role relationships (see Leitner, 1985). Because process cannot be understood independently of content, the issue of what content we need to understand to construe another's process inevitably arises. I have argued (Leitner, 1985) that understanding another's core constructs leads to an understanding of the other's process of construing. However, as core constructs *"govern a person's maintenance processes—that is, those by which he maintains his identity and existence"* (Kelly, 1955, p. 482), our most central constructs are on the line when we engage in a role relationship.

The issue of construing process as well as the content of constructs also implies that we cannot construe individuals as static and have a role relationship with them. The "other" is an evolving, growing, changing organism (cf. Kegan, 1982), and a relationship that does not appreciate that is, in reality, not a role relationship. As a matter of fact, if we begin to construe the other as more static, then we are beginning to develop a less extensive understanding of the other's construing process: We are limiting the role relationship. On the other hand, construing the other as in continual motion also leads to the possibility that our understandings of the other will be invalidated. Because our core may be involved when we try to understand another's core, this in turn can threaten our most central processes with invalidation. In my earlier work (Leitner, 1985), I have detailed how role relationships carry the risk of a conglomeration of threat, fear, anxiety, hostility, and guilt that I have termed *terror*.

The sociality corollary also implies that two people are involved in a role relationship (one person construing the construction process of another person). Thus, although connection is an important characteristic of deep role relating, a role relationship also involves an understanding of the separateness of the other from you. The other is a unique, evolving organism who is simultaneously linked to, yet apart from, you. This simultaneous experience of sharing closeness and the mystery of distance is an important component of role relationships, a topic to which I return later.

Kelly (1955) explicitly stated that roles involve "an ongoing pattern of behavior" (p. 97). In other words, in a role relationship, we place our most important constructs on the line by way of our interpersonal actions. We are then faced with the potential validation or invalidation of these central constructs in the public domain of interpersonal actions—not only in the private confines of our thoughts. Furthermore, the ongoing nature of personal investment within role relationships implies that we are risking major invalidation for extended periods of time.

In summary, role relationships are important for experiencing meaning in life yet are potentially terrifying. Faced with this challenge, many people decide to limit their investments in role relationships. When such limitations characterize a person's relationships, psychopathology can be said to exist. When individuals globally avoid role relationships, the resulting deprivation of meaningful interpersonal understandings is often experienced as meaninglessness and emptiness (see Leitner, 1985; cf. Yalom, 1980).

Experiential personal construct psychotherapy responds to this psychopathology by helping the person struggle with the dilemma between the terror of risking and the emptiness of avoiding role relationships. It focuses more on the process of construing that is the person than on the specific content of the constructs that are created. This does not imply that content is ignored. The content of one's constructs is the outcome of the process of construing and gives important clues to that process. Indeed, for certain types of problems, an emphasis on the content of constructs may be more necessary than an emphasis on the process of construing. However, I feel that focusing therapeutic attention on the process of construing brings the choice corollary into play.

Kelly's (1955) choice corollary essentially states that each person chooses in the direction of elaboration of the construct system. In other words, each person's creative process always moves in the direction of greater growth among its creations (i.e., the construct system). For me, this implies a respect for the wisdom of the other in the choices that each person makes. If the therapist can establish an appropriate atmosphere, then the process of construing that is the other will develop in ways that will make life richer, more meaningful, and (alas) more risky. (After all, greater richness and meaning implies that a person is using more central meanings in the world. Invalidation of these meanings could have profound consequences.) These implications of the choice corollary are particularly useful to me when I experience the great confusion and disorganization of severely disturbed persons. They allow me to continue to believe in the creative process of the other.

In this regard, one important struggle in experiential personal construct psychotherapy involves the therapist exploring the nature of the role relationship that he or she has established with the client. The client, having been centrally invalidated in previous intimate relationships, will bring his or her struggles about risking role relationships into the therapy relationship. How the therapist deals with this issue may very well determine the outcome of the entire therapy, particularly for the more disturbed person.

The therapist, then, must understand the core role constructs of the client. Because the potential for massive invalidation exists, the client will not allow just any person access to his or her core. Rather, clients will risk such exposure only as they decide that the therapist, as a person, is worth such a risk. This implies that the therapist's own core role constructs are on the line in any therapy that attempts to help the other rebuild the core. Obviously, the therapist also is confronted with the choice of risking versus avoiding a role relationship with the client.

Thus, the therapist's experiences form an integral part of the process of experiential personal construct psychotherapy. For example, the therapist's experiences can provide important clues to the nature of the role relationship being formed. Furthermore, the client will use the therapist's experiential reactions to determine whether the client's central constructs are being validated or invalidated. In the remainder of this chapter, I deal with these two points—the first point quite directly and the second more implicitly.

THERAPISTS' EXPERIENCE AND NATURE OF THE RELATIONSHIP

Let me begin this section by discussing theoretically the specific ways in which the nature of role relationships affects the experience of the therapist. In particular, I focus on the simultaneous experience of connection and separateness that is the hallmark of role relationships. Because, ideally, therapists have already had such experiences, they have the opportunity to understand the quality of their relationship with a client by becoming aware of their own experience. Indeed, one could argue that therapists have an obligation to engage in such introspection. The quality of therapists' experience can then be used to facilitate the development of a role relationship with the client. Therapists who ignore their own experience in the relationship may hinder significantly their ability to help their clients.

I am aware that many people feel most uncomfortable with such an assertion. They believe that this position introduces a subjectivity into psychotherapy that makes it more of an "art" than a "science." Personal construct psychologists should take exception to this arbitrary division. Rather, our belief that all interactions are tied to the construing process allows us to look at the many different ways and levels of construing. In other words, our subjective reactions in the therapy relationship are based on some constructions of self and other. When properly construed, these reactions may tell us profound things about ourselves and our clients that we had not noticed. Furthermore, they allow for deeper access to personal meanings as well as the therapeutic elaboration of such meanings.

With this as background, I examine next some experiential qualities of the optimal relationship between therapist and client. The reader should be aware that I make the deliberate error of speaking in all-or-none terms for the sake of clear presentation. After this discussion, I present two types of experiences that point to problems in the therapy role relationship. All of these points are illustrated with clinical examples.

Optimal Therapeutic Distance

Optimal therapeutic distance is the term I use to construe the optimal blending of connection and separateness associated with a therapy role relationship. The term implies being close enough to the other to experience the other's feelings while being distant enough to recognize them as the other's feelings—not the therapist's own. It should be kept in mind that this is an experiential–poetic definition, not a literalistic one. Although I am well aware of the logical contradictions should one take the definition literally, I believe that the definition experientially captures what I am trying to communicate. Such optimal distancing is very demanding of the therapist, requiring him or her to be willing and able to enter into the most intimate of mutual constructions.

Let me illustrate with an example. Judy referred herself to therapy because she was feeling extremely depressed and suicidal. She had been in therapy 3 times previously and had been hospitalized for depression twice. As we discussed her life, she recalled incidents of horrendous physical abuse. She had been hospitalized 3 times with broken ribs during her childhood. Her mother had locked her in closets for extended periods of time. Her mother had also burned her with cigarettes and once had left Judy in a forest because, although she "loved" Judy, Judy could not come home. Despite these incidents, Judy could recall pleasant times when her mother gave her bubble baths. One day, while discussing the bubble baths, Judy began to look quite distressed. She reported that she was remembering that, after each bubble bath, she was dressed in a nightgown and sexually abused by her stepfather. At this moment, I became aware of feeling a combination of sadness, shock, pain, outrage, and (unexpectedly) guilt. My emotional reactions permeated my interventions. For example, when she said, "Why did this happen?" I replied, with great tenderness, "You blame yourself for it, don't you?" Judy began sobbing. After 10 minutes, she said that she had always felt that it was her fault because, if she could have been "good enough," they would have treated her like the other children. I would argue that the guilt I felt was me therapeutically experiencing Judy's emotion.

My beliefs about Kelly's (1955) sociality and choice corollaries obviously influence my ability to be optimally distant as a therapist. However, Kelly's notion of the "credulous approach" also plays a critical role. The credulous approach emphasizes believing that the client means exactly what he or she says. Through this approach, I can attempt to understand the world as if I had the same experiences as my client. Relying on my construing of myself, my client, other clients, students, friends, and so on, I then can imagine what my client is going through. I become aware of my empathic imagination (Margulies, 1989) through my experiences with the client in therapy.

After I act, on the basis of how I construe my client's process, I have fulfilled the parameters of a role relationship. At this point, the client's response can validate or invalidate my constructions. Because clients have innumerable responses to interventions, a detailed listing of different validators and invalidators is beyond the scope of this chapter. As a general rule, however, I experience validation in any client actions that both increase the depth of the role relationship and help the client master the emptiness and symptomatology of his or her life. I experience invalidation when neither of the above occurs. When invalidated, I may experience anxiety, threat, fear, hostility, and guilt—as any person might. After all, I may need to reconstrue self and other (possibly in fundamental ways) if I am to be of help to my client. Therein lies the risk to the therapist.

When the therapist is optimally distant, the client can potentially grow. At that moment, the therapist has access to the most central processes of the other. The therapist experiences the client's experience and acts in a way that simultaneously communicates an understanding of the other's pain (connection) and a profound respect for the other's integrity, strength, and ability to transcend the distress (separateness). The optimal blending of connection and separateness by the therapist validates the parameters of a role relationship with the client. At the same time, nonrole aspects of the relationship (e.g., client or therapist constructions negating this optimal blending) are being invalidated.

As the client construes this validational process, the choice and experience corollaries would suggest that therapeutic growth occurs. After all, the client's system evolves as events are successively construed (experience corollary). Furthermore, this evolution will be in the direction of a more optimal engagement with the world (choice corollary). Unfortunately, though, all too much of therapy is spent with the relationship being less than optimal. Let me turn to the first of the two general problems in this area to expand on this point.

"Therapeutic" Strangers

The first error involves the therapist being too distant. I use the term *therapeutic strangers* to describe the status of the participants in this mode of relating, because I think it captures the essential contradictions of the therapeutic misalliance (Langs, 1974). After all, the relationship is supposed to be therapy (and therefore connected) but is not. The failure to connect causes serious problems in experiential personal construct psychotherapy. The therapist cannot construe the central processes of the other without engaging his or her central processes. Because process is intimately linked to emotion, the therapist and client should be experiencing similar emotions. Because the reality being construed actually has been cocreated through a dynamic interaction between the participants, if the therapist does not connect with the client's experience, this implies that neither participant is experiencing the "process" inherent to a role relationship. Both participants probably are experiencing self and other as static. This is a kind of "objectivity" that destroys the healing alliance.

In this regard, consider Jane, a client I have written about previously (Leitner, 1988). She came into therapy severely depressed because of marital problems. Shortly after treatment started, her husband (who had been in therapy with another therapist) committed suicide. I construed that she was a highly dependent person who had spent most of her life wanting others to take care of her and feeling sorry for herself when they failed her. I found it very difficult to experience Jane's construing process. Rather than trying to understand the bases of her profound dependency, I spent my efforts engaging her intellectually. Jane's response was to become more depressed and suicidal. This resulted in panicky phone calls to my house at all hours of the day and night, with desperate pleas for extra sessions.

Many important points can be made with this vignette. First, my inability to empathize with Jane reflected the state of our role relationship. She was looking for a rescuer rather than someone to struggle with her over her issues in life. As such, she was experiencing both of us in static ways. She was the injured victim, and I was cast in the role of the perfect rescuer. (She even nicknamed me "God.") Once I gave her "the answer," she could solve her problems.

Second, my unwillingness to connect with her overwhelming dependencies was invalidated by her. As a matter of fact, my excessive intellectual distance had the effect of increasing her dependent demands on me—not decreasing them, as I had hoped. These increasing demands for dependence and the experience of helplessness can be seen as invalidating me. After all, her experience of separateness was decreasing during these episodes. Thus, the role relationship was not deepening. Furthermore, her symptoms were increasing.

A third important point can be made with this example. By accepting her panicky calls as invalidation, I was able to reconstrue my approach to her. For example, when she would call in a panic, I agreed to see her. In other words, I accepted the dependency instead of running from it. Amazingly, by the time she arrived at my office, the crisis had passed. After a few such instances, I was able to point out the pattern to her. This enabled her to see her suicidal crises as angry interpersonal demands—not an inevitable part of her life. Having had the courage to accept her dependency, I had gained the moral authority to comment on her processes more intellectually. In other words, I had become a validating agent (Landfield, 1988) to her.

My experiences with Jane were tied to my reactions to her excessive dependencies. A different set of issues can be seen by considering John, a highly successful businessman. John came to see me at the insistence of his wife. He had no need for therapy; he was quite satisfied with life. He just wanted to know why his wife was so dependent on her therapist. One session could get his questions answered. I asked why his wife wanted him seen. He did not know why; she said he needed to deal with some issues. He was willing to solve any problems I might see.

Despite his protestations of optimal psychological health, he compulsively worked 14–16 hours per day, was 40 pounds overweight, had a blood sugar problem, and had suffered one heart attack and three angioplasties. After the third angioplasty, his physician told him to modify his diet. When he said, "Why haven't I been told this before?" his wife and his physician became angry and informed him that he had indeed been ordered to engage in this life-saving change many times before.

When the conversation turned to his family, he talked of being a "good" husband and father. Being good meant providing them with material possessions. I commented on what they might say about him, should he die. I focused on how deprived they might feel because of the lack of relational experiences they had experienced with him. When he acknowledged that this was true, I wondered aloud what it would be like for him to die a stranger to his own family.

At this point, both of us were feeling the tragedy of his life (optimal therapeutic distance). However, our time was about up, and I asked if he felt the need to come back for another session. Subsequently, all experience of tragedy disappeared, and John said, "If you think I need to. I don't think I have anything to work on." I then pointed out his inability to experience his problems, as shown both by his inability to hear his dietary orders and by how rapidly he had shed his experience of aloneness. I also wondered out loud what these issues said about his life. He was intrigued enough to agree to another session.

In contrast to Jane, the difficulties in the role relationship with John stemmed from his problem with the connection side of the connection–separateness dialectic. I used my experience of him as distant and problem focused in an attempt to engage him in a role relationship. His responses (sharing a sense of tragedy and agreeing to return) can be seen as validating my interventions. Sharing a sense of tragedy allowed us to connect. Returning for another session continued the relationship. Both of these events increased the depth of the role relationship and provided an opportunity for symptom relief.

Experientially, if not corrected, being therapeutic strangers, as a mode of relating, results in a therapy stalemate. When the therapist is too distant, the client may become frustrated with the fact that, although they talk about things, nothing changes. The therapy relationship may continue indefinitely without the core of the client being touched. Alternatively, the client may terminate "prematurely" (i.e., after the client realizes that therapeutic growth will not occur in the relationship but before the therapist does).

The too-distant therapist may focus on techniques to change clients as opposed to experiences of being with clients. These techniques often are cognitive–behavioral, chemical, or paradoxical. They can, though, include relational techniques. Unfortunately, although these techniques sometimes succeed in alleviating the symptom, the client still is limited in role relationships. However, without a presenting complaint, the client may live out life in this limited manner. Such moral and ethical issues must be considered by the experiential personal construct therapist.

Therapeutic Unity

The second general problem in maintaining optimal therapeutic distance involves the experience of excessive closeness by the therapist. The term *therapeutic unity* can be used to describe this misalliance. Although closeness is encouraged, the closeness is such that the separateness of the client is not validated. Experientially, the therapist is unable to experience the client's struggles as the client's, feeling instead that they are his or her own dilemmas. Sometimes the problem is manifested blatantly (e.g., the therapist's own feelings are so intense that no therapeutic action is possible). At other times, the manifestation may be more subtle (e.g., the therapist might feel excessively responsible for the client's experiences). Furthermore, as with the problem of being therapeutic strangers, the therapist's struggles may be based on the client's striving for excessive closeness or distance.

To illustrate, consider Tom, a mental health professional in a neighboring town. He sought treatment because of severe marital problems caused by his excessively busy work schedule. Although he loved his family and wanted to be with them, professional responsibilities pulled him away. He was most depressed over this distance from his family. In my therapeutic practice, I am also extremely busy and sometimes struggle with feeling deprived of intimacy with my family. I found it very easy to "experience" Tom's distress. However, I also found it very difficult to "act therapeutically" on my experience. I alternated between excessive silence, agreeing that it is tough to be a professional, cognitive techniques designed to help him develop more free time, and wondering why he experienced his work schedule as a problem. None of these interventions helped either of us enrich our understanding of his despair. Thus, they all were invalidated. I could not be optimally distant until I had gained enough perspective on my own struggles to use my experience as a reflection of Tom's reality.

As another example, let us return to Judy, the woman who, as a child, had been sexually abused after her baths. After a great deal of hard work, Judy exhibited tremendous personal growth. Many disowned experiences had been reintegrated into her system. Suicidal ideation had disappeared. Furthermore, she had, for the first time, fallen in love with a man. Both of us felt very proud of her accomplishments.

At this time, a crisis occurred in her relationship with her lover. She fled to the Arizona desert for a week. Upon returning, she informed him (and me) of her inability to live in relationships as there could be no true commitment. However, without relationships, she felt she might as well die, because life was meaningless. I could experience her anger and disappointment. However, I could do little with it because of my anger and disappointment; after all, I take pride in being a skilled therapist. Months of very hard work had gone into helping her risk role relationships. I had written about her progress in other contexts. Now, all of my hard work (and a core definition of myself) felt invalidated. My response consisted of trying to show her that she was misconstruing commitment. She became quite angry and withdrew emotionally from me. Our relationship became so tenuous that she began to consider terminating therapy quite seriously.

One of the important points in this vignette involves the "factual correctness" of interventions. Technically, I was quite correct in my view that Judy had a simplistic view of commitment and meaning. However, I was too close to her experience myself to have transcended it in some way. The net result was that I failed to communicate both an experiential understanding of her anger and disappointment and a deeply felt faith (expectation) that she (we) could therapeutically act on it. As with previous examples of failures in optimal distance, my interventions were invalidated. Once again, my client was challenging me to work through some of my own issues in order to be of help to her. Her invalidations can be seen as messages to me about my personal retreat from a role relationship.

Some Theoretical and Technical Implications

The foregoing construction of psychotherapy has many theoretical and technical implications. In particular, I believe that it has implications for the construct of validation and invalidation of the therapist's constructions of the client as well as for the therapist's own personal growth.

Validation and Invalidation of a Therapist's Constructions

Let me first address some implications of these ideas for the therapist's experience of validation and invalidation. This construction of psychotherapy implies that the therapist is invalidated when she or he is not optimally distant. Many failures in optimal therapeutic distance occur when the therapist quite simply is wrong in his or her construction of the client. In other words, the therapist believes that the client is using Construct A when the client actually is using Construct B. However, more subtle failures occur when the therapist is using the client's constructs accurately yet either is too close or too distant to fully implement a role relationship.

These latter failures may be more destructive to the client than the therapist simply being wrong. After all, the client is aware that the therapist understands the client's construction of things. However, the client's experience of the problem is that he or she is not changing in productive and meaningful ways. Moreover, the client may not be able to verbalize why the pathology is not improving. Because role relationships are complex and abstract, the client may not be able to conceptualize clearly what is missing. Also, role relationships are terrifying, so a part of the client may be content to have a therapy relationship that fails to establish the parameters of a deep role relationship. The net result may be that the client decides that therapy cannot help because the therapist understands the problem yet the problem has not improved.

All of this implies that interventions are less useful when the therapist is not optimally distant. It also implies that many different interventions can be therapeutic when the therapist is optimally distant. Because optimal therapeutic distance occurs through the engagement of the person of the therapist with the person of the client, different therapists can use different interventions and still be therapeutic. (Note, however, that this does not imply an anything-goes approach to therapy, because validation and invalidation of therapeutic interventions leads to rigor in the choice of techniques.) Moreover, some techniques cannot be used by a given therapist as they are incompatible with the person of the therapist. Each therapist must accept the responsibility of integrating his or her own person with the techniques used. When done successfully, the techniques are no longer merely techniques; they are behavioral manifestations of the person of the therapist.

It should be emphasized that failures in optimal therapeutic distance are not inherently bad. They can be most beneficial for the therapy process if the therapist reconstrues his or her self and the client following invalidation. As a matter of fact, one way of understanding experiential personal construct psychotherapy is as a process in which the therapist continually invites self and other into such a process of reconstruing. When the therapist retreats into hostility instead of looking inside himself or herself, the therapy process is injured. Thus, the therapist must have the courage to confront his or her own personal issues when he or she feels invalidated.

Therapist's Personal Growth

The discussion above leads to a consideration of the impact that therapy has on the personal development of the therapist. Indeed, it can be argued that the therapist is obligated to use the experience of being a therapist to continue his or her growth as a person. In this regard, the therapist's willingness to reconstrue possible central aspects of self validates a similar process in the client.

The notion of "reflexivity" also is important here. In this regard, the therapist who demands that only the client face the anxiety and threat of reconstruing is nonreflexive. Many clients will construe that such a therapist is hypocritical. As long as the therapist does not acknowledge his or her contribution to the client's construction, the therapy process will be jeopardized. Although this argument may be valid, it may, in fact, be irrelevant if optimal therapeutic distance implies that the process of the therapist engages the process of the client. In so doing, both people are changed by the reality created between them. The therapist can avoid this only by distorting the relationship such that optimal distance is not achieved. Put simply, if I am unwilling to use the reality created between us to change me, then I should not see you in psychotherapy.

Experiential personal construct psychotherapy humbles me. I am continually more aware of the many nuances of my experience as well as of my limited ability to use this experience therapeutically. I am also increasingly aware of how fleeting my "answers" to many of life's dilemmas are. Once I arrive at a "solution," I become aware that my answer creates the possibility that I might cheat (harm) a future client. After all, answers tend to be static; people always are changing.

Finally, great experiences of guilt can arise out of therapeutic failures. Because, as a therapist, I am as responsible as the client for the reality created between us, I bear part of the responsibility for every therapeutic failure. In the overwhelming majority of therapeutic failures, I can find ways in which I contributed to the failure. One of the greatest burdens

of the experiential personal construct psychotherapist is having contributed to the failure of a venture entrusted to you by society and the client.
To compound this, the process of therapy is among the most frightening
of experiences because it leads the therapist to reconstrue his or her
role (and role relationship) in fundamental ways. On the other hand,
contributing in some small way to the growth of another person is among
the most moving of human experiences. As Jackson (1990) has stated,
"they honor us with an invitation into the rare intimacies of their
personal lives." Let us hope that, as a rule, we psychotherapists will find
the courage to apply Kelly's (1955) ideas more systematically. In so doing,
we may very well create ways of touching more human beings in more
powerful ways than is now believed possible.

REFERENCES

Button, E. (Ed.). (1985). *Personal construct theory and mental health*. Beckenham,
    Kent, England: Croom Helm.

Dunnett, C. (Ed.). (1988). *Working with people*. New York: Routledge, Chap-
    man & Hall.

Epting, F. R. (1984). *Personal construct counseling and psychotherapy*. New
    York: Wiley.

Jackson, J. (1990, April). *Agoraphobia as an elaborative choice*. Paper presented
    at the Second British Conference on Personal Construct Psychology, York,
    Great Britain.

Kegan, R. (1982). *The evolving self*. Cambridge, MA: Harvard University Press.

Kelly, G. A. (1955). *The psychology of personal constructs* (2 vols.). New York:
    Norton.

Landfield, A. W. (1988). Personal science and the concept of validation. *Interna-
    tional Journal of Personal Construct Psychology, 1*, 237–250.

Langs, R. (1974). *The technique of psychoanalytic psychotherapy* (2 vols.). New
    York: Jason Aronson.

Leitner, L. M. (1985). The terrors of cognition: On the experiential validity
    of personal construct theory. In D. Bannister (Ed.), *Issues and approaches
    in personal construct theory* (pp. 83–103). San Diego, CA: Academic Press.

Leitner, L. M. (1988). Terror, risk, and reverence: Experiential personal construct
    psychotherapy. *International Journal of Personal Construct Psychology, 1*,
    251–261.

Mair, J. M. M. (1977). Metaphors for living. In A. W. Landfield & J. K. Cole
    (Eds.), *Nebraska symposium on motivation* (Vol. 24, pp. 243–290). Lincoln:
    University of Nebraska Press.

Mair, J. M. M. (1989). *Between psychology and psychotherapy: A poetics of experi-
    ence*. New York: Routledge, Chapman & Hall.

Margulies, A. (1989). *The empathic imagination*. New York: Norton.

Yalom, I. (1980). *Existential psychotherapy*. New York: Basic Books.

17

CONSTRUING ON THE EDGE: CLINICAL MYTHOLOGY IN WORKING WITH BORDERLINE PROCESSES

STEPHANIE L. HARTER

In this chapter, I draw on theoretical approaches of constructivist, storytelling psychology (cf. Harter, 1988; Kelly, 1955, 1969; Mahoney, 1982, 1988, 1991; Mair, 1988, 1989; Neimeyer & Harter, 1988) in addressing clinical dilemmas encountered while working with clients psychiatrically categorized as having borderline personality disorders. I use the vehicle of myths—personal, societal, and professional—to describe impasses and future directions in psychotherapy. Rather than developing or reviewing specific techniques, I attempt to illustrate and elaborate potential contributions of a constructivist stance to a creative therapeutic relationship as well as the potential contributions of an intriguing group of clients to the development of constructive therapists.

I relate constructivist theory to the general literature on borderline personality disorder and my experiences with clients diagnosed with this constellation of symptoms. Many of my observations arose from work with one particular client, who served as a salient prototype for me because I encountered her early in my practice and because her engaging personality, high level of intelligence, and excellent educational background contrasted sharply with her intense, chronic suffering and resulting severe disability in activities of daily living and social relationships. I call her *Laura*, although I have removed or changed all identifying information in this chapter to protect her anonymity. Many of the processes and content discussed could apply to a number of clients with whom I have worked. As I have continued to work with this disorder, my construction of these clients has differentiated beyond any single prototype, such as that presented by Laura or by diagnostic manuals. Therapists must still look to the individual person for his or her personal history and other constructions of experiences.

Asking you to keep the above cautions in mind, I present a brief case summary of Laura, so that you might better relate my experience of treating her to your own experiences with clients. Although she met criteria in the *Diagnostic and Statistical Manual of Mental Disorders* (American Psychiatric Association, 1994) for borderline personality disorder, she also met criteria for major depressive disorder, single episode, chronic (with a duration of over 2 years). Like many other clients with borderline personality disorder, Laura had a number of deficits on neuropsychological testing (e.g., memory, attention and concentration, and motor integration) for which no organic cause could be detected in spite of extensive evaluation. Descriptively, she was similar to the clients with borderline personality disorder described by Linehan (1993) as chronically depressed, hopeless, and parasuicidal. She had continual suicidal obsessions over the time I worked with her. In the 2 years preceding our work, she had made multiple suicidal gestures and attempts and had repeated, lengthy psychiatric hospitalizations. I saw her initially as an inpatient and continued to follow her on an outpatient basis for about 1 1/4 years. She made no actual suicidal attempts during this time, although suicidal thoughts and a few related behaviors (e.g., loading a gun) continued. I did help her obtain two brief hospitalizations because of increased suicide ideation that arose as we worked toward terminating therapy because I was relocating to another state. Central themes in therapy included validating emotional experiences and their expression, validating personal protection and elaboration, making a commitment to live (at least for the present), construing memory fragments of childhood abuse that began to spontaneously emerge, and reconstruing other family members and family relationships that she had previously viewed in extreme, idealized terms.

MYTHOLOGY

There is a myth deeply ingrained in Western civilization, that sin is the cause of death. As the story goes, there were two children who lived in a perfectly beautiful garden, built for them by a perfectly wise father. In the midst of this garden, the father, God, planted two trees. One was the tree of the knowledge of good and evil. The other was the tree of life. The father warned the children: "you may eat of any tree, except the tree of good and evil, for if you eat of it, you will die."

A smooth-talking snake came along and beguiled the children, saying, "if you eat of this fruit, you will be like God, knowing good from evil." And the children, being curious and desiring to imitate their parent, ate the fruit, knew they had sinned, and were ashamed. The father cursed the snake and drove the children from the garden and the tree of life to encounter many hardships and, eventually, to die. The story of Christianity is the sequel—the father's efforts to regain his children and to reestablish his family. In the process, he himself became a child, was brutally sacrificed, and conquered death to rise again.

Myths endure because they speak to human experiences on many levels. They embody processes, images, wishes, and themes that are difficult to articulate in the more logical, practical language of everyday life. They carry in shorthand form the beliefs of a people—their explanations of life and their anticipations for salvation.

As we grow more civilized, we institutionalize our myths. We develop rules for mythmaking and refer to our myths as history, facts, and science. These tools create an increasingly complex way of life that may appear far removed from the lives of the two children who were thrown from the garden. But when we face issues of life and death and of good and evil, scientific theories take us no farther than the primitive myth of the garden.

Mair (1988) reminded us that we are lived by the stories we create; not only our own stories, but the stories of our parents, our grandparents, our colleagues, and our civilization. Prigogine (1980; Prigogine & Stengers, 1984) described living systems as irreversible processes. Myths share this property with the individuals, families, and societies that create them. We create new myths, but we do not reverse the old. If we choose to discard them, the process of renouncing our myths is itself a change process.

The power and poignancy of myth has never been more evident to me than when I am working with a client diagnosed as having a borderline personality disorder. I included in this chapter the story of the garden because the work that Laura and I did reminded me again and again of the story's themes, images, and paradoxes. And, in the course of our work together, I found myself and Laura playing each of the characters—the child, the snake, and the father—as we struggled to transcend the roles, and endings, that our myths prescribed.

The Garden

The context of our work was the psychiatry service of a university hospital. It is a service that lives myths of curing what others cannot cure and of seeing where others are blind. It is a service—in a profession, in a society—striving to actualize a mythical garden where it is possible to know what is right, to do it, and to live happily and healthily ever after.

In this case, the fruits of science included many eminently qualified psychiatrists and psychologists, multiple medication trials, electroshock therapy, family therapy, and individual and group cognitive therapy. Laura became "like us," knowing good from evil. She could identify her own distorted thinking and maladaptive behaviors—and ours as well. She could "therapize" other clients as well as or better than I. But in spite of her intelligence and perceptiveness, she could want only one thing—to die. I began beguilingly, like the snake, but often felt that I was trying to force the fruit of life down her unwilling throat.

Our therapeutic experience may be unique in its own ways, but it is also similar to the experiences of many other clients with many other therapists. There are rich stories of borderline personality disorder in different languages: psychoanalytic (Adler, 1985; Kernberg, 1984; Masterson, 1976, 1988), behavioral–dialectical (Linehan, 1993), and empirical–descriptive (Gunderson, 1984; Gunderson & Zanarini, 1987). The explanations differ, but the characters are strikingly similar: young adults, predominately women, with extreme difficulty forming a stable, positive identity and a history of intense, unstable relationships. They are said to be exquisitely vulnerable in relationships, responding to any threat of loss or separation with intense negative affect and self-destructive behavior. Perhaps for this reason, they may protect themselves from relationships with angry, demanding, critical interpersonal styles or distant, superficially competent and cheery styles. They have a history of impulsive behavior that is often inexplicable and unpredictable even to themselves. They are also notable for extremely dichotomous thinking and dissociative episodes.

For all the apparent chaos that surrounds these clients, there is a remarkable stability in their instability. They may be described as moving between extremes on a limited set of fixed axes. Masterson (1976, 1988) described the prime issues as abandonment versus autonomy, explaining their alternation between fearful flight from dependency and demands for exclusive, unconditional relationships. They may act arrogantly entitled or describe themselves as absolutely, irretrievably wicked, perverse, and unworthy. They may be aggressively attacking and controlling or passively unprotesting of victimization. They may be extraordinarily competent, particularly in caretaking roles, but their competence crumbles when they are asked to care for themselves.

Professionals caring for those with borderline personality disorder often join in the dance, taking complementary extremes (Gunderson, 1984). They may be relentlessly, professionally detached and confrontative. They may insist on rigid control of therapy structure and limits and may terminate the client without discussion or recourse at any hint of infraction. On the other extreme, they may offer themselves as unconditionally available and empathetic. They may exhaust themselves answering late-night phone calls and meeting crisis appointments. Their involvement may overflow professional boundaries to become a friendship or sexual relationship (Guthiel, 1989; Linehan, 1993).

Perhaps because the latter extreme is so unacceptable a threat to therapists' personal autonomy and professional values, we often take a defensive position toward these clients. There is a pervasive belief that, without united, consistent, vigorous assertion of clinical authority, this group of clients will split treatment teams, manipulate therapists, demand the unreasonable, and remain angry when they receive it. I have sensed that colleagues would interpret a therapist's expression of affection for a borderline client as incompetence, weakness, gullibility, or a sign of serious personality disturbance. I have seen therapists who expressed empathy and positive regard for a client with this diagnosis accused of overpermissiveness and splitting the treatment team.

Few mental health practitioners are eager to work with a borderline client. The term *borderline* itself often seems to be used interchangeably with *unlikable* and *manipulative*. Gallop and her colleagues (Gallop, 1988; Gallop, Lancee, & Garfinkel, 1989) have found that psychiatric nurses, responding to hypothetical client statements, are more likely to offer nonempathetic, belittling, and contradictory responses if the client is labeled *borderline* rather than *schizophrenic*. These clients are not only seen as difficult and untreatable but as deliberately, maliciously, and manipulatively choosing to be ill.

The Father

A hierarchical relationship is implicit in the practice of psychotherapy in most institutions. The therapists' assumed role in the relationship is the delivery of psychological techniques to the client. In some cases, institutional policies may require the therapist to create a treatment plan specifying the client's problems and corresponding methods and goals of treatment. At an extreme, the objectives must be measurable and begin with "The client will." Therapists' participation in such rituals enacts the myth that we, as knowing authorities, are scientifically administering a procedure that will alter the client in a predictable, desirable direction.

Debates surrounding the correct treatments for borderline personality disorder may implicitly assume that the therapist can and should make the right choice for the client, who is incapable of choosing wisely. The therapist may play the critical, emotionally distant, disciplinarian parent or the praising, understanding, ever-giving parent. Each extreme assumes that the therapist dispenses wise control or support and that the client must only cooperate to be healed.

Transference is an unavoidable process in psychotherapy, especially in a societal context that shrouds healers with authority. When we are working with borderline clients, we may anticipate specific transference themes to emerge, including the perfect, powerful, or punishing parent and the sinful child. A very large majority of borderline clients have been severely abused as children. It has been estimated that up to 86% of female clients with this diagnosis have been sexually abused (Herman, Perry, & van der Kolk, 1989; Stone, 1981; Zanarini, Gunderson, Marino, Schwartz, & Frankenburg, 1989). This abuse may not emerge, or even be remembered, in the early stages of treatment. The nonabused remaining clients are thought to have experienced more subtle forms of systematic emotional invalidation, such as that offered by the parent who professes to be perfect (Linehan, 1987c, 1993). Whether to conceal their own guilt or to glorify themselves by creating a perfect child, both groups of parents may dictate their child's feelings, wants, and thoughts and label any independent deviation or self-protection as "bad." In this process, it is not only the child's specific constructions that are invalidated, but their construing process—their life.

Borderline clients may be seen as having shattered myths and shattered faith in their ability to create new ones. They may come to therapy remembering perfect parents in a supportive family. Then, as my client did, they find themselves shocked by vivid memories of cruel abuse and perpetual terror. In contrast, clients may report a history of proceeding apparently unscathed through repeated trauma as children, but of crumbling into helpless depression as adults with the realization that other ways of life exist that were denied to them.

The interaction between the life experiences of borderline clients and our myths as therapists results in stormy transference relationships. We may inevitably find ourselves cast in a parental role, but we can suspend reenacting the perfect or blaming parent. Our clients know that role by heart and repeatedly enact it for themselves.

The Child

Descriptions of borderline personality disorder assume that these clients have failed to learn the lessons that are crucial to functioning as a healthy adult. Masterson (1976, 1988) attributed these deficits to a failure in the separation–individuation stage of child development. Linehan (1987a, 1993) attributed them to a biological deficit in emotional regulation and an invalidating early learning environment. Such views assume that therapists should teach the client skills that they learned as children.

As constructivists, we might consider that the therapy relationship can be asymmetrical without being hierarchical in every aspect. Therapists may have answers because their experiences have posed easier questions: The client may be struggling with quantum mechanics whereas the therapist has mastered plane geometry. Philosophers and theologians abstractly debate questions of suffering and evil, with generally unsatisfying results; borderline clients live the questions. Theologians say that sin is the cause of suffering and death; Laura, and others like her, conclude that they are evil and must die. Therapist and client each struggle to create myths for living in a relationship, in a world, that they cannot control. They may both experience themselves as children, trying to recover a garden in which things turn out better, if not always perfect.

Laura, more realistically cynical than I, often saw our quest as hopeless, labeling me "Pollyanna" for my optimism and naïveté in the face of despair. Some loss of innocence is inevitable in treating survivors of abuse. With this loss of innocence, the therapist may also lose the vital imagination of his or her own childhood. Struggling with the difficulty of treating this disorder and the issues it poses, the therapist may be drawn into experiencing the helplessness and powerlessness of childhood. Engulfed with the evil that has been and the suffering that is, the therapist may not see possibilities of what might be, given developmental changes in the client's context and roles. If the client perceives helplessness on the part of the therapist, then he or she may enact a well-learned parental-child role. Many clients were encouraged as children to attend to the needs of their parents while ignoring their own needs, emotions, and interpretations of experience. Laura was vigilant for any opportunity to assume the more comfortable role of ministering to me, rather than asking for my help. Because she was naturally kind and gentle, this temptation might have been difficult to resist if her need for new ways of relating were not so desperately apparent. As long as the client is firmly fixed in the role of helpless child or responsible child, he or she cannot experiment with new aspects of the child role, such as play, curiosity for its own sake rather than for self-protection, exploration, hopeful anticipation, and trust. The therapist's own childlike qualities might best be used to model these constructs.

The Snake

Clients with borderline personality disorder also often feel that they are somehow irretrievably different from others. The distaste with which mental health practitioners react to this diagnosis reminds one of the curse put on the snake in the garden—that he would crawl on his belly in the dirt and that there would be everlasting enmity between him and humankind. This group of clients disrupts the myths that we construct around our profession and our treatment systems. Our theories are often unable to grasp them, and our techniques are ineffective to cure them, reminding us that our professional garden is far from the myth we prefer to present.

Professionals may communicate their distaste to clients by telling them that they are manipulative. Laura often asked me, having received this feedback from others, if she was being manipulative. She would also at times label her own behavior, usually a new self-protective or self-expressive act, as manipulative. Other times, meekly asking for help, she would reassure me and herself that she was not trying to manipulate. This label seems especially painful to many borderline clients—possibly because they have had multiple experiences as victims of exploitative manipulation. I honestly tell them that I do not see them as any more manipulative than I am. I remind them of the many things I have done to "manipulate" their behavior. They may have difficulty seeing my inevitable attempts at influence as manipulative, but they can almost always find something manipulative about the behavior of the person who attached that label to them.

The frequent accusations of manipulation that Laura received seemed related to her difficulty in knowing what she felt and in asking for anything she might want. She would act suicidally before she realized that she felt depressed and hopeless. As therapy progressed, she learned to talk about feelings before they became actions. She would express intolerable pain and helplessness but would have difficulty identifying anything specific that she wanted or asking anything of the therapist. Mental health professionals may construe such helpless, suffering behavior as a demand for a fixer-upper response on their part. If they do not have a readily available remedy, they may label the client manipulative rather than face up to their own discomfort and human limitations.

In refusing to acknowledge our own human interests and limitations, we may neglect an important teaching experience and inadvertently assume the deceptive role of the snake. Therapists have difficulty acknowledging acts for their own self-interest. Borderline clients often have particular difficulty applying their apparent competencies on their own behalf. It is an interesting paradox that we ask our clients for behavior that we are reluctant to own ourselves. In an extreme example, a therapist's refusal to take on or decision to stop treating a seriously suicidal client may be framed as being in the client's best interest whereas it is actually the therapist's response to his or her own emotional fears and concern with legal liability. Less extremely, a therapist's limitation of late-night phone calls may be exclusively presented as discouragement of unhealthy dependency on the part of the client.

Therapists probably fool themselves and their colleagues more often than they fool their clients. Although borderline clients are often oblivious to their own emotional nuances until overwhelmed by them, they are often extraordinarily perceptive of others' nonverbal, emotional cues (Frank & Hoffman, 1986). If we honestly communicate our attempts to influence the therapy relationship for our own benefit, we may provide a model for new roles that would allow the client to better influence others' behavior for his or her protection and benefit.

This direct self-protection on the part of the therapist contrasts with the seductive manipulation of the snake. That manipulation often takes a subtle disguise, in which the therapist's agendas are presented as beneficial for the client. For instance, the client may be asked, or may perceive that she is being asked, to improve in order to please or to validate the competence of the therapist. She may hide pain and turmoil behind a facade of improvement, enacting a role into which she is unable to fully invest important aspects of herself. Her core constructions of herself and her experiences may remain unexperienced, unexpressed, and unvalidated. When the resulting anomie becomes intolerable, she may unexpectedly behave suicidally in a desperate, unplanned attempt to validate her pain and her identity.

The Trees

Therapists often get bogged down with their colleagues and their clients in questions related to the troublesome tree that defeated the children in the garden: What or who is good or evil, right or wrong, true or false? Borderline clients are noted for dichotomizing experiences, people, and themselves at the extremes of these poles. Therapists often construe the client in similarly extreme terms. If therapists are less extreme, they may at minimum expect themselves to know how to accurately nail down experiences, behaviors, and therapies along these dimensions.

Clients with borderline personality disorder may be limited to describing experiences by using highly evaluative constructs. They see themselves, others, and experiences as good or bad. Laura gave up most of the activities that she had previously enjoyed because her symptoms hindered her performance. She was unable to tolerate playing the guitar, working, or even doing routine housework badly. When I asked her to imagine an activity in which she could participate without giving herself a "grade," she was unable to give any examples.

Clients may look to therapists to validate or invalidate their evaluative constructions. "Praise" for "good" performance may validate a judgmental approach to experience and a metaphor of therapist as judge (judgmental father) rather than as healer, experimenter, cocreator, or other, more elaborative roles. Even attempts to modulate appraisals may keep clients stuck on the evaluative axis. Rather than focusing exclusively on moving black-and-white constructions into the "gray zone," therapists might also direct attention to the other tree in the garden. Many aspects of life are more richly described in reds, blues, and yellows. If therapists fail to recognize this complexity of life and of themselves, they offer oversimplified, one-dimensional myths that their clients, wisely, do not believe.

The primary task of the therapist is not to validate or invalidate the client's constructions but to validate the client's construing process itself. Rather than labeling the client's theories as veracious or distorted, the therapist validates the client as a theory maker and remaker. The healing power of therapy may be accessed through participation in elaborative or creative processes rather than through accurate application of the technical rules with which we evaluate the experience.

Beyond the Garden

In the original tale, rebirth was only possible when God became human. Suffering and death were the door to a new life. The emotional, cognitive, behavioral, and relational turbulence of borderline clients may be an integral aspect of a creative process (cf. Mahoney, 1982, 1988, 1991). As therapists, we may hinder this process and recapitulate old myths if we overvalue our techniques and our clinical–scientific role. Perhaps the most important experience we can hope to offer is validation of the client as construer. This entails respectful attention to the wisdom in the emotions that clients experience and the behavioral questions they pose. The belief in themselves as construers is probably fundamental to exposing specific constructions to invalidation, revision, or re-creation. We may thus facilitate new ways of being as we create a safe, collaborative, experimental relationship, that is, a context in which the client is secure enough to ask questions that challenge and re-create the roles we enact. Kelly (1955) made a still-pertinent first step in reminding us that when we describe our clients, we describe ourselves as well.

CONCLUDING REMARKS

One of the persisting controversies in stories of borderline personality concerns the label of borderline itself, which has been repeatedly criticized as pejorative and inadequately descriptive. The resistance of the label to revision through constructive criticism and significant changes in definitions of the diagnostic category over the past 50 years suggests that it conveys some important tacit meaning to mental health professionals beyond the formal definitions that they use. Instead of expressing some essential attribute of the clients described, the label may express the experiences of professionals working with them. These are clients who test the borders of psychotherapists' theories, techniques, acceptance, and caring. We may label them *borderline* not only for the instability of their own self and relational boundaries but also for the challenges they pose to the boundaries that we construct for ourselves. Our work together tests assumptions on which our identity as therapists and our practice of psychotherapy depends. We may hostilely locate our limitations within the client or elaborate new boundaries. Aronson (1989) attributed a revitalization of psychoanalysis to exploration of this disorder. Linehan (1993) has developed a radical elaboration of behavior therapy, integrating dialectical and systems theories, in the process of working with this population. Researchers in both traditions are developing an increasing respect for constructive processes of both therapist and client.

The 1970s and 1980s produced a rich clinical mythology of borderline personality disorder (cf. Adler, 1985; Gunderson, 1984; Gunderson & Zanarini, 1987; Kernberg, 1984; Linehan, 1987a, 1987b, 1987c; Masterson, 1976). Professional theories abstracted from long-term relationships with many clients provide therapists important tools as they cocreate their own roles with each client. However, it remains vital that therapists maintain a hypothetical stance toward their professional and personal constructions. In particular, we should be aware that our theories both allow us to see and blind us to the individual client, with his or her own unique stories.

REFERENCES

Adler, G. (1985). *Borderline psychopathology and its treatment*. New York: Jason Aronson.

American Psychiatric Association. (1994). *Diagnostic and statistical manual of mental disorders* (4th ed.). Washington, DC: Author.

Aronson, T. A. (1989). A critical review of psychotherapeutic treatments of the borderline personality: Historical trends and future directions. *Journal of Nervous and Mental Disease, 177*, 511–528.

Frank, H., & Hoffman, N. (1986). Borderline empathy: An empirical investigation. *Comprehensive Psychiatry, 27*, 387–395.

Gallop, R. (1988). Escaping borderline stereotypes: Working through the maze of patient–staff interactions. *Journal of Psychosocial Nursing, 26*, 16–20.

Gallop, R., Lancee, W. J., & Garfinkel, P. (1989). How nursing staff respond to the label "Borderline Personality Disorder." *Hospital and Community Psychiatry, 40,* 815–819.

Gunderson, J. G. (1984). *Borderline personality disorder.* Washington, DC: American Psychiatric Association.

Gunderson, J. G., & Zanarini, M. C. (1987). Current overview of the borderline diagnosis. *Journal of Clinical Psychiatry, 48*(Suppl.), 5–11.

Guthiel, T. G. (1989). Borderline personality disorder, boundary violations, and patient–therapist sex: Medicolegal pitfalls. *American Journal of Psychiatry, 146,* 597–602.

Harter, S. (1988). Psychotherapy as a reconstructive process: Implications of integrative theories for outcome research. *International Journal of Personal Construct Psychology, 1,* 349–367.

Herman, J. L., Perry, J. C., & van der Kolk, B. A. (1989). Childhood trauma in borderline personality disorder. *American Journal of Psychiatry, 146,* 490–495.

Kelly, G. A. (1955). *The psychology of personal constructs* (2 vols.) New York: Norton.

Kelly, G. A. (1969). Sin and psychotherapy. In B. Maher (Ed.), *Clinical psychology and personality: The selected papers of George Kelly* (pp. 165–188). New York: Wiley.

Kernberg, O. F. (1984). *Severe personality disorders: Psychotherapeutic strategies.* New Haven, CT: Yale University Press.

Linehan, M. M. (1987a). Dialectical behavior therapy for borderline personality disorder: Theory and methods. *Bulletin of the Menninger Clinic, 51,* 261–276.

Linehan, M. M. (1987b). Dialectical behavior therapy: A cognitive behavioral approach to parasuicide. *Journal of Personality Disorder, 1,* 328–333.

Linehan, M. M. (1987c). Dialectical behavior therapy in groups: Treating borderline personality disorders and suicidal behavior. In C. M. Brody (Ed.), *Women's therapy groups: Paradigms of feminist treatment* (pp. 145–162). New York: Springer.

Linehan, M. M. (1993). *Cognitive–behavioral treatment of borderline personality disorder.* New York: Guilford Press.

Mahoney, M. J. (1982). Psychotherapy and human change processes. In J. H. Harvey & M. M. Parks (Eds.), *Psychotherapy research and behavior change* (pp. 77–122). Washington, DC: American Psychological Association.

Mahoney, M. J. (1988). Constructive metatheory: II. Implications for psychotherapy. *International Journal of Personal Construct Psychotherapy, 1,* 299–315.

Mahoney, M. J. (1991). *Human change processes: The scientific foundations of psychotherapy.* New York: Basic Books.

Mair, M. (1988). Psychology as storytelling. *International Journal of Personal Construct Psychology, 1,* 125–137.

Mair, M. (1989). Kelly, Bannister, and a story-telling psychology. *International Journal of Personal Construct Psychology, 2,* 1–14.

Masterson, J. F. (1976). *Psychotherapy of the borderline adult: A developmental approach.* New York: Brunner/Mazel.

Masterson, J. F. (1988). *The search for the real self: Unmasking the personality disorders of our age.* New York: Free Press.

Neimeyer, R. A., & Harter, S. (1988). Facilitating individual change in personal construct therapy. In G. Dunnett (Ed.), *Working with people: Clinical uses of personal construct psychology* (pp. 174–185). New York: Routledge, Chapman & Hall.

Prigogine, I. (1980). *From being to becoming: Time and complexity in the physical sciences.* New York: Freeman.

Prigogine, I., & Stengers, I. (1984). *Order out of chaos: Man's new dialogue with nature.* New York: Bantam Books.

Stone, M. H. (1981). Borderline syndromes: A consideration of subtypes and an overview, directions for research. *Psychiatric Clinics of North America, 4,* 3–13.

Zanarini, M. C., Gunderson, J. G., Marino, M. F., Schwartz, E. O., & Frankenburg, F. R. (1989). Childhood experiences of borderline patients. *Comprehensive Psychiatry, 30,* 13–25.

18

THE PSYCHOLOGICAL DEMANDS OF BEING A CONSTRUCTIVE PSYCHOTHERAPIST

MICHAEL J. MAHONEY

Being a psychotherapist is a formidable challenge in and of itself. Practicing psychotherapy in the constructivist tradition amplifies those challenges considerably. Several years ago, I concluded an article on the therapeutic implications of constructive metatheory with the following observations:

> *The psychological demands of constructive metatheory are unsurpassed by those of any other contemporary perspective.* No other family of modern theories asks its adherents to maintain such a degree of self-examining openness, to so painstakingly tolerate and harvest (rather than eliminate) ambiguity, or to so thoroughly question both the answers and the questions by which they inquire. It is not easy to be a constructivist—a point that may help explain why, until recently, it has also been less popular than other approaches. Popular or not, however, it continues to appeal to a sizeable and growing minority of both theorists and therapists—a minority, I might add (with conscious bias), whose products are disproportionately represented

at the frontiers of modern inquiry. Whatever developments emerge in our next century of study and service, many will have been offered or influenced by those who have accorded the human knower a proactive role in the knowing and the known. (Mahoney, 1988, pp. 312–313)

These are strong assertions, to be sure, but I believe that they remain warranted in light of the conceptual and practical differences between constructivist and nonconstructivist psychotherapies.

In this chapter, I hope to convey some of the challenges involved in and amplified by practicing psychotherapy from a constructivist perspective. It is not my contention that all of these challenges apply exclusively to constructivist therapists, but only that many of them are considerably more formidable when life counseling is conducted from such a perspective. My remarks are organized around four interdependent themes: (a) epistemological and ontological issues; (b) phenomenological and existential challenges; (c) issues of strategy, technique, and praxis; and (d) ethical issues. I conclude with a brief epilogue and a venture into the poetics of developmental processes.

EPISTEMOLOGICAL AND ONTOLOGICAL ISSUES

Epistemology is a term frequently used in discussions of constructivism; it refers to the nature of *knowing*. I emphasize the present progressive ("ing") verb form here because this tense is central to constructivist contentions about the present and ongoing nature of the activities operative in knowledge. *Ontology* refers to theories of existing (not just "existence") and realizing (in the sense of "making real"). In most nonconstructivist psychotherapies, knowing is presumed to reflect a valid correspondence between the knower's representations and the true nature of the known—hence the emphases on objectivity, the validation of knowledge, and the central role of "reality contact" in psychopathology and psychotherapy.

Constructivist psychotherapists, however, reject the assumptions of traditional objectivism and what are called *justificational* epistemologies (Bartley, 1984; Weimer, 1977). A constructive psychotherapist does not believe that there is one true appraisal of reality or that any claims to knowing can be ultimately justified by unequivocal appeals to an absolute authority (whether such authority be science, scripture, numbers, sense data, expert consensus, or whatever). Indeed, in constructivism, the distinction between issues of knowing (epistemology) and the known (reality) is ambiguated, as are the boundaries between subject and object and between internal and external.

Among other things, these nontraditional ways of construing knowledge processes place considerable burdens on the constructivist counselor.[1] Although accepting the culturally defined role of a professional authority, the counselor cannot rest assured that he or she truly knows what is wrong with or best for a given client. The constructive counselor cannot fall back on the collected works of a chosen leader as a bedrock of reassurance or authorization for what she or he is doing as a life counselor. Nor can the counselor naively trust that his or her own perceptions or experiences are unbiased (or less biased) efforts at knowledge. These are not simply abstract issues without practical implications, as I illustrate later with remarks on ethical issues in constructivist psychotherapy. First, however, I address the phenomenological and strategic challenges facing the constructive practitioner.

PHENOMENOLOGICAL AND EXISTENTIAL CHALLENGES

It does not require a substantial leap from the foregoing remarks to realize that constructivist psychotherapy must necessarily deal with individual experience (phenomenology) and the challenges of existential consciousness. Even though constructive counselors realize that they cannot completely bridge the gap between their own experiential processes and those of their clients, they also assume that their professional services and helpfulness to clients are likely to be facilitated by their imperfect-but-important efforts to know these individuals. Those efforts toward knowing, in turn, require that counselors be capable of encouraging an intimate level of self-description and self-presentation on the part of clients. Some of those descriptions and presentations are difficult to follow or painful to witness. They may include emotionally intense and vividly detailed reports of abuse, cruelty, injustice, and tragedy. Not only are such life stories painful to hear, but the emotional pain of the client in the process of relating them can also be formidable. And just as the words and "voice" of the counselor go with clients into their lives outside and after psychotherapy (Rosen, 1982), so do their words, their stories, and their heart-wrenching tears remain with the counselor throughout his or her career.

Like our humanist, existential, and experiential colleagues, we constructivist counselors sometimes achieve a privileged proximity to our clients' "secrets of the heart" (Bugental, 1978, 1981). Those secrets—particularly the most painful ones—tend to be shared only when a deep

---

[1]Hereinafter, I use the terms *counselor* or *life counselor* because they offer a much broader characterization of the psychotherapy practitioner.

bond of caring and trust has been developed between counselor and client. That bond, in turn, seems to emerge most profoundly when the counselor is emotionally present and compassionately responsive to the client's struggles and suffering. In contrast with the emotional distance prescribed by early and orthodox psychoanalytic theory, it has become increasingly apparent that the counselor's emotional presence is a powerful facilitating factor in individual psychotherapy (Greenberg & Pinsof, 1986). Paradoxically, maintaining that presence is often an emotionally depleting challenge for the psychotherapist (Guy, 1987; Norcross & Guy, in press). Thus, one of the most valuable contributions that the counselor can make to the therapeutic process turns out to be one of the most difficult to sustain. It is for this reason, among others, that I believe that counselor self-care is a central priority for all mental health practitioners (Mahoney, 1991).

Besides the emotional demands of optimal psychotherapy, there are limits to what any individual counselor can understand or fathom. Sometimes this is because a phenomenology is involved that is difficult or impossible for the client to convey. Even in the presence of clear communication, however, constructive counselors are aware that their ability to understand the experience of a client will always be constrained by their own range of personal experience. The counselor who has never personally struggled with issues of trust or hope or control, for example, may have greater difficulty being compassionate, patient, or reassuring with clients for whom these issues are pervasive or immediately overwhelming. At the same time, of course, the counselor who is overwhelmed—by these or other personal issues—is unlikely to be optimally helpful to anyone.

ISSUES OF STRATEGY, TECHNIQUE, AND PRAXIS

Given the above constraints and challenges, professional practice for the constructivist counselor is not a simple or linear activity. In more traditional psychotherapies, the tacit or explicit role of the mental health professional is to cure, correct, or teach the client. In constructivist therapy, some teaching may occur, but it is seldom didactic and often bidirectional. The constructivist counselor and his or her client collaborate in explorations and experiments that are intended to enhance the life quality of the latter. This is the primary purpose of their interaction. Inevitably, however, the counselor is given opportunities to learn valuable lessons in the process. Many of those lessons will have to do with the individuality—the existential uniqueness—of each client. Other lessons may teach the counselor more about herself or himself. In my own experience as a practitioner, some of the most important lessons I have learned seem to emphasize the limitations of explicit understanding and the importance of what might be called *an active trust* in the process and the possibility of human development (Mahoney, in press-a, in press-b, in press-c).

Consciously Respecting Unconscious Processes

One of the most difficult challenges facing the constructivist counselor involves the act of practicing psychotherapy in a way that respects what Hayek (1978) has termed "the primacy of the abstract"—that is, the extent to which the most basic and important human processes of organizing our moment-to-moment experience operate at levels far beyond what we consider conscious awareness (Guidano, 1987, 1991; Kelly, 1955; Weimer, 1982). The practical implications of this contention include the following: (a) Both client and counselor are always communicating far more than they are explicitly verbalizing; (b) the learning that takes place in the context of therapeutic interaction is always more profound than either the client or counselor consciously realize—for better and for worse; and (c) the reorganization of a client's personal experience patterns tends to be holistic rather than circumscribed. Among other things, these acknowledgments encourage constructive counselors to balance their attention between relatively more and less conscious aspects of their work with a person. In other words, they attend to their explicit formulations of a given client's situation and resources (e.g., as reflected in their private verbal reflections and case notes) as well as to a multitude of less specifiable impressions and inclinations (e.g., intuitions, "feeling tones," and personal dreams). For counselors trained in other traditions, this may not be an easy balance to achieve or maintain; the need for explicit understanding may far exceed the yield of clinical work. Hence, tolerance for ambiguity is a critical skill in constructivist therapies, and its development does not usually emerge quickly or without distress. Harking back to the opening remarks of this chapter: It is not easy to be a constructive counselor.

Sensing and Moving With the Balance of Novelty and Familiarity

Another challenge that the constructivist counselor encounters is that of facilitating a balance between old and new ways of experiencing. Novel experience is a necessary aspect of learning. Without the contrast of thinking, feeling, or acting in new ways, the client is likely to remain mired in familiar, "life-as-usual" ways of experiencing. This is now a widely acknowledged generalization across different systems of psychotherapy (Lyddon, 1993; Mahoney, 1991, in press-a). Alternatively, if life circumstances or the demands of psychotherapy push the client too far or too quickly beyond familiar ways of experiencing, then self-protective resistance is likely to be exacerbated. Hence, the constructive counselor tries to assess each client's tolerance for and capacity to integrate novel experiences. This challenge is complicated by the fact that these tolerances and capacities not only differ from one client to the next but may also change over time within the same individual.

The Metaphor of Movement in Constructive Psychotherapy

Some of the complex demands of being a constructive counselor may be illustrated with the metaphor of movement. Psychotherapy is like a journey in that it usually involves a quest for change through some form of movement—symbolic or otherwise (Bugental, 1978). To stretch this analogy, the metaphor of travel also carries considerable baggage in the form of hidden meanings. In most instances of contemporary travel, for example, there is a conscious itinerary, a destination, and a means of movement (often powered by energies that derive from sources other than the traveler). Implicitly, at least, this analogy emphasizes the importance of knowing where we are in the overall scheme of things, where we would like to be, and (consequently) the direction of activity necessary for movement from a current position to a desired destination. This rendition of the travel metaphor is technically termed *teleological*, meaning end- or goal-oriented. There is a clear direction of desired movement defined by an explicit destination. Indeed, the essence of teleology is this "end game" orientation: All efforts are oriented to achieving movement toward and accomplishment of a specifiable goal of arrival at an explicit destination. Most psychotherapy, I believe, begins as a teleological enterprise—the client presents with explicit hopes of acting, feeling, or thinking differently in certain circumscribed domains of experience. More often than most textbooks acknowledge, however, many of these same clients shift their interest in the course of therapy from one indisputable goal to many more important, but less specifiable, directions. In technical terms, they exhibit differentiation in the course of their psychological development. In so doing, they exhibit a shift from teleological to teleonomic directionality.

Whereas *teleology* refers to movement with directionality determined by an explicit destination, *teleonomy* refers to movement that reflects directionality that is not defined by an explicit destination. In teleonomy, directionality reflects an ever-evolving and dynamic interaction between a system and its changing medium. Two of the best known examples of teleonomy are biological evolution and life-span personality development. Both exhibit unmistakable patterns or paths of movement, yet their directionality is not predictable on the basis of an explicit or final destination. In teleonomic counseling—that is, counseling that appreciates these dynamic, complex, self-organizing, and evolving aspects of human lives—there is a respect for the power and continuing contribution of novel experiences as they challenge and otherwise revise old and established patterns of experiencing self, others, the world, and the possible relationships among them.

Pulling these themes together, a basic strategy of the constructivist counselor is to respect and facilitate a dynamic balance among clients' teleological and teleonomic activities. This is more easily said than done, of course. I shall try to communicate my current understanding of this strategy by further extending the travel metaphor. Imagine, if you will, that life is an unfolding landscape and that the psychotherapy client is a traveler in trouble. Frightened, tired, and often feeling lost, the lone traveler witnesses the movement of humanity all around. He or she sees other travelers moving in different directions—some racing with haste and others crawling with pain. Most of these individuals travel well-worn paths; some travel lonely, difficult courses; and some are not moving at all. It can be a bewildering panorama. Along the way there are many people asking for help and many others offering assistance. Among the latter are psychotherapists, many of whom establish themselves at choice points along the most frequently used paths. And it is here that life counselors exhibit some of their most important differences in strategies of helping.

Some life counselors are essentially selling maps or information about the terrain ahead. They may claim to be well traveled and to know the best route for traveling to the destinations sought by their clients. They may offer advice and opinions on the merits of the destinations themselves. They are, in a sense, travel agents or guides. Those counselors who practice from a constructivist metatheory, however, are seldom seen selling maps or advocating particular destinations. What distinguishes constructivists from other kinds of counselors, in my opinion, is their willingness to temporarily join their clients in the processes of teleonomic travel. Such a counselor is willing to take turns leading and following. He or she respects the client's need to rest. He or she is compassionate and comforting when clients feel frightened or are despairing. If a client feels that he or she cannot move on, the counselor is willing to wait, or offers to carry some of the client's burden for a while. But the power for movement and the responsibility for choices of direction always return to the client. When there are dangers or falls—which are inevitable—the counselor remains focused on the safety and well-being of the client. And, when it is time, the counselor and client take their separate life paths, both having been enriched by their time and travel together.

This is, to be sure, an idealized caricature. However, it is a clarifying exaggeration, and it highlights the ideological kinship of constructivist, existential, humanist, and transpersonal counselors (Bugental, 1978, 1981; Friedman, 1992; May, Angel, & Ellenberger, 1958; Rowan, 1993; Walsh & Vaughan, 1993). Each in his or her own way respects the dilemma so poignantly described by Fitz-James Stephen in 1874:

> In all important transactions of life we have to take a leap in the dark. . . . We stand on a mountain pass in the midst of whirling snow and blinding mist, through which we get glimpses now and then of paths which may be deceptive. If we stand still we shall be frozen to death. If we take the wrong road we shall be dashed to pieces. We do not certainly know whether there is any right one. What must we do? "Be strong and of a good courage." Act for the best, hope for the best, and take what comes. . . . If death ends all, we cannot meet death better. (cited in James 1896/1956, pp. 30–31)

Whether we move by leaping quickly or by slowly inching our way into the darkness, we are forever traversing the unknown of the arriving moment. This appreciation, with its decidedly existential and postmodern corollaries, casts both new light and long shadows on the dimensions of ethics and values in professional psychological practice.

ETHICAL ISSUES

There was a time—not all that long ago—when a significant portion of the world's psychotherapists believed that their activities and professional services were essentially value-free. That illusion was a costly one for many clients. Fortunately, this illusion is no longer unchallenged. Ethical and value issues are increasingly acknowledged as pervasive in all forms of psychotherapy (Cushman, 1993; London, 1964; McNamee & Gergen, 1992; Prillitensky, 1989; Sampson, 1993a, 1993b). The constructivist life counselor strives to maintain an active appreciation of this realization. Three of the implications of such an appreciation are as follows:

1. Values, like objective truth, cannot be justified or otherwise unequivocally authorized. What is good or bad, sacred or profane, and right or wrong is always framed within individual, social, and historical contexts.
2. There is not, never was, and never can be a truly "nondirective" or value-free form of human dialogue. All human perception, learning, knowing, and interaction is necessarily motivated by and permeated with biases, preferences, and valuations (which are usually implicit).

3. As socially sanctioned experts in human experience, psychotherapists often play an important role in their clients' examination and experimental exploration of personal values (i.e., their morals and ethics).

These generalizations do not necessarily imply, however, that clients in psychotherapy are passive victims of their counselors' values. Contrary to earlier notions that psychotherapy inevitably leads to clients compromising their values in the direction of the values held by their counselors, more recent research has suggested that there is a selectivity in this influence (Kelly & Strupp, 1992). The point here is that the counselor's values are not necessarily overwhelming: Clients show a considerable degree of ethical autonomy.

Even if this is an accurate depiction of the therapeutic enterprise, it does not negate the fact that clients' values in some domains may be significantly influenced by the values expressed, affirmed, and challenged by the professional practitioner. The constructivist counselor is particularly sensitive to this fact, and this sensitivity may create ethical challenges in his or her activities as a mental health service provider. I shall illustrate this point with a clinical case of more than 15 years ago in which I served in the role of psychotherapist.

Dolly T. was a 46-year-old music teacher whose personal traumas were substantial. In the process of our work together, she gradually reconstructed memories of having been physically and sexually abused by her father. Months later, it also became apparent to her that her mother had colluded in her abuse, at first by not protecting her from her father and later by sexually abusing her herself. Dolly's pain was excruciating. She struggled with suicidal depression and feelings of hopelessness for a long time. I struggled along with her, not knowing what I could do to ease her pain or to accelerate her psychological movement. In the course of all of this, Dolly became increasingly interested in spiritual works on the phenomenon of reincarnation. Over many months, her own spirits began to lift as she developed an elaborate scaffolding of past lives in which she believed that she had been both the victim and perpetrator of abuses. She consulted a mystic, who encouraged her dawning awareness.

Meanwhile, I changed my academic home. Accepting an offer from another university forced me to inform Dolly that our work together would have to end. I explored possibilities for her referral and eventually recommended a local counselor who was relatively liberal in the realm of religious and spiritual scaffoldings. Dolly was not happy that I was leaving, but she later reported very positive results from her work with this transpersonal counselor.

I was, to say the least, relieved. At the same time, however, I was challenged. If the circumstances had been different, and I had remained her counselor, what could or should I have done? Given the limitations of my own spiritual education and personal experience, I was not prepared to openly accept or affirm her constructions about reincarnation and karma. At the same time, however, I had developed enough self-awareness and epistemological conscience to realize that I could not claim any guaranteed (authorized) warrant for rejecting or discouraging her conceptual scaffoldings. Who was I to tell her that her mystical explorations were not acceptable or healthy in her attempts to organize the experience of having been abused by both of her parents?

In the years that have ensued, I have paid close attention to the writings and reports of other psychotherapists in the domains of mysticism, religiosity, and spiritualism. What have been the experiences and lessons of my colleagues in these domains? I am sure that my readings have been selective, of course, but the essence of those lessons warrants reflection. Although their quantity is small relative to the literatures on perception, learning, and psychopathology, scholarly writings on the significance of mystical, religious, and spiritual experiences in personal development are not difficult to find (e.g., Allman, de La Rocha, Elkins, & Weathers, 1992; Bergin, 1991; Heery, 1989; Park & Cohen, 1993; Shafranske & Malony, 1990; Spanos, Cross, Dickson, & DuBreuil, 1993; Vaughan, 1991). My readings and reflections have rendered a greater personal appreciation and respect for the diversity of belief systems that may assist individuals in their attempts to cope with the circumstances of their lives.

The ethical challenges of constructivist psychotherapy are perhaps no different from those encountered in any other form of mental health practice (American Psychological Association, 1992). Human dignity and the right to be different are foundational assumptions. What may be different for the constructivist counselor is the relative power of these issues in daily practice. She or he is sensitive to the complex and changing matrix by which diversity is defined. He or she realizes that being different is always relative to community norms and that those norms are increasingly evolving at an unprecedented pace. The phenomenon of globalization in communication, travel, technology, economics, and political ideology has dramatically challenged identities and the ethical norms associated with nationalities, races, cultures, religions, physical abilities, age, and lifestyles (Balibar & Wallerstein, 1991; Gergen, 1991; Mahoney, 1993; Mato, 1993; Maturana & Verden-Zöller, 1993; Montero, 1991; Zambrano, 1988). Never before has the act of balancing individual rights and social responsibilities required such a comprehensive appreciation for the dynamic complexities of life on this planet.

EPILOGUE

In the preceding pages, I have outlined what I believe to be some of the major challenges of being a constructivist life counselor. As I said earlier, I do not claim that these challenges are distinct from the challenges of practicing psychotherapy from any other perspective; but I do believe that constructivist metatheory and attempts to put it into practice often involve a magnification of those challenges. There is much that constructivist counselors do that is exploratory, experimental, and otherwise fundamentally existential. This being the case, I shall conclude by relating an exchange with a client whose process taught me much about myself and my role as a constructivist life counselor.

Mary G. was a 35-year-old multiply diagnosed professional woman with problems that ranged from alcohol abuse and anxiety to depression and obsessive–compulsive patterns. She had been in therapy many times before, and she was still seeking a state of being in which she felt capable of resting, relaxing, and enjoying herself. The particulars and process of our work together are less relevant here than the reflections we shared at the conclusion of that work. As has been my habit for many years now, in anticipation of our final sessions together, I asked Mary to prepare some kind of summary of how she had experienced our work together. She arrived for our final scheduled meeting with a narrative that concluded with the following poem:

> You asked me to write
> And this I have done
> My pain and my progress
> Are they not but One?
>
> I've cried out my heart,
> I've vented my rage,
> And you have stood by me
> Part friend and part sage.
>
> I know that I've changed
> In ways I can't say;
> I know that I'm more
> Than I was yesterday.
>
> I thank you, my friend,
> For being so true;
> I thank you, I guess
> For just being You.

For your being You
Has helped me to see
That I can find peace
In just being Me.

Enclosed with her poem was a request that I share with her my experiences of our work together. I was touched by her poem and by her request. I responded with a poem that has grown considerably over the ensuing years. It conveys my continuing respect for the challenges of constructivist counseling as well as my deep appreciation for the complexities of developmental processes. I therefore conclude with "The Pilgrim in Process":

It's a season of transition and you're on the move again
  On a path toward something you cannot disown;
Searching for your being in the labyrinths of heart
  And sensing all the while you're not alone.

Yes, you seem to keep on changing for the better and the worse
  And you dream about the shrines you've yet to find;
And you recognize your longing as a blessing and a curse
  While you puzzle at the prisons of your mind.

For as much as you seek freedom from your agonies and fears
  And as often as you've tried to see the light,
There is still a trembling terror that your liberation nears
  And you struggle with the edges of your night.

For your Reason is a skeptic and rejects what it desires,
  Playing hard to get with miracles and signs;
'Til a Witness gains momentum and emerges from within
  To disclose the patterns well above the lines.

Then a window has been opened and you've let yourself observe
  How the fabric of your Being lies in wait;
And you want to scream in anger and you want to cry for joy
  And you worry that it still may be too late.

For the roller coaster plummets with a force that drives you sane
  As you tightly grasp for truths that will abide;
Never fully understanding that your need to feel secure
  Is the very thing that keeps you on the ride.

You survive the oscillations and begin to sense their role
  In a process whose direction is more clear;
And you marvel as your balance point becomes a frequent home,
  And your lifelong destination feels like "here."

So with gentleness and wonder, with questions and with quests
  You continue on the path that is your way;
Knowing now that you have touched upon the shores of inner life,
  And excursions deeper can't be far away.

There will be so many moments when an old view seems so strong
  And you question whether you can really change;
And yet, from deep within you, there's a sense of more to come
  And your old view is the one that now seems strange.

Take good care, my friend, and listen to the whispers of your heart
  As it beats its precious rhythm through your days;
These warm thoughts and hopes are with you on your journeys
  through it all
  And the paths of life in process find their ways.

So be gentle, Process Pilgrim; learn to trust that trust is dear.
  The same is true of laughter and of rest;
And remember that the living is a loving in itself
  And the secret is to ever be in quest.

(Mahoney, 1994)

REFERENCES

Allman, L. S., de La Rocha, O., Elkins, D. N., & Weathers, R. S. (1992). Psychotherapists' attitudes toward clients reporting mystical experiences. *Psychotherapy, 29*, 565–569.

American Psychological Association. (1992). *Ethical principles of psychologists and code of conduct.* Washington, DC: Author.

Balibar, E., & Wallerstein, I. (1991). *Race, nation, class: Ambiguous identities.* London: Verso.

Bartley, W. W. (1984). *The retreat to commitment.* Peru, IL: Open Court.

Bergin, A. E. (1991). Values and religious issues in psychotherapy and mental health. *American Psychologist, 46*, 394–403.

Bugental, J. F. T. (1978). *Psychotherapy and process.* Reading, MA: Addison-Wesley.

Bugental, J. F. T. (1981). *The search for authenticity.* New York: Irvington.

Cushman, P. (1993). Psychotherapy as moral discourse. *Journal of Theoretical and Philosophical Psychology, 13*, 103–113.

Friedman, M. (1992). *Dialogue and the human image.* Newbury Park, CA: Sage.

Gergen, K. (1991). *The saturated self.* New York: Basic Books.

Greenberg, L. S., & Pinsof, W. (Eds.). (1986). *The psychotherapeutic process.* New York: Guilford Press.

Guidano, V. F. (1987). *Complexity of the self*. New York: Guilford Press.

Guidano, V. F. (1991). *The self in process*. New York: Guilford Press.

Guy, J. D. (1987). *The personal life of the psychotherapist*. New York: Wiley.

Hayek, F. A. (1978). The primacy of the abstract. In F. A. Hayek (Ed.), *New studies in philosophy, politics, economics and the history of ideas* (pp. 35–49). Chicago: University of Chicago Press.

Heery, M. W. (1989). Inner voice experiences: An exploratory study of thirty cases. *Journal of Transpersonal Psychology, 21*, 73–82.

James, W. (1956). *The will to believe*. New York: Dover. (Original work published 1896)

Kelly, G. A. (1955). *The psychology of personal constructs* (2 vols.). New York: Norton.

Kelly, G. A., & Strupp, H. H. (1992). Patient and therapist values in psychotherapy: Perceived changes, assimilation, similarity, and outcome. *Journal of Consulting and Clinical Psychology, 60*, 34–40.

London, P. (1964). *The modes and morals of psychotherapy*. New York: Holt, Rinehart & Winston.

Lyddon, W. J. (1993). Contrast, contradiction, and change in psychotherapy. *Psychotherapy, 30*, 383–390.

Mahoney, M. J. (1988). Constructive metatheory: II. Implications for psychotherapy. *International Journal of Personal Construct Psychology, 1*, 299–315.

Mahoney, M. J. (1991). *Human change processes*. New York: Basic Books.

Mahoney, M. J. (1993). The postmodern self in psychotherapy. *Journal of Cognitive Psychotherapy, 7*, 239–248.

Mahoney, M. J. (1994). *Poems of process*. Unpublished manuscript.

Mahoney, M. J. (in press-a). *Constructive psychotherapy*. New York: Guilford Press.

Mahoney, M. J. (in press-b). *Constructive psychotherapy techniques*. New York: Guilford Press.

Mahoney, M. J. (in press-c). *Embodying the mind: Constructive health psychology*. New York: Guilford Press.

Mato, D. (Ed.). (1993). *Diversidad cultural y construcción de identidades* [Cultural diversity and identity construction]. Caracas, Venezuela: Fondo Editorial Tropykos.

Maturana, H., & Verden-Zöller, G. (1993). *Amor y juego: Fundamentos olvidados de lo humano* [Love and Play: Forgotten fundamentals of being human]. Santiago, Chile: Instituto de Terapia Cognitiva.

May, R., Angel, E., & Ellenberger, H. F. (Eds.). (1958). *Existence*. New York: Simon & Schuster.

McNamee, S., & Gergen, K. J. (Eds.). (1992). *Therapy as social construction*. Newbury Park, CA: Sage.

Montero, M. (1991). *Ideología, alienación e identidad nacional* [Ideology, alienation, and national identity] Caracas: Universidad Central de Venezuela.

Norcross, J. C., & Guy, J. D. (in press). *Leaving it at the office: Understanding and alleviating the distress of conducting psychotherapy.* New York: Guilford Press.

Park, C. L., & Cohen, L. H. (1993). Religious and non-religious coping with the death of a friend. *Cognitive Therapy and Research, 17,* 561–577.

Prillitensky, I. (1989). Psychology and the status quo. *American Psychologist, 44,* 795–802.

Rosen, S. (Ed.). (1982). *My voice will go with you.* New York: Norton.

Rowan, J. (1993). *The transpersonal.* London: Routledge & Kegan Paul.

Sampson, E. E. (1993a). *Celebrating the other: A dialogic account of human nature.* New York: Harvester Wheatsheaf.

Sampson, E. E. (1993b). Identity politics. *American Psychologist, 48,* 1219–1230.

Shafranske, E. P., & Malony, H. N. (1990). Clinical psychologists' religious and spiritual orientations and their practice of psychotherapy. *Psychotherapy, 27,* 72–78.

Spanos, N. P., Cross, P. A., Dickson, K., & DuBreuil, S. C. (1993). Close encounters: An examination of UFO experiences. *Journal of Consulting and Clinical Psychology, 102,* 624–632.

Vaughan, F. (1991). Spiritual issues in psychotherapy. *Journal of Transpersonal Psychology, 23,* 105–119.

Walsh, R., & Vaughan, F. (Eds.). (1993). *Paths beyond ego: The transpersonal vision.* Los Angeles: Tarcher.

Weimer, W. B. (1977). *Notes on the methodology of scientific research.* Hillsdale, NJ: Erlbaum.

Weimer, W. B. (1982). Hayek's approach to the problems of complex phenomena: An introduction to the theoretical psychology of *The sensory order.* In W. B. Weimer & D. S. Palermo (Eds.), *Cognition and the symbolic processes* (Vol. 2, pp. 241–285). Hillsdale, NJ: Erlbaum.

Zambrano, M. (1988). *Persona y democracia: La historia sacrificial* [The individual and democracy: The history of sacrifice]. Barcelona, Spain: Anthropos.

GLOSSARY

Several of the terms below refer to constructivist concepts and procedures that can be only briefly summarized here. For a more complete explication of theoretical terminology and therapeutic techniques, consult the various chapters of this book as well as the volumes by Mahoney (1991)[1] and Neimeyer (1993).[2]

AUTOPOIESIS [from Greek *auto* (self) and *poiésis* (creative power or construction)]   A term introduced in biology and other fields by Maturana to denote the ongoing activity of self-organization in living systems.

BIPOLAR SCULPTURES   A group or family therapy technique in which the therapist designates the walls of the room as the poles of prominent family or group constructs (e.g., one wall may represent "people who are like me" and the opposite wall "people who are unlike me," with the other two walls labeled "people who understand me" vs. "people who do not understand me"). The therapist then asks one member to physically guide each of the other members to his or her place in the room to depict how that individual other is viewed on each dimension by the group member doing the arranging. This form of family or group sculpting physically instantiates the construing of the sculptor on the stage of public awareness, and the exercise can be followed by group members noting their feelings and reactions to being placed in that configuration.

---

[1]Mahoney, M. J. (1991). *Human change processes*. New York: Basic Books.
[2]Neimeyer, G. J. (Ed.). (1993). *Constructivist assessment: A casebook*. Newbury Park, CA: Sage.

BOW-TIE DIAGRAMS   A means of mapping the relative positions of various members in a family system at the level of their constructions of one another and the actions that cohere with these constructions. A unique feature of this diagramming strategy is that it graphically displays the way in which the actions of one family member unintentionally validate the constructions of another embroiled in the problem system, providing a detailed (bow-tie-shaped) "map" of potential therapeutic interventions (see Neimeyer, 1993, for examples).

CHANGE, FIRST- AND SECOND-ORDER   A differentiation introduced by Gregory Bateson to emphasize that changes in systems may vary depending on their centrality to the functioning of the system. Superficial changes represent first-order changes: minor adjustments to or realignments of current system elements, as when one changes the locations of system components. Second-order changes, which are qualitatively revolutionary, involve changes not just in the components of a system and their relative location, but also in the entire web of relations that define the system.

CHOICE COROLLARY   In personal construct theory, the axiom that a person chooses to construct his or her experience and action in such a way that he or she anticipates the greatest possibility for extension and definition of the construct system. In less technical terms, this implies that a person's choices invariably represent his or her best attempt to enhance or preserve some sense of meaning, however "illogical" such choices might seem to the outside observer.

CIRCULAR QUESTIONS   Inquiry strategies used by constructivist family therapists to elucidate family members' constructions of one another and their relationships.

CONSTRUCT [Latin *con* and *struere* (to arrange together or to build)]   A term with a varied history in psychology and philosophy, sometimes used as a synonym for *concept* (e.g., by Karl Pearson). In psychology, the term is probably most frequently associated with the tradition of George A. Kelly, who used it as a cardinal concept for the individual's active processes of "channelizing," or organizing, experience. Personal constructs in this sense represent individual or shared distinctions imposed on experience as a way of anticipating it and defining one's options for action.

CONSTRUCTIVE   A term associated with "constructivism" or "constructive metatheory" in psychology, a tradition emphasizing the active participation of each person in his or her own life organization and development.

CRITICAL CONSTRUCTIVISM   asserts that the individual is synergistically interdependent with his or her environment and that there are, indeed, "external" (extrasystemic) constraints (call them physical, material, or whatever) that importantly constrain and influence each person's continuing constructing.

RADICAL CONSTRUCTIVISM   asserts that the individual is self-sufficient in these processes and that his or her physical environment or medium of existence is a relatively insignificant factor in the construction of experiences. However, some radical constructivists strongly emphasize the role of language in shaping the constructions of human individuals and groups, even to the point of shaping their most basic sense of self and relations.

CORE ORDERING PROCESSES   Powerful and mostly nonlinguistic processes of human self-organization; proposed by Mahoney and others, these processes tend to be dichotomous (Kelly) and directional. Mahoney proposed at least four such processes: (a) those that render perceptual and experiential order itself and, hence, pattern, meaning, and experienced reality; (b) those that order experiences emotionally or evaluatively, along dimensions of good–bad or right–wrong; (c) those that serve the lifelong differentiation from and communion with others—the dynamics of I–thou and me–you; and (d) those that organize people's activities in styles that reflect their remembered or anticipated experiences of empowerment and reciprocity.

CREDULOUS APPROACH   George Kelly's injunction for the therapist to treat the client's disclosures and formulations "as if" they were valid from that individual's standpoint rather than to treat client verbalizations as products of "cognitive distortions" or "unconscious dynamics."

CYBERNETICS   [Greek *kybernetes* (steersman)]   A term introduced by Norbert Weiner and Arturo Rosenblueth for the study of feedback mechanisms in computational machines. Goal-directed machines can be organized and assembled in ways that allow them to use information from their own ongoing activities such that they can continually adjust their direction of activity according to convergence (vs. divergence) from a specified end state.

DEEP STRUCTURES   A term primarily associated with Chomskian linguistics and the observation that all "surface structure" expressions of language necessarily reflect the operation of "deeper" organizing processes that constrain the forms of surface structure while still affording an infinity of expressions. In constructive metatheory, deep structures are the engines that drive one's lived experience. *See also* SUPERORDINATE CONSTRUCTS.

DIALECTICS [Greek *dialektos* (discourse, debate)]   A tradition as well as a process in both philosophy and less formalized communication. Originating in the writings of Zeno, Socrates, and Plato, dialectical processes were central to Karl Marx's socialism. Formalized by Fichte as involving three phases—thesis, antithesis, and synthesis—this triad became the center of both Marx's and Hegel's popularization of this idea. Dialectics honors the dynamic role of contrast in generating development.

EMBODIMENT   "Bodily situated" or otherwise grounded in the indwelling activities of the body; its current popularity may derive in part from its emphasis on the bodily nature of mind, that is, its intrinsic relationship to motor behavior in contrast to a Cartesian separation of psyche and soma.

ENACTMENTS   An inclusive term covering a broad spectrum of dramatic techniques in individual, family, or group psychotherapy—ranging from brief, casual therapist and client role playing to more elaborate exercises enlisting several group members. As used by constructivists, enactment exercises are meant to enhance the client's (and therapist's) awareness of alternative ways of construing life and the outlooks of others, instead of having the client practice an approved set of skills offered by the therapist (as in assertiveness training). *See also* FIXED-ROLE THERAPY.

EPISTEMOLOGY [Greek *episteme* and *ology* (the study of foundations)]   Theories of knowing, knowledge, and (more recently) the knower's participation in those processes.

EQUILIBRATION [Greek *equi* (equal) and *libre* (freedom)]   The concept that all human experience, and particularly learning and development, involves a dynamic balance between what can be assimilated as familiar and what must be accommodated ("made room for") by revising current operational rules. The idea was introduced by Johann Herbart and was later elaborated by Jean Piaget and others.

FAMILY CHARACTERIZATION SKETCH   An adaptation of Kelly's self-characterization sketch, which instructs a client to write a free-form description of himself or herself (or family), as it might be written by someone (real or imagined) who knew the client (or family) intimately and sympathetically—perhaps better than anyone really could. To promote a sense of perspective, the client is asked to write the sketch in the third person, beginning with "[client's name] is." The resulting sketch is itself a useful assessment device, and it can be used to prompt the construction of an alternative sketch as a basis for fixed-role therapy.

FIXED-ROLE THERAPY In personal construct theory, the development and enactment of a hypothetical identity or role, carrying novel implications for viewing and living life differently. The alternative identity is given a different name from the client's and is organized around ways of construing life that are "orthogonal" to (i.e., neither isomorphic with nor in opposition to) the client's own habitual ways, as represented in a self-characterization sketch. The client enacts the role in daily life without informing others of the experiment, but only for a fixed period of time (e.g., 2 weeks), after which the hypothetical identity is set aside, and therapist and client discuss the implications of the exercise for reinventing the client's biography.

HERMENEUTICS [Greek *hermeneutikos* (interpretation)] A field of study that originated in the interpretation of sacred scriptures and has more recently become a secularized analysis of the meaning or meanings of texts and how text and reader interact to create unique meaning systems.

HIERARCHICAL STRUCTURAL ORGANIZATION A form of self-organization within complex systems (especially human systems) in which categorical functions are operationally nested at levels that can be described as differentially central or peripheral to the activities within those systems. *See also* CORE ORDERING PROCESSES and SUPERORDINATE CONSTRUCTS.

HISTORIOGRAPHY The "writing of history," as distinguished from history, which is defined by what "really" happened.

IDIOGRAPHIC [*ideo* (personal, distinct, or peculiar)] Term introduced in 1894 by Wilhelm Windelband of the Baden School, a late-nineteenth-century German center of constructive thinking. The term was used by Allport to describe methods of inquiry that emphasize the uniqueness of the individual as a primary focus.

INTENTIONALITY [Latin *in* and *tendere* (to stretch into or toward)] The tendency of self-organizing systems to be anticipatory—that is, to integrate memory and anticipation in relatively selective ranges of all levels of activity.

INTERSUBJECTIVITY [Latin *inter sub* and *ject* (literally, "between under throwings")]   The domain in which humans relate to one another. It implies the human tendency to recognize and take into account the personal or subjective experience of others and not to merely adjust to their observable behavior.

LADDERING TECHNIQUE   A form of recursive (repeated) questioning used to elicit a hierarchy of the personal constructions that regulate an individual's choices and anchor his or her identity in a certain life context. It represents a technique for eliciting the higher order implications of a given construct in a person's system of meaning.

LANGUAGING   Any form of symbolic display, action, or communication within human communities—verbal or nonverbal—intended to establish, question, or otherwise negotiate social and personal meanings and coordinate behavior. *Languaging* includes, but goes beyond the content and grammar of formal languages defined by linguists. Languaging also makes possible the phenomena of self-referencing and self-awareness and, therefore, it is a central concern of constructivist therapy.

LIFE REVIEW   The process of systematically reflecting on one's own life, sometimes structured through such diverse exercises as current autobiographical constructions, self-interpretations of dreams, journal writing, and other symbolically "sentimental journeys."

MIRROR TIME   A method of self-observation in which the individual is asked to spend time in front of a mirror reflecting on experiences of his or her self.

MOVIEOLA TECHNIQUE   A method of self-observation popularized by constructivist Vittorio F. Guidano. The essence of the technique is to develop a capacity to phenomenologically move "in and out of" experiences and their explanations.

NOMOTHETIC   In contrast to *idiographic*, this term denotes the search for general "covering laws" of human behavior.

OBJECTIVISM   A set of assumptions and assertions about both methods of knowing (*see* EPISTEMOLOGY) and the nature of reality (*see* ONTOL-

OGY). Objectivists hold that a reality exists outside the human knower that can be known in principle and that "truth" coincides with the accurate apprehension of this reality.

ONTOLOGY   Theories (or the study of theories) of reality.

PERSONAL EPILOGUE   An exercise often used in life-review methodologies, in which individuals are asked to reflect on and diversely express their desires about their own eventual funeral services.

PHENOMENOLOGY [from Greek *phainomenon* and *logos* (literally, "the study or knowledge of appearances")]   A term introduced by J. H. Lambert in 1764 in reference to the theory of appearance. Its contemporary meanings are spread across traditions that have respected the prevailing power of immediate experience in both short- and long-term navigations of individual development. Phenomenologists focus on human experience and its situated meanings, rather than on only overt behavior and its environmental contingencies.

POLARITY [from Greek *pelo* (I turn; I am in the motion of a wheel)]   A contrast that is defined by (two) opposites.

POSTMODERN   That perspective in philosophy or worldviews that acknowledges the complexity, relativity, and intersubjectivity of all human experience. Postmodernism accepts the lack of any ultimate foundation for the multiplicity of human belief systems and calls into question the idea of an essentialized self, in contrast to the modernist belief in a knowable world and in self-contained individualities having specifiable characteristics. Postmodernists also advocate that science is essentially an interpretive, rather than computational, enterprise, and they judge the adequacy of a position in part by whether it yields a useful critique of unquestioned dominant practices and ideologies.

PRAXIS [Greek *prassein* (habitual action)]   Active doing.

REFLEXIVITY (REFLECTION, ETC.) [from Latin *re* and *flectere* (to bend back upon self)]   The phenomenon of self-reference or self-relatedness. A psychological theory is considered reflexive to the extent that it can account for the theory-making capacities of its originator or originators.

REPERTORY GRIDS   In personal construct theory, a set of techniques used to elicit and map those dimensions of meaning by which an individual, family, or group organizes his or her (or its) perceptions of some domain of experience. A typical repertory grid might consist of a dozen or more "elements" (important people, social situations, and occupations) that are then compared and contrasted to elicit the respondent's constructions of their similarities and differences. Elements are then ranked or rated on each construct, and the resulting matrix is mathematically analyzed to yield various indexes of the complexity and hierarchical arrangement of the respondent's belief system, commonality in construing with others, and so on. Also referred to as *role construct repertory grids*, or *rep grids*.

RITUAL PRESCRIPTION   A technique often used by constructivist family therapists to provoke movement or reflection in family members. For example, a family of a depressed patient might be prescribed the ritual of treating his depression as biological on even-numbered days and reactive to social circumstances on odd-numbered days. Rituals can take many forms, and they can be assigned by the therapist or worked out collaboratively with the family.

ROLE RELATIONSHIP   In personal construct terms, the process of relating to another person with the intent of subsuming or understanding his or her constructions of experience. This pattern of "role making" in the discursive context of relating to concrete others is in contrast with the more extraspective definition of "role taking" as a set of socially or culturally prescribed behaviors.

SELF-SCHEMAS (OR SCHEMATA)   A term borrowed from social–cognitive psychology to depict the organized matrix of meaning used to direct attention to and to prompt memory of self-relevant information.

SOCIALITY COROLLARY   In personal construct theory, the axiom that one person can enact a role relationship with another to the extent that he or she construes the other's construction processes. It thus has to do with the significance of developing a "metaperspective" on the other's constructions, rather than merely responding to the other's behavior.

STREAMING   An abbreviation for "stream-of-consciousness reporting," in which an individual is asked to report the spontaneous flow of his or her immediate experience in the nonevaluative, noninterpretive presence of a therapist.

SUPERORDINATE CONSTRUCTS   The highest order or most central constructs in a person's belief system. These are typically the anchors to an individual's identity and basic values, carrying sweeping implications for his or her more peripheral constructs. *See also* HIERARCHICAL STRUCTURAL ORGANIZATION.

TELEOLOGIC [from Greek *telos* and *logos*]   Goal-directedness relative to a specific, external "destination."

TELEONOMIC [from Greek *telos* and *nomos* (lawful end or purpose)] Developmental directionality that is not primarily determined by a single, specific, external goal or concrete destination; for example, the evolutionary development of species in a patterned, nonrandom direction, but not toward some preenvisioned ideal form.

TEXTUALITY   A consequence of contextual theories of meaning, referring to the fact that all particulars of experience exhibit meaning only within specific and individual boundaries of discourse.

TIME AND PLACE BINDING   In personal construct therapy, the strategy of validating a construction as appropriate to a particular time or place but questioning its application to other domains of experience. For example, a therapist might validate the pervasive distrust felt by an adult survivor of childhood incest, indicating the appropriateness of construing all relationships in childhood in terms of the trustworthiness of the other person; however, at the same time, the therapist gently encourages the client to give other dimensions of relating at least equal salience in the context of contemporary adult relationships.

VALENCE [Latin *valere* (to govern or have power)]   A basic dimension of contrast, usually carrying evaluative implications.

AUTHOR INDEX

Numbers in italics refer to listings in reference sections.

SUBJECT INDEX

Borderline personality disorder (*continued*)
mythology and, 373–374
transference relationships in, 376
Bow-tie diagram
in couple therapy, 322–323, 326
definition of, 402
Brain as computer metaphor, 74–75
Brain function, connectionism and, 43

Categorical constructivism, 175–176
categories in, 175
limitations in, 175–176
reality in, 177
Causality
Aristotle and, 83
efficient, 71, 266
final, 267
formal, 71–72, 266
material, 71
narrative metaphor and, 266–267
teleologic, 72
types of, 71–72, 83
in world hypotheses, 71–72
Change. *See also* Therapeutic change
constructivist, 6
first-order
definition of, 402
of meaning of clinical problem, 255
processes in, 80
resistance to, 17, 18
second-order, 18
definition of, 402
therapeutic, 100–104. *See also* Therapeutic change
Chaos, complexity specialization and, 47
Choice corollary
definition of, 402
in experiential personal construction therapy, 360
in personal construct theory, 311
Circular questions
in conversational elaboration therapy, 23–24
definition of, 402
Client
as coinvestigator, 267, 268, 269
interaction with therapist. *See also* Collaboration
balance of novelty and normality in, 389–390

communication and learning in, 389
in meaning-making psychotherapy, 141
as self-investigator, 268
Cognition, in external and internal dialectics, 179
Cognitive paradigm
ontology and epistemology in, 211–212
research implications of, 212–213
selfhood in, 209–210
textuality in, 208–209
Cognitive psychotherapy, 47–54
cognitive behavior modification, 49–51
origins of, 49–50
constructivism and, 15
constructivist and complex systems therapies, 52–54
mind cure movement in, 48
personal construction therapy, 49
personal scientist model in, 19
rational emotive therapy, 48–49
selfhood development in, 20
Cognitive sciences
cybernetics in, 41, 42
dialogue with cognitive psychotherapy, 56
information theory in, 41, 42
key features of, 41
twentieth-century developments in, 40–47
complex systems approaches, 46–47
connectionism and computational neuroscience, 42–44
constructivism and evolutionary epistemology, 44–45
hermeneutics and narrative, 45–46
Collaboration
client–group, 244
client–therapist, 19
credulous approach in, 17, 114, 363, 403
in exploration, 388
in self-investigation, 267–269
in self-observation therapy, 160
in therapeutic narrative, 243–244, 267
Complex systems psychotherapy, 52–54
Complexity
and complex systems, 46–47

applications of, 47
roots of, 46–47
internal
definition of, 170
symbolization from, 181
Connectionism
associationism and, 43–44
definition of, 42
origin of, 42–43
Consciousness
dialectics of, 186, 187
infantile, 97
self-construction in, 186–187
Construct, definition of, 402
Constructivism, 175, 176
categorical, 175–177
characteristics of, 82
construction in, 53
constructivist versus rationalist cognitive psychotherapies, 53–54
contextualism, 71–72, 264, 267
critical, 403
development of, 4–5
dialectical, 175, 176
epistemology and, 44–45
forms of, 72–81
efficient, 74–75, 81, 83, 84
final, 78–81, 83, 84
formal, 75–78, 83, 84
material, 72–74, 81
influence on psychology, 70
internal tensions in, 30–32
origins of, 69
principles of experience in, 44–45
problems with, 53–54
psychoanalysis in, 4–5
and psychotherapy integration, 27–30
radical, 275–302, 403. *See also* Radical constructivism
root metaphor theory and, 70–72
techniques in, 16–18, 113
view of psychotherapy, 2–3, 4
Constructivist paradigm
ontology and epistemology in, 218–219
research implications of, 220–221
selfhood in, 217–218
textuality in, 215–217
Constructs
anticipations as, 316
dichotomy of, 316–317

relationships among, 317
superordinate, 408
Construing process
therapist in
in change model, 315
reflexivity of, 319–320
Containing metaphor
dichotomy of inside–outside, 201
hermeneutic alternative to, 201–202
Content, in personal construct theory, 328
Context
of construing, 315
in personal construct therapy, 317–319
Contextualism
description of, 71–72, 264
historical act and narrative in, 264
meaning changes in, 265
versus mechanism, 26, 265
self-confrontation in, 267
valuation theory and, 267
as world hypothesis, 71–72
Conversation
client–therapist, 298, 301
in constructivist therapy, 278, 301
in family system therapies, 23–24, 290
in group and family therapy, 290
meaning and, 31
psychotherapy as, 23–24
Core ordering processes, 16
definition of, 403
Covert conditioning, 49–50
Creativity
characteristics of, 137
definitions of, 135, 136–137
dialectic of unique and universal in, 134–135
manifestations of, 137
mindfulness in, 138–139, 148
in personal styles and life, 135–136
wisdom in, 133–134, 136, 137–138, 148
Credulous approach
in assessment, 114, 330
to client, 114
definition of, 17, 403
in experiential personal construction therapy, 363
Critical constructivism
definition of, 403
environment interdependence in, 403

Cybernetics, 41, 42
  definition of, 403
  family therapy and, 314
  first- and second-order, 314

Death of self, 30
Deep structures. *See also* Superordinate
      constructs
  definition of, 403–404
Depression, cognitive therapy and, 51–52
Determinants, innate, 175, 176
Development
  cognitive
    equilibration and dialectics in,
        78–79
    definition of, 133
    of human potential, 133–134
    map of, 135
    theory of, 78-79
Developmental history, client restructuring
      of, 166–167
Dialectical constructivism, 175, 176
Dialectics
  definition of, 169, 404
  of experience and explanation, 170
  integrative, 28–29
  of selfhood development, 21
Differentiation, subjective–objective,
      158–159
Discovery versus confrontation in ther-
      apy, 20
Distinction making
  in formism, 71
  in reality construction, 73

Efficient constructivism
  information processing in, 74–75, 82
  social learning theory in, 75, 82
Embodiment
  of action, 283
  definition of, 404
  issues in, 55
Emotion
  action and, 282
  Aristotelian trichotomy, 282
  client effect on psychotherapist,
      387–388
  in constructivism, 281
  in creative aging, 141
  disturbance of
    rationalist–cognitive view of, 100

  in psychotherapy for creative aging,
      141
  in radical constructivism, 281–284
  role in change, 54–55
Emotion schemes, 184–185
  complex, 174
  description and function of, 184–185
Enactments. *See also* Fixed-role therapy
  casual, 118, 119
  definition of, 404
  in exploration, 117–119
  unverbalized, 118
Endogenic knowledge theory, 76
Environment
  in critical constructivism, 403
  in knowing, 75, 81–83
Epistemology
  in constructivism, 13–15
    versus nonconstructivism, 386–387
  definition of, 404
  dialectical constructivist, 169, 187
  evolutionary, 44–45
  objectivist, 30
  participatory, 16
  in radical constructivism, 73
  sensory order and, 44
  social constructivist, 76
Equilibration
  definition of, 78, 404
  in systems perspectives, 79
Ethical issues
  belief systems and, 394
  case history, 393
  individual rights and social responsi-
      bilities, 394
  values and, 392–393
Existing. *See* Ontology
Exogenic knowledge theory, 76
Experience, 15–16
  as bodily felt sense, 170, 185
  as circular process in change, 315–316
  as cycle, 316
  dialectical synthesis of, 184
  dialectics of scheme and hardwired
      operators and, 171–172
  immediate
    reordering of, 162–163, 165
  intersubjective, 96
  as language, 185
  linguistic distinctions and, 171
  meaning and, 407

novel
   balance of, 389–390
   as dialectical synthesis, 180–181,
      182–183
   principles of, 44–45
   reordering of, 101–104
   roots of, 183
   selfhood dynamics and life-span devel-
      opment, 98–100
   structure and dynamics of change
      and, 162–163
   symbolization of, 181, 242
   of therapist, 362–370. *See also* Thera-
      pist experience of personal con-
      struct therapy
Experiencing and explaining
   awareness of bodily sense in, 170
   in constructivist therapy, 94–95
   dialectics of, 170
   in self-observation therapy, 156–157
   immediate, 162–163
   vital reason in, 184
Experiential personal construction psychotherapy
   choice corollary and client creativity
      in, 360
   role relationships in
      connection and separateness in, 359,
         362, 363
      terror of risk in, 359, 360
      therapist experience in development
         of, 361
   role relationships in construing of con-
      struction process, 359
   sociality corollary in, 358, 359
   therapist experience of, 357–370. *See
      also* Therapist experience of per-
      sonal construct psychotherapy
Exploration
   for change, 113
      enactments in, 117–118
      fixed-role therapy in, 119–122
   client–therapist collaboration in, 388
   of hypothetical worlds, 116, 117
   personal, 114
   in psychotherapy, 55
   types of, 118–119

Facial recognition, 96
Family characterization sketch, 327
   definition of, 404–405

Family construct therapy (FCT), 317–319
   anticipation in, 320
   childhood development and, 318–319
   overlap with personal construct sys-
      tem, 318
   role relationships in, 319
Family therapy. *See also* Family construct
   therapy (FCT)
   bow-tie diagram in, 322–323, 326,
      401–402
   circular questions in, 402
   family characterization sketch in, 327
   language in, 23–24
   ritual prescription in, 408
   systemic constructivism in, 310
   therapist hierarchy-power in, 327–328
Family-characterization sketch, 327
FCT. *See* Family construct therapy (FCT)
Feeling, as process, 55
Feelings, self-referencing, 163, 164
Final constructivism
   developmental and dialectics theories
      of, 78–79
   forms of, 78
   organic process metaphor and, 78
   systems perspectives in, 79–80
   transpersonal psychology in, 80–81
Fixed-role therapy, 119–122
   client self-characterization sketch in,
      120, 326
   definition of, 405
   evaluation of, 121–123
   implementation of, 121
   as personal inquiry process, 296–297
   therapist fixed-role sketch in, 120–
      121, 326
Formal cause, contextualism and, 71–72
Formal constructivism
   definition of, 78
   narrative psychotherapy in, 77–78
   reality in, 75
   root metaphor and causality in, 75
   social constructivist theory in, 76–77
Formism, 71

Goals
   definition and accomplishment of,
      293
   of therapy, 17

reconstruction of, 21–23. *See also* Narrative reconstruction therapy

Life-review
    definition of, 406
    personal epilogue in, 407

Life-span development, selfhood dynamics and, 98–100

Love and need, 299–300

Maturana, H., 311-314

Meaning
    of clinical problem, 255
    construction of, 170, 181, 317
    continuity of and narratives, 233–234
    dialectical, 170
    irreducibility of, 268
    locus of, 31
    networks of, 116
    personal. *See also* Valuation theory
      in self-narrative, 247–269
    reflexive, 181
    search for in narrative, 233–234, 241
    self-reflective versus conversational techniques and, 31

Meaning-making psychotherapy
    client–therapist relationship in, 141
    closure in, 143
    data gathering in, 141–142
    disintegration–transformation in, 144
    levels of change in, 143–145
    life as story in, 132
    metacognitive awareness in, 144–145
    modification in, 143–144
    patterning in, 142–143
    as proactive, creative process, 140
    therapist in, 147–148

Mechanism, 71

Metaphor or metaphors. *See also* Life, metaphors for; Root metaphor or metaphors
    black box, 41, 42
    brain as computer, 74–75
    embodiment of, 200–201
    generation in therapy, 220–221
    historical event, 71, 75, 77–78
    for life, 131–133
    as meaning transports, 131–133
    person as scientist, 18–20, 316, 324–325
    for psychotherapy, 18–24. *See also* Psychotherapy

reincorporation, 343–351

rite of passage, 341–342

root and world hypotheses, 71–72, 75, 82

for termination of therapy, 340–341, 343–353

for therapy, 341–342

travel as movement in therapy, 390–392

Mind cure movement, 48

Mindfulness
    in creative aging, 138–139, 148
    definition of, 138
    mindlessness versus, 139

Mirror time, definition of, 406

Modernism, in early psychology, 12, 13

Modulation corollary, in personal construct theory, 311

Movieola technique, 17
    in affective style study, 165
    definition of, 406
    description of, 157–158
    in developmental history analysis, 166
    differentiation of subjective-objective in, 158–159
    "how and why" of experience in, 158
    in selfhood development, 21

Narrative
    constructions of reality in, 209
    in formal constructivism, 77–78
    hermeneutics in, 46, 199–200
    therapeutic, 231–244. *See also* Therapeutic narrative
    therapy as, 198–199

Narrative reconstruction therapy
    bases of, 22
    techniques in, 22, 23
    therapist role in, 22–23

Nomothetic, 406

Novel performance
    generation of, 177, 178
    gestalt, field factor in, 173

Objectivism
    assumptions of, 93
    versus constructivism, 12–16
    definition of, 406

Observer
- characteristics of, 93
- person as, 94–95

Ontology. *See also* Reality
- in constructivism versus nonconstructivism, 386
- definition of, 407

Ontology and epistemology
- behavioral–objectivist paradigm, 204–205, 211, 218
  - absolutist versus dialectical, 205
- cognitive–subjectivist paradigm, 211–212
  - equilibrium maintenance in, 212
  - relativism versus absolutism in, 211, 218, 219
- constructivist–hermeneutic paradigm, 218–219
  - dialectics in, 219–220
  - knowledge in, 219
  - radical versus critical constructivists, 219
- definitions of, 204–205

Organicism, 72

Organization of behavior theory, 43

Patterning
- of experience, 76
- in meaning-making psychotherapy, 142–143
- in therapy for aging, 142–143

Performance
- affect influence on, 174–175
- cognitive-finding executive, 174–175
- generation of, 177, 178
- novel, 173, 177–178
  - gestalt and field factor in, 173
- scheme overdetermination of, 172

Person as scientist metaphor, 18–20, 316
- criticism of, 19
- logical–empiricist conception of, 19

Personal construct theory (PCT)
- behavior-meaning interchange in, 320–327
  - position for intervention, 323–327
  - position in assessment of, 322–323
- change and, 311
- choice corollary in, 402
- constructive alternativism in, 308–310
- content and process issues in, 327–329

client as content expert, 328
- hierarchy and power of therapist and, 327–328
- therapist as construing process expert, 328–329
- family construct therapy overlap with, 318
- fixed-role therapy in, 326
- history in, 49
- knowledge in, 307–308, 311
- ontological contrast in, 312–314
- reality in, 311, 312–314
- repertory grids in, 407–408
- research in
  - client-centered, 330–331
  - investigator-centered, 330
- sociality corollary in, 408
- systemic constructivism in, 310–311
- systemic therapies and, 305–331
  - differences in, 305–306
  - similarities in, 306, 307
- techniques in, 324–327
- therapy model in
  - behavior-meaning interchange in, 320–321
  - contextualist, 317–319
  - process-oriented, 315–317
  - reflexive, 319–320
- time and place binding strategy in, 409

Personal epilogue, definition of, 407

Personal scientist metaphor, 18–20, 316
- hypothesis testing and, 324–325

Personality psychology, 268

Personhood. *See also* Selfhood
- individual conception of, 341
- life story effect on, 22

Phenomena, patterning of, 76

Phenomenology, definition of, 407

Philosophy, constructivism and, 11, 13–14

Piaget, J., 78-79

Polarity
- in affective reports, 102
- definition of, 407

Position
- in personal construct therapy
  - for assessment, 322–323
  - for intervention, 323–327

Positive thinking movement, 48

Postmodernism
- constructivism and, 12
- definition of, 407

Praxis of life
    definition of, 407
    of living, 94, 96, 97
Problem
    conversation elaboration and, 24
    in family therapy, 305-306
    language dependence of, 279–280
    redefinition in self-observation ther-
        apy, 160
Process
    in dialectical constructivism, 171–172
    in personal construct theory, 315–317
    therapeutic
        behavioral research in, 205–207
        cognitive research in, 212–213
        constructivist paradigm in, 220–221
        covert mechanisms in, 212–213
        hermeneutics and metaphor genera-
            tion in, 220–221
        research limitations in, 220
        stimulus–response conditions in,
            206–207
Psychology
    constructivism influence on, 70
    methodology in early, 12, 13, 14
    modernism in, 12, 13
    scientist–practitioner gap in, 269
Psychotherapy. *See also* Termination of
        therapy
    constructivism and, 2–3, 4, 11–12,
        27–30
    constructivist, 52–54
        experience and, 94–105
        experiencing and explaining in,
            94–95
        self and intersubjectivity, 95–98
        selfhood dynamics and life-span
            development, 98–100
        strategies and techniques in, 16–
            18, 113
        structure and dynamics of change,
            100–104
    as conversation, 23–24
    dialectical constructivist epistemology
        in, 187
    of inclusion versus isolation, 340, 341
    integration of
        with constructivism, 27–30
        movement and schools for, 29–30, 55
    metaphors for, 18–24
    as narrative, 198–199, 222

phenomenological and cognitive
    perspective, 199
structuralism and, 198–199
as narrative reconstruction, 21–23
as personal science, 18–20
research in, constructivist contribu-
    tion, 24–27
as rite of passage. *See also* Reincorpora-
    tion
    liminal space in, 342–343
    reincorporation, 343, 344
    separation in, 342
    stages of, 341–342
as selfhood development, 20–21
stages in
    closure in, 143
    data gathering in, 141–142
    establishment of client–therapist
        relationship, 141
    patterning in, 142–143
task of, 112

Questions
    clarification of in constructivist ther-
        apy, 279
    in family construct therapy, 402
    in repertory grid, 231–232
    in self-investigation, 278
    in termination interview, 346–354

Radical constructivism, 275–302
    contexts in, 300, 302
    defined, 403
    emotion in, 281–282, 283–284
    in social reticence, 294–300
        cognitive-behavioral approaches,
            294–296
        constructivist fixed-role therapy in,
            296, 297–298
        objectivist imitation approach,
            294–296
    individual choice and ecological
        imperative, 288–294, 301
    interdependence of language, emo-
        tion, action, 276–285
    language in, 403
        as action, 276–277, 279, 301
        reframing versus verbal magic in,
            291–292
    personal projects in, 300

Radical constructivism (*continued*)
  problems, language dependence of, 279–280, 301
  reality of constructions in, 285–288
    individual experience and, 287
    invented, 292
    labels and social consensus, 286–287
    understanding versus change of, 286
    responsibility and blame in, 288–289
    self as authority in, 293
    therapist function in, 293–294
Rational emotive therapy (RET), 48–49
  task of, 211
Rationality
  as mood, 282
  as unresolved quandaries, 280
Reality
  categorical versus dialectical, 176–177
  construction of, 176–179
    dialogical distinction in, 201–202
  in constructivism, 3, 69, 93–94
    versus nonconstructivism, 386
  in efficient constructivism, 75
  external, 176-179
  in formal constructivism, 75
  harsh, 285-288
  in informal constructivism, 76
  internal and internal dialectic, 179–182
  intersubjective, 96, 97
  in material constructivism, 73, 74
  as narrative, 209
  in objectivism, 93
  objectivism and, 406
  in radical constructivism, 285–288, 292
  realist–idealist dichotomy in, 176–177
Reflexivity
  definition of, 407
  of meaning, 181
Reincorporation
  consulting your consultants in, 344–345
  obstacles to, 343–351. *See also* Termination interview for reincorporation
  practices in, 344–345
Repertory grid
  in assessment and research, 320
  client narrative on, 232–233
  definition of, 407–408

  as research technique, 25
  in therapeutic narrative, 231–232
Research
  behavioral, 205–207
  cognitive, 212–213
  constructivist, 24–26, 220–221
  paradigmatic and narrative approaches to, 27, 31
  personal construct theory and, 330–331
  repertory grid in, 320
Resistance
  to change, 17, 18, 116
  in psychotherapy for aging, 143
  to reality, 176, 178, 179
RET. *See* Rational emotive therapy (RET)
Rights and responsibilities, client and therapist, 394
Ritual prescription, definition of, 408
Role relationship, 408
Roles. *See* Fixed-role therapy
Root metaphor or metaphors
  historical event, 71
  machine, 71
  organic process, 72
  similarity, 71

Scheme or schemes
  accommodation principle of, 177
  affective, 174–175, 184–185
  assimilation principle and, 172, 173
  of body experience, 201
  in dialectics
    external, 178–179
    internal, 179–180
  dialectics of and hardware operators, 171–172
  dynamic choice of, 172
  emotion, 184–185
  emotion-releasing, 179–180
  executive cognition-finding, 174–175
  healing, 180
  in information processing, 74–75
  as knowledge unit, 178–179
  neuropsychological interpretation of, 173
  overdetermination principle and, 172, 173
Scheme's overdetermination of performance (SOP) principle, 172

Self
centrality of, 30, 55
community of selves in, 236
in constructivism, 13
death of, 30
deconstructionism and, 30
individual versus language based, 30–31
as observer, 94–95
as process, 21
as project, 196
as protagonist, 22
roles of, 22, 94–95
as subject and object, 96–98, 102
in valuation theory, 248–249
Self-awareness
attentional allocation in, 183
in therapeutic change, 101
Self-characterization sketch
client, 326
therapist alternative, 326
Self-confrontation assessment, 251–255, 267, 268
combination of valuation and affect, 253–255
matrix of, 252
follow-up self-investigation, 255
self-investigation in, 251, 253, 272
valuation construction in, 251, 253, 272
Self-control, in therapeutic change, 100–101
Self-deception, 163–164
Self-development, in transpersonal psychology, 80
Self-exploration
narrative examples of, 234–249
repertory grid in, 232–233
Selfhood. See also Personhood
behavioral–objectivist approach
self as object, 204
cognitive–subjective
central assumptions of, 210
self as subject, 209–210
constructivist–hermeneutic approach
self as project, 217–218
self-knowledge in, 218
development of
versus cognitive or behavior change, 20
dynamics of, 20, 21

stream of consciousness technique in, 20
dynamics in movieola technique, 158–159
life-span development and, 98–100
Self-individuation, 96, 97
Self-investigation
as collaboration, 267–269
in self-narrative, 251, 253, 255, 272
Self-management, behavioral, 49–50
Self-narrative
affect in, 251, 253–255
changing meaning in: case histories, 255–264
meaning change in, 255–264
conflict avoidance case, 256, 257, 258–259
fear of death case in, 259, 260, 261
psychosomatic problem and stress, 261, 262, 263–264
motives in, 249, 250
personal meaning in, 247–269
self-confrontation in, 251–255. See also Self-confrontation
in self-exploration, 234–249. See also Therapeutic narrative
self-investigation in, 251, 253, 255, 267–269, 272
valuation process in, 251, 252, 253–255, 272
valuation theory and, 248–251
Self-observation, definition of, 406
Self-observation psychotherapy, 155–167
in assessment and intervention, 155–156
differentiation in, 158–159
experiencing and explaining in, 156–157
mirror time technique in, 406
movieola technique in, 17, 157–159, 406
therapeutic process in
construing of therapeutic setting in, 161–165
developmental analysis in, 165–167
focusing and reordering immediate experiencing, 162–163, 165
preparation of context in, 160–161
reconstruction of client's affective style in, 163–165
therapist and, 156–157

dialectical synthesis of emotion and reflection in, 182–183
experience in
as circular process, 315–316
focusing and reordering of, 162–163, 165
symbolization of, 181, 242
generation of, 187
rationalist–cognitive approaches to, 100–101
reflective processing in, 181
self-control strategy in, 100–101
structure and dynamics of, 100–104
techniques in, 181–182
Therapeutic narrative
client examples, 231–232, 234–239
client–therapist collaboration in, 243–244
functions of
attending to experience, 242
intrapersonal, 233–234
search for coherence and meaning, 233–234, 241
symbolization of experience, 242
hermeneutics of, 199–200
versus nonnarrative techniques, 240–241
repertory grid in, 231–232
techniques
client-generated, 242–243
client–group, 244
cognitive, 243–244
journaling, 244
versus nonnarrative techniques, 240–241
therapist role in, 234, 235, 236, 242
therapist-generated, 243
Therapeutic relationship. *See also* Collaboration
in family therapy, 327–328
function of, 114
in self-observation therapy, 160
Therapist
for aging client, 146
attitudes of, 115
toward aging, 147-148
challenges to constructivist, 385–397
emotional demand on, 387–388
epistemological and ontological issues and, 386–387
ethical issues and, 392–395
explicit goal-oriented, teleologic, 391
as participant in client change, 19

phenomenological and existential challenges to, 387–388
role in radical constructivism, 293–294
in self-observation therapy, 156–157
strategy, technique, praxis of, 388–392
balance of novelty and normality, 389–390
movement, teleonomic versus teleologic, 390–391
respect for unconscious processes, 389
in teleonomic enterprise, 390–392
Therapist experience of personal construct therapy
guilt for therapeutic failure, 369–370
optimal distance in
client evolution and, 363
connection and separateness in, 363
credulous approach in, 363
example of, 362
failures in, 368–369
personal growth in, 369–370
role relationships in, 359–361
stranger relationship error in, 363
client connection problem in, 365–366
dependence case, 364–365
therapist failure to connect in, 363
unity in excessive closeness in, 366–370
examples, 366–367
invalidation of client separateness, 366
invalidation of intervention, 367
validation and invalidation of, 368–369
Therapy. *See* Psychotherapy
Thought control, 50
TOTE (Test, Operate, Test, Exit), 43
TPI. *See* Theoretical progressive integrationism (TPI)
Transformation
in creative aging, 135–136
as human capacity, 136
Transpersonal psychology, self-development in, 80

Understanding
in constructivism, 215, 216
hermeneutics in, 199–200

ABOUT THE EDITORS

Robert A. Neimeyer is a professor in the Department of Psychology, University of Memphis, Tennessee. Since completing his doctoral training at the University of Nebraska in 1982, he has drawn on concepts and methods in personal construct theory and related constructivist approaches to personality and psychotherapy in the majority of his research. He has published 12 books, including *The Development of Personal Construct Psychology* (University of Nebraska Press, 1985), *Casebook in Personal Construct Therapy* (Springer, 1987), and *Advances in Personal Construct Theory* (Vols. 1–3; JAI Press, 1990, 1992, 1995). The author of over 150 articles and book chapters, he is currently attempting to refine methods for constructivist assessment, to develop a constructivist basis for psychotherapy integration, and to pursue empirical research on such topics as depression and suicide and the outcome of cognitive therapy. Neimeyer is coeditor, with Greg J. Neimeyer, of the *Journal of Constructivist Psychology*, and he serves on the editorial boards of a number of other journals. In recognition of his scholarly contributions, he was granted the Distinguished Research Award by Memphis State University in 1990.

Michael J. Mahoney is currently a professor of psychology at the University of North Texas, Denton. After earning his doctorate at Stanford University in 1972, he accepted faculty appointments at Pennsylvania State University and the University of California—Santa Barbara, before moving to North Texas in 1990. As a pioneering contributor to the development of cognitive-behavioral therapies, Mahoney has published over 200 articles on such topics as the psychology of science and, particularly, on psychotherapy theory and research. His current scholarly work focuses on constructive-developmental psychotherapies, as well as on broadly constructivist trends in neuroscience, philosophy of mind, and artificial intelligence. His books include *Scientist as Subject* (Health Science Systems, 1976), *Psychotherapy Process* (Plenum, 1980), *Cognition in Psychotherapy* (Basic Books, 1985), *Human Change Processes* (Basic Books, 1991), and *Cognitive and Constructivist Therapies: Recent Developments* (Springer, 1994). Mahoney was the founding editor of *Cognitive Therapy and Research* and has received numerous scholarly awards for his distinguished contributions to the profession.